ARCHITECTURE, TOWN PLANNING AND COMMUNITY

Edited and with an Introduction by
DONALD G. WETHERELL

ARCHITECTURE, TOWN PLANNING AND COMMUNITY

Selected Writings and Public Talks by Cecil Burgess, 1909–1946

CECIL SCOTT BURGESS

The University of Alberta Press

Published by
The University of Alberta Press
Ring House 2
Edmonton, Alberta, Canada T6G 2E1

Copyright © Introduction and supporting materials, Donald G. Wetherell 2005
Copyright © Burgess Papers, University of Alberta Archives 2005
ISBN 0-88864-455-8

LIBRARY AND ARCHIVES CANADA CATALOGUING IN PUBLICATION DATA

Burgess, Cecil Scott, 1870–1970.
    Architecture, town planning and community : selected writings and public talks by Cecil Burgess, 1909–1946 / Cecil Scott Burgess ; edited and with an introduction by Donald G. Wetherell.

(University of Alberta centennial series)
Includes bibliographical references and index.
ISBN 0-88864-455-8

    1. Architecture—Canada—20th century. 2. City planning—Canada—History—20th century. I. Wetherell, Donald G. (Donald Grant), 1949– II. Title. III. Series.

NA745.B87 2005   720'.971'09041   C2005-907170-2

Printed and bound in Canada.
First edition, first printing, 2005
All rights reserved.

No part of this publication may be produced, stored in a retrieval system, or transmitted in any forms or by any means, electronic, mechanical, photocopying, recording, or otherwise, without the prior written consent of the copyright owner or a licence from The Canadian Copyright Licensing Agency (Access Copyright). For an Access Copyright license, visit www.accesscopyright.ca or call toll free: 1-800-893-5777.

The University of Alberta Press is committed to protecting our natural environment. As part of our efforts, this book is printed on stock produced by New Leaf Paper: it contains 100% post-consumer recycled fibres and is acid- and chlorine-free.

The University of Alberta Press gratefully acknowledges the support received for its publishing program from The Canada Council for the Arts. The University of Alberta Press also gratefully acknowledges the financial support of the Government of Canada through the Book Publishing Industry Development Program (BPDIP) and from the Alberta Foundation for the Arts for our publishing activities.

Title page: Sundial by University Residence. (71.213–415, UAA)
Title page and background illustrations for sections: Burgess's sketch of decorative plaster at McGill. (71.213–178, sketchbook, UAA)

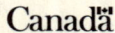
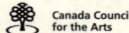

As Always, for Irene Kmet

Contents

IX	*Abbreviations*
XI	*University of Alberta Centennial Series*
XIII	*Preface*
XV	*Acknowledgements*
XVII	*Cecil Burgess's Architectural Career and Writings*
XCIX	*Editor's Notes on The Burgess Papers*

PART I 1909–1920

3	DOCUMENT 1	Old Buildings of the Province of Quebec (1909)
15	DOCUMENT 2	Applications of the Lessons of History (1909–12)
31	DOCUMENT 3	Architecture (1913)
51	DOCUMENT 4	The Old House and the New (1913)
71	DOCUMENT 5	Hygiene in Architecture (1920)

PART II 1921–1939

89	DOCUMENT 6	Modern Architecture (1925)
105	DOCUMENT 7	The Town (1928)
117	DOCUMENT 8	Civic Pride (1929)
127	DOCUMENT 9	Relation of Architecture to Town Planning (1930)
141	DOCUMENT 10	Architecture as a Profession (1931)
153	DOCUMENT 11	Appreciation of Architecture, Lecture 1: Architecture and the Arts (1932)

177	DOCUMENT 12	Appreciation of Architecture, Lecture 4: *Architecture To-Day* (1932)
217	DOCUMENT 13	Recent Domestic Architecture (1932)
227	DOCUMENT 14	City Improvement (1935)
249	DOCUMENT 15	Garden Cities (1939–40)

PART III 1940–1946

261	DOCUMENT 16	Home Building Exhibition (1940)
269	DOCUMENT 17	The New Town Planning (1941)
273	DOCUMENT 18	Housing Present and Prospective (1941)
285	DOCUMENT 19	What Zoning Does for Edmonton (1943)
293	DOCUMENT 20	Improvement of Business Street Fronts (1946)

PART IV Recollection of a Half Century

317	DOCUMENT 21	Recollections of a Half Century (1957)

325 *Bibliography*

331 *Index*

Abbreviations

AAA	Alberta Association of Architects
CEA	City of Edmonton Archives
GA	Glenbow Archives, Calgary
MIT	Massachusetts Institute of Technology
MoMA	Museum of Modern Art
RAIC	Royal Architectural Institute of Canada
RIBA	Royal Institute of British Architects
PAA	Provincial Archives of Alberta
PQAA	Province of Quebec Association of Architects
UAA	University of Alberta Archives

University of Alberta Centennial Series

As the University of Alberta looks forward to its centennial in 2008, it is time to also look back at the history of this campus. The University of Alberta Centennial Series will celebrate the University's 100 years of academic excellence with a variety of books about the people and events that have shaped this institution.

It is fitting that this centennial series start with a book from one of the University's own centenarians—Cecil Scott Burgess—an early visionary of the University of Alberta. Although he came to Alberta for what he thought would be only a few years when the University was just five years old, he remained in Edmonton until his death in 1970 at the age of 101. Burgess's ideas on architecture helped shape this University and landmark buildings in downtown Edmonton including the Birks Building and the Bowker Building. Appointed by Henry Marshall Tory as Resident Architect and Professor of Architecture in 1913, Burgess influenced the planning and development of our campus, exemplified in the graceful Arts Building and stately Pembina Hall. He retired from the University in 1940 but continued to practice architecture until he was 90 years old. His writings collected in this book reflect a man dedicated to the ideals of fine architecture.

Today, as the University's collective memory fades, few know that the University Cup, awarded annually to a member of the academic staff for outstanding distinction in areas of scholarly research, teaching, service to the University and the community at large, was designed by Burgess as a soup tureen in 1925. He would be proud to know that his work remains highly valued on this campus although not many know his name today. *Architecture, Town Planning and Community: Selected Writings and Public Talks by Cecil Burgess*, edited by Donald G. Wetherell, the first book in the University of Alberta Centennial Series, lets the reader experience Burgess's philosophy on architecture through his lectures on campus and public talks around the province.

Commissioned specifically for the University's centennial, Professor Rod Macleod's *All True Things: The University of Alberta 1908–2008* will delve into the community of scholars, researchers and students at the University of Alberta over the past century. Dr. Macleod states that to be able "to reflect on the history of your own institution is a real priviledge." Lively first-hand accounts filled with an abundance of historic photographs tell the history of the University of Alberta from its earliest days to the Class of 2008 in Ellen Schoeck's *I Was There: A Century of Alumni Stories About the University of Alberta*. Forthcoming in 2006 to celebrate the creation of the University in 1906, *I Was There* captures the decades of experiences on campus. As honourary editor of the University of Alberta Centennial Series, I am delighted to present our collective history to our alumni, students and staff in these and other new books planned in this series over the next three years as we lead up to our celebrations in 2008.

HON. JIM EDWARDS, PC
Chair, University of Alberta Board of Governors

Preface

CECIL SCOTT BURGESS became professor of architecture at the University of Alberta in 1913. Before his arrival at the University of Alberta, he was active in the architectural circles of Montreal, and his career, lectures and thinking between 1909 and 1946, the years of his most active practice and teaching, are a unique source for many of the topics that animated architectural discussion in Alberta and English Canada. Burgess's wide-ranging interests are one mark of his importance in the architectural and town planning history of Canada, but his work in training future architects, his involvement in the development of professional architecture in Alberta, his tireless promotion of town planning, and his general efforts to broaden Canadians' understanding of architecture and the built environment give him a unique place in the history of Canadian architecture.

I first encountered Burgess's writings over fifteen years ago when carrying out research on the history of domestic architecture in Alberta. While Burgess's papers at the University of Alberta Archives are an excellent source on the history of housing in Canada, they deal with far more than domestic architecture. They also contain extensive material on many of the wider concerns on architecture and town planning that were being discussed in English Canada. In his talks and lectures, including, after the late 1920s, those over the brand new medium of radio, Burgess discussed many of the dominant ideas of his age about the meaning and potential of architecture and town planning. And because Burgess wrote out his lectures in long hand, the transcripts of these talks now offer a window into this past world.

While other projects and responsibilities kept me from realising the publication of a selection of Burgess's talks and writings, I remained convinced that a book of original documents drawn from the Burgess papers would provide a unique insight into the history of Canadian architecture and town planning. In my view, such a book was further justified because contemporary reference to Burgess's activity and thinking is sparse. Since public addresses were rarely recorded, knowledge of his many lectures and talks is now limited. Moreover, many of the buildings he designed or worked on have been demolished, most of the furniture and household objects he designed are lost or no longer identified, and many of his town plans were imperfectly realised or have now been significantly altered. Burgess wrote clearly and beautifully, but he published relatively little, other than a few articles and his regular monthly column in the RAIC *Journal*. The record of his activity is thus accessible mainly through archival records, but such collections are by their nature difficult to access for many people.

Any selection of documents runs the risk of being a medley, and the Introduction to the volume has been designed to help orient readers, fill gaps and to link the reprinted documents to Burgess's broader thinking and activity. It also provides an outline of the national and provincial framework that helped condition Burgess's activities and thinking as well as a context for the issues raised in the reprinted documents. The illustrations have also been chosen to offer visual context for the documents. Special effort has been made to use, when possible, photographs or drawings that Burgess used in his talks, or which illustrate his buildings and other activities.

Acknowledgements

I OWE, AS ALWAYS, special thanks and gratitude to Irene Kmet. Her encouragement, her help with the research, and her knowledge have helped me realise this project. The dedication of this book to her reflects her contribution to it. I wish also to thank the staff at the University of Alberta Archives, especially Bryan Corbett, Raymond Frogner and Kevan Warner. During her transcription of the documents, Catherine Ivany became an expert at deciphering Burgess's handwriting. I appreciate her excellent and careful work. The Alberta Historical Resources Foundation provided financial assistance for completion of the research on Burgess's papers and for the publication of the book; its support is gratefully acknowledged. I am also grateful to the University of Calgary which provided support through the Research Excellence Envelope. I am indebted to Janice Dickin for her assistance and encouragement in securing this funding. Among many others, Jim Corrigan, Marianne Fedori, Robert Geldart, Ken Tingley and Mike McMordie contributed to the realisation of this book. And as in the past, Mary Mahoney Robson's editorial skills and Alan Brownoff's design skills and the work of other staff at the University of Alberta Press have made this book better.

Cecil Burgess's Architectural Career and Writings

His was a familiar story. When Cecil Scott Burgess emigrated from Montreal to Alberta in 1913 he planned, like so many emigrants, to stay only a few years. Alberta would be only a short stop in his career. But history, circumstance and the comforts of familiarity changed these plans, and when he died in Edmonton in 1970—at the age of 101—Burgess had spent almost six decades in Alberta. By then he had become a formative figure in the development of architecture and town planning in the province. During his career, he gave dozens of public talks, acted in an official capacity with the Alberta Association of Architects and the provincial Examining Board for Architecture, lectured on architecture at the University of Alberta and directed its architecture programme, served as the university's resident architect, and designed numerous buildings at the university and elsewhere. He also acted as the supervising architect on other buildings, drew town plans for a number of towns and cities in western Canada, served on the Edmonton Town Planning Commission, and, among many other activities, wrote a monthly column for many years as the Alberta

Burgess made this drawing of the west doorway of Holyrood Abbey in Edinburgh in 1894 while serving his apprenticeship in architecture. (71.213-191-21, UAA)

correspondent for the *Journal* of the Royal Architectural Institute of Canada (RAIC).

It is a significant mark of Burgess's privacy that almost no personal correspondence is included in the archival collections of his papers. He carefully arranged his papers before depositing them in the archives, with the apparent intention that they would form a public record of his professional rather than his personal life. This strict separation of the personal and the professional was a mark of cultural and class attitudes of the time. The personal had no place in public life, and his lectures and public talks are devoid of personal references. We thus now know little of his private life—nor would he have believed that such knowledge was relevant. As revealed in tape recorded interviews with him late in his life, he spoke with a soft Scottish brogue. He never married, and his biography in *The Canadian Who's Who* in 1938 listed golf and curling as his recreational activities. In interviews later in his life, he recalled outings with colleagues from the university: taking the train to fish at Jasper; golf games at the Mayfair country club; suffering through the occasional hunting trip taken out of social pressure rather than pleasure for he "didn't like to shoot wild animals"; and social events, dinners and lectures at the homes of colleagues.[1]

Details of Burgess's childhood and early life are also only broadly known. He was born, as he always carefully noted, "to Scottish parents," in Mumbai, India in 1870. His father, James Burgess, was the director of the Archaeological Survey of India. But India played little part in Cecil Burgess's life for, when he was two, his family returned to Scotland. Thus, Britain shaped his formative years, and he never lost his sensibility and pride of being British or the belief that British culture and history offered a model to the world.[2]

From 1887 until 1891, Burgess attended the Royal High School in Edinburgh, graduating with a gold medal. A good draughtsman, he concluded that he had the makings of an architect, and in 1892 he secured an apprenticeship in the office of George (later Sir) Washington Browne (1853–1939), a rising Edinburgh architect. Apprenticeship was then the route to a career in architecture in Britain—there were yet no British schools of architecture—and during the four years of his apprenticeship, the aspiring architect took morning classes in decoration at the Edinburgh School of Art, worked in Browne's office in the afternoons, and for three years filled his evenings with technical classes at Heriot Watt College. At Heriot Watt, he studied building construction, as well as historical architecture and geology.

At this time, Edinburgh was a vibrant architectural centre.[3] Especially influential was Arts and Crafts thinking, which was more a set of assumptions, shared attitudes and approaches than a formal theory. Especially important in the evolution of Arts and Crafts thought was the writing and practice of the English architectural and art critic, John Ruskin, and the socialist designer, poet, critic and builder, William Morris, whose dictums about the personal satisfaction and social value of meaningful work and the importance of "truth" in architecture were highly influential. They also expressed distress, and often despair, about the environmental and social ugliness that industrialisation had brought, and promoted a countervailing emphasis on the social and aesthetic values of craftsmanship and hand work and extolled the products of earlier times, especially the middle ages. They argued that, while people had an innate need for beauty, industrialisation and mass production had crushed such needs or, at best, left them unsatisfied. Nonetheless, most Arts and Crafts practitioners accepted the realities and benefits of modern industrial materials and of scientific knowledge, although they also strongly stressed the value of using local materials and building traditions to create an "authentic" architecture. This appeal to tradition and history was sometimes consciously directed at creating a distinctively national architecture that was relevant to its place and time and that would contribute to national identity. Indeed, as architectural historian Nicola Spasoff notes, the supposed Britishness of buildings and artefacts was a significant measure of its quality for many British Arts and Crafts architects who, with few exceptions, saw these models not only as "fine examples of architecture and design" but as "fine *British* examples." Arts and Crafts proponents were also careful to stress that good design was holistic—excellence resulted from expressing a unity and relationship among all the design elements of a building and its contents. Integral to this attitude was a view that materials and methods of construction (whether of a building, a chair or a coffee pot) should be honestly reflected in design. Ideally, this would bring about unpretentious design that eschewed gratuitous decoration and met human yearning for beauty, social meaning and practicality. Architecture and its related arts such as town planning were thus not mere technical matters, but socially useful and even moral undertakings in which the expression of an individual's innate creative instincts would help bring about a better society. In keeping with broader currents of thinking in the late nineteenth century, there was a strong belief in Arts and Crafts thinking that the physical environment influenced character and behaviour. Accordingly, it was assumed that when people lived in creative, beautiful and suitable environments, their lives and character would become more expressive and meaningful and thus more fulfilled.[4]

Such ideas deeply influenced Burgess, who successfully completed his apprenticeship in 1896 when he was admitted as an Associate of the Royal Institute of British Architects (RIBA). He subsequently worked in architects' offices in Edinburgh, London, York and Liverpool. This itinerant life was typical for many young architects at the time, and Burgess found it an invigorating way to gain the skills of his craft. Indeed, forty years later in a radio talk about careers in architecture, he advised prospective architects that work in different practices and cities would give them a "variety of experience" that would be of great value in their future careers.[5] He also travelled widely, sketching and studying British, French, Greek and, chiefly, Italian cities, historical buildings, paintings and sculpture. Such trips were part of the ongoing education of British architects, and the conventions of the time held that sketching, not photography, was the best way to appreciate architectural history and to learn the essence of a building's design.[6] On one trip in Italy in 1903, he met up with Percy Nobbs, an acquaintance from Edinburgh.[7] Burgess and Nobbs shared an enthusiasm for Arts and Crafts approaches, and their shared sentiments were confirmed when Burgess showed Nobbs his recent watercolour sketch of the tower of the municipio in Verona. As Burgess later told it, it was a serendipitous exchange. Nobbs was about to leave for Montreal to teach at the school of architec-

As a young architect, Burgess travelled widely in Europe, sketching monuments and buildings such as the Arche Scaligere, the tomb of the Scaligeri family in Verona, Italy. Drawing dated October 11, 1900. (71.213–191, UAA)

ture in the Faculty of Engineering at McGill University. Impressed with Burgess's quick and competent sketch, he invited Burgess to move to Montreal where he could find work as an assistant draughtsman at McGill.[8]

Burgess found the prospect attractive. He later observed that he had already concluded that his prospects as an architect were limited "in the old country," and since RIBA Associates could gain admission to architectural associations throughout the British empire, he would be able to practice immediately upon his arrival in Canada. Thus, with Nobbs's invitation in his pocket, he moved to Montreal the same year.[9] He at once became involved in the architectural life of the city. He designed several buildings for the Boys Farm and Training School at Shawbridge, Quebec, as well as several houses (one in association with Nobbs) in Montreal. He also served as a member of the Council of the Ordre des Architectes du Québec (then called the Province of Quebec Association of Architects, or PQAA), and in 1908 he organised a junior PQAA Sketch Club. As a collegial forum, it organised outings to sketch and study historical buildings and landscapes and held meetings at which members gave talks on architecture.[10] Burgess naturally delivered talks at the Sketch Club, but he also spoke in other venues, such as the Grand Trunk Literary Institute and the St. James Literary Society. In 1907, he also served as assistant on the construction of the new Macdonald Engineering Building at McGill, and by 1909 he was, as he phrased it, an "assistant to Professor Nobbs," lecturing on building construction, architectural history, "historical drawing" and freehand drawing. In 1909, despite his concern that he would not be able to handle it along with his other teaching responsibilities, he also taught a course in ornament and decoration.[11]

While Burgess taught again in 1910–11, he was considering other alternatives. His prospects at McGill seemed limited, which was reflected by the increasingly frequent reassignment of his responsibilities to accommodate the permanent faculty who were being hired. When Philip J. Turner was hired in 1909 to teach building construction, for example, Burgess took charge of medieval and renaissance architecture, which he then "relinquished a year later to Thomas Ludlow, a newly appointed assistant professor."[12] He did not teach at McGill in 1912, and when invited that year to apply for a teaching position at the University of Michigan, he noted that teaching held little promise for him as "my training has been strictly practical." With characteristic modesty, he noted that while he had been on the staff at McGill University for four or five sessions, this was "a side line and one which offers no eventual prospect from the fact that I have no University degree."[13]

Burgess was being somewhat disingenuous. He did not want the Michigan job because he did not want to live in the United States. He had not come to Canada, he recalled a half century later, only to end up in the United States. He wanted "to stick to Canada because I am a Britisher."[14] And clearly the lack of a degree did not hold him back the next year when he was offered the position of professor of architecture and resident architect at the University of Alberta in Edmonton. Nobbs (who had formed a partnership with George Taylor Hyde in 1910) had been commissioned to plan the new university, and he heartily recommended Burgess to its president, Henry Marshall Tory. As Nobbs confided to Tory, Burgess was a shy man, but "in pure architectural scholarship, I know of no one in the country who is his superior."[15]

Nobbs no doubt also wanted a competent architect on site at the University of Alberta to supervise construction of the buildings and landscaping for which he was responsible. And on Burgess's part, the Edmonton position promised adventure in a new part of the country, some social status and a decent salary—$2,500 for the first year and $2,600 for the second. So too, the position was ideal for a man of "practical experience" since he would be the university's superintending architect as well as teach courses in the winter under "the title Professor of Architecture." Nonetheless, Burgess was unwilling to make a long-term commitment, sight unseen, and agreed only to take a two-year appointment. Seemingly, he saw the Edmonton position as a bit of an adventure and a place to make some money and sort out his future. In accepting these terms, President Tory insisted that Burgess be settled in by April 1 because he was leaving for the summer and wanted Burgess on site to plan a third residence

In 1913 Edmonton was growing rapidly. The steel frame just visible on the mid left of the photograph is the Macleod Building, where Burgess would establish his office in 1940 after his retirement from the University of Alberta. (NC-6-386, GA)

building for the university. Thus, in mid-March 1913, Burgess stepped off the train in Edmonton. The city was in the midst of an unprecedented economic boom and was growing rapidly, and Burgess took a room at the King Edward Hotel, then the best in the city. The next day, he travelled to the site of the new university on the south bank of the river. Crossing the North Saskatchewan River over the Low Level Bridge in a horse-drawn cab, he wound his way along the river valley where the grip of winter was beginning to loosen, then up the steep banks to the scrub-covered land where the new university was being built.[16] Whatever plans about the future were in his mind that day, this journey to the new campus proved no short-term adventure, for the unforeseen vagaries of war, circumstance and time meant that he would be associated with Edmonton and the University of Alberta for the rest of his long life.

The First Years at the University of Alberta

The University of Alberta was chartered in 1906, and the first classes were held in 1908 in the Strathcona High School. The next year Premier Rutherford, who had championed the establishment of the university, as well as its location in his riding of Strathcona on the south bank of the river across from Edmonton, turned the sod for a new campus. Looming over the whole enterprise was President Henry Marshall Tory who had arrived in 1908 as the university's first president.[17] Trained at McGill where he was also professor of mathematics, he had already been instrumental in establishing the University of British Columbia. Tory was an ambitious and energetic figure who Burgess described as "a most remarkable man" who could "get things done" and was driven by a desire "to promote education throughout Canada." Perhaps someone gripped by such a personal mission also needed a strong, even self-centred, personality. As Burgess recalled, he and Tory "would walk together and he would ask, 'What do you think?' I would tell him what I thought. Several weeks later Dr. Tory would say, 'I have been thinking', then present the ideas as if they were his own."[18]

Tory's commitment to the future included plans that the University of Alberta would become one of the premier universities in Canada. This entailed the development of a campus to accommodate such ambitions, and in this connection Nobbs reworked the general plan for the university that he had earlier prepared. Developed in 1912 in partnership with Frank Darling of the prominent Toronto firm, Darling and Pearson, this new plan proposed a series of monumental brick and stone buildings laid out on a formal grid around squares and quadrangles. Nobbs rejected the popular Gothic style then favoured by many North American universities as unsuitable to the prairie climate and as too American a fashion. Instead, he favoured an "elastic free classical style in accordance with modified English traditions." The look of the campus would thus assert those elements of Canada's traditions and connections that were British, which implicitly also expressed and legitimised the social and political dominance of Anglo Canadians in a province with an increasingly mixed ethnic and racial population.[19] The campus would not only shelter the university, but a

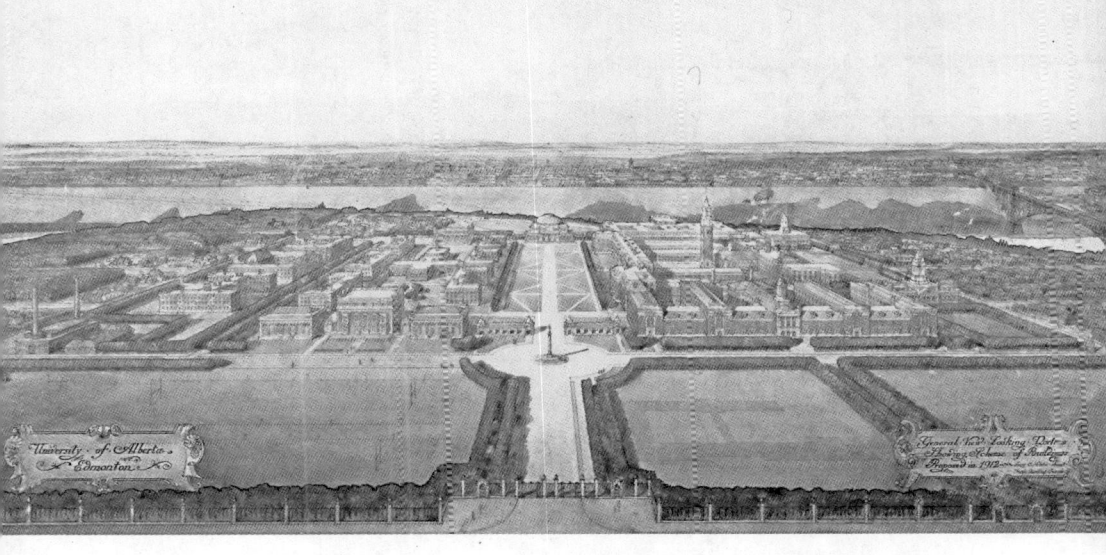

The Nobbs and Darling plan for the University of Alberta is shown in this watercolour rendering in 1912. (73.124, UAA)

provincial library, medical centre and other facilities. The Nobbs and Darling plan was designed to guide this development into the future and prevent problems encountered in older universities, such as McGill. There, piecemeal development had destroyed any possibility of a consistent design identity for the university and had created a confused and often conflicting layout that served little purpose other than, as Nobbs knew from personal experience, to pose problems for architects designing new buildings on the campus. Thus, as Nobbs observed, a long-range plan for the University of Alberta would "obviate the growth of a museum of detached architectural modernities by providing for large connected elements capable of expansion by units without disturbance of the general scheme."[20] When Burgess arrived in early 1913, this plan guided the building of the campus, although, as with so many efforts to develop long-range plans for complex sites, the Nobbs and Darling plan ultimately had only limited impact on the campus's physical evolution.

The Arts Building opened in 1915. Designed by Nobbs and Hyde, Burgess acted as supervising architect. (69.97–1 UAA)

The belief in the desirability of a long-term plan to guide future growth and establish the new university's identity through a coherent architectural statement was one indication that the University of Alberta was at a unique point in its history when Burgess arrived to supervise its architectural development. The population of the prairies had increased from 419,000 to 1,328,000 between 1901 and 1911, a period in which the region's social, economic and political life had been transformed. Growth in Alberta was slightly slower, but still spectacular, with the population almost doubling to just over 374,000 in 1911. Forecasts that such growth would be sustained well into the future were common, and it was assumed that a university that would match and ultimately exceed those of eastern Canada was needed. Thus, while the university's first faculty was arts and science, the range of teaching and research expanded quickly; law was added in 1912, as were civil engineering (under a new Faculty of Applied Science) and medicine in 1913. As well as these familiar faculties, the University of Alberta also established an architecture programme.

In contrast to France, where formal academic training in architecture had been the rule since the late eighteenth century, Britain, the United

States and Canada were only beginning in the late nineteenth century to abandon apprenticeship in favour of comprehensive university training. Such training was believed necessary to raise professional standards, to produce sufficient well trained graduates for a growing nation, and to help Canadian architects meet American competition.[21] The enhancement of architecture as a profession was also believed to be at stake. The first school of architecture in Canada was established in 1890 at the School of Practical Science (later the Faculty of Applied Science and Engineering) at the University of Toronto and schools followed in Montreal at McGill in 1896 and the Ecole Polytechnique in 1907, and at the University of Manitoba in 1912. In the United States, the first such school had been established at the Massachusetts Institute of Technology (MIT) in 1865, and by the 1890s architecture schools were appearing at many major American universities. In Britain, the same pattern was repeated. Architectural courses were being offered at various institutions and schools, such as King's College, London, by the late 1890s, and the first British school of architecture was established at the University of Liverpool in 1895.[22] Tory's ambition to establish an architectural school in Edmonton was thus part of the trend in the English-speaking world for universities to assume new responsibilities in professional education. And in this context, it also reflected another aspect of Tory's determination to make the University of Alberta into a first rank Canadian university.[23]

Burgess later recalled that the programme was probably premature since "the population of the province at that time was scarcely sufficient to support such a course," but its creation was inspired by the character of the time, not foreknowledge of the future.[24] The programme also reflected that Tory was too pragmatic to ignore that it had benefits aside from its educational value. True, a "considerable number" of students had said that they wanted to study architecture, and Tory noted that a programme, at least on a trial basis, was justified to meet this demand. But he also carefully calculated how it would contribute to the prolonged period of construction of new buildings that was assumed to lie ahead at the university. As he informed the university's Board of Governors, "the building operations going on at the University required the continuous presence of a competent architect for consultation and advice." This Burgess could provide at the same time that he taught architecture. Indeed, with Burgess as the "supervising architect for the University, the saving on architect's fees alone would be more than sufficient to pay the necessary salary during the opening trial years of the [architecture] Department." Moreover, as part of its role as a provincial centre of learning, the university was eager to have a hand in licensing professional activity in the province, including architecture. Thus, it had agreed to help regulate architecture in Alberta by examining applicants for membership in the Alberta Association of Architects (AAA), which had been established in 1906 to regulate the practice of architecture in the province. Again, the new professor of architecture and supervising architect of the university could administer and co-ordinate these examinations.[25]

Despite the many predictions of the university's future eminence, Burgess thought the campus was a "waste land" when he first saw it. While the city of Strathcona was building a hospital on university land at the south end of the campus, the university itself had only three buildings: Athabasca Hall and Assiniboia Hall (opened in 1911 and 1912 respectively), both designed by A.M. Jeffers, the chief architect in the Alberta Department of Public Works, and Alberta College (now St. Stephen's College), a Tudor revival-style brick building designed by the Edmonton firm of Magoon and Macdonald as a Methodist residential teaching college.[26] Athabasca and Assiniboia Halls met the university's needs for classrooms, administrative offices, and residential space for students and staff. Featuring a Jacobean revival-style, Jeffers had apparently applied ideas proposed by Percy Nobbs, and both buildings respected the "English" brick–with–stone appearance that Nobbs had specified in the general plan of the university.[27]

Burgess was given a north-facing room in Assiniboia Hall from which he could "hear the coyotes calling in the river valley" at night. He set to work immediately and accomplished an astonishing amount of work in his first two years at the university. He immediately put his stamp on the campus by designing exterior metal fire escapes for both Athabasca and

Assiniboia Halls, which, as wood frame buildings veneered with brick and stone, were not fire resistant. Reflecting his Arts and Crafts predilections, the fire escapes were designed specially and featured a distinctive cartouche, intertwining the letters U and A, on the landing of each level. In 1913 he also put in almost 300 hours drafting plans and elevations and drawing perspective views of Nobbs and Darling's general plan. As well, he and William Muir Edwards (professor of civil engineering 1908–1918) laid out, graded and seeded to grass the rest of the campus. Further, Burgess drew plans for horse and cattle stables and other buildings for a proposed university farm. He also designed seven detached houses for professors and staff. Later known as the Ring Houses, they were built along a cul de sac on the campus's west end. Rented to faculty, these were two-storey, three-bedroom houses with basements and featured floor plans that were then widely popular in the English-speaking world, especially in North America. Bedrooms were placed on the second floor, and living areas were on the first, with the kitchen at the back looking out onto the garden. The exterior of the buildings featured locally-made brick on the first floor and wood shingle on the second floor, which conveyed a welcoming, picturesque mood.[28] And along with these various projects, Burgess drew scale plans and elevations for the Arts Building. Designed by Percy Nobbs, and in keeping with the "free classical" style he favoured for the university, the building was planned as the campus's main teaching and administrative building. Contracts were let in 1913, and as the university's architect, Burgess supervised construction. The building opened in late 1915.[29]

Another major project in 1913 and 1914 was the design and construction of Pembina Hall, a third student residence that Burgess named after a local geographical feature. He devised a restrained and elegant Jacobean revival-style for the building, distinctive from, but compatible with, the two existing residential buildings. Clearly, the building was another part of the visual assertion of the Britishness of Canada, and it also respected Arts and Crafts beliefs by utilising locally-made brick and locally-quarried stone. Decorative elements were pared to a minimum in service of the principles of honesty and directness in design that Burgess so earnestly supported. Some areas

Pembina Hall was one of the largest buildings Burgess designed in his first years at the University of Alberta. Photo dated 1928. (69.18–36 UAA)

The lobby of Pembina Hall was not merely a reception area but was an architectural element that helped promote air movement in the building. (ND–3–2692, GA)

were ready for classroom use by the fall of 1914, although the building was not completed until 1915. Built with steel framing and concrete veneered with brick and stone, Pembina Hall was more fire resistant than the other two residence buildings. Showing the wisdom of Tory's desire for a resident architect at the university, it cost just over 37 cents per cubic foot, considerably less than comparable fireproof buildings in the city. Moreover, Burgess paid special attention to the provision of adequate ventilation. This was a topic of increasing importance given new scientific understanding about the role of germs in spreading communicable disease as well as more general contemporary theories about the value of fresh air for healthy living and working environments.[30] Lacking the mechanical means to ensure adequate air circulation in buildings, ventilation was promoted by planning the interior layout so as to encourage the natural movement of air throughout the structure. The same system that he described in his 1920 essay, "Hygiene in Architecture," was applied in Pembina Hall, and air circulated naturally through the building in both horizontal and vertical directions due to the design of the lobby, stairwells and corridors.[31]

In addition to his responsibilities for new buildings, Burgess quickly became immersed in the educational work of the university and seized the opportunity of establishing the architectural programme. The first student, Walter Thomas Middleton, enrolled in the architecture programme in the fall session 1914. As Burgess later recalled, the architecture programme was feasible because "the students in architecture could take courses along with students in engineering in theory of structures, surveying, geometrical drawing and other general subjects."[32] Beneath this simple description of an educational programme lay often acrimonious debates that had dominated thinking about architectural education in Britain and the United States in the late nineteenth century.

Beginning in the late 1800s, Arts and Crafts proponents had advocated various systems of training that would broadly link in a practical way the art of craftsmanship (the handling of materials such as brick or stone) with expression in design. In this view, design could not be approached separately from the nature of materials, craftwork and expression, and it was often seen as a fluid and applied activity. This was a logical expression of the holistic view that building was both art and science, although the most profound aspect of building was art, which expressed the unification of materials and sentiment. This was, despite the language in which it was often clothed, a pragmatic and applied approach to building. In contrast, the French Beaux Arts approach to education, which had become dominant in American architectural schools by about 1900 and in British schools by about 1920, stressed that architecture was about formal public design and grand planning. In Beaux Arts education, composition held first place in the curriculum and students were given a "design problem" that they sketched and then developed into detailed drawings. Often, little attention was paid to the specifics of site and function or the economic or constructional practicality of the project. The system was highly competitive and complex and the student's final design was juried. In the Beaux Arts view, "study in schools was considered more professional the more elevated it was from hands-on building; it had to have less emphasis therefore on construction." In the view of Arts and Crafts thinkers, such architectural training failed to give students practical experience or a mastery of the building process. Nor did it teach them respect for a meaningful context through a studied application of materials and design suited to specific places and times.[33]

Even so, at the same time that Arts and Crafts architects rejected Beaux Arts methodology and the sort of designs it produced, architectural schools in English Canada incorporated some Beaux Arts teaching methods into their curriculum, especially an increased emphasis on design. But despite the triumph of Beaux Arts approaches in the U.S. and later in Britain, English Canadians before World War II tended to cling to Arts and Crafts approaches overall, although they modified them by including some Beaux Arts pedagogical thinking. Nonetheless, a crucial difference remained between Canadian approaches to architectural education and those adopted in the United States, and after 1920, in Britain. McGill provided important precedents for Canadian architectural education, and its Scottish-based tradition became highly influential in Canada.[34] Thus, English-Canadian pedagogy continued to stress the practicality of the design process through the use of applied, rather than theoretically inspired, design projects.

To a significant degree, the system that Burgess implemented at the University of Alberta reflected these broadly understood Canadian approaches to education, and he (like most other schools in English Canada) continued to endorse them throughout the 1920s and 1930s. Thus, the first year of the four-year programme corresponded generally with that of civil engineering, but Burgess added courses in architectural drawing, history and French. In the remaining three years, students progressively completed more specialised architecture courses, such as building construction, architectural history and architectural design, as well as more advanced engineering courses and classes in public hygiene offered through the medical faculty.[35] Except for the University of Manitoba, where architecture was part of the Faculty of Arts until it joined the engineering faculty in 1920, this approach to architectural training was typical in English Canada at the time. At McGill and the University of Toronto, for example, architecture was embedded in the engineering faculties and students took courses in civil engineering, applied mathematics and arts in addition to specialised courses in architecture. Alberta's programme was clearly inspired by the precedent of McGill and its Scottish academic tradition. It was also a pragmatic response to the newness of the university and the fact that the architecture department consisted only of Burgess Thus, while he taught subjects in which he felt competent, such as architectural history, specifications, design, drawing and building construction, more "scientific" subjects were taken in the engineering faculty and at the medical school.[36] Similarly, Burgess asserted that the primary objective of the programme was to give students skills in "what to do" as practising architects. As he observed, "my idea was that an architecture department should be as near to what I had done as an apprentice and an architect in an architect office." The students were, as he termed it, "serving an apprenticeship under me," and so they were given a practical training in "work of a class that they would get to do" after their graduation.[37]

A practical training did not, however, mimic that which might be had at a technical or vocational school. As taught in the university, practice also included theory, which meant analysing why architecture mattered and why architectural practice took the forms it did. Achieving a balance between theory and practice was never easy. It was never safe from the complaints of those who thought that architectural education should be practical and thus reject the "scholasticism" of architectural history and theories about proportion, symmetry and balance that were part of the "secrecy and mysticism" of architectural professionalism. Opposing such views, others argued that architectural training needed to be a highly intellectual and theoretical pursuit.[38] Devising an acceptable programme for architectural training thus involved balancing a complex interplay of factors that defined and shaped both theoretical and practical concerns. Was a concern for beauty, for example, a practical aspect of designing a building, or was it only incidental to more important technical things? As well, how could the professional status of architecture be enhanced through formal training? And among other concerns that needed to be weighed, what was the social meaning of architecture and its connection with a society's character and outlook?

These were not simple questions, and Burgess made sense of them by appealing to his humanist belief that while architecture was obviously about putting up buildings and ensuring that they were put up well, it was also a social act in which people's creative, aesthetic and social needs were central. This philosophy—which owed so much to Arts and Crafts thinking—informed his teaching at the University of Alberta. Consistent with current beliefs that physical surroundings and social context helped shape character and human behaviour, this philosophy asserted that the built environment influenced behaviour and that designing it offered the individual an opportunity to express and develop his or her character. As Burgess had told an audience in Montreal in 1908, "the home expresses the character of its owner as a mirror reflects what stands in front of it." And, he rhetorically asked, could a well-designed home improve the character of its owner? "Why surely," he answered, for "the work and thought he has expended has helped him to know himself, what he really likes and wants, and his wits have been improved" by completing the work to his satisfaction.[39]

In the same sense, but at a less personalised level, architecture was a measure of the quality and attainment of a civilisation because it enriched society by giving it pride in its accomplishments and by creating a legacy worthy of the future. Burgess was fond of saying that "manners maketh the man," and when taken to its fullest meaning, this suggested that architectural education needed to prepare architects to participate thoughtfully and responsively in their society. But the participation of the architect in society was not that of the solitary creative genius battling to achieve his or her personal vision. Analogous to the way that the home mirrored the character of its owner, the creative work of the architect mirrored the architect's interpretation of society. This was a crucial issue for determining the sort of education that an architect needed. Over his life, Burgess remained firm in his assertion that society, not architects, created architecture. This was, at the time, a common view, and it led to an assertion that the architect's task was to express—as a sort of seer—his or her society's desires, sentiments and needs. Thus an architect needed to be trained to be a full and active participant in his or her society, to work to make it better and to understand and express its aspirations in an artful manner. As Burgess succinctly remarked in 1925, architecture was "the human intelligence and sentiment that is built into buildings."[40]

The assumption that architecture expressed both individual and collective character also revealed those things that a society truly valued. Some societies had pursued beauty (which Burgess thought was the highest aim of architecture and was best expressed in the classical Greek "discovery" of "the harmonious relationship of all component elements"), others (such as Rome) had valued the grandeur and power of the state, while still others (such as Byzantium or Medieval Europe) had valued religious life. In each case, these values were revealed by the architecture of each civilisation; an expressive capacity that made architecture an "art." Integral to this was craftsmanship—the way in which expression was shaped materially—

which Burgess, faithful to Arts and Crafts principles, believed was one of the central dimensions of practice. Indeed, craftsmanship was a force broader than architecture itself, for it was essential for the personal fulfillment and gratification that came from expressing "the human appetite to record emotion and to express the joy the world inspires us with." This in itself promoted social well-being, but, as well, a class of crafts workers who gained their living and self-respect from the skill of their hands was essential for social order and dignity. This followed the thinking of John Ruskin and William Morris. Also faithful to Morris, Burgess accepted the dictum that architecture needed to be created by the people for the people and to be a "joy to the maker and the user." Because beauty was an innate need that enriched and expressed the most profound human motivations, this made a concern for beauty in architecture a practical quest.[41]

The assertion that the meaning of architecture lay in its social context and expressed individual as well as community character elevated the study of history to a central place in the education of architects. Architectural history was a required course in three of the four years of the University of Alberta programme, a requirement premised on the belief that history made architecture intellectually meaningful by enhancing architects' skills in critical thinking. As Burgess noted, "it is easier to come to right, fair, unbiased opinion regarding old work. It has taken its place in historical perspective, and we know the effect it has produced on the minds of men of various temperaments. Having an outside knowledge of the spirit of the times, we can estimate how far it has clearly embodied that spirit."[42] Moreover, historical knowledge helped link theory (the "why" of architecture) with practical applications (the "how") because it involved learning the "lessons" taught by historical events and facts. Such lessons were different for different generations, but the historical study of architecture demonstrated the ways that buildings revealed the character of their times and how architecture arose from a social context. It was also a practical way to teach about the performance over time of a wide range of building technologies and materials.

But of all of these justifications for historical study, the most important, Burgess argued, was that history helped broaden the sensibility of the architect. Such sensibility was crucial for all great architecture, for, as history demonstrated, the greatest architecture was that which appealed to the mind by having an emotional impact upon the observer. This was the sentiment, or feeling, of a building. Indeed, codes of architectural practice or rules of design could never teach what history demonstrated: that inventiveness, flexibility and passion were the roots of great architecture and one of the sources of sentiment. As Burgess concluded in a lecture to the University of Alberta Philosophical Society in 1913–14, this realisation was important for the education of the architect. As he observed, "we may create schools and elaborate rules of art, we may develop the technical part of it to high and curious pitches of excellence, but it is impossible for any school to be as broad as humanity. In the outside multitude lives the root of all learning and in them in ages yet to come shall time and time again be begotten these influences which shall revivify a world grown weary with old learning and old customs and old art."[43]

Yet for all its promise to create a vibrant and living architecture, the emphasis on history in architectural education was a very conservative technique for broadening and deepening the study and practice of architecture. In conjunction with Arts and Crafts thinking, Burgess at times romanticised poverty as a source of honesty, patience and the dignity of working with one's hands, although it also led him to urge that crafts workers deserved decent wages, for, when one purchased the products of their labour, one also bought "the lives and thoughts of men."[44] But conjoined with this attitude was an assumption, especially common among Arts and Crafts proponents, that personal and collective character was formed within a matrix of tradition, and that the accretions of the past incrementally enriched individual and collective experience. And as the character of a people matured, the architecture they produced also became more subtly expressive. Despite the evidence of the transformation wrought by industrialisation and urbanisation, this argument presumed the existence of a relatively static society in which "progress" gradually unfolded through living amidst the material evidence of the past as well as an intellectual familiarity with the society's history and achievements.

Such a rationale for architectural history was consistent with widely held social views among members of the English-speaking dominant culture of Alberta and Canada. It was accepted that, outside of Egypt and the ancient Middle East (which were important because they had influenced classical Greek architecture and therefore were relevant to European development), most of the models of architecture deemed worthy of study were European-inspired. This focus asserted a particular hierarchy in the value and importance of various civilisations because its exclusive focus on European forms placed European civilisation as the highest expression of human development. Canada, as a relatively recent but remote fragment of this older source civilisation, was an inheritor of this tradition, especially its British variants. But in light of the separation that distance imposed, the arrival of new Canadians who had no connection to Britain or its traditions and the inevitable erosion of the immediate relevance of the British source culture for Canada, how could this tradition retain its vitality and vigour for Canadians? This was an especially pointed issue in a place such as Alberta where European settlement was recent, the population was ethnically diverse, and the assimilation of non-English-speaking peoples was a concern to the English-speaking group that dominated the province. Burgess assumed that, through education and the transmission of values by family and social institutions (such as universities, museums and schools), these connections would be maintained and strengthened. Architecture too was part of this transmission of culture, since the form, style and sentiment of buildings expressed cultural values and continuity. This was, it can be recalled, one aspect of Nobbs's use of the English free classical design for the University of Alberta where the buildings had been envisioned not merely as functional structures, but also as promoting and displaying social and political power and viewpoints.

In light of these beliefs, Burgess assumed (as did many Canadian architects) that a Canadian architecture would evolve within a British mould in response to the unique climatic demands, variations in building materials and social conditions of the country.[45] This would not necessarily produce buildings that would be particularly distinctive in style from those of Britain or Europe, but they would modify the European template. An appeal was also made to Euro-Canadian traditions, especially the old architecture of Quebec. Arts and Crafts assumptions that historical architectural forms could inform the present inspired architects such as Percy Nobbs and Ramsay Traquair, who succeeded Nobbs as the head of the architecture programme at McGill, to argue that Quebec's early French building traditions offered a model for a distinctively Canadian architecture. This was coupled with an admiration for old Quebec furniture and hand crafts, which were seen (in defiance of historical evidence) as honest expressions of a culture uncorrupted by industrialisation and commerce.[46]

Burgess too shared kindred sentiments in his admiration for hand craft and for the material culture of the pre-industrial world, and in his disdain for most forms of advertising and modern commercial life. But while he expressed some excitement about old Quebec building traditions as models for the present, his enthusiasm for local building traditions did not survive his move west in 1913. Although he continued to endorse the Arts and Crafts dictum that buildings should reflect their site and the character of local materials, he showed almost no interest in western vernacular traditions. The reasons for this are unclear, but perhaps he assumed that the west was a *tabula rasa*, or that its traditions or human culture were unworthy of inspiring the present. Perhaps, as well, his vision was ethnically and racially too narrow to pick up on older Métis building traditions of the west or to be inspired to devise new regional forms based on older Aboriginal responses to the western land and climate. Such an inability to stretch outside one's cultural references was a mark of Euro-Canadian thinking, not only in the west but on the national stage as well, and Burgess seems to have shared this attitude. This may also have explained his lack of interest in more recent vernacular building traditions that had been brought to the region by non-English-speaking migrants from various parts of the world, especially central Europe. Whatever the case, Burgess perceived no need to break away from the European canon or, more specifically, the models of the British past. In this, he differed little from the widely held belief among the English-speaking dominant culture in western Canada that the region would be remade in the image of the British and English-speaking world.

These attitudes were given added credibility by Burgess's assumption that architecture reflected the preoccupations and the dominant character of a society. All architecture, even if wholly imitative, reflected the character of place and time, and one of the ways of obtaining a better architecture was through public education about the meaning and sources of architectural design and its connection to broader cultural concerns. As a consequence, Burgess saw one of his responsibilities as giving expression to the particular requirements of the new land in a way that would link them to Canada's cultural traditions as he understood them. This ambition was always coloured by his lens of "Britishness" and his belief that Canada was a British society, albeit one with a North American face. It was part of the self-assumed task of the English-speaking intellectual vanguard (such as professionals and educators) of the new settler society to cultivate the emerging culture of the west so as to give these European and British traditions fertile ground in which to grow and evolve. Such a task suited Burgess perfectly for his training in Edinburgh had imbued in him the Scottish ideal of the architect as both a technically competent builder and a "scholar, historian and polemicist."[47]

Such assumptions informed his participation in a lecture tour by university professors organised by the university's extension department shortly after his arrival in Alberta. The Department of Extension had been established in 1912 "to take the university to the country," and over the next several decades it met this goal through a varied and often imaginative array of programmes. A lending library that sent books (and later slides and films) on request to people and organisations in rural communities, the sponsorship of debating, drama and handicraft clubs, a radio station, as well as lectures by university professors in small towns were all used over the years to help spread learning throughout the province and to mitigate the isolation and loneliness of people in remote communities. In the 1913 lecture tour by professors, Burgess spoke about architectural history and its meaning in various locations in southern Alberta. His talk at the Claresholm Agricultural School was not a rousing success—the local newspaper reported that it was not as well patronised "as its quality deserved"—but at Fort Macleod he drew an audience of about 50 people and he earned a glowing write up in the local paper.[48]

One of the themes that Burgess emphasised in this lecture tour concerned the Arts and Crafts emphasis on the importance of craftsmanship in architecture and the need to develop an educated aesthetic judgement. As he told his listeners, it took effort and knowledge to appreciate good workmanship, and using the example of a well-laid brick wall, he advised his audience that "you cannot see the beauty of a brick wall without knowledge and intelligence and a sense of the beauty of shapes and colours and an appreciation of human industry and the character that goes along with it." This was so for all the arts, and "the poet is simply a man like the bricklayer who builds up beautiful thoughts line by line, well laid in the courses, well bonded together line answering to line." But craftsmanship was only one part of architecture. Greater still was its contribution to civilisation. Architecture, he observed, created a "lasting monument of fine ideals and enthusiasms otherwise passing [and] incorporates them into [the] traditions of the race." Thus, great buildings were "a means of holding the ground that civilisation has gained" for they helped people to realise "how large and grand a thing human life may be."[49]

World War I and After

The architecture programme was no sooner in place at the University of Alberta when World War I changed the direction of Canadian life. By the war's end, the university had contributed 438 undergraduates, alumni and staff to the war effort, 82 of whom never returned. Burgess was one of those swept up by the demands of war, and in 1915, at the age of 45, he joined the Canadian Officers Training Programme at the University of Alberta. Later that year—about the time his contract with the university expired—he joined the war effort. Failing to gain a commission, he served in the 66th Overseas Battalion. After a short training period in Calgary, he went overseas, although it seems that he did not serve in France. His contribution, however, did not end with the armistice. In 1919 he joined the staff of the Khaki College, in Ripon, England, which had been created by President Tory to occupy men waiting to return to Canada from overseas. As Burgess observed, "there were not enough ships to bring the men home" and the young men "left in England were restless." In Tory's view, schooling would keep them busy and interested, and would improve their minds. Burgess found it an inspired project and immediately signed up to help. There were about eight instructors at Ripon, and Burgess taught building construction and architecture. Classes were small and allowed personalised instruction as well as tours of the countryside to study historical buildings; on one occasion Burgess and his students ventured as far as Lincoln to see the cathedral.[50]

In late 1919 Burgess returned to the University of Alberta. There are no clues about why he decided to make Edmonton his permanent home. He had already accomplished much there in his first years, and perhaps the fact that he was now almost 50 years old helped decide the matter. Whatever the case, he was no longer interested in a short-term contract, and he resumed his duties on a permanent basis, "although there had been no formal arrangement to that effect." But as he wryly recalled many years later, he seemed to be expected, and so he settled into the life that he had left almost five years before.[51]

This was the opening of a highly productive phase in Burgess's life, and for the next thirty-odd years he was fully involved in the architectural life of the university, the province and the country. He served as President of the Alberta Association of Architects in 1923 and 1924, and also served for many years on the provincial examining board for architects in Alberta. In 1930 he was elected a Fellow of the RAIC, and in 1933 a Fellow of RIBA. He also continued to deliver public talks on architecture and, increasingly after the mid-1920s, on town planning. An added venue for such work came in 1927 when the university established its own radio station, CKUA, to use the new technology of radio to expand the reach of its extension programme and to help broaden the cultural and social horizons of rural Alberta. Through affiliations with local stations, CKUA reached most parts of the province, and offered a mix of classical music, drama, information features and lectures on a vast range of topics. Over the years, Burgess gave a number of lectures on architecture and town planning, some of which are reprinted in this book.[52]

The architecture programme was resumed after Burgess's return in 1919 in the form established six years earlier; students took courses in engineering and medicine as well as the architectural courses taught by Burgess. As in earlier years of the programme, students took courses in design, specifications and, among others, building construction. And, of course, they took architectural history. In the conventional format used at architectural schools elsewhere, lectures were illustrated with lantern slides or illustrations from books, and historical precedents were further incorporated into the curriculum in the drawing courses where students used historical models, plaster casts and images. This did not entail mere copying of past forms and styles, but involved learning how to adapt historical precedents into a culturally responsive architecture that, while rooted in tradition, was sensitive to contemporary needs.

The second student, Andrew Giffen, graduated in 1922, but then the programme declined precipitously. The reasons for this are unclear, but potential students may have worried that the university's architecture programme had an uncertain future since the provincial government had recommended in 1923 that it be discontinued "on the grounds of economy." While lobbying by the AAA (of which Burgess was President at the time) helped defeat the proposal, it was a discouraging development.[53] Students may also have had fresh in their minds the lessons of World War I. During the war building activity slowed dramatically.[54] Although conditions improved after the war, employment opportunities for architects in the province remained limited, and Alberta architects often struggled to make a decent living. Although there were times in the 1920s when building was active, architects were often bypassed. The provincial government no longer employed any architects in its public works department, and while some urban centres required that architects be hired for the construction of buildings over a certain value, these requirements were often ignored. In Edmonton, for example, where a bylaw required that buildings costing over $10,000 had to be designed by an architect or engineer registered in Alberta, the law was often evaded. Sometimes this was done with collusion of registered architects (which revealed the weakness of professional ethics and enforcement) or by contractors flouting the law to save money and eliminate competitive tendering.[55]

All of these factors may have deterred students from taking up architecture as a profession. Indeed, no one entered the programme until 1928 when John Ulric Rule enrolled. But enrolment then began to increase steadily. The reasons for this are also unclear—while the early 1930s saw a serious decline in building construction, perhaps the programme by then was perceived as more stable. Whatever the reason, there were students continuously enrolled in the programme during the 1930s. By 1940 a total of twenty-one students had graduated since the programme's inception.[56] Nonetheless, the university did not hire additional staff to assist Burgess, who alone continued to shoulder the whole of the architectural programme. Whatever his strengths or energy, a single individual could not constitute a coherent or balanced school of architecture. As Percy Nobbs remarked in 1930 in a survey of architectural education in Canada, training was focused at McGill and the École des Beaux Arts (established in 1923) in Montreal, at the Universities of Toronto and Manitoba, and with the beginnings of schools in Saskatchewan and Alberta. None of these schools, however, sustained or nourished each other as part of a national effort in architectural education. As Nobbs noted, there was no contact among them: they were far apart, and seemingly there was a degree of defensiveness and parochialism that led them to stick to their provincial boundaries.[57]

While the University of Alberta programme remained under-funded and rested entirely on Burgess's shoulders, the steady stream of graduates it produced in the 1930s indicated that it was beginning to find its feet. In the 1930–31 session the programme was made into a five-year one, which brought it into conformity with other architecture programmes in Canada.⁵⁸ It offered a solid training and produced some notable architects. John Ulric Rule graduated in 1932, Lloyd George MacDonald, John Stevenson and Gordon Wynn graduated in 1936, and, among others, Peter Rule and Jean Wallbridge graduated in 1939; all of them made important and distinguished contributions to Alberta's and Canada's architectural record. The alumni of the programme included three women, Margaret Buchanan, who graduated in 1937, and Margaret Findlay and Jean Wallbridge, both of whom received their degrees in 1939. While the student body almost entirely reflected the dominant Anglo-Canadian ruling group in Alberta, two graduates broke this pattern: Nobuichi Yamaoka graduated in 1935 and Edward Yee Wing graduated in 1936.⁵⁹

The presence of three women—about 14 percent of the graduates of the programme—also spoke about the wider context of the practice of architecture in Canada. Put simply, the architectural profession in mid twentieth century Canada was a hostile place for women. The first woman graduated from architecture at the University of Toronto in 1920, and the first woman to be admitted to a professional association was Esther Marjorie Hill, who was admitted to the AAA in 1925. Hill had applied in 1921, but her application caused such "consternation" that it took the association until 1925 to admit her. The next breakthrough for women architects in Canada came only in 1931 when the Ontario Association of Architects admitted two women members. Such restrictive conditions reflected wider currents in the society that defined women's role as that of homemakers. As Burgess concluded in his 1930 talk to the Edmonton Household Economics Association, some people resented the saying that a "woman's sphere is the home," but then there were "some people who would turn their backs on heaven." He was, nonetheless, willing to accept women applicants for the University of Alberta programme, and the first woman, Margaret Buchanan, enrolled in 1932. Indeed, the highest percentage of women admitted to professional architects' associations before 1960 was in western Canada, while the highest number of graduates in architecture was also from the western schools at the University of Alberta, the University of British

Columbia and, especially, the University of Manitoba. Nonetheless, these early women graduates often left the profession or were effectively confined to areas of practice such as domestic architecture and interior decoration, which were the least profitable and prestigious areas of practice.[60] This was the experience of Jean Wallbridge (class of 1939) and Mary Imrie. Imrie was admitted to the University of Alberta architecture programme in 1938, but she transferred for her second year to the University of Toronto when it was announced that the University of Alberta programme would be closed. She returned to Edmonton in 1944 and by 1951 had set up practice with Wallbridge. The firm designed many houses and apartments, but despite the quality and thoughtfulness of their work, they had difficulty in finding larger or more lucrative commissions.[61]

Burgess was proud of his students and of the education that he helped them acquire. Late in his life he recalled that his students, largely because of their training, had found work immediately upon graduation. Moreover, since he ran the architecture programme "like an office," he was successful, despite the protests of some architects in the province, in persuading the Alberta government to allow University of Alberta students to enter practice directly without an apprenticeship.[62] And some of his students also fondly recalled their years with him. Burgess's personality and the small classes allowed an "Oxford-type education." As Gordon Wynn, who joined John and Peter Rule, two other University of Alberta architecture graduates, to form the firm Rule Wynn Rule in 1938, recalled, "Burgess could talk for two hours about manufacturing lead for lead pencils and be fascinating."[63]

In the 1920s, when enrolment in architecture was low or nonexistent, Burgess taught ancient, medieval and renaissance history in the history department. After about 1930, when students were almost continuously enrolled in architecture, he taught all of the architecture courses, about 15 courses per year when there were students enrolled in each year of the programme. He also taught an introductory architecture course, simply called Architecture.[64] Designed for students in the Faculty of Arts, the course was sufficiently popular that it was offered almost continuously during the 1920s and 1930s. It featured lectures, with a heavy emphasis on the history of architecture, as well as extensive sketching. As Burgess noted, "architecture is pre-eminently a subject of material forms" and sketching was an important way to understand it. Although there may have been hopes that this general course would help broaden the reach of the architecture programme, it aimed to teach nonspecialists about architectural forms and principles of design. Crucial in this respect was the pursuit of beauty, which Burgess defined as a quality immune to time or fashion. As he told his students in the opening lecture, "the appreciation of what is beautiful is constant—proportionate, dignified, expressive of intelligence acting in a healthy, happy and congenial manner." The search for beauty was an appetite existing "in all healthy and well trained minds," which needed to find expression in everyday life if people were to lead contented and fulfilled lives. Since individuals were responsible for their material surroundings, training in aesthetics would lead them to create pleasing and beautiful environments in which their "minds can take delight." At the most immediate level, this would find expression in the home, which had become "a matter of highest consideration" in an age when "all wish to be rich and highly considered." Indeed, Burgess contended that "at the present-day it would be almost true to say that architectural design begins at home."[65] It was a further assertion of his enduring belief that the pursuit of beauty was of singular importance for society because people would be improved spiritually and intellectually by living in well-designed and appointed homes. The corollary was that if people also demanded beauty, excellence and efficiency in public spaces and took pride in their communities, society would be made that much better.[66]

An Emerging Interest in Town Planning

The concern about the importance of well-designed public space expressed Burgess's belief in the importance of town planning. This had long been a personal interest: he had joined the Town Planning Institute of Canada in 1920, one year after its founding.[67] The context of buildings had, of course, always been a concern for architects who were naturally concerned that buildings be placed to best show themselves. The growth of urban planning as a distinct field of study after the 1880s, however, had broadened their involvement in planning urban space. Moreover, for those architects coming from an Arts and Crafts background, the assumption that architecture was concerned with the social, as well as the physical, context of buildings was only a logical extension of a holistic view of architecture as a social art. Indeed, as Burgess noted in 1930, town planning and architecture operated together seamlessly, and one could define architecture as including "the design of the open spaces as well as the buildings of a town."[68] So too, he applied the same principles that he used to judge the quality of individual buildings to assess the quality of town plans: order, purpose and, among other criteria, utility. Aside from such thinking, some architects also saw town planning as a chance to broaden their practices. As E. Underwood, a past president of the AAA, noted in 1930, town planning offered new opportunities for architects. While the ways that planning regulations influenced construction were of obvious significance for an architect's practice, Underwood contended that architects were "exceptionally well-equipped" to educate the public about urban planning. Consequently, he believed that architects needed to become involved with the various planning agencies that were springing up because the raising of the public's "appreciation of aesthetics" would simultaneously help to "create greater desire to obtain the advice of architects."[69]

In the late nineteenth century, urban planning theories that stressed architectural harmony, visual beauty and public grandeur had often become absorbed in an idealised quest for civic beauty or in grandiose plans such as those drawn by Thomas Mawson for Calgary just before World War I.[70] While many of the concerns of this approach, such as the arrangement of streets and the provision of parks and services for public sanitation, remained important, planning was also evolving into a broader effort to make urban life more rational, healthy, efficient and pleasant. For some critics, such as the English planner and social activist, Ebenezer Howard, the best solution for the problem of the modern industrial city was to abandon its further development and build new towns with their own economic base some distance away from the cities. He called these Garden Cities because of their extensive use of green belts and open space. This was a bold experiment in regional planning, and Howard successfully implemented these ideals at Welwyn and Letchworth, north of London.[71] Another popular argument among many planning advocates was that one of the greatest barriers to the improvement of city life was unrestricted control of private property by landowners. Indeed, in Alberta the tension between public regulation and an exaggerated commitment to individual rights over private property was one of the reasons why planning efforts there had historically failed.[72]

Planning theories in the interwar years continued to show a varying emphasis on different activities, procedures and justifications for planning. Some planners, such as Thomas Adams, the British planner who was associated with the Canadian Commission of Conservation between 1914 and 1920, argued that the social benefits of planning could be realised without challenging the economic and political pre-eminence of the individual in society. While Adams recognised that some aspects of planning (such as zoning) inevitably diminished private rights over property, this was mitigated by the increased property values and social stability that planning brought.[73] Others, such as Burgess, were less certain that planning could achieve its social goals without challenging liberal individualism. While both Adams and Burgess agreed that economic benefits could flow from urban planning and that the ultimate goal was to make cities and towns more wholesome, efficient and respectful places in which to live and work, Burgess assumed that this would inevitably involve more collective solutions. As he observed in 1941 in a talk to the Edmonton Rotary Club, "the town planner must realise that he is the builder of the home of civilised man. Such is the *ideal* function of town planning."[74] While he did not adopt socialist approaches, he believed that one of the purposes of planning was to ensure good living environments for all members of society. As he noted in a speech at the Men's Faculty Club in 1935, the infringement of rights of private property was sometimes necessary for the public good.[75]

Burgess was also willing to curtail individual economic rights in the case of advertising. At the beginning of the twenty-first century, when people have been inured to advertising and promotion of commercial interests in almost every aspect of their daily lives, concerns in the 1920s about billboards and rooftop advertising signs seem an over-reaction. But Burgess, like many observers, was deeply offended by the increasing scale of these intrusions into public life, which he viewed as demeaning human potential and intelligence. He saw the growing chorus of advertising as a social failing and believed that it had become a "disease with us." Indeed, along with unplanned building and thoughtless design, advertising was a major contributor to the "great menace of general ugliness" that was "threatening our civilization" and spoiling the natural beauty of the world.[76] The threat that ugliness posed to civilisation was a further expression of Burgess's belief in the power of environment to shape behaviour and thought. He stated this concisely in a 1942 talk when he observed that human ideas came through all five senses, but mainly hearing and sight. As he noted, "upon the right functioning of these, the rootlets of thought, depends the maintenance of our whole mental constitution." Thus,

> Words convey to us ideas—but only at second hand; for the ideas are independent of the sound of those artificial contrivances that we call words. All ideas are founded originally upon what our senses directly perceive. Vision and hearing are the chief ultimate bases of thought. Hence the great importance which the Greeks attached to music and architecture, the chief direct appeals of art to hearing and to sight.[77]

Such reasoning explained the importance of visual culture and how it directly shaped society. Ugliness was to be resisted, not from an abstracted pursuit of beauty, but for the social good. People needed to be educated in visual terms and taught to incorporate sentiment in a controlled way into their daily lives. Once this was done, they would demand better environments that would in turn produce clearer thinking citizens.

The realisation of social goals through planning also applied to housing, a subject particularly close to Burgess's heart. Arts and Crafts thinkers placed heavy emphasis on the need for well-designed houses to bring tradition, efficiency and beauty into everyday life. Nonetheless, how could good house design be achieved when most architects could not afford to build a practice around domestic work? The answer was to educate the public to recognise good design to give them the confidence to demand it. This explains the frequency with which Burgess spoke publicly about housing and domestic architecture. He had a strongly materialist view on the matter, and argued that while the "house" was merely a type of building that offered shelter, a "home" was the beneficent influence of the material surroundings of family life—the fireplace, the furniture, the particular rooms that sheltered special activities, the books and pictures, and, outside, the garden. Burgess saw this expression as particularly English in its origin and character, and claimed that these material objects and places shaped family life, giving it expression and focus. The idealised home thus became yet another expression of the place of British values in Canada. The home also had to meet practical concerns about sanitation, efficiency and cost because such matters had a direct practical impact on health and thus happiness. Accordingly, design was of the highest importance in the making of homes, and Burgess was insistent that it should be founded on the ambition of creating an environment that expressed tradition, sociability and comfort so that the family would find happiness and contentment. This also led to his support for the detached single family owner-occupied dwelling and his condemnation of apartment living for families. Children needed safe and private outdoor play space, which they could not have in apartments. While apartments met the housing needs of some specialised groups in the society, he agreed fully with the then popular Canadian assumption that owner-occupied houses entailed commitment and pride of ownership, created social cohesion, and best sheltered family life.[78]

While Burgess tended in his earlier years to focus on design, decoration and the personal and social meaning of "home," after about 1930 he began to broaden his thinking about housing in terms of its integral role in urban planning and as confirmation of the architect's mandate to address social needs. This was a logical expression of his belief in the identity of purpose of architecture and urban planning. Although Burgess remained concerned about the "home" as a private repository of social virtue, he increasingly spoke about housing in terms of social justice. While he was perhaps influenced by modern approaches that saw housing as inseparable from planning (such as those posed by European Modernists from the German Bauhaus), it appears from his talks on the subject that this shift was also part of his response to the intensification of social inequality brought about by the Depression. By the mid 1930s, inspired by social housing initiatives in Britain and Sweden, and encouraged by the social housing possibilities of the *Dominion Housing Act* of 1935, he had become a strong advocate of the necessity for public initiatives, especially co-operative arrangements on the Swedish model, for ensuring adequate supply and conditions of owner-occupied single family detached dwellings.[79]

Such housing issues were intimately connected to zoning. Zoning plans—which were only adopted to any appreciable extent in Canadian cities and towns during the interwar years—set out allowable uses of urban land within broad categories such as business, residential and industrial. This grew in part from the functional planning techniques that had been promoted and developed by planners such as Thomas Adams. In this approach, districts of a city were designed to match their unique functions, whether they were commercial, residential or industrial, and all were tied together by an efficient transportation network. Burgess supported both zoning and transportation planning, which placed him firmly within the Thomas Adams functional approach to planning. But while Adams tended to justify zoning as a regulatory process that would preserve property values, Burgess pointedly observed in 1935 that the problems of crowded, inadequate housing could not be solved through zoning alone. Housing had special needs and its own dynamic, and while zoning could bring about better housing conditions in some respects, he recognised that more proactive state initiatives were necessary because the effect of zoning on housing "is salutary but chiefly restrictive and something more than restriction is needed to ensure good housing for all."[80]

While there seems to have been a popular view that zoning and civic beautification through parks development and tree planting were the sum total of urban planning, planning advocates such as Burgess insisted that these things were only single elements among many. By about 1930 most planners were pressing for the use of more comprehensive urban planning, or what was then called City Planning Procedure. Rather than planning a city in segments and ensuring connections among these parts through transportation and other services, City Planning Procedure offered a more sophisticated methodology for co-ordinated long-range planning of the multifarious needs of entire urban areas. Further, there was growing support for regional planning, which dealt in a similarly comprehensive manner with a number of related adjacent urban and rural areas of differing density and function. In both cases, the resulting planning documents would be inclusive, incorporating zoning provisions as well as those for transportation, street layouts, housing and sanitation. Among many other considerations, parks and recreational and educational needs would also be addressed, thus creating a rational plan that treated the whole of an urban area as an integrated unit.[81]

A central aspect of such planning initiatives was street layout. Almost all places in Alberta were laid out on a gridiron—a relentlessly expandable system of rectangular blocks surveyed on a strict north-south and east-west axis. Burgess was another of the many critics of the soulless monotony that the gridiron created and its waste of the natural advantages of a site. He endorsed popular proposals for alternative street layout that would bring visual variety and increase the amount of sunshine available to both sides of the street.[82] More imaginatively planned streets would also bring a more socially interactive urban landscape by creating convenient and visually interesting streetscapes built on a human scale, thus permitting people to develop closer connections with the life of the community.[83]

The creation of social space through more imaginative street planning was only one route to stimulating a more engaged citizenry. Burgess also strongly supported the concept of a civic centre, a central focal point (aside from the central business district) in an urban area. This concept was somewhat popular among planners during the interwar years, but it especially appealed to Burgess's belief that society would be made better through the appropriate design of the physical environment. The civic centre concept commonly drew upon European traditions of town squares where the most important institutions of the town were located in conjunction with open space. It was reasoned that, as community focal points, town centres helped create civic identity and pride by bringing a personal sense of belonging and commitment to the city or town. While Burgess thought that country life was best for physical well being, he recognised that urban places not only fulfilled crucial economic roles but cultivated thinkers and artists. The city was not just a place to do business; it more importantly met instinctive human needs for social context and interaction, all of which the civic centre would promote. Such civic centres were difficult to establish after the fact in built-up areas, but possibilities remained even within established urban environments. Edmonton was particularly fortunate in this respect. There, land had been reserved downtown for a civic centre, and though nothing had been done to implement the plan, Burgess lobbied constantly in the 1930s and 1940s for its realisation.

Hopes about the possibility of implementing many of these planning concepts were raised in 1929 when Alberta passed new town planning legislation. Alberta's earlier legislation in this respect had been piecemeal and ineffectual, and by the late 1920s lobbying by local organisations that endorsed town planning helped to bring the matter to public attention. This, along with other factors, persuaded the Brownlee government in 1929 to bring in new town planning legislation that ostensibly encouraged both rural and urban planning.[84] While Alberta's legislation drew heavily on existing town planning legislation in British Columbia and Saskatchewan, it was the most comprehensive in the country, and the inclusion of rural planning differentiated it from other town planning legislation in Canada.[85] Nonetheless, while a concern for rural planning widened the scope of Alberta's legislation, Burgess noted that it did not amount to genuine rural planning in the form of regional planning. Thus, rural planning in Alberta remained concerned with restricting billboards along highways and regulating roadside service stations, both of which Burgess welcomed, and offering advice on farmstead layout. With respect to urban planning, however, the legislation incorporated many popular contemporary planning concepts such as zoning, transportation plans and encouragement for civic beautification projects such as parks and boulevards.

Administratively, town planning in Alberta was approached from the bottom up by giving local governments the authority to establish local planning commissions. A central co-ordinating office in Edmonton was established, and a prominent Canadian urban planner, Horace Seymour, was hired as Alberta's Director of Town Planning. Seymour, advised by a Provincial Town and Rural Planning Advisory Board, provided advice and guidance to municipal councils on preparing zoning bylaws and general plans, and met farm needs with advice on farmstead planning. The local planning commissions were voluntary and advisory, which meant that local government officials were able to ignore their recommendations if they wished. Nonetheless, local planning commissions were an important step towards implementing town planning initiatives, and Edmonton, like many cities and towns in the province, immediately established a commission. The Edmonton Town Planning Commission was an advisory body staffed by volunteers, and Burgess was appointed for a three-year term by the city council. He chaired the zoning committee, and was responsible for the development of Edmonton's first zoning plan, which was adopted by the city in 1933. And in keeping with the functional type of planning that this presumed, he was also heavily involved in the development of Edmonton's first transportation plan that was adopted in 1930.[86]

The development of planning initiatives in Alberta led directly to a town planning course at the University of Alberta. Town planning was first offered in 1929–30 in the civil engineering department by Horace Seymour, and Burgess immediately added Seymour's course to the required list of courses for architecture students. Seymour dealt with a variety of topics, including the history of planning, the situation in Alberta, rural and farmstead planning, highway development and control, and, among others, subdivision design and control and housing controls.[87] This planning course, however, was short-lived. Seymour left Alberta in 1932 when his position was abolished as part of government retrenchment because of the Depression. Despite this setback, Burgess did not allow his interest in town planning to wither. He continued to lecture publicly on town planning, and in 1938 he attended a summer programme in planning at MIT to acquire formal skills. He sat the examination at the conclusion of the course and received a certificate in "Techniques of Town Planning." Upon his return to Edmonton, he began teaching town planning as part of the architecture programme.[88]

Architecture in the Interwar Years

Throughout the 1920s and 1930s, Burgess continued to serve as the university's resident architect. The first large project upon his return from the war was the Medical Building (now Dental Sciences Building). The Faculty of Medicine had expanded steadily after its establishment in 1913 with new programmes such as pharmacy and dentistry. By the end of World War I, it was evident that the faculty needed its own space. Nobbs and Hyde designed a building in the "English" brick and stone look that Nobbs had specified for the university a decade before. The building was highly specialised, with labs, classrooms and, for the first time at the university, two lecture theatres, each with a capacity of 200 students. Nobbs and Hyde prepared the preliminary sketches and cost estimates for the project, but the major task of preparing the working drawings (which would have been drawn to a scale of 1/8 or 1/4 inch to the foot) was done by Burgess, who also drew up the specifications setting out in detail the materials and the construction techniques to be used. As part of preparing the working drawings, Burgess would have drawn large-scale and full-scale drawings to guide the contractors in the detailed elements of the project. Further, he would have hired the structural and service engineers to plan the heating, ventilation, electrical and plumbing aspects of the building. His final responsibility was to work with the project's general contractor. General contractors had emerged in the nineteenth century, but by the interwar years they were taking on projects that had formerly been handled only by architects. In the case of the Medical Building, a general contractor from Winnipeg (then the most advanced professional and technical centre in

The Medical Building in 1922, the year after it was completed. (81-145-16 UAA)

prairie Canada) was retained to hire the trades and take charge of construction. The use of general contractors was a boon to architects. It relieved them of much time-consuming and tedious work during the construction phase and left them free to concentrate on ensuring that plans and specifications were properly carried out.[89] The Medical Building was a large undertaking and the CPR built a spur line onto the campus to bring building materials (including brick from a brickyard in Redcliffe near Medicine Hat) directly to the building site. Burgess seems to have fretted about the project, especially with respect to the bearing strength of the clay, and he calculated every foot of the building.[90]

Following the completion of the Medical building there was little new construction at the University of Alberta for almost three decades. President Tory's plans for decades of expansion and new construction had stalled. Nonetheless, Burgess remained active. In 1927 he designed a new skating rink for the university, which gave him the opportunity to design the largest roof span (at 104 feet) in the city. The roof was a wooden latticed bow roof, and as he recalled, "I saw them hoist the roof. It went up, shaped like an S, then it straightened out perfectly."[91] A more consciously stylised

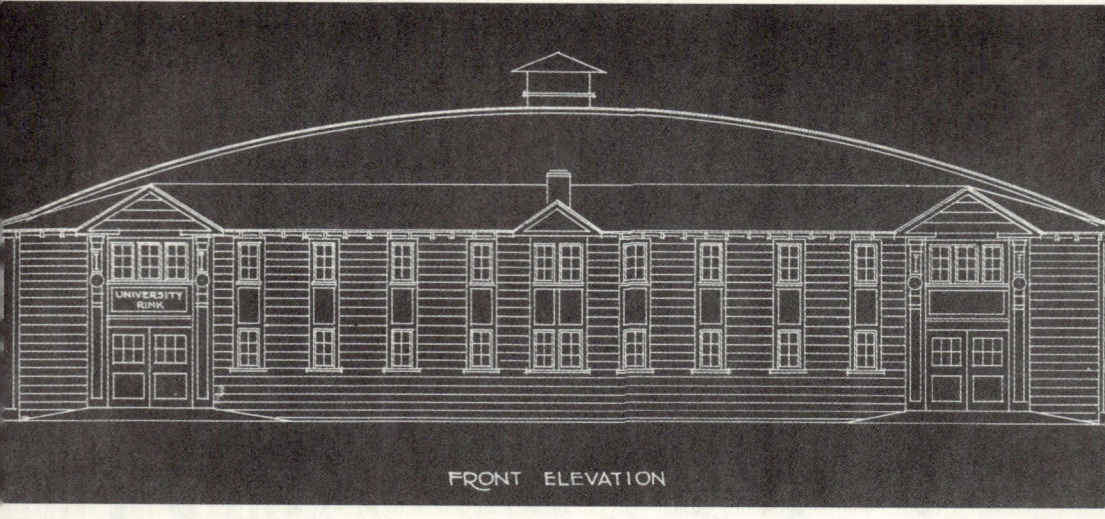

Burgess designed a skating rink for the University of Alberta in 1927. This elevation is taken from the blueprint. The building has been demolished. (72.209, UAA)

The skating rink during construction. Its span was the longest of any building in the city. (demolished) (71.213–281, UAA)

This 1960 photograph shows the University Hospital addition. The building exterior shown was little changed from Burgess's original plan. (demolished) (74.154–32 UAA)

Burgess was fascinated by sundials. He drew these sketches in 1932. (71.213–193, UAA)

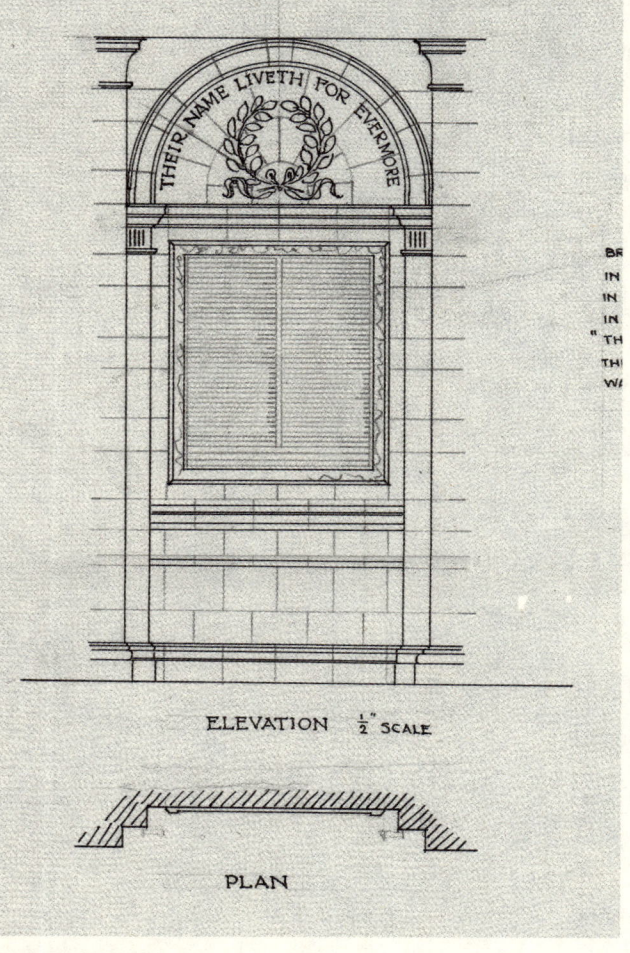

The War Memorial Tablet Burgess designed for the lobby of the Arts Building in 1925 was a testament to the deep resonance of World War I in the 1920s. (71.213–208, map case, UAA)

Burgess was supervising architect on the Birks Building, Edmonton, designed by Nobbs and Hyde. (ND-3-5546, GA)

The Provincial Government Administration building (now Bowker Building) which opened in 1932 had many of the qualities that Burgess ascribed to a "modern" building.
(71.213–288, UAA)

building was his extension to the university hospital, which had been built by the city on university land in 1913 and then transferred to the university in 1922. Here he repeated, to a modest degree, some of the Jacobean stylistic elements that he had earlier used on Pembina Hall. He also designed many buildings that were not intended to be built immediately, but were designed so that "ideas of cost or placement might be clarified." These included a student's union building, a library, a residential Anglican college, and, among others, a residential Presbyterian college and residence. As well, he was involved in a number of other projects. He apparently designed several houses, although details on them have not been located.[92] He was also fascinated by sundials, designing several for various locations in Edmonton (including one on the south wall of the Arts Building and another for the garden of the power plant in the river valley) and yet another for a site in Aklavik. In 1925 he also designed a memorial wall in the lobby of the Arts Building in honour of the 82 University of Alberta men killed in World War I. And among many other similar projects, he designed a silver service for the university as well as some furniture, including a convocation table for the Arts Building and furniture and bookcases for the President's office.[93]

In addition to these responsibilities, Burgess served as supervising architect on two other major projects. His contract with the university allowed him to take on private work as long as it did not interfere with his university responsibilities. The construction of the Birks Building in Edmonton in 1929 was one such project. The building was designed by Nobbs and Hyde (who had designed the Birks store on Cathcart Street in Montreal in 1911), but the AAA required that buildings designed by firms outside of Alberta have a resident Alberta architect.[94] Another private project was the Alberta Government Administrative Building (later called the Natural Resources Building and now known as the Bowker Building). It was built between 1929 and 1932 to serve as the main office building in Edmonton for the provincial government. It was designed by the provincial department of public works, but since there were no trained architects in the department at the time, Burgess was named as consulting architect.

He was forced to make many changes and to redesign substantial parts of the plan. These changes were apparently so extensive that the building design in many respects can be said to be his. Faced with Tyndall limestone, the building had wide stone steps flanked with banisters leading to the main entrance from which rose four columns topped with a small pediment. With a design inspired by the English free classical style, it echoed the most conservative historical traditions of Canadian and British architecture. The building was, nonetheless, in keeping with contemporary construction practices and utilised a structural steel frame. At about 87,000 square feet with a 275 foot frontage, the project was valued at almost $1 million. Showing the development of the building industry in Edmonton, a local contractor, H.G. Macdonald and Co., acted as general contractor.[95]

Burgess saw the Bowker Building as a "modern" building. In some ways, he viewed "modern" and "contemporary" as synonymous terms, but he clearly interpreted modernity as much more than a mere style or point in time. Modern architecture, he had argued in 1925, was different from any that had come before because of the changes brought by industrialisation, urbanisation, mechanisation and scientific discoveries in the health sciences. Modern buildings were distinctive because of their reliance on "modern services" such as electricity (which allowed unprecedented types of infrastructure such as elevators) and water and sewer systems connected to mains. This brought the skill of the engineer into architecture in a wholly new way, increasing the responsibility of the architect as a co-ordinator of trades. Such buildings also met new demands for efficiency and economical use of space to serve an increased population connected to ever more centralised state, economic and communications networks. Related to this more complex social context and function, modern architecture demanded close integration with urban planning. This further reinforced the principle that architecture was a social art in which an architect expressed his or her social responsibility. Moreover, an increasingly central element in the definition of modern architecture, Burgess argued, was the new knowledge derived from biology. In 1920 he published an essay, "Hygiene in Architecture," in which he argued that architects needed to recognise that concerns about hygiene and health were now central influences in architectural design. It was the first systematic statement of his belief that a broadly conceptualised concern about hygiene was the greatest contemporary force shaping architectural expression. Significantly, he noted that the need to incorporate features to promote hygiene meant that buildings increasingly functioned like living organisms.[96] So too, modern buildings made use of materials in new ways (such as in structural steel framing), or at least used older types of materials in new ways.[97] All of these forces demanded a complexity of building form and layout that few architects had previously been forced to provide. Modernity was thus about new purposes, functions and expectations.

In Burgess's mind, however, this did not mean that past architectural styles were irrelevant and should be discarded. New demands and conditions could be met by adapting and reworking traditional forms and styles at the same time that new materials and services brought improved performance in buildings. Agreeing with popular views in Canada, Burgess argued that this meant that rules long used to judge the quality of architecture, and which were demonstrated in the "great" buildings of the world, still held merit.[98] It is important to observe in this connection that modernity for Burgess—and the same could be said for many other Canadian architects of his generation—was not a concept with firm boundaries. The task of modern society was to assert control over the immense technological, social and scientific changes that had taken place in the last half of the nineteenth century by correcting their faults and taking advantage of their virtues. While Burgess celebrated hand work and the culture that pre-industrial times supposedly embodied, and denigrated much of the industrial production of his own time, he was also eager to find meaning and architectural expression in science and the new materials and techniques of the industrial age. All these modern developments could be fitted, he contended, within the forms and dictums of the past.[99] As he told his audience at the Edmonton Museum of Art in 1932, good architecture had to meet six qualities. In inverse order of importance these were workmanship, display of materials, usefulness, stability, composition and proportion, and, at the pinnacle, emotion or sentiment.[100]

In 1932, the same year that Burgess delivered these talks in Edmonton, an exhibition, The International Style: Architecture Since 1922, opened at the Museum of Modern Art (MoMA) in New York. Curated by Philip Johnson and Henry-Russell Hitchcock, the exhibition helped launch and formulate the International Style.[101] The exhibition featured work that had come out of the interwar ferment of various European avante garde architectural and intellectual movements. Although it featured some contemporary architecture from the United States, it drew most significantly on the work of European figures such as Walter Gropius, Mies van der Rohe and others at the German Bauhaus of the 1920s, the DeStijl movement in the Netherlands, and Charles Edouard Jeanneret, known as Le Corbusier, in France. These movements can, for the sake of discussion, be called Modernism.[102] While most of these architects had stressed the social meaning of architecture and its power to express and stimulate social change, such intention was stripped from the exhibition at MoMA, and the work was presented purely as an aesthetic form devoid of social intention. This view came to define the International Style even though it represented a recasting of the original meaning and vitality of Modernism.

It was, in any case, easy to present these Modernist buildings simply as new forms. They looked entirely different and consciously rejected the traditional styles, decorative elements and forms that architects, such as Burgess, favoured for their "modern" buildings. Rather, the new architecture stressed that buildings were not about beauty, art or sentiment; they were instead to be viewed like machines, whose purpose was to provide efficient, hygienic and productive environments in which to live and work. Function would lead design, not history, tradition or emotion. New materials produced by industrialisation were used in an honest, direct and sometimes lavish manner to reinforce the functional needs of the building. Moreover, architecture was not "art" according to the Modernists, it was more akin to engineering. And part of this definition was that older architectural elements and forms were obsolete in an age dominated by utility, function and the ethos of the machine.

For some of the Modernists, architecture was part of the remaking of European society to meet the needs of a democratic, egalitarian (and often socialist) future. The European modernists tended to brag that theirs was a uniquely revolutionary approach to building in an industrial age. In some ways this was so, but such claims were often overstated and their dogmatism ignored that modernity wore many guises. Concerns about hygiene, the linking of function and appearance, the connection between materials of construction and expression, and, among others, the integration of social space through urban planning and building design also concerned most contemporary architects, such as Burgess, who were clearly not part of an avante garde but nonetheless still saw themselves as "modern" architects. Such architects also resented the Modernist appropriation of the word "modern," which made everyone else "pre-modern" and thus, by definition, unprogressive and backward. It remained true as well that the Arts and Crafts philosophy of Ruskin and Morris, for example, had many points of agreement with the Modernism that came later, such as the need for honesty of expression in terms of materials. Indeed, some of the Modernists consciously applied the dicta of Ruskin and Morris.[103] The rub was that appearance always matters. Modernist buildings looked different and were justified with different language and emphasis than earlier buildings, and even when stripped of social meaning in the form of the International Style, the new aesthetic occasioned a deep schism in the architectural community. These differences were never resolved; they only became irrelevant with the complete triumph of the Modernist aesthetic in the form of the International Style after World War II, and then by its eclipse thirty years later by various postmodernist schools.[104]

The reaction in the architectural establishment in the Anglo-North American world to the new ideas coming out of Europe evolved from an insular ignorance in the mid 1920s, to a halting awareness in the late 1920s, and to full scale debate in the 1930s. Burgess was slightly ahead of this curve, and in the 1920s he expressed a degree of sympathy with the ideas of the European modernists as far as he knew about them. But his knowledge of what was going on in Europe would have been sketchy. His scholarly reference points were British, and in contemporary criticism and reporting on architectural issues he drew on British and Canadian sources such as the RAIC *Journal*, the *Architectural Review* (the most important architectural journal in Britain at the time), and the RIBA *Journal*. On the whole, these sources, and the architectural communities which they informed, remained aloof from the happenings on the continent until the early 1930s.[105] Thus, it was perhaps not surprising that Burgess at first saw Modernism as something of a fad. But he also found elements with which he agreed, parts that he disliked from the beginning, and others that he was willing to tolerate. Modernism was a house of many rooms, and there were parts of it in which he was comfortable. His view of the indispensable connection between architecture and town planning was not at odds with what most Modernists argued. Le Corbusier would state in 1943 that it "is no longer possible to separate architecture and town planning—they are one and the same thing," a position that Burgess had expressed in similar terms in 1930.[106] So too, Burgess had strongly advocated Swedish Modernist social housing programmes in his lectures at the University of Alberta and in his public talks. Nor did he disagree with the Modernist position that architecture needed to respond to social conditions and their amelioration by linking planning, architectural design and social policy into a coherent approach. Moreover, though he sometimes saw it as self-conscious and precious, Burgess found the Modernist experimentation with new forms and materials intriguing and at times exciting.

But ultimately, the points of disagreement outweighed any common attitudes and linkages that existed. Burgess did not become as contemptuous of the Modernists as some critics, including his old colleague Percy Nobbs, who in 1930 charged the Modernists with deliberately promoting cultural illiteracy because "the difficulty about putting scholarship and tradition in the waste paper basket is that we deprive ourselves of the very phrases out of which we make up the sentences, the paragraphs and whole compositions." Indeed, Nobbs contended, "tradition is not incompatible with evolution, but connotes it."[107] Burgess agreed, but less harshly. He agreed with the Modernists that utility (or function) was an important element in architecture, but he disagreed profoundly that this was its highest aim. Conspicuously lacking in the criteria of architecture espoused by the Modernists was sentiment (or emotion), which Burgess—as so many others, including Nobbs—continued to define as the highest quality that a building could possess. In a related vein, he fundamentally disagreed with the notion that a building could be judged without reference to place, historical time or tradition. Buildings could not be appreciated in the same fashion as a machine: as a technical process whose output could be measured in quotients of light, germs and square feet per inhabitant, and whose appearance matched this purpose. As early as 1920 in his essay, "Hygiene in Architecture," Burgess had complained that the quest for a hygienic environment would produce homes that were sterile and hard. The architect's task, he argued, was not to reject the evidence of science, but to use it as far as possible without sacrificing comfort and traditional aesthetic values and preferences. The Modernists, however, embraced clean lines, light colours and hard surfaces, and Burgess complained that their view of the world was cold, comfortless and lacking in social grace and cultural context. When taken to their logical extent, such buildings were virtually unliveable. Buildings were not machines to live in, he argued, they were things that one could love and grow old with.[108]

By 1932, the rising prominence of Modernist ideas seems to have intensified Burgess's belief that architecture was an "art." This was a logical stance: the Modernist idea that architecture was more engineering than art and akin to constructing machines could best be refuted by asserting the artistic and sentient value of architecture. This was not a novel position for Burgess, but while he had long expressed such views, they now became more pointed.[109] The canon by which he tested this argument remained largely Euro-centric, and the 1932 lecture series at the Edmonton Museum of Art was essentially a sustained argument about Modernism—a debate, it can be hazarded, that his audience was probably only dimly aware of. Burgess argued that, while architecture was not a fine art, it was an art nonetheless because it expressed human creative needs that were basic defining human qualities. This also served, in Burgess's terms, to refute the Modernist assertion that utility, or function, was the highest quality in architecture, and that the visual meaning of a building was irrelevant to its form, function and geographical place. As Burgess asserted, buildings needed to express their purpose, which served to unify form, utility and sentiment. This was basic in architecture's role as a social art. A library should look like a "resort for literary enjoyment" rather than a storage place for books, Burgess observed, while a city hall "should speak of civic control and order, rather than a mere convenience for collecting taxes." And in the most telling example, he contended that a house needed to look like a "home," not "a machine to live in."[110]

A New Path

In 1939, facing declining enrolments and the challenge of the war, the University of Alberta abolished its department of architecture. Burgess had reached retirement age and would soon be leaving the university. Dean Robert Wilson of the Faculty of Applied Science (and conterminously Head of the Department of Civil Engineering) seized the opportunity to recommend to President Kerr that the architecture programme be abolished.[111] In a memo to Kerr, Wilson observed that at least two people would be needed to replace Burgess, who had been able to carry the programme alone because he had "an extraordinary background of education, training and experience, and is equipped with a fine private library, including also an extensive series of his own notes written over a long period of years." Moreover, he noted, Burgess's "work is his hobby." In any case, Wilson saw the architecture programme as draining the university's resources. While its direct costs were $4,180 per year, it produced revenue of only about $1,200. And if two faculty were hired to replace Burgess, the direct costs of the programme would reach about $7,000. But space was as valuable as money at the University of Alberta, and Wilson clearly resented that, while eight architecture students occupied one drafting room "suitable for twelve students," fifteen civil engineering students were "crowded into one room across the hall." And all this was happening for a group with only dismal job prospects. As Wilson informed President Kerr, "the condition of the profession of Architecture in Alberta is not good at present from the point of view of new graduates. There is very little demand for the services of architects and the outlook for the next few years is not encouraging." Clearly, Dean Wilson saw architecture as a losing proposition, which further sustained his case for abolishing the architectural programme. For those Alberta students wishing to pursue architecture, he noted that the University of Manitoba programme was a convenient alternative.[112]

In declaring its limited short-term prospects, Wilson may also have been suggesting that architecture was no longer a discipline with much of a future at all. Other architecture programmes were also under assault: McGill toyed with the idea of closing its architecture school in 1938–39, although wiser counsel prevailed.[113] This was, perhaps, one of the ironic legacies of Modernism and the doctrine that architecture was, in essence, only a form of engineering. As the prominent Toronto architect, A.S. Mathers, noted in 1941, the professional status of architects was increasingly challenged by civil engineers. Architects were content, Mathers noted, to leave the science and mathematics of building to civil engineers, concerning themselves with interior decoration, mortgage law, real estate valuation and other such matters. This was not a subtle statement at the time—such activities were all of lower rank within the profession. Mathers drove this point home with his concluding remark that the architect needed to assert technical building skills, "otherwise he must shortly find himself in the employ of Decorators where he will consort only with drapers and dressmaking."[114] Murray Brown, Chairman of the Committee on Architectural Training of the RAIC, made much the same claim the next year. He, however, drew upon Modernist approaches to urge reform of the profession. As he noted, past efforts to elevate architecture to an art had merely convinced the public that architects were impractical and should be hired only when "a building was to be decked up with all sorts of ornamental 'doo-dabs.'" Architects need to establish, Brown claimed, that they were expert builders who could ensure suitability and efficiency.[115] Such sentiments expressed an anxiety that architecture needed radical revamping if its future was to be assured.

The university's decision to end its architecture programme—then one of the oldest at the university—now seems parochial and short-sighted.

Yet no one at the time could foresee the building boom that would grip the province after 1947 and the thirty years of extraordinary economic growth that would follow the discovery of oil at Leduc and Redwater. As Burgess noted in 1957, the boom that came in the late 1940s would have justified maintaining the architecture department, but such knowledge was "being wise after the event."[116] But not surprisingly, the university's decision rankled, and as Burgess noted in his recollections in the RAIC *Journal* the same year, perhaps President Tory—who Burgess credited with thinking fifty years ahead—had been correct all along when he had established an architecture programme that would have come fully into its own only by the early 1960s. Indeed, the University of Alberta's loss proved to be the gain of the upstart University of Calgary which established an architecture programme in 1971; a programme that continues to be the only one in the province.[117]

Burgess went on pension in November 1939 but stayed on staff until the end of the 1939–40 academic session to see his third year architecture students through their programme. In return, he received the annual tuition fees of the students in his classes and was allowed to continue to rent one of the Ring Houses (which he had designed twenty-five years before).[118] Later that year he was made Professor Emeritus of Architecture. He moved out of his university house in the spring, relocating to a two-storey house of traditional design near the campus. He also immediately established an office in the Macleod Building in downtown Edmonton, "doing such work as he could accomplish without assistance." He described it as "a trickle of varied work," mostly small projects such as designing small stores, office buildings and additions and renovations to office buildings and homes. There were also some larger projects, such as community hospitals in Eckville, Coaldale and Elnora, typical of the small local hospitals that were being built in the postwar years in small town Alberta.[119]

While architectural projects were still part of his professional life, his interests were becoming ever more focussed on town planning and housing issues. As he noted in 1946, "I live and work with the promotion of good town planning" as the "principal object of the remainder of my life."[120] An essential part of this concern was affordable housing. As a

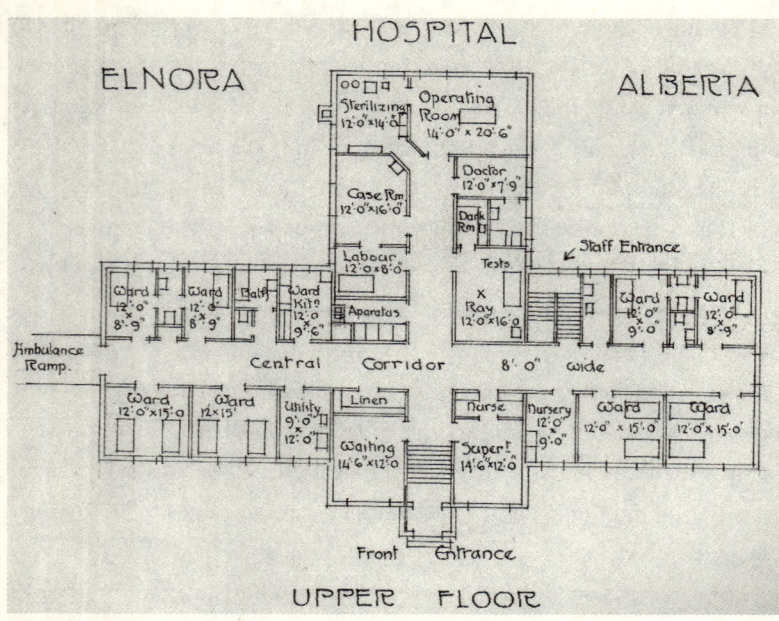

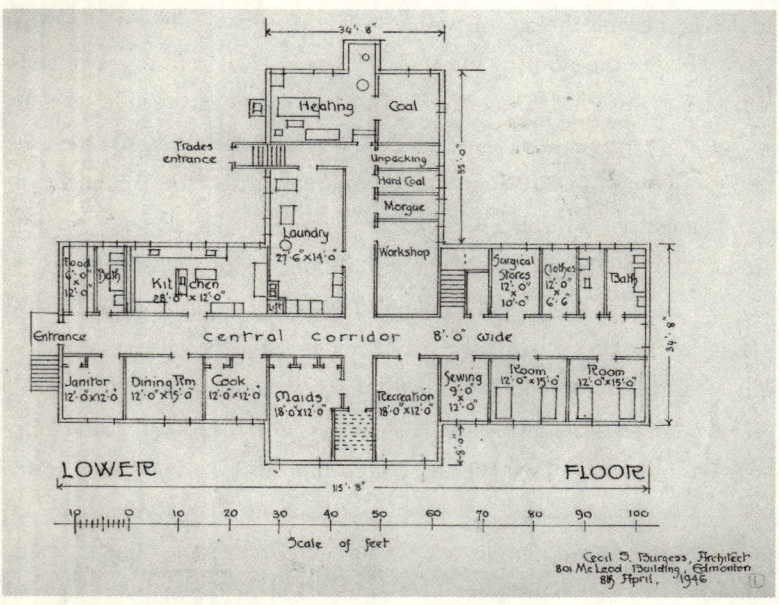

Burgess designed this hospital for the small community of Elnora in central Alberta in 1946. (71.213–193–4 and 71.213–193–5, UAA)

professor, Burgess had always enjoyed the luxury of being able to deal with unprofitable activities such as domestic architecture. The need for improved housing was intense during the 1940s when Edmonton, like many Canadian cities, faced almost continual housing crises because of the war and the economic boom that followed after 1947. Burgess toyed with many concepts of how to design housing to meet these needs, and he continued to draw plans and to promote various schemes; even having a model of one proposal built for display at the Edmonton Exhibition in 1940.[121]

Burgess's low-cost housing proposals tended to share certain basic principles. They drew on his long-held assumptions about the nature of a home and how its design could promote familiarity and comfort and serve as a social anchor. The houses, often in the form of duplex and row houses, promoted his social ideals by featuring a separate kitchen, dining room, living room, bathroom, several bedrooms and a full cellar with laundry facilities. All of the proposals also featured playgrounds where children could play safely and under adult supervision. In one proposal in 1941 he also included a limited number of small apartments in a complex sited on a relatively large block of land. This mix of housing types was designed to meet various social needs, but all would, as he phrased it, "provide homes with a healthy environment and with community interest." Reflecting a long-held hostility to children living in apartments, he specified that the houses would be reserved "for families with children under fifteen years of age," while the apartments would be occupied by people without young children. This mix of housing types was designed to allow the community to replicate "a typical residential cycle." As he envisioned it, "young couples, without children, should occupy the apartments until they have a child of not more than one year old and after that they should then occupy a house. The families should live in the houses until the youngest child is fifteen years of age. They may then move into an apartment."[122]

It was not only apartments that Burgess generally objected to in affordable housing schemes. He was also opposed to rental housing. Pride of ownership was crucial for building community and reinforcing individual pride and self-respect. Burgess was certain that people, regardless of income, were not interested in giving up control over their daily lives to a landlord, whether it was the state or otherwise. Burgess insisted that affordable housing, however it was achieved, needed to be owner-occupied in order to build up "social sentiment, whereas the ordinary renter-tenant housing belongs to the character of the sapping and exhaustion of society."[123] In this connection, he continued to find inspiration in Swedish housing precedents that featured co-operative approaches, with public support provided in the form of land and maintenance subsidies. In the late 1930s and early 1940s, the city of Edmonton still owned large amounts of land as a result of forfeitures for nonpayment of taxes during the years after 1913. Concerned individuals like Burgess often made proposals that it should use this land to subsidise low-cost housing projects, but ultimately the city sold most of the land to developers, rarely turning it over to low cost or social housing. In any event, assistance for housing was available after 1943 in Alberta through subsidised mortgages under the *National Housing Act*, and these provisions helped stimulate building in the province.[124]

In addition to low-cost housing schemes, Burgess also believed that affordability could be increased through such things as the standardisation of materials, prefabrication of some component parts and tract building. Such industrialised approaches to reducing construction costs were only commonly discussed in Canada by the 1940s. Canadian wartime housing projects had employed prefabricated standardised components to speed up construction, but Burgess's suggestions for more efficient sequencing of construction, the use of a few standardised plans and standardised building components, and the construction of several houses at the same time by a single builder operating under a single contract all represented a more radical industrial model of organisation. Such approaches did not become part of the Canadian building industry until the 1950s. Burgess showed little interest, however, in the popular preoccupation of the 1940s—the dream of prefabricating entire houses. His silence on a matter of such widespread debate in the construction industry suggests a scepticism on his part about the feasibility of prefabrication and claims that it would bring reduced building costs.[125] Perhaps he foresaw its practical limits, which did indeed prove to be immense, but perhaps more important in shaping his attitude towards prefabrication was his long standing commitment to building as a craft. As well, he continued to resist the modernist idea that houses were "machines to live in," an attitude he saw as socially sterile.

Such a social perspective also continued to inform Burgess's thinking about town planning. While he never described himself as a professional town planner because he did not have professional training, other than the MIT summer school certificate he had earned in 1938, he believed that his long experience in "accessory work" entitled him "to give advice, always pointing the way towards the ultimate employment of the professional city planner." In 1945 he prepared a town plan for Jasper, and in 1945–46 he drew one for Banff. The federal government commissioned these plans in an attempt to improve conditions in the park townsites and make them "more attractive and more convenient to residents and tourists" by directing commercial development along lines that would least detract from the natural beauty of the surroundings. In both cases, Burgess drafted zoning and building regulations and bylaws to control commercial signs in the townsites. These were followed in 1946 by planning guides for Medicine Hat and Lethbridge. These were not formal town plans. Rather, he sketched in broad strokes an outline with planning concepts, approaches and methods that would meet local conditions. In each case, he demonstrated the benefits that could be expected from the application of professional planning principles by a resident professional town planner. Indeed, the city of Lethbridge inquired about Burgess's interest in such a position, but as he noted, "at the age of 75 and with my chief interests in the city of Edmonton, I am not in a favourable position to undertake the duties of a resident town planner in Lethbridge."[126]

One expression of this "chief interest" in planning in Edmonton was his convening of a committee in 1947 to establish a local branch of the Community Planning Association of Canada—a new agency that aimed to promote professional planning in Canada.[127] Sufficient public interest could not be found in Edmonton to form a branch, and Burgess thus continued to direct his primary efforts on behalf of the Edmonton Town

Planning Commission, to which he had been reappointed to successive three-year terms since 1929. By this point, however, the weakness of Edmonton's approach to planning was becoming apparent. While the city was making some steps to professionalise its civil service (including the creation of a Parks and Recreation Department staffed with trained workers), its town planning commission remained staffed by volunteers who served only in an advisory capacity at the will of city council. By the 1940s, the commission had to its credit a major street plan, a zoning bylaw (now over fifteen years old), a zoning appeal process as well as the reservation of land for extensive parks throughout the city. Burgess had been directly involved in all these developments. But by the end of World War II, both the street and the zoning plans were becoming threadbare. Neither constituted a general plan that could guide development or respond flexibly to rapid growth. All the while, Edmonton had grown quickly, expanding well beyond the scope of both of these early plans.[128]

The town planning commission's lack of authority was an important failing of Edmonton's system, as was the lack of sympathy on the part of civic executives and officials for its work.[129] This came to a head in 1949 over plans for Edmonton's civic centre, a cause that Burgess had long championed. He had increasingly been at odds with the city over this issue: in 1943 he had formally protested the construction of a temporary recreation building for U.S. troops on the site where the town planning commission had planned the civic centre. As Burgess argued, this was short sighted, especially since there were other vacant lands for such a building.[130] Then, in 1949, the city announced that a long-awaited federal building would be constructed on the site. In protest, Burgess resigned from the commission, publicly rebuking the city's administration about how it had made the decision and for its plans for siting the proposed building on the land. He clearly saw it as a final humiliation of the town planning commission and the culmination of many years of frustration with the politics of Edmonton planning. As Burgess stated, the town planning commission had "been gradually forced into a situation in which it cannot perform its principle duties" because civic administrative and political leaders were making decisions on planning without consulting the commission. "The city is being chewed to pieces by people who know nothing of town planning," Burgess fumed, observing that while he had spent twenty years studying planning, "every alderman knows more about it than I do." The planning commission publicly supported Burgess and underlined that it too was frustrated by the attitude of city officials. While the Edmonton *Journal* joined the commission in urging Burgess to withdraw his resignation, he refused.[131] Reconsideration was unlikely. The issues at stake concerned his deepest convictions that planning should express a social ideal: a properly designed civic centre would help the city mature into a truly civic environment, while professional planning would allow the city to regulate growth and free it from the randomness of whimsical and self-interested decision-making.

Burgess's departure and the struggle over the direction of planning helped to force the city to admit that its planning initiatives needed revision. The crisis demonstrated the need to professionalise and curtail political partisanship in the city's planning process. In late 1949 John Bland, the director of McGill's school of architecture, and Howard Spence-Sales, who taught at McGill's recently established town planning programme, were hired by the city to make recommendations about urban planning in Edmonton. They recommended replacing the town planning commission with a professional technical planning board made up of representatives from various city departments, a professional planner and other technical experts. Such a professionally constituted group would be equipped to prepare a general plan for the city. While they commended the work of the town planning commission over the previous twenty years, they noted that a voluntary and essentially amateur approach to town planning was no longer adequate and that planning had to be professionalised and separated from the political proclivities of the mayor and council. Many of these recommendations were implemented, most importantly, in the hiring of a professional planner, Noel Dant, in late 1949. Other changes, including a professional town planning board as well as regional planning, were gradually implemented following amendment of the provincial enabling legislation in 1950.[132]

Burgess's departure from the planning scene in Edmonton reflected a changing course in his life. He maintained his professional practice, continuing to work on small architectural projects and in 1951 prepared a town plan for Whitehorse, Yukon.[133] But he was beginning to disengage from professional life. In 1950 he began donating his copies of architectural journals and books to the University of Alberta library, some of which continue to be important holdings. He also presented his father's books to the university, noting that the addition of some of the journals (such as those of RIBA) made the university's collection one of the finest of such materials outside London.[134] In 1953 he resigned from the Board of Examiners in Architecture because "being over four score years of age, I think my resignation must be fully due so that some younger person may take over the duties."[135] In 1958, at the age of 88, the University of Alberta conferred on him a Doctor of Laws *honoris causa*. In the convocation address, President Robert Newton praised Burgess for having "given us a well-established heritage of beauty, the work of his hands, and the record of a personal life to match his work." "He wears well," said Newton, "in every sense of that expression."[136]

Burgess went into full retirement in about 1960, and showing pride in defeating age and the ravages of time, he noted that "I retired from the University of old age at 70. I then set up an office from which I retired at 90."[137] In 1969, two years before his death, he was interviewed by Ruth Bowen, who conducted a lengthy interview with him on behalf of the university archives. During the interview he got up from his chair and took down a watercolour from the wall of his home to show Bowen. It was the sketch of the municipio in Verona that had set in motion his coming to Canada in 1903.[138] Shortly, he would lose his sight, entertaining himself by listening to books recorded by the Canadian National Institute of the Blind.[139]

Cecil Burgess's Thoughts and Views on Architecture and Town Planning
Cecil Burgess was a significant figure in Canadian architecture and his life and work reflect a number of important themes in the cultural development of Alberta and prairie Canada. To be certain, no single individual can ever reflect all of the aspects of such a complex field. But Burgess's thoughts and views form a record of many of the important issues in the first half of the twentieth century that dominated thinking on the shaping of the physical environment that people lived with—urban spaces and landscapes, buildings and the material objects of everyday life. In the course of his career, Burgess grappled with the meaning of architecture and its relationship with society; the perplexities of training future architects; the challenge posed by new architectural thinking and forms coming out of Europe in the 1920s and 1930s; and, among many other concerns, the planning of towns and cities. This range of concerns and issues offer insight into an important period in Canadian architectural development.

The built environment is a cultural and historical artefact, and Burgess's thinking and attitudes form a part of our understanding of how it was constructed in Alberta during the early years of the twentieth century. Burgess exemplified many of the cultural assumptions that informed the physical transformation of the prairie region. Like many European settlers in Alberta and on the prairies, he assumed that the region's culture began with his own historical epoch. And it was the English-speaking group (whether from Montreal, Ontario, England or even the United States) who were in control of this era. They dominated the political, economic and social structures of the new province and thus held the key to making it in an image of their liking. This was predicated in part on the view that the region was historically empty. What had gone before and the lives that had been lived there for many thousands of years were colourful and perhaps provided contemporary entertainment, but they did not inform or inspire the present. The fur trade had been an exciting episode, one that in a limited fashion had paved the way for the present, while the Aboriginal past barely existed, and when it did, it was seen as having no merit in guiding or informing the culture of the present. It was the region's future that concerned Albertans in the early twentieth century, and Burgess, despite his erudition, shared this view. When the past of the region was symbolically annihilated or presumed to be of no value, only the future, or the past of other places, was left as a source of inspiration. In light of these assumptions, the obsession with the future of so many people on the prairies was not merely a product of the mentality of "making good," or of a rampant materialism, or of the insecurity of life on farms and in a cyclical economy in an often harsh and hostile land. It was also a particular view of history and culture. In this sense, Burgess was as much a part of the pioneer myth—however far apart they may have been in the veneer of their lives—as any homesteader. Both saw themselves as a vanguard, the bringers of culture and meaning to the province and as the planters of an older culture in a new place. Burgess never lost faith in the assumption that British culture and precedents offered a model for the world, and that they offered a basis for the future. The prairies would be made in a British, or at least a European, mould.

As Burgess's public talks reveal, his references remained British or European throughout his life. The hierarchy of values that his approach to the history of architecture asserted was one measure of this attitude, and there is no record that this discomfited his listeners or that they held particularly different perspectives. In fact, it is remarkable that the United States provided relatively few of Burgess's references on the shaping of the physical environment. While American-style housing was a dominant pattern in prairie Canada from an early date, this passed without comment. When American precedents were cited, they were often found wanting. Burgess admired American skyscrapers for their bravado and technical boldness, but they were not, he thought, a sane model for city development because they brought unmanageably high urban density. Other American buildings drew his attention from time to time, but the Beaux Arts classicism that dominated much of the United States in the first part of the twentieth century was not to Burgess's taste or philosophy, although he praised the head office of the Bank of Montreal designed by the famous New York firm, McKim Mead and White. He paid more attention to

American urban planning experiments (and it will be recalled that he even studied town planning at MIT), but, again, he often compared American experiments in design of suburban developments unfavourably with British sources such as those pioneered by Ebenezer Howard in his Garden Cities. Of mid twentieth century American architectural writers, he seems to have had the greatest fondness for Lewis Mumford, the prescient arch-critic of the International Style and proponent of an organic, culturally informed architecture. Mumford too was an early proponent of town planning (he had been involved in the development of Radburn, New Jersey), and Burgess found his views on the nature of planning and its relationship with architecture and society sympathetic to his own.[140]

While Burgess and his generation implanted a culture that was British and European, they assumed that it would evolve and develop in terms of the landscape and resources of the prairies, but always within the parameters of the source culture. Indeed, Burgess's nostalgia for the vanished pre-industrial English past, not the Canadian one, is one mark of this attitude. What was relevant about Alberta was its landscape and climate, stripped of its human history. As he argued in a lecture in 1932 to the Edmonton Museum of Arts, painting should respond to Alberta's natural environment—to land forms, plants, colour and climate. While he did mention history as part of this representation of place, he did so only in a vague and uncommitted fashion. His silence about what this history included and what it meant reinforced that landscape primarily defined the region and its contribution to present-day culture.[141]

While Burgess firmly accepted that human intellectual and social thought, as well as social mannerisms and attitudes, were formative forces in social development, he also believed that the physical environment played an important role in framing these forces and in shaping character and behaviour. Indeed, he tended to endorse the view that the physical environment was the source of human thought. This view was revealed in many ways: in his concern for town planning, in his assertion that architecture was a social art and in his views about how architects should be educated. It also helped to condition his beliefs about the importance of craftsmanship. As with many Arts and Crafts thinkers, he accepted that craftsmanship was of social as well as aesthetic importance. True, Burgess clearly found joy in looking at and using well-made things and in appreciating the skill behind their creation. But craft was always more than a mere individualistic indulgence and source of personal pleasure. Instead, the pursuit of excellence and quality was one way to defeat what was viewed as the chaos of nature and a means to create a model of thought. Good workmanship was also a source of personal pride and a way to create self-confidence, and it expressed a commitment to the future because well-made things were meant not to be thrown out under the dictates of fashion but to endure and form a legacy for the future.

All of these attitudes informed Burgess's contribution to the shaping of the built environment in Alberta. In a more direct fashion, his involvement with the construction and design of various buildings at the University of Alberta and elsewhere in Edmonton helped create the look of these places and asserted a self-consciously British architectural model. He was also the most consistent and vocal figure to advocate for the need for town planning in the province from the 1920s to the 1940s, a period that was formative in the history of planning in Alberta and in Canada. His service of almost twenty years with Edmonton's Town Planning Commission allowed him to implement many of his ideas and approaches. While he failed to achieve his goal of a town centre for Edmonton, he was instrumental in the adoption of the reservation of park land and open space as a basic feature in the city's planning approach. So too, his service in an official capacity with the Alberta Association of Architects and the provincial Examining Board for Architecture gave him scope to implement his ideas about professional conduct and standards. More direct scope for the dissemination of his ideas came in his role as professor of architecture. Although the University of Alberta's architecture programme did not survive his retirement, he trained a generation of architects who contributed to the application of professional standards in the province.

On a broader level, Burgess was representative of certain schools of thought on architecture and town planning, and his work demonstrates the translation of broadly held ideas into practice. Throughout his life, Burgess remained faithful to many of the basic tenets of Arts and Crafts thinking that he had embraced in his early days in Edinburgh and Montreal at the turn of the century. Especially important was the sense of architecture as an organic expression rooted in place, culture and history. He applied many of these ideas over his life, and they helped him make sense of his craft and its evolving standards. He agreed, as did many of his contemporaries, that architecture found its best justification as a social art, an activity that served its community by bringing about more beautiful, healthy, culturally appropriate, and satisfying physical environments that would allow people to live more fully. This was intimately connected to his belief that architecture was an interdisciplinary activity. In one sense, this was expressed in his Arts and Crafts belief that architecture, like all art, elevated the manipulation of materials and the integration of emotion into a single unified expression. Architecture also drew upon science to understand the nature of materials and natural forces. In combination, all these disciplines and approaches made architecture greater than the sum of its parts. Burgess's expression of these beliefs in lectures, public talks, writing, buildings, town plans and furniture design confirmed his assumption that architecture could not be easily compartmentalised or reduced to a single focus.

Burgess's beliefs also provided him with a framework with which to respond to new approaches to architecture and to try to sort out the meaning of new ideas and methods. This was part of the reason that Modernism posed such a challenge: how could one debate with people when the very ground rules of debate had changed? Thus he continued to fight by the rules that he understood. In 1948, for example, he called for the enforcement of what he described as adequate standards for admission to the AAA because while architects were still technically well trained, he believed they were now unfamiliar with matters of architectural culture, by which he probably meant a culture that was historically grounded.[142] And in another typical assertion of such views, in 1958 he decried the lack of monumental effect in International Style buildings, arguing that they were monotonous and uninteresting and that they would not adapt well to the social and institutional change that they would inevitably face.[143] In light of Burgess's belief that the built environment mirrored the thoughts and sentience of its society, this was also a critique of a society that Burgess believed had become too commercialised and too infatuated with machines and mass production. His penchant for architectural history, his love of hand work and craftsmanship, and his disdain for treating architecture, urban space and life as commodities to be bought and sold, or things whose true value could only be judged if measured by money or by scientific quantification, continued to inform his view about his society and its buildings.[144] As he wrote in 1953 in an unpublished essay on architects and architectural practice, architects were inheritors of a noble tradition that should inform their response to new conditions. They were "not mere mechanics" but people of feeling who had "a great part to play in forwarding civilisation and culture."[145]

Burgess's ideals for architecture and community were frequently tested by the ease with which English Canadians allowed money, status and fashion, instead of reason and humanitarianism, to guide the building of their homes, towns and cities. This distance between professional and popular opinion suggests that there was never a single community of opinion in Canada about the practice of architecture. Professional opinion was never united in all particulars either, as the rise of the Modernist movement in the interwar years revealed. Burgess thus reflected one part of the various communities that responded to the built environment and the world that architects, builders and town planners had created and continued to create. Indeed, the assumptions that informed his life and the issues he grappled with are ones that, although often expressed in different language, continue to perplex and challenge Canadians' interaction with landscape and the built environment, with the shape and meaning of their communities, with the place of history in their lives, and with the shape and character of their buildings. This does not mean that his ideas should be copied or revived—they were of a different place and time—but they can continue to inform and enrich contemporary debates about place, time and the structures of daily life. This was the lesson that Burgess always claimed was the most important in the history of architecture, and his assertion of the importance of the past in informing contemporary perspectives remains one of the lasting contributions of his views and thought.

NOTES

1. "Excerpts from Interview with Burgess by Ruth Bowen," 1969, Tory Papers, 79.112, file 8, University of Alberta Archives (UAA); *The Canadian Who's Who*, Vol. 3, 1938–39 (Toronto: Trans-Canada Press, 1939), 96.
2. Biographical information in this and following paragraphs is drawn from the autobiographical files in Burgess's papers, 71.213, files 2 and 130, UAA, and various archival interviews. Interviews with Burgess include "Excerpts from Interview with C.S. Burgess by Ruth Bowen," 1969, Tory Papers, 79.112, file 8, UAA; Interview with C.S. Burgess, October 1969, 74.19, UAA; and Interview with C.S. Burgess, May 1969, 69.361, Provincial Archives of Alberta (PAA).
3. On Edinburgh's architectural and town planning culture at this time see Nicola Justine Spasoff, "Building on Social Power. Percy Erskine Nobbs, Ramsay Traquair, and the Project of Constructing a Canadian National Culture in the Early Decades of the Twentieth Century," Ph.D diss., Queen's University, Kingston, Ontario, 2002, 44–68.
4. Spasoff, "Building on Social Power," 226 [italics in original]. There is a huge literature on the Arts and Crafts movement. See for examples, Peter Davey, *Arts and Crafts Architecture* (London: The Architectural Press, 1980) and Robert Winter, "The Arts and Crafts as a Social Movement," *Record of the Art Museum, Princeton University* 34, no. 2 (1975): 36–40. There are a number of biographies of William Morris, including E.P. Thompson, *William Morris: Romantic to Revolutionary* (New York: Monthly Review Press, 1961) and Fiona McCarthy, *William Morris. A Life for Our Times* (London: Faber and Faber, 1994).
5. "Architecture as a Profession," Talk on Radio Station CKUA, April 27, 1931, 71.213, file 143, UAA. (Reprinted as Document 10.)
6. See Gwendolyn Wright, "History for Architects," in *The History of History in American Schools of Architecture 1865–1975*, edited by Gwendolyn Wright and Janet Parks (New York: The Temple Hoyne Buell Center for the Study of American Architecture, 1990), 14–16, 22–23.
7. Percy Erskine Nobbs (1875–1964) had an early successful career in Edinburgh and London that led to his appointment in 1903 to the Macdonald Chair of Architecture at McGill. He directed the architecture programme until 1910. Thereafter he served as

professor of design at McGill. He also pursued an active private architectural practice with George Hyde after 1910.

8. "Percy Erskine Nobbs Biography," at http://cac.mcgill.ca/nobbs/bio-pen-english.htm (current 2005); Interview with C.S. Burgess, October 1969, 74.19, UAA.

9. "Excerpts from Interview with Burgess by Ruth Bowen," 1969, Tory Papers, 79.112, file 8, UAA.

10. Kelly Crossman, *Architecture in Transition. From Art to Practice 1885–1906* (Kingston and Montreal: McGill-Queen's University Press, 1987), 104; Interview with C.S. Burgess, May 1969, 69.361, PAA.

11. Nobbs to Tory, 1912. In "Excerpts from correspondence between H. M. Tory and Percy Nobbs," Tory Papers, 79.112, file 4, UAA; Burgess to Nobbs, May 6, 1909 (Letter Book), 71.213, file 6, UAA.

12. *McGill's School of Architecture: A History by Norbert Schoenauer.* "Legacy of Nobbs," Montreal: McGill University, School of Architecture, at http://www.mcgill.ca/architecture/introduction/history/nobbs/ (current 2005).

13. Burgess to Lorch, January 27, 1912 and Burgess to Burell, May 1, 1912 (Letter Book), 71.213, file 6, UAA.

14. Interview with C.S. Burgess, October 1969, 74.19, UAA.

15. Nobbs to Tory, 1912. In "Excerpts from correspondence between H.M. Tory and Percy Nobbs," 79.112, file 4, UAA.

16. Tory to Burgess, March 3, 1913, 71.213, file 7, UAA; Burgess to Tory, March 11, 1913 (Letter Book) 71.213, file 6, UAA.

17. Henry Marshall Tory (1864–1947) was professor of mathematics at McGill until 1905 when he moved to Vancouver and helped establish UBC. He was President, University of Alberta 1908–1923, Chair and then President of the National Research Council of Canada, 1923–35, and President (unpaid), Carleton University 1942–47. E.A. Corbett's 1954 biography has been reprinted as *Henry Marshall Tory A Biography,* with an introduction by Douglas Owram (Edmonton: University of Alberta Press, 1992).

18. "Excerpts from Interview with Burgess by Ruth Bowen," 1969, Tory Papers, 79.112, file 8, UAA.

19. See Spasoff, "Building on Social Power," 253, for other examples of this thinking. As a further example of the connection between ethnicity, power and architecture, Nobbs was highly critical of the Beaux Arts design for the Alberta Legislative Building, which he saw as too American in its inspiration. Instead, he recommended a "free classic" English style. This advice was not followed (Harold Kalman, *A Concise History of Canadian Architecture* (Don Mills: Oxford University Press, 2000), 391).

20. Percy Nobbs, "The General Scheme for the University of Alberta," *Journal* RAIC, 2 (1925): 159; Susan Wagg, *Percy Erskine Nobbs, Architect, Artist, Craftsman* (Kingston and Montreal: McGill Queen's University Press for the McCord Museum, Montreal, 1982), 47–51; O.S.E. Bilash and O.F.G. Sitwell, "Words into Buildings: The University of Alberta, 1906–28," *SSAC Bulletin* 20, no. 1 (March 1995): 4–8.

21. Crossman, *Architecture in Transition*, 51–63.
22. Mark Crinson and Jules Lubbock, *Architecture. Art or Profession. Three Hundred Years of Architectural Education in Britain* (Manchester: Manchester University Press, 1994), 65–86.
23. Percy Nobbs, "Construction at the University of Alberta Edmonton," *Construction*, January 1921, 3; Wright, "History for Architects," 13–22.
24. Hand written autobiography, n.d., 71.213, file 2, UAA.
25. President's Report, *Report of the Board of Governors of the University of Alberta For the Year Ending June 30, 1913* (typescript), UAA. Candidates applied for admission to the AAA that then recommended to the Senate of the University of Alberta their eligibility to sit the examinations. Success in the exams allowed application for membership in the association.
26. Allan Merrick Jeffers came to Alberta from the U.S. In 1907 he was hired by the provincial government to design the new legislature building. The same year, he was made provincial architect, a position he held until 1912 when he became the city of Edmonton architect. R.P. Blakey then became provincial architect. Jeffers went into private practice in 1915. In 1923 he moved to California, where he died in 1926 (Michael Payne, "Allan Merrick Jeffers: One of Alberta's First Architects," *Alberta Past* (Winter 1994)). On Magoon and Macdonald, see Percy Johnson, "George Heath Macdonald (Class of 1911) The Story of One Graduate from McGill University's School of Architecture," *SSAC Bulletin* 21, no. 3 (1996): 74–76.
27. Autobiographical notes, n.d. 71.213, file 2, UAA.
28. Two types of houses were designed. Both had similar layout, differing mainly in size. In both types, a central main entranceway opened onto a foyer from which the stairs ran up to the bedrooms on the second floor. The foyer also served as the focal point of the main floor, giving access to the rooms on that floor. Burgess also designed a scullery in each kitchen, "for the rough work, the peelings, carrots, etc.," but most of the occupants of the houses soon tore out the scullery and incorporated this space into the kitchen.
29. Letter Book 1913 passim, 71.213, file 6, UAA ; *Report of the Board of Governors of the University of Alberta for the Year Ending December 31, 1915*, 18, UAA; "Excerpts from Interview with Burgess by Ruth Bowen," 1969, Tory Papers, 73.112, file 8, UAA; Interview with C.S. Burgess, May 1969, 69.361, PAA.
30. Annmarie Adams, *Architecture in the Family Way* (Montreal and Kingston: McGill-Queen University Press, 1996), 9–72; Donald G. Wetherell and Irene R.A. Kmet, *Homes in Alberta. Building, Trends and Design* (Edmonton: University of Alberta Press, 1991), 49–53, 82–93. Especially important knowledge developed from Pasteur's germ theory.
31. Letter Book 1913 passim, 71.213, file 6, UAA; *Report of the Board of Governors of the University of Alberta for the Year Ending December 31, 1915*, 18, UAA. "Hygiene in Architecture" is reprinted as Document 5.
32. Hand written autobiography, n.d. 71.213, file 2, UAA.

33. Crinson and Lubbock, *Architecture. Art or Profession,* 81. On challenges to Beaux Arts approaches in the U.S. see Mary N. Woods, *From Craft to Profession The Practice of Architecture in Nineteenth-Century America* (Berkley: University of California Press, 1999), 66–81. See also Spasoff "Building on Social Power," 174.
34. Crossman, *Architecture in Transition, 59.*
35. Hand written autobiography, n.d. 71.213, file 2; UAA; *The University of Alberta, Edmonton. Calendar 1914–15,* 66.
36. Interview with C.S. Burgess, 1969, 69.361, PAA; *McGill's School of Architecture: A Retrospection by Norbert Schoenauer* (1987). There is no history of the University of Manitoba school of architecture, but see the brief historical note about the faculty at http://www.umanitoba.ca/faculties/architecture (current 2005). On Toronto see Geoffrey Simmins, *Ontario Association of Architects. A Centennial History 1889–1989* (Toronto: The Ontario Association of Architects, 1989), 31–32.
37. Interview with C.S. Burgess, October 1969, 74.19, UAA. See also Interview with C.S. Burgess, May 1969, 69.361, PAA and "Excerpts from Interview with Burgess by Ruth Bowen," 1969, Tory Papers, 79.112, file 8, UAA.
38. *Calgary Herald,* April 14, 1922 (syndicated).
39. "Art in the Household," a talk to the Grand Trunk Literary Society, March 4, 1908, 71.213, file 118, UAA.
40. "Modern Architecture," a talk to an unidentified audience, ca. 1925, 71.213, file 85, UAA. (Reprinted as Document 6.)
41. Ibid.; "Two Ideals in Architecture 1913–14," a talk to Philosophical Society, 71.213, file 94, UAA.
42. "Applications of the Lessons of History," a talk to an unidentified audience, possibly Montreal Sketch Club, 1909–12, 71.213, file 126, UAA. (Reprinted as Document 2.)
43. "Two Ideals in Architecture," a talk to the University of Alberta Philosophical Society, 1913–14, 71.213, file 94, UAA.
44. See for example "Art in the Household," a talk to Grand Trunk Literary Institute, Montreal, March 8, 1908, 71.213, file 118, UAA. The phrase about "lives and thoughts of men" was from Sir Walter Scott.
45. Kalman, *A Concise History of Canadian Architecture,* 466.
46. On this topic, see Spasoff, "Building on Social Power."
47. Isabelle Gournay, "The First Leaders of McGill's School of Architecture: Stewart Henbest Capper, Percy Nobbs, and Ramsay Traquair," SSAC *Bulletin* 21, no. 3 (September 1996): 60.
48. *Claresholm Review,* December 4, 1913; *Macleod Spectator,* December 14, 1913. On the Department of Extension, see Donald G. Wetherell and Irene Kmet, *Useful Pleasures. The Shaping of Leisure in Alberta 1896–1945* (Regina: Canadian Plains Research Centre, 1990), 51, 56, 89.
49. "Architecture," University of Alberta Extension Lecture Tour 1913, 71.213, file 93, UAA. (Reprinted as Document 3.)

50. "Excerpts from Interview with Burgess by Ruth Bowen," 1969, Tory Papers, 79.112, file 8, UAA; Interview with C.S. Burgess, October 1969, 74.19, UAA; Hand written biography, n.d., 71.213, file 2 UAA.
51. "Recollections of a Half Century," 71.213, file 177, UAA. (Reprinted as Document 21.)
52. Wetherell and Kmet, *Useful Pleasures*, 89–91.
53. "Reports on Activities of Provincial Associations, The Alberta Association of Architects," RAIC *Journal* 1 (1924): 32.
54. "The Alberta Association of Architects, President's Report to Annual Meeting, September 23, 1938,"RAIC *Journal* 15 (1932): 253.
55. "Status of the Profession in the Province of Alberta," RAIC *Journal* 7 (1930): 195–96.
56. Harris (Assistant Registrar) to Burgess, August 26, 1958, 71.213, file 10, UAA; Hand written autobiography, n.d., 71.213, file 2, UAA.
57. Percy Nobbs, "Present Tendencies Affecting Architecture in Canada. Part II, Modernity," RAIC *Journal* 7 (1930): 315–16.
58. The five-year programme was abolished by 1937–38 when the programme returned to a four-year format.
59. Harris (Assistant Registrar) to Burgess, August 26, 1958, 71.213, file 10, UAA. In 1958, of the twenty-one students who graduated in architecture at the University of Alberta, two had died, twelve were working in Alberta and seven were in other provinces. Five had been elected Fellows of the RAIC (Hand written autobiography, n.d., 71.213, file 2, UAA). For biographies of John Rule, Jean Wallbridge and Gordon Wynn, see Marianne Fedori, Ken Tingley and David Murray, *The Practice of Post-War Architecture in Edmonton, Alberta. An Overview of the Modern Movement, 1936–1960* (Edmonton: n.p., 2001), 60–61, 63–64. Biographies on other graduates of the programme have not been located.
60. Annmarie Adams and Peta Tancred, *"Designing Women" Gender and the Architectural Profession* (Toronto: University of Toronto Press, 2000), 16–18, 36–58; "The Home," a talk to Household Economics Association, Edmonton, March 24, 1930, 71.213, file 98, UAA.
61. Erna Dominey, "Wallbridge and Imrie. The Architectural Practice of Two Edmonton Women 1950–1979," SSAC *Bulletin* 17, no. 1 (March 1992): 12–18.
62. "Excerpts from Interview with Burgess by Ruth Bowen," 1969, Tory Papers, 79.112, file 8, UAA; Interview with C.S. Burgess, May 1969, 69.361, PAA.
63. Tony Cashman and Norman Croll, *50 Years in Architecture* (n.p.: Schmidt Feldberg Croll Henderson, 1958), 30.
64. "Notes for Talk to Faculty Club," ca. 1958, 71.213, file 130, UAA. The architecture course for arts students was part of the revision of the university's curriculum in 1920 when students were given greater opportunity to take elective courses ("Organization of the University," *The University of Alberta, Edmonton, Calendar*, 1926–27, 30).
65. "Lecture Notes," Architecture 62, n.d., 71.213, file 9, UAA.

66. "Modern Architecture," a talk to an unidentified audience, ca. 1925, 71.213, file 85, UAA. (Reprinted as Document 6.)
67. The Town Planning Institute of Canada was established in early 1919 to advance the study of town planning, carry out public education on planning, housing and land development and promote Canadian training of professional town planners (*Calgary Herald*, May 31, 1919).
68. "Relation of Architecture and Town Planning," a talk to an unidentified audience, Edmonton, ca. 1930, 71.213, file 87, UAA. (Reprinted as Document 9.)
69. "Status of the Profession in the Province of Alberta," RAIC *Journal* 7 (1930): 196.
70. See Geoffrey Simmins, *Documents in Canadian Architectural History* (Peterborough: Broadview Press, 1992), 77–78. On Mawson, see Max Foran, "The Mawson Report in Historical Perspective," *Alberta History* 28, no. 3 (Summer 1980): 31–39.
71. Gordon E. Cherry, *The Evolution of British Town Planning* (Leighton, England: Leonard Hill Books, 1974), 34–39.
72. Wetherell and Kmet, *Homes in Alberta*, 164: Donald G. Wetherell and Irene R.A. Kmet, *Town Life: Main Street and Evolution of Small Town Alberta 1880–1947* (Edmonton: University of Alberta Press, 1995), 164–71.
73. On Adams's political views, see Michael Simpson, *Thomas Adams and the Modern Planning Movement: Britain, Canada and the United States 1900–1914* (London: Mansell, 1985), 79.
74. "The Science and Art of Town Planning," a talk to Edmonton Rotary Club, July 24, 1941, 71.213, file 135, UAA.
75. "City Improvement," a speech to the Men's Faculty Club, 1935, 71.213, file 133, UAA. (Reprinted as Document 14.)
76. "The Town," a talk on radio station CKUA, June 4, 1928, 71.213, file 155, UAA. (Reprinted as Document 7.); "Civic Pride," a talk on radio station CKUA, May 27, 1929, 71.213, file 156, UAA. (Reprinted as Document 8.)
77. "Criteria of Architecture," a talk to an unidentified audience, January 1942, 71.213, file 113, UAA.
78. Wetherell and Kmet, *Homes in Alberta*, 46–49, 152–53. Current interpretations about late nineteenth century housing no longer reflect Burgess's sanguine view of the home. As Nicola Spasoff notes, rather than a "domestic haven," the home is now often seen as a battleground where public debates were waged about health, hygiene and the position of women in society (Spasoff, "Building on Social Power," 4).
79. "Housing and Related Problems in Britain," a talk to an unidentified audience, ca. 1935, 71.213, file 132, UAA; "Housing in Sweden," town planning lecture, n.d. (ca. 1939–40), 71.213, file 65, UAA.
80. "City Improvement," a speech to the Men's Faculty Club, 1935, 71.213, file 133, UAA. (Reprinted as Document 14.)
81. See "City Improvement," a speech to the Men's Faculty Club, 1935, 71.213, file 133, UAA. (Reprinted as Document 14.)

82. See for example: Horace Seymour, "Town Planning Includes 'Sunlight Engineering,'" *The Canadian Engineer*, 36 (April 10, 1919): 363–66; and Percy Nobbs, "Planning for Sunlight," *Journal of the Town Planning Institute* 1, no. 9 (April 1922): 6–12.
83. "Relation of Architecture and Town Planning," a talk to an unidentified audience, Edmonton, ca. 1930, 71.213, file 87, UAA. (Reprinted as Document 9.)
84. "The Town," a talk on radio station CKUA, June 4, 1928, 71.213, file 155, UAA. (Reprinted as Document 7.)
85. Horace Seymour, "Technical Observations on Town Planning Progress in Alberta," (typescript), Department of Municipal Affairs Papers, 71.4, PAA.
86. "The Place of Parks and Playgrounds In Town Planning: Edmonton," a talk to the Property Owners' Association, April 2, 1948, 71.213, file 140, UAA.
87. *The University of Alberta, Edmonton, Calendar, 1930–31*, 156–57.
88. "For the Record," hand written autobiographical notes, ca. 1958, 71.213, file 174, UAA.
89. On an architect's day-to-day responsibilities during the interwar years, see John M. Lyle, "Architecture—A Vocation," RAIC *Journal* 10 (1933): 34–35. On the rise of the general contractor, see A.S. Mathers, "Thirty Five Years of Practice," RAIC *Journal* (December 1955): 462–64.
90. "Excerpts from Interview with Burgess by Ruth Bowen," 1969, Tory Papers, 79.112, file 8, UAA.
91. Burgess to Criaf, October 26, 1928, 71.213, file 25, UAA; "Excerpts from Interview with Burgess by Ruth Bowen," 1969, Tory Papers, 79.112, file 8, UAA.
92. File 137 of the Burgess papers (71.213, UAA) contains clipping of house designs from newspapers such as the *Western Canada Contractor*. His notations on these clippings indicate that he used these as models. It is unfortunately impossible to tie specific house designs to these plans, which would have offered a test case of how popular design was internalised by an architect.
93. File 23 of the Burgess papers (71.213, UAA) concerns plans and correspondence on sundials. See also "Excerpts from Interview with Burgess by Ruth Bowen," 1969, Tory Papers, 79.112, file 8, UAA.
94. Interview with C.S. Burgess, May 1969, 69.361, PAA.
95. Interview with C.S. Burgess, May 1969, 69.361, PAA; General Correspondence 1931, City of Edmonton Papers, MS 209, file 449, City of Edmonton Archives (CEA); "Alberta Government Administrative Building, Edmonton," RAIC *Journal* 8 (1931): 352–56.
96. "Hygiene in Architecture," a typescript for publication in AAA Yearbook, January 30, 1920, 71.213, file 95, UAA (Reprinted as Document 5.)
97. The use of steel was modern, but to define frame building (in which the frame, not the wall substance, was load bearing) as uniquely "modern" is problematic. To be sure, modern architecture has increasingly utilised frame structure in novel ways, but Burgess would have recognised Medieval frame timbering as the same principle on a different scale and using different materials. So too, frame construction had been

characteristic of domestic architecture in western Canada since the beginning of Euro-Canadian settlement.

98. Kalman, *A Concise History of Canadian Architecture*, 466.

99. The pursuit of modernity through an appeal to the past is sometimes called anti-modernism. This term is not employed here because it seems to take too closed a definition of the word "modern"—a word whose meaning has continually changed over the past 200 years. For application of the concept of anti-modernism, see Spasoff, "Building on Social Power," and Donald A. Wright, "W.D. Lighthall and David Ross McCord: Antimodernism and English Canadian Imperialism, 1880s–1918," *Journal of Canadian Studies* 32, no. 2 (Summer 1997): 134–53. On use of the word "modern" see Raymond Williams, "When Was Modernism?" *New Left Review* 175 (May/June 1989): 48–52.

100. See "Appreciation of Architecture, Lecture 1: Architecture and the Arts," a talk for the Edmonton Museum of Arts, October 27, 1932, 71.213, file 99, UAA. (Reprinted as Document 11.); and "Appreciation of Architecture, Lecture 4: Architecture To-day," a talk for the Edmonton Museum of Arts, November 18, 1932, 71.213, file 102, UAA. (Reprinted as Document 12.)

101. On this exhibition at MoMA, see Hasan-Uddin Khan, *International Style. Modernist Architecture from 1925 to 1965* (Cologne: Taschen Books, 1998), 65–87.

102. The terms modern and Modernism are vague. Nicholas Pevsner, *The Sources of Modern Architecture and Design* (London: Thames and Hudson, 1968), sees modernity as connected with industrialisation and the creation of an architecture for "the masses." He thus includes the Arts and Crafts Movement as "modern." Henry-Russell Hitchcock simply defines "modern" as twentieth century architecture (*The Pelican History of Art. Architecture: Nineteenth and Twentieth Centuries* (Markham: Penguin Books, 4th edition, 1977), 419). In the case of Alberta, Trevor Body sees Modernism as ahistorical function-alism, especially as represented by the International Style (*Modern Architecture in Alberta* (Regina: Canadian Plains Research Centre, 1987), 15–17). Harold Kalman takes much the same position, seeing Modernism in Canada as a self-conscious expression of the principles of the European Modernists and the later International Style (*A Concise History of Canadian Architecture*, 535). This is also essentially the position (with a broader range of styles and precedents) of Alan Colquhoun, *Modern Architecture* (New York: Oxford University Press, 2002), 9–11.

103. Alexander F. Gross, "Witness to the Passing of Victorian Architecture—The RAIC Journal, 1924–1935," *SSAC Bulletin* 12, no. 1 (June 1987): 14.

104. When Modernism became only another "style" of architecture it rapidly lost some of its original purpose of addressing contemporary life. By the 1970s, a full revolt against the International Style was underway. This would not have surprised Burgess. He had warned in 1909 of a too uncritical acceptance of the contention by some Arts and Crafts supporters that truthful expression of structure, function, and craftsmanship through the appropriate use of materials was "the ultimate salvation of modern architecture."

He did not disagree, but he observed that this quest had also been a motive in Gothic architecture and central to its glory. Asserting the centrality of sentiment in architecture, he noted that, when any one value became the objective of architecture, it lost its social complexity and relevance. This had been the case, he argued, with Gothic architecture, for when workmanship itself had become its dominant objective, Gothic had been undone because it lost its emotion and thus its social and intellectual meaning ("Applications of the Lessons of History," paper to unidentified audience, Montreal, 1909–12, 71.213, file 126, UAA. (Reprinted as Document 2.)

105. Gross, "Witness to the Passing of Victorian Architecture," 9–14; Anthony Jackson, "The Politics of Architecture: English Architecture 1929–1951," *Journal of the Society of Architectural Historians* 24, no. 1 (March 1965): 97–98. A brief survey of the *Architectural Review* shows Modernist building featured in any significant number only after about 1932.

106. "Relation of Architecture and Town Planning," a talk to an unidentified audience, Edmonton, ca. 1930, 71.213, file 87, UAA. (Reprinted as Document 9.); Le Corbusier, "If I Had To Teach You Architecture," RAIC *Journal* 20 (1943): 17–18.

107. Percy Nobbs, "Present Tendencies Affecting Architecture in Canada Part II," RAIC *Journal* 7 (1930) 315–16.

108. This was a widespread argument in Canada in the 1930s (Gross, "Witness to the Passing of Victorian Architecture,"13).

109. In 1909, for example, Burgess had stressed in a talk ("The Value of the Arts," 71.213, file 119, UAA) to the St. James Literary Society in Montreal the value of the "humbler arts," or crafts, in contrast to "fine arts." Many of these arguments were repeated later the same year, again at the St. James Literary Society, in "The Aims and Uses of Art" (71.213, file 120, UAA). And in 1923 a similarly broad view of art as expressing sentiment had been discussed in the "Function of Art" at the Philosophical Society at the University of Alberta (71.213, file 121, UAA).

110. "Appreciation of Architecture, Lecture 4: Architecture To-day," a talk for the Edmonton Museum of Arts, November 18, 1932, 71.213, file 102, UAA. (Reprinted as Document 12.)

111. Robert Starr Leigh Wilson, professor of civil engineering, 1919–20, Head, Department of Civil Engineering, 1920–46, Dean of Applied Science, 1929–46.

112. Wilson to Kerr, March 8 1939 and attachment, "The Position of Architecture in the University," President Kerr's Papers, University of Alberta, 68–1, Box 2 3/3/4/3/1–1, UAA.

113. *McGill's School of Architecture: A History by Norbert Schoenauer.* "Legacy of Turner," Montreal: McGill University, School of Architecture, at http://www.mcgill.ca/architecture/introduction/history/nobbs/ (current 2005).

114. Guest Editorial, RAIC *Journal* 18 (1941): 16.

115. Report, RAIC *Journal* 19 (1942): 16.

116. Vita (hand written), 1957, 71.213, file 1, UAA.

117. "Recollections of a Half Century," 71.213, file 177, UAA. (Reprinted as Document 21.)

118. Kerr to Burgess, April 10, 1939, and Kerr to Burgess, November 4, 1939, 71.213, file 8, UAA.
119. For a history of the Elnora hospital, see Margaret Hughes, *Off the Record. A View of Hospital Happenings From Behind the Medical Record Desk* (n.p.: Goosehaven Publishing, 1998). Thanks to Colleen Hepburn for this reference.
120. Burgess to Watson, November 6, 1946, Cecil Scott Burgess Papers, 69.190, file 3, PAA.
121. Burgess to Abbott, June 20, 1940, 71.213, file 166, UAA. The model measured 6'x 3'6" and stood 2'6" inches high. Photos or drawings of this model have not been located. Drawings in file 72.28.142 UAA may be related to this but are unidentified.
122. "Housing Plan. CSB 10.8.39 April 1941," 71.213, file 166, UAA.
123. Cecil Burgess, "Housing," RAIC *Journal* 17 (October 1940): 182.
124. Many lenders refused to advance mortgages on property in Alberta after the 1935 election of Social Credit in protest of the government's economic policies. This made the provisions of the federal housing schemes inoperative in Alberta. The impasse was broken under the premiership of the more business-friendly Ernest Manning in 1943 (Wetherell and Kmet, *Homes in Alberta*, 189–91).
125. Clayton Research Associates and D.G. Wetherell and Associates, *Two Decades of Innovation in Housing Technology, 1946–1965* (Ottawa: CMHC, 1994), 19–34.
126. Burgess to Ferguson, June 29, 1946, 69.190, file 3, PAA;. "For the Record," hand written autobiographical notes, ca. 1958, 71.213, file 174, UAA.
127. Burgess to Secretary, February 26, 1947 and passim, 71.213, file 174, UAA.
128. Wah May Chan, "The Impact of the Technical Planning Board on the Morphology of Edmonton" (M.A thesis, University of Alberta, 1969), 4–7; Cecil Burgess, "The Place of Parks and Playgrounds In Town Planning: Edmonton," A talk to the Property Owners' Association, April 2, 1948, 71.213, file 140, UAA. The Edmonton zoning plan had been designed for a city with a future population of 217,000. By 1949 Edmonton had a population of around 118,000 and by 1951 it reached 172,000.
129. Chan, "The Impact of the Technical Planning Board," 3.
130. Burgess to Chairman, October 8, 1943, City of Edmonton Papers, RG11, Class 204, file 74, CEA.
131. Clippings: "Civic Town Planning," 1949, CEA; *Edmonton Bulletin*, February 26, 1949; *Edmonton Journal*, February 16 and February 17, 1949.
132. Chan, "The Impact of the Technical Planning Board," 7–12.
133. Burgess's Edmonton projects 1948–1953 can be pieced together from building permit records in the City Clerk's Papers, RG 17, various items in boxes 17–195, CEA.
134. Sherlock to Burgess, July 4, 1950 and May 15, 1952, and Peel to Burgess, September 16, 1959, 71.213, file 14, UAA.
135. Burgess to Chairman, September 1, 1953, 71.213, file 9, UAA.
136. "Presentation of Cecil Scott Burgess," *The New Trail* 16, no. 1 (1958): 15.
137. "Excerpts from Interview with Burgess by Ruth Bowen," 1969, Tory Papers, 79.112. file 8, UAA.

138. "Excerpts from Interview with Burgess by Ruth Bowen," 1969, Tory Papers, 79.112, file 8, UAA.
139. "Cecil Burgess Reaches 100," *Folio*, October 22, 1970.
140. For an analysis of Mumford's thinking in the context of the debate over Modernism see Gail Fenske, "Lewis Mumford, Henry-Russell Hitchcock, and the Bay Region Style," in *The Education of the Architect, Historiography, Urbanism and the Growth of Architectural Knowledge, Essays Presented to Standford Anderson*, edited by Martha Pollak (Cambridge: The MIT Press, 1997), 37–85.
141. "Appreciation of Architecture, Lecture 4: Architecture To-day," a talk for the Edmonton Museum of Arts, November 18, 1932, 71.213, file 102, UAA. (Reprinted as Document 12.)
142. Fedori, Tingley and Murray, *The Practice of Post-War Architecture in Edmonton*, 9.
143. Outline of talk to Faculty Club, n.d. (ca. 1958), 71.213, file 130, UAA; Interview with C.S. Burgess, May 1969, 69.361, PAA.
144. See also Ronald Rees for suggestive comments on the way that postwar commercial architecture reflected the culture of North America (Ronald Rees, "Reconsidering Antiurban Sentiment" *Landscape*, 28 (1985): 26–29).
145. "Expression in Architecture," unpublished essay (ca. 1953), 71.213, file 149, UAA.

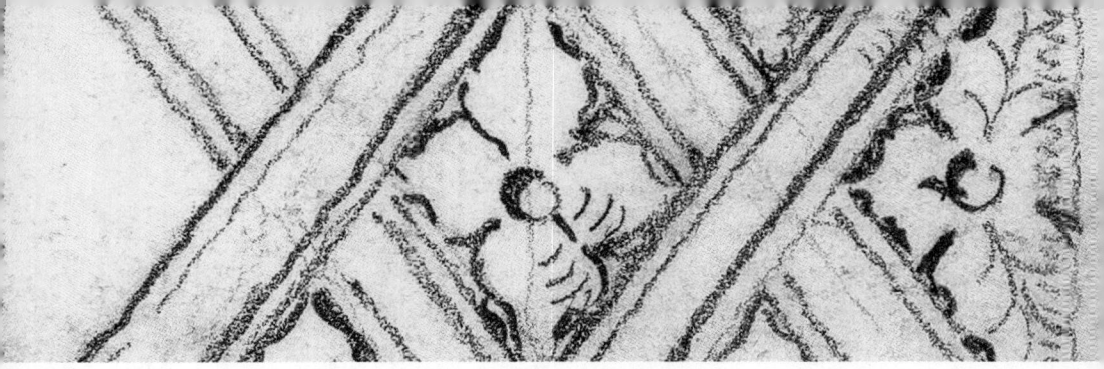

Editor's Notes on the Burgess Papers

THERE ARE VARIOUS ACCESSIONS in the Burgess fonds at the University of Alberta Archives. The collection consists of a small amount of personal correspondence and a very extensive range of transcripts of lectures and talks, notes on poems and books, photographs, postcards and illustrations, drawings, tracings and sketches, and blueprints. Additional Burgess records from the 1940s and 1950s on town planning are held at the Provincial Archives of Alberta. There is also scattered material at the City of Edmonton Archives about his involvement with town planning in Edmonton.

I have selected materials from this extensive body of material that are representative of Burgess's public addresses and which would best convey an understanding of the issues that animated his approach to architecture and town planning. I have been concerned to avoid repetitive materials, although this is difficult in some cases because Burgess, like all lecturers, often reworked previous materials. Rather than university lectures, I have stressed unpublished materials and talks of a public nature, which better illustrate the ideas that Albertans and Canadians were exposed to during the period between 1909 and 1946. This book thus includes only a small part—perhaps no more than 20 percent—of the material in the Burgess fonds at the University of Alberta Archives.

One of the guiding editorial principles for this book has been the preservation of the original character of the materials. All documents are published in their complete form. Burgess wrote out a complete text of many of his talks in longhand. These texts were not intended as publications and some editorial intervention has been necessary. Thus, abbreviations in the original text have been spelled out and most spelling has been standardised to current Canadian standards. Punctuation has been standardised and very long sentences have been split for coherence and to reflect how Burgess would likely have delivered the lecture. These editorial interventions have been done silently, but any words that have been inserted are enclosed in square brackets. Press style has been followed for numbers, percentages, hyphenation and similar matters. Annotations in the text are numbered as endnotes. I have tried to keep annotations to a minimum, but all of Burgess's notations in the original manuscripts are included in the endnotes, as are explanatory or biographical notes to clarify those cases that would not be readily apparent to most readers. The introductory capsules for each document are designed to provide context, to create connections among the documents and to refresh the reader's memory of material discussed in the Introduction. For this reason, I have not, in most cases, provided endnotes for the capsules, assuming that the reader can revisit the Introduction to find citations or broader discussion of the points raised.

The organising principle of the archival collection is not a suitable form for this book. The archival collection is organised with materials grouped functionally: correspondence makes one set of files, notes another, while lectures, talks, radio talks and so on make up others. While rational, this division is too fragmented to facilitate an easy understanding of Burgess's thinking because it requires a solid grasp of the total collection. Materials chosen for reprinting have thus been organised in a chronological fashion, which allows the progression of Burgess's interests and ideas to emerge most clearly. While it would also have been possible to organise the materials on a topical basis around architecture and town planning, this organization would fragment the unity of the materials because Burgess never saw a firm distinction between the two, viewing each as taking essential reference from the other. Thus, materials have been grouped in three temporal units that reflect important divisions in Burgess's life. Part I contains materials up to 1920. This covers the period from his early years in Montreal to his return to Edmonton after World War I and his decision to make his future at the University of Alberta. Part II deals with the highly productive period between the mid 1920s and 1939, the year Burgess retired from the university. Part III contains materials from the time of his retirement from the university until 1948. Part IV consists of a single document, Burgess's recollections published in the RAIC *Journal* in 1957.

PART I

1909–1920

Overleaf: Cecil Burgess with an unidentified woman, ca. 1917–19. (71.213-273, UAA)

DOCUMENT 1

Old Buildings of the Province of Quebec

ARTS AND CRAFTS praise of craftsmanship and authenticity often led its proponents to express admiration for past vernacular building traditions. Such building practices, which had developed without the aid of architects or formal training, were said to be honest, unassuming expressions of society and the builder's art. Supposedly rooted in simpler times, such building traditions appealed to people disenchanted with urban industrialised times whose machine-made products were said to lack the integrity of hand-made things. The study of how earlier builders had solved problems of design and construction was believed to offer models of how to create better and more authentic contemporary architecture. It was also believed that this study of local traditions might also inspire the development of a distinctive Canadian architecture.

Some Arts and Crafts proponents in Canada found such building traditions in the early architecture of Quebec. Percy Nobbs and Ramsay Traquair, both of whom taught at McGill with Burgess, were admirers of these buildings, and

Traquair devoted his life to discovering and cataloguing them; work that he published in 1947 as The Architecture of Old Quebec. *Burgess's talk on these buildings to the Province of Quebec Architect's Association Sketch Club (which he had organised as a collegial forum for members) was thus part of a broader trend in early Canadian architectural criticism. By drawing parallels with Greek and Gothic architecture, Burgess was validating the worth of old Quebec architecture. But as well, Greek, Gothic and French Canadian building traditions, despite coming from such widely dispersed places and times, offered models to present-day architects of how creativity, honest use of materials and the clear expression of a building's purpose could produce buildings that spoke to the unique needs of their place and time.*

Document 1 is a talk to the PQAA Sketch Club, October 28, 1909, 71.213, file 91, UAA.

IF YOU WERE TO ASK any distinguished architect's views on the matter of domestic work, he would probably preface his remarks by saying that this is a class of work which it does not pay an architect to undertake. Or, if he was a very distinguished architect indeed, he might say he always charged 10 percent when he took on that class of work. No doubt it is for this reason that so much domestic work is built without the mediation of an architect at all. A larger part of the work of which I have slides was no doubt built in this way, and yet not without success.[1] I fear no architect got even 5 percent for it.

It has sometimes been admitted even abroad that no architects are so successful with domestic [work] as are the English. This is so far admitted in Germany and in America that in both countries there are many recent houses which are obviously built with the intention of looking as like

English houses as possible, and there are few who will not admit that in France, where the training of architects is more thoroughly looked after than in any other country, there is a conspicuous failure in domestic architecture. Something seems to have gone all wrong about the French idea of a house to live in with comfort.

Some attribute this to the absence of family life amongst the French. But if this is at all the reason, it is not, I am convinced, the whole reason. Possibly the men who work out their architecture belong to classes who have no private family life, but that any healthy country can be wholly or chiefly composed of people who have no private family life I cannot think credible. Least of all can I believe it of a nation possessing the superlative qualities of the French of the present day.

I think it is rather because the elements out of which a genuine domestic style of architecture [arises] are so humble that academic schools overlook them as not seeming to belong to their sphere. I think it is by condescending to take notice of, and to make the most of, some very humble things that the English architects have succeeded in domestic work. It is a matter of frequent recurrence in the history of art that some fresh discovery of beauty is first made by the efforts of humble craftsmen working along lines that the great schools take no note of or despise as not rising to the dignity of their ideals.

I suppose the great historic instance of this in connection with architecture is that of the rise of Gothic architecture—barbarous and uncouth forms according to those of classic training. I think anyone who has seen the old Gothic building will admit their majesty of outline, the beauty of their parts and the charm of their detail. The intelligence of their construction and its frank expression is their distinguishing feature, which all must perforce admit. Yet we find such an appreciation of them as this in an old edition of the Encyclopedia Britannica:

> when the empire was entirely overrun by the Goths the conquerors very naturally introduced their own method of building. Like the ancient Egyptians. the Goths seem to have been more studious to

amaze people with the greatness of their buildings than to please the eye with the regularity of their structure or the propriety of their ornaments. They corrected themselves, however, a little by the models of the Roman edifices which they saw before them, but these models themselves were faulty and the Goths being totally destitute of genius neither architecture nor any other kind of art could be improved by them.

This masterpiece of mistaken history and failure in architectural appreciation was probably compounded by some distinguished architect who may have keenly appreciated classic work and possibly could do excellent work within his own limits. I quote it to show how one school of thought often entirely fails to see any virtue in the work of another school. I do not think that the modern academic school fails in this colossal way to appreciate the beauty of successful domestic architecture. But I do think that architects successful along academic lines fail usually to make their domestic architecture a success. I believe this arises from the fact that the principles underlying successful work in these two lines are not contrary, but indeed very diverse, and an academic training as at present understood does not fit a man for doing the ideal domestic work.

Academic training is singularly absent in England. The Englishman clings to the apprenticeship system. He loves to potter over his architecture, not to go about it systematically. Hence he is apt to remain an amateur at his own business all his days. He is apt not to have very clear ideas about the standard solution for each problem that comes in his way and he attacks it from a personal viewpoint of his own that often fails in largeness and all-roundness and mechanical adequateness but has a certain merit of freshness and originality and individuality and personal joy in the work. And these are precisely the qualities that are the delight of good domestic work and they are qualities which broad schools will always hail with pleasure and encourage and cultivate but which, of course, they cannot implant or teach. There are many other useful things which they can and do teach and therefore these three—freshness, originality and individuality—are not apt to show up too largely in their results.

Now I think that for all great monumental work academic training is not only good, I think it is absolutely essential. But even the greatest monumental work must take its inspiration in its origins from humbler works, just as surely as the sublimest temples of the Greeks have written upon their face the fact that the lines of beauty there immortalised in marble were first developed by the handy craftsmen who long before had shaped log huts into things of beauty—into homes of such simple and satisfactory beauty that the people of the keenest intellect the world has ever seen accepted the form as being so excellent that they could not improve upon it and they only set to work to refine its details in proportion and subtlety of line.

It is this fine craftsman spirit that underlies the Greek temple and all other noble and highly developed forms which I think is still a mine, and by no means a worked out mine of beauty. Such fine work as has been produced so far in this world owes its origin to this, but I think more remains than ever came out of it, and I think all this delightful domestic work of the present day derives its virtue from the fact that it draws its inspiration from this inexhaustible source. The early, perhaps prehistoric, Greeks had their wooden huts which they loved. They were not very elaborate affairs but there was something about that crowning member with beam ends regularly spaced and the mutules and guttae and all the rest, probably made brilliant with colour we should remember, that charmed the very hearts of these old people, just as the gable and the rows of mullioned windows charm the hearts of the Englishman of the present day till he thinks there is no place like home.

I have said that the humble prototype of the Grecian temple was a very simple affair and that the great virtue of it was that it had a charm—a charm like some simple melody "that's sweetly played in tune"—and it had a few intelligible features founded on constructive motive. The greatest temples of the Greeks have hardly any more features, and in them the constructive connection has disappeared. It is only quasi-constructive for the wood members are petrified and make no elaborate attempt to seem really structural—they are obviously no longer so.

The province of Quebec has her own forms of simple building; they have their own characteristic features, simple and few, no doubt. So simple and so few that the architects of the present day, not being of the same metal as the ancient Greeks, find little hope of brilliant inspiration in them.

I am not going this evening to advocate the establishment of a Quebec style based on the habitant's cottage. The only effectual way of advocating such a thing is to go and do it and show in practice that it can be done successfully. I can even give some reasons [why] we should not base a domestic style for the present day on these very simple works. The principle one is that solid stone is the usual construction in these buildings, and expense must bar out solid stone in a great many buildings of the present day. Again, I think that with our smaller stock of genius than the Greeks, and with our hearts that cannot find delight in such severe simplicity as filled theirs to the brim, we must have more variety in our structures, both of features and of structural motif. And at all cost we must build such buildings as our hearts and eyes can take delight in.

What I do want to point out, however, is that even these buildings have their charm, and that in ours we ought not to be satisfied with less. If we fail, it will probably be because we have not had the sense to realise what the true principles of a humble scale of art are. They are really expressed in the word I have been using—good craftsmanship. The Greeks borrowed all they knew of decorative motif from a piece of good carpentry work. The Gothic builders took their most favourite, though perhaps not their only, decorative motif from a little structural device that was the stone mason's pride, the arcade. Constructional, or as the merest decoration, we get the arcade, the arcade, the arcade always before our eyes in Gothic buildings. The best modern domestic work does the same thing, not in one or two ways merely, but in many ways. To take one instance, in bricklayer's work there are many craftsmen's structural expedients which are

Burgess's photo of an old Quebec house with a double chimney. Not dated, ca. 1903–1912. (71.213-311, UAA)

realised as presenting a charming appearance to the eye. By noting these and employing them, not flagrantly or wantonly (for one of the first rules of good manners in craftsmanship, as in anything else, is not to obtrude itself gratuitously and not to be fussy or irritating), but with moderation and when circumstances really seem to call for or excuse them, we may build brickwork that is delightful to the eye. The same applies to the treatment of all materials, external and internal, and in such features as doors, porches, roofs, etc., different craftsmen's methods of solving the structural problem are full of suggestions for interesting treatment. Indeed, if you want another source of inspiration you have to fall back on the pilasters and entablature, and I think you will find that even these look best when they appear to have some structural propriety. Now there is much satisfaction to be got out of our old friends the pillar and entablature, big and little, and I don't want to turn down such useful members of society, but I find that human nature, or at any rate human clients, seem often enough to feel they could do without such purely ornamental company.

I have spoken of the Englishman's lack of admiration for academic training. What is his idea of training? I don't know that I ever heard it very clearly described, but I have some notion of what it is. Of course, in his apprenticeship he does his "five orders" very faithfully and becomes an accomplished and commonly useful practical draughtsman.[3] But the English architect generally can't take much interest in architecture until he sees some work he has schemed on paper taking shape in substance. Then he at once becomes intensely interested and his interest as often as not takes the form of taking down what he had put up and reconstructing it some other way. I have known one of the best known English domestic architects spend a good deal of his time, for which he could command a good many guineas per hour, I say, I have known of this man spending a good part of a day along with a bricklayer, constructing a little row of labourer's cottages, picking out bricks that had ends rather blacker than their neighbours and directing the man just how to work them so as to get a good haphazard, nicely sprinkled effect in the facework. No doubt, both man and architect became so keen on the job that for a while there seemed to be nothing else in the world desirable but nicely dappled brickwork. This, I think, is the training of the good domestic architect. The principle involved affects the masonry, the brickwork, everything down to the painting, carpets and furniture. Some do not stop till the table covers, plates, knives and spoons are to their taste, and if they were allowed, they would probably have the meals cooked so as to be in harmony with the brickwork and would investigate along with the cook the best process of getting the toast of the proper colour and speckle. Only he must never forget his 5 percent.

Well, to return to our old Quebec buildings. I have said that they are mostly of stone of the simplest class of building and they do not afford a great many motives which can even be glorified into decoration. So simple are they that I believe the style might even be called trabeated, for arches are rare, with the exception of the flat arch with one keystone and two side pieces, an arch that is handy to build with, for the pieces are more easily lifted than [is] a big lintel. When in place it has more elasticity and is less likely to crack than a lintel, especially in the somewhat rigid and

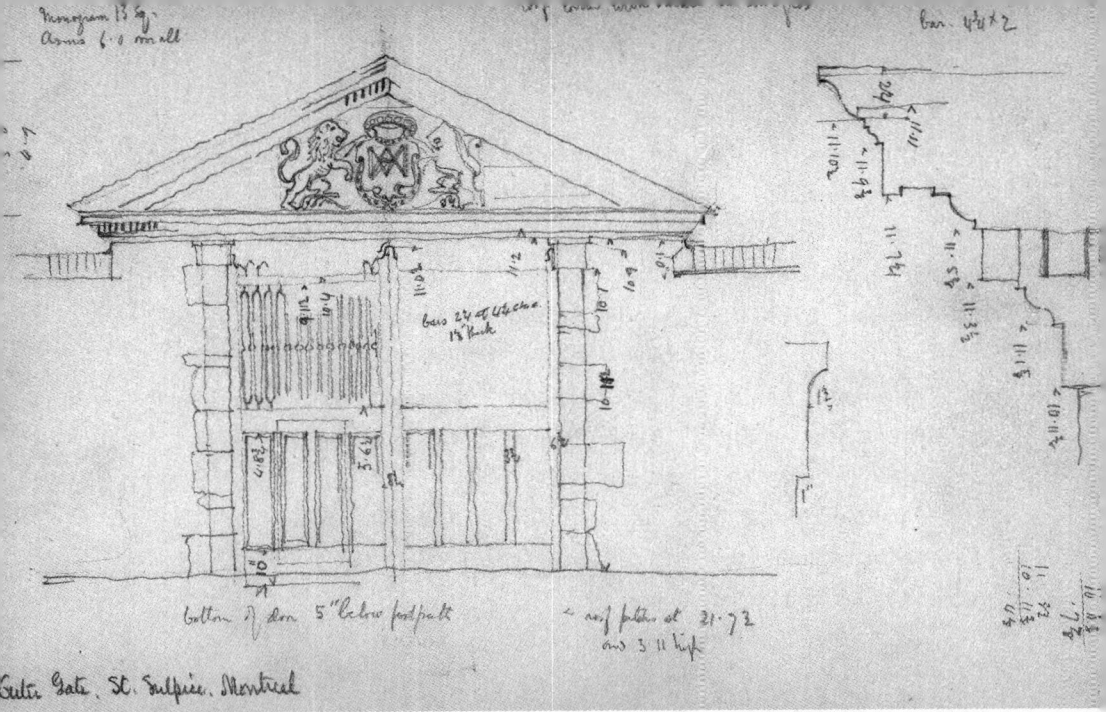

Burgess's measured sketch of the outer gate, St. Sulpice, Montreal, ca. 1909–13. (71.213–184, sketchbook, UAA)

faulty limestone of Montreal.[4] It has the merit of the lintel in having a straight soffit to suit simple sashes, and lastly it has in it a decorative motif which has received attention from some of the greatest architects of the present and of the past. Certain features will be more easily referred to on the screen. The great gables carried their entire thickness above the roof and [were] shingled on edge with the great moulded corbel carrying a projection at the foot of the gable against which to stop the eaves of the roof. All this forms a kind of gable which I do not remember having seen outside of this province, and one that is full of character and strong architectural effect. One feature common in these gables is the double chimney with a horizontal wall between. I wish someone here could explain to me the reason for this form. There are variants on it, but it is remarkably frequent in occurrence. Does it represent a back room or a front room each with a chimney? Did old houses in this province have a fireplace in each room, and in any case, what difficulty was there in the way of having two flues carried over into one central stack as is general in other countries? The wall was surely thick enough for the purpose.

The eyelash roof of the little cottages is a very charming feature which one appreciates all the more when seen beside the more modern and improved style of [the] so-called flat roof which slopes backwards at the smallest angle and is adorned along the front edge with tin gimcrackery. The verandah in front of some of these old Quebec houses is an interesting feature. As often as not, it has neither railing in front nor posts to support the roof, which comes out in cantilever.

I should like to ask if anyone can tell us what the two little square buildings were for that one occasionally sees a little distance off from each end of an old stone farmhouse.

I have been speaking of the older buildings, and especially the country buildings. I should like to mention that some of these exist in the town, such as the Chateau de Ramezay, the Seminary of St. Sulpice and many other interesting examples in the neighbourhood of the Court House and lower St. Urbain Street. Later buildings are not so characteristic of this province—their inspiration from old France and old England is evident. Many of the houses on St. Denis Street and neighbourhood are quite in the style of streets still existing in many towns in France built about the time of Louis XV. I think the Bonsecours market might be classed along with these, whilst the Inland Revenue office, McCord Building on St. Gabriel Street, and others in Beaver Hall Hill, Sherbrooke Street and elsewhere resemble Georgian buildings in England and show the delicate profiles and exceeding restraint of that period of gentility when people set such store by refinement of manners that they were afraid to let themselves go or even to express themselves with freedom and frankness. The house at the corner of St. Lawrence Boulevard and Sherbrooke Street is a good example of Adams style and other examples occur. There is a chimney piece of this style on an old house on St. Jean Baptiste Street which was measured and drawn by Mr. J.R. Smith and illustrated in the PQAA Annual in 1906.

In the province there are many churches of excellent architecture as I think I can demonstrate by one or two examples. I do not know the dates of these in all cases, but the church of Pointe-aux Trembles is dated 24th June 1705, which I take to be the date of dedication, and the style of work is similar to that being executed in France at that date. The others which I have to show are probably a good deal later, but I think they show admirable arrangement and good judgement in the scale on which the classical pillars are introduced and their general proportions are most satisfactory. The lighting too is quite skilfully and beautifully arranged.

NOTES

1. The list of slides that Burgess used to illustrate this talk is not in his papers.
2. This was a modest criticism of the École des Beaux Arts, one of the dominant French architectural schools. A highly centralised institution, it stressed monumentalism and neo-classicism, taught through appeal to formal rational analysis of what were thought to be universal principles of architectural design.
3. The five orders were the Tuscan, Doric, Ionic, Corinthian and Composite. It was believed that through the proper proportioning of these orders, the highest expression of beauty and harmony could be achieved. The Roman architect Vitruvius, in the *Ten Books on Architecture*, offered the ideal proportion for each order. Vitruvius's model was reworked during the Italian Renaissance, and studying the correct proportion and harmony of the orders remained a central feature of architectural education until the mid twentieth century.
4. Note in margin: "McCord's House."

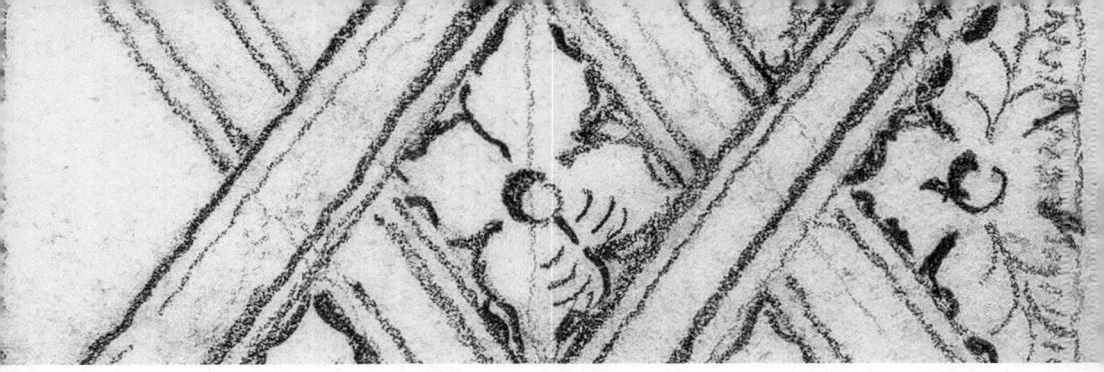

DOCUMENT 2

Applications of the Lessons of History

THE OLD BUILDINGS of Quebec demonstrated for Burgess that the sensibility of a society—in his terms, its culture—was the basis for honest architectural expression. This, he claimed, was one of the lessons of history. Writ large, this was one reason, he argued, why architectural history lay at the heart of architectural practice. This did not mean that architects should copy past architectural styles and forms. Rather, as he asserted in this lecture to a Montreal audience, they should attempt to understand what forces had made past buildings great, how materials had been used and had stood up over time, and then apply these approaches and lessons in their work. Architectural history was thus of immediate and direct application to architectural practice because it helped broaden the cultural sensibility as well as the technical competence of an architect. Accordingly, lectures in architectural history, as well as the use of photographs, models and casts of historical buildings, sculpture and building details in drawing courses was part of the curriculum in

McGill's architecture programme where Burgess taught architectural history, drawing and building construction. When he set up the architectural programme at the University of Alberta several years later, he followed this model by incorporating such subjects and approaches in the curriculum.

Document 2 is a paper to an unidentified audience, possibly the Montreal Sketch Club, 1909–12, 71.213, file 126, UAA.[1]

HERE IN CANADA we are separated by 3,000 miles of water from the older traditions of our race; but we have at our disposal many means of annihilating the distance. The value of tradition is incalculable. Men have died gladly because it was the tradition of their family or of their regiment to do so. Men have devoted themselves to various forms of work, with a zeal that carried them to the highest point of excellence, because it was the tradition of the firm they worked for to do excellent work. Kindness, patience and forbearance, in a word "character," is not to be taught by precept; it is part of the tradition of a civilised race handed on to the children by their fathers from a third and a fourth generation reckoning backwards.

We may have at our birth good constitution of body, mind and spirit, but for the methods by which these are to be brought into full play we look to that experience which we inherit from past times. If we burn to attain ideals of any worth, we may enter the lists with high hearts and make straight into the fight. Soon we shall be seeking a salve for wounded hopes, providing ourselves with the most efficient arms we can possibly obtain, observing the bearing of the older soldiers whom we see standing their ground where we have failed. We may even find it wise to retire to study how battles have been fought and won, and campaigns successfully carried through. The knowledge of these things is the tradition of warfare. Tradition is not a muttered spell that being repeated will bring to us success, and history is not the bare chronicle of facts—it is the lesson that these facts teach. The past is irrevocable, what is done cannot be changed. But history is not of the past; it is part of the present, and is always changing. The history that is written today is very different from the history that was being written half a century ago. Changed circumstances have given us a new viewpoint from which to judge the same old past events. Men who made much noise in their own day are often of little interest to us; and others who were despised and rejected we look on as the givers of good gifts to men.

That the past keeps turning to us another and another side may be very clearly seen in the matter of architectural history if we compare the views of Chambers in his work on *Civil Architecture* with James Fergusson's *History of the Styles*, and these again with the writers of our own day—Blomfield, Anderson, Russel Sturgis, Lethaby and Choisy.[2] Sir William Chambers lays down rules for architecture with all the dogmatism of an orthodox believer in that one true style of which he was himself so great a master and Gothic is a name abhorred.[3] Fergusson attacks this complacent attitude of mind, fighting for a broader view and endeavouring to formulate rules based on pure reason. We today reap the benefit of Fergusson's iconoclasm and conceive of architecture as having a range wider than his rather dryly intellectual theories included. A right appreciation of history demands, therefore, that we survey the past from the vantage point of the present. We must bring our own thought to bear upon the events of the past and examine them in view of our situation and our needs today; otherwise we shall not be studying the lesson to us of past achievement, but its lesson to someone else of another place and time.

The quality of endurance is the first quality that impresses itself upon us in those sights we see when we venture forth from our little circle of present-day interests into the larger world of history. It is also the quality that men seem first to have striven with any force to attain in the dawn of architectural aspiration, as we see in the pyramids or the stone circles of Stonehenge and elsewhere. It is well to observe this for we are apt, in reading history, somewhat loosely to suppose that beauty has always been one aim of architectural design. History tells us another tale. Neither the pyramids nor the Egyptian temples had the slightest intention of being beautiful. They were intended to express the might and mystery and even the terror of the unseen and unknown and they were the tributes of humble men to the higher powers earthly and heavenly. In the same way, I cannot imagine that the Assyrians aimed at beauty in their architectural work. They wanted to give the impression of dazzling splendour and of transcendent kingly power. For beauty they probably had a somewhat supercilious patronage. It was a little thing to them, not worth a great effort to attain. They spent their energy on other qualities.

To the Greeks we owe the discovery of that harmonious relationship of all component elements that we call beauty. The intellect of this people was of a finer mould than that of any of their predecessors or successors, and this discovery was much more important to human progress than was Newton's discovery of the laws of gravitation. Like gravitation, this too was a quality which had always been in existence; but no men had heretofore been bred of fine enough mind to stamp it into current coin and of set purpose to breathe it into the work of their hands. Not every nation since has equally realised this quality. To the Roman the whole worth and interest of life was not comprised in its immutable ideas, the glory of power, nor in its harmonious refinements. The men that quelled earth's warring tribes, commanded peace by force of arms, gave stability to those nations that would consent to live by law, and shattered those who had no occupation but rapine, were not the equals of the Greeks in their perception of beauty. They had their own architecture, however, expressing their own great qualities. The monuments of Rome bear witness to the largeness of mind and varied interests of her men. To organise into a unity many diverse elements, to command respect by power physical and intellectual, to create order out of disorderly and apparently conflicting requirements—these are the triumphs equally of the Roman empire and of Roman architecture. The Thermae of Rome had been erected to satisfy the physical and intellectual wants of a vast imperial people to whom the earth was tributary. The Byzantine Church was built to the glorification of an ideal and moral controller of the world and its destinies, to whom belonged the earth and the fullness thereof. The first essential thought was unreserving homage to the great spiritual power to whom all honour was due.

The mediaeval church established a well-ordered and far-reaching hierarchy over Europe, inculcating its moral teachings in city, town and cottage—a hierarchy that in its scheme of design and in its adaptation to purpose has its exact expression in the cathedral which sheltered its sacraments. The crowning vault [was] forethought in every detail before the foundations were laid; its weight and thrusts maintained by a structure of many ramifications, each of its many parts having its allotted form and function. It represents the social scheme as pictured by the mediaeval mind—each unit is assigned its sphere and its task and is free to attain such excellence as it may within and whilst it performs that task. In turn, the mediaeval church, by putting in practice her systematised order, had succeeded in drilling men up to a degree of excellence at which the individual asserted his independence. Society lost its classified system and architecture was now no longer an affair of buildings whose structural problem controlled the form and disposition of all their parts and in which the duty of each workman was but to construct and shape these parts well and perhaps to superadd some pleasant fancy.

The main formative element of the building was now no longer the structural problem expressing the general structural principle of the social system, but was the character of man, its maker and its user. If these are pleasant fancies now, they are no longer essentially based on some structural groundwork; they spring directly out of human, not structural, demands. As we watch the masters of the Renaissance struggling with this problem of the deliberate self-conscious expression of human character, we see the stern simplicity of the early Florentine palaces transformed by their efforts into the broader urbanity of Bramante, the sweet, firm, gentle refinement of Peruzzi, and the manly grace and vigour of San Michele. Michelangelo's colossal work at St. Peter's is brought to completion, demonstrating what great things men, not systems, can dare and do; and amidst her waters, Venice expands herself in wealth and ease and dignity. So great is the charm of these deliberately self-conscious expressions of sentiment and of thought, and so strong is the demand for them in human nature, that for their sake the whole current of men's thoughts was turned aside from the old mediaeval ways, even in France and England, where men were so steeped in the delight of craftsmanship and the loveliness of materials. Much was obviously lost thereby, as Gothic revivalists have rightly insisted and as all that love beauty must admit; but the Renaissance took place in answer to a human need then first realised, and needs once realised will not be forgotten at the bidding of those who hope to praise past times.

I have taken up a great deal of your time in making so cursory a review merely of ancient architecture. To continue into the more complex and fascinating story of more recent times—the expression for example in later civil architecture of the life politic of the people, and the phases represented by the erection of picture galleries wherein the people may take delight and moral instruction, and public libraries where all classes may sit as guests at the tables of imagination and of science—all this would require several course of lectures. I wish, however, to draw attention specially to certain points:

1. That the study of the history of architecture is not merely the study of the outward shapes of buildings, of things we can measure with a footrule, and having done so, can go and reproduce as the natural purpose of our studies. This sort of thing has been tried over in Europe since the time when Stuart and Revett brought back their measured drawings of the Parthenon and dazzled the eyes of scholarly architects. The reaction of mediaeval revival followed and, as a result of the drawn battle of these styles, all other styles—Egyptian, Francis I, Old Dutch, Louis XIV, Queen Anne, Georgian and even Adams—were galvanised into wonderful counterfeits of life. Whilst a more rational style of things seems to be setting in in England, this galvanic process seems in the United States not yet to have run its

full course; and not merely individual men, but whole communities have become such worshippers of past forms of expression that a brilliant traveller summing up his impressions of Boston society says that whilst attending a meeting at which cultured Bostonians were feasting upon their favourite diet of history worship, he had a sort of uneasy feeling "that mind was now dead and the souvenirs were being distributed." Gentlemen, this is a pitfall into which we must not allow our study of the past to lead us. History is the background against which the living present is to be viewed; we must not allow our lives to be merged into that background. The dead hand must not be allowed to chill our living hearts. The student who sets before him a piece of ornament, which he means to study by drawing, has a snare similar to this. If he copy merely the form though ever so faithfully, the result may be correct but it will be dead. If, on the other hand, he realise the principles of design and live them over again in his own mind so to speak, re-designing the object as he makes his copy, he will have some chance of putting some spirit and life into his work. Of course, this humble process of copying, though it has its own excellent uses as study, is not a means at all of producing real and living work, whether it be the copying of buildings or of ornament.

2. The second point I wish to note, as being one of the broad lessons of history, is that the thing to look for in old architectures is not a vague something called beauty. What we find there recorded are all the sentiments of human nature. Beauty is truly the highest quality we shall there find, giving worth to all the others. It stands in relation to those others somewhat as balance does to mental qualities, or as conscience to our moral qualities.

3. A third general point is that, when we survey the different stages of the world's architectural development, it is startling to observe how little some of these stages have consciously derived from their predecessors. Each age addresses itself to its peculiar work as a man rises fresh in the morning, the sleep and the forgetting of the night having

renewed his powers of mind and body; but he must not come to his work in entire forgetfulness or dire will be the consequences. For this reason we must study well our history—lest we forget.

There is gladness in remembrance. History offers us a great and delightful panorama, full of sights strange and at first apparently inexplicable. They awaken and train our faculties of appreciation. It is easier to come to a right, fair, unbiased opinion regarding old work. It has taken its place in historical perspective, and we know the effect it has produced on the minds of men of various temperaments. Having an outside knowledge of the spirit of the times, we can estimate how far it has clearly embodied that spirit. Being outside the stress and strain of our daily work, one can enjoy old architecture as an entertainment in the same way as one can enjoy good literature. It is a recreation of a liberal education. It furnishes us with edifying society and with standards to live up to. It is an open book for our instruction.

History speaks, as we have seen, of human effort and human character. Ideas that occur to us as new and tempt us to experiment may be there seen worked out to splendid developments or to dismal failures according to their inherent worth. We can see the temptation to piquant and exaggerated detail besetting the men of the later periods of the Renaissance, and producing the extravagancies of the baroco and rococo styles—extravagancies which in their day no doubt had their admirers as exhibitions of virility and originality. Whilst we realise how this crazy search after novelty arose out of a praiseworthy desire to escape from dullness and commonplace, we can at the same time observe how the greater masters avoided these same faults by satisfying themselves with excellence of proportion applied to dignified and worthy motifs.

These are temptations which are liable to beset all periods of art, and it is one of the best uses of our study of history that one may be warned against thinking that mere oddities are new revelations in art. We can, by careful study of mediaeval work, come to some approximate estimate of the value and the limitations of the development of structure as a means

Burgess's sketch of the southern doorway of Lincoln Cathedral. Not dated. (71.213–182, sketchbook, UAA)

of beauty, and, what is more important, as a means of expressing human mind and sentiment. We shall find, I think, that it is in the last matter, that of sentiment, that it has its strictest limitations—in deliberate, human, individual, self-conscious sentiment that is.[4] This is observable in two directions. First, the tendency of mediaeval craftsmanship, delightful as it is, to usurp too large a share of the interest of the work; thrown deliberately into prominence it becomes tiresome. Second, the tendency of purely structural features to be the whole building—as when the buttresses and flying buttresses are multiplied and extended with such bewildering cleverness as we see them in many of the French cathedrals.

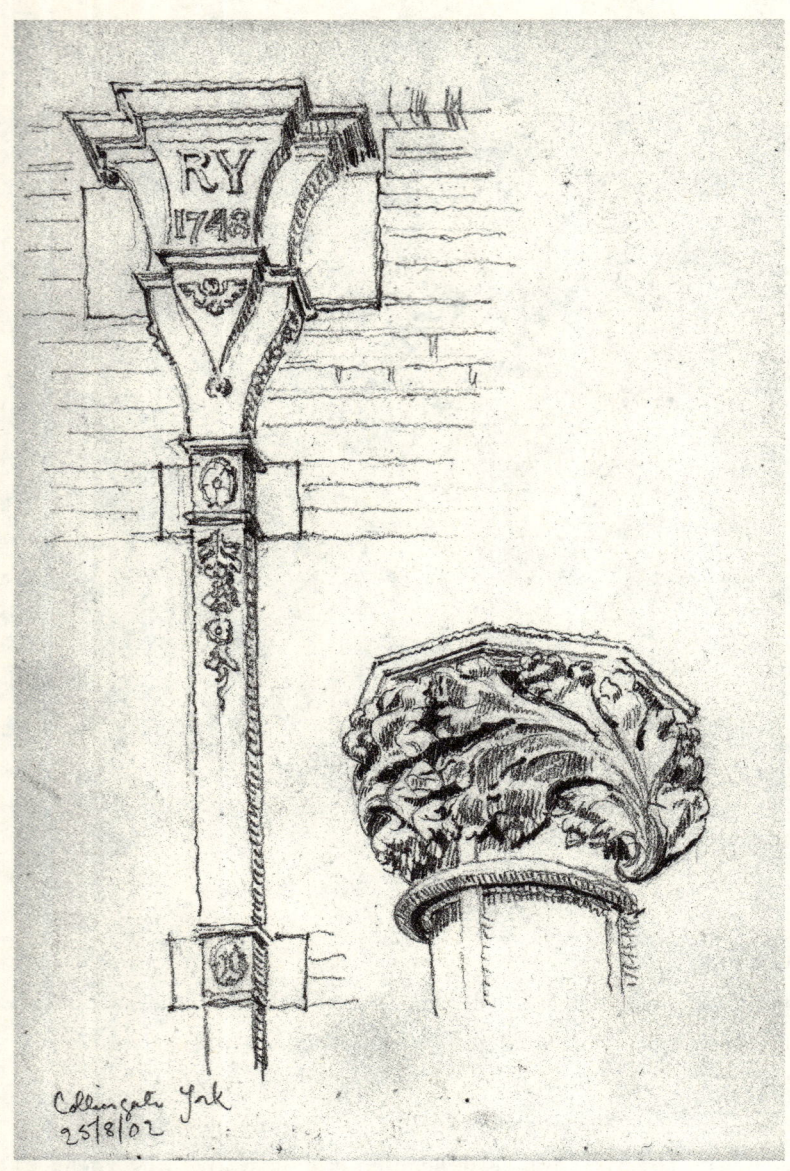

Burgess's 1902 sketch of architectural elements in York, England.
(71.213–183, sketchbook, UAA).

24   ARCHITECTURE, TOWN PLANNING AND COMMUNITY

The fact that the English mediaeval builders did not work their structural principles so hard as did the Frenchmen, and that either their fingers or their materials did not lend themselves to such marvels of craftsmanship, or perhaps an inherent distaste in the English nature for carrying things to extremes, results in a style in which qualities are more balanced; one in which the design, or beauty and harmony, holds a better control over other desires. This is probably one of the reasons why in France Gothic work today fails to be popular, whilst in England it still holds a powerful sway in the hearts and imaginations of the mass of the people.

The truthful expression of structure, of function, and of craftsmanship, displaying itself in the appropriate treatment of the various building materials (including steel and concrete), is spoken of by many as being the ultimate salvation of modern architecture. These qualities were the backbone of Gothic work. They are the lesson of that age, and we cannot afford to neglect the lessons of that age any more than of any others. It is essential that we learn it thoroughly. These, however, are not the only elements of good expressive architecture. The triumph of Renaissance over Gothic teaches us that human nature demands still other qualities, and architecture is the expression of human nature. A work of architecture, if it is to be of the best class, must be the expression of the being that is its tenant; and this applies to the humblest dwelling and to the most magnificent temple. We are perhaps too much inclined to think that such an idea has no application to buildings for manufacture and for other purely utilitarian purposes. But the acceptance of even so much limitation would imply that certain men can become merely utilitarian creatures. This view is not, I think, a part of the ideals of our civilisation. There is an ever-gathering demand amongst working men and factory hands for better and more cheerful conditions in which to carry on their daily toil. I have myself listened to an orator, who was commanding the respectful attention of a large open-air audience, arguing that if it was food for us to have flowers and other beautiful objects to make our dwellings brighter and more cheerful, why should the factory hand not have some similar elements in the scene where he is spending the best of his days and his strength to render his life less merely mechanical, less dull and monotonous, in a word, more human.

The shocks that new ideas give hitherto established views are but part of our process of education. With a knowledge of history at our backs, we shall have some kind of touchstone to try the value of ideas that present themselves to us. In some of them we shall be enabled to see that what claims to be a new truth is merely an old deception ever reappearing in varying guises, to deceive a number and in time to be discredited by consensus of opinion.

Thus, a prevalent idea at the present moment is the transcendental virtue of the simple life. This is an excellent idea which is sometimes worked so hard as to become an error. The "simple life," as a prevalent idea in the thought of our day, has naturally its reflection in the architecture of our day, and we find architects cutting out feature and ornament till there is no interest left. The simple life was probably an old idea in the time of Diogenes, who lived in a tub and spurned the beautiful works with which Plato was proud to surround himself. In doing so he only displayed a grosser and less worthy pride. In a less ignoble spirit, the Cistercians banished carved ornament from their churches and puritannic minds have conceived the idea that a barn was the most suitable type of building in which to worship God. Following out a similar idea, men have thought the most excellent way of living was in isolation in a cabin in the wilderness. Not the avoidance of life's complexities, not the repression of life's desires, but their wise control and healthy development should be our aim in life. In architecture, the past examples of history teach us how a true simplicity is attained not by the omission of the element of expression but by their high development under just control and co-ordination. This power of expression and balance is not to be acquired without study and effort.

I began by saying that we have many means of annihilating the distance that separates us from the architectural record of civilisation, and I have tried to show that it is well worth our while to put these means in operation. They consist in all that can aid us in travel and in home study. When we travel, it is well to be prepared by study to read aright the records which we shall see when abroad. In our home studies much remains to be done to make them more effective. That no architectural library is complete without an ample supply of photographs of old work is so thoroughly recognised at the present day that many important recent publications consist of little but collections of photographs with a minimum of explanatory text. I have tried to point out the danger of the superficial study of the merely outward form and letter of old work. Photographs are great aids to study, but they will not take the place of real study of the essence of things.

Besides books and photographs, we could be aided to take firmer hold of all worthy traditions by means of good collections of casts and models. I believe such collections would be found to be of surprisingly little cost and surprisingly great value. In these days we have attained a high proficiency in the production of shams and imitations of many kinds. What an excellent and legitimate field for the exercise of our talents in this direction the making of a museum presents. A plaster cast very naturally presents the texture of its original; and I have known the ingenious, by means of a little simple tinting, to carry the delusive effect of these facsimile copies to a wonderfully fine point.

In the ordinary British policy of letting art look after itself, the British government has done comparatively little towards illustrating the traditions of the country by means of casts; so that even in the South Kensington Museum, Englishmen may study the arts of all countries but their own.[5] This may not matter very seriously where the actual examples are not far to seek, but of course many are not accessible to the ordinary traveller; and when one goes into other countries the result is that, whilst all are well supplied with reproductions of their own work as well as of their neighbours, the place of British art, which is often very naturally taken to be a new representation of British architecture, is represented by a blank. This is of a piece with the Englishman's well known unfortunate habit of parading his objectionable qualities and keeping his amiable ones buttoned up under his coat for private consumption only. My friend Professor Nobbs of McGill College has been exercising his influence, and is hopeful of good success in the effort to persuade the British authorities to get casts of their architectural work made, if not for themselves, at least for the benefit of their friends across the sea.[6]

All art is the expression of character. We get the best idea of the British character from her literature, for that readily disseminates itself broadcast—no false modesty restraining the bookseller from distributing his wares. Shakespeare, Milton and Burns go round the world, whatever the virtues of other literatures may be. All round the world these are acknowledged to be singers of sweet and gentle voice, matchless in range and radiant with all kindly humour and sympathies. Art is one. Architecture too is the expression of character; and the architecture of the mother land will on a closer view be found to possess this same high character, this same wide range and gentle tone. In studying the history of other races, it will be well not to neglect our own.

Here in Canada we have conditions that differ at every point from the conditions that produced the old styles, varied as these styles and their conditions are. We have a climate that is all our own; and if this limits us, for example, to a certain simplicity in our forms of roofs, we shall find that in history severe limitations have ever served great workers not as clogs but as preservatives, to keep sweet their work and curb all tendencies to run riot. We have our own conditions as regards materials and methods of production. History teaches us that the skilful scientific use of materials is of the very essence of some of its grandest examples. Above all, we have our own problems of thought and social manners, and all that constitutes life to the modern Canadian mind. History teaches us that these are the elements that shape all true architecture; we read there how civilisations of all times lived their own lives whilst absorbing the tradition of their predecessors.

In order that we too may take hold of the great traditions, a broad and liberal knowledge and understanding of history is necessary lest we forget, and lest, instead of taking part in the good fight, we struggle from the line of march of the great army and as a nation take no part in the great forward movement of the human race.

NOTES

1. The hand-written original document was heavily edited by Burgess, seemingly at the time he delivered the paper. About 30 percent of the text was marked to be omitted. The edited text is the one reproduced here since this was likely the one he delivered.
2. William Chambers (1723–1796) wrote *A Treatise on Civil Architecture*. He was a proponent of classically inspired forms and with the patronage of the British royal family became an influential figure in late eighteenth century British architecture. A recent study on him is *Sir William Chambers: Architect to George III*, edited by John Harris and Michael Snodin (New Haven: Yale University Press in association with the Courtauld Institute of Art, London 1996). James Fergusson (1808–1886) published his *Handbook of Architecture* in 2 volumes in 1855, with the third and final volume appearing in 1862 as *A History of the Modern Styles of Architecture*. Reginald Blomfield (1856–1942) wrote *A History of Renaissance Architecture in England 1500–1800* (2 vols., 1897) and *Studies in Architecture* (1905).William James Anderson (1864–1900) published *The Architecture of the Renaissance in Italy: A General View for the Use of Students and Others* in 1896 as well as *The Architecture of Greece and Rome. A Sketch of its Historic Development* in 1907. Russell Sturgis (1836–1909) published *European Architecture. A Historical Survey* (1896) and the heavily illustrated *Dictionary of Architecture: Biographical, Historical and Descriptive* (1901–02). William Richard Lethaby (1857–1931) authored *Architecture, Mysticism and Myth* (1891) and *Form in Civilization* (1922) His *Philip Webb and His work* was published posthumously in 1935. A recent study on his work is *W. R Lethaby 1857–1931: Architecture, Design and Education*, edited by Sylvia Backemeyer and Theresa Gronberg (London: Lund Humphries, 1984). Auguste Choisy (1841–1909) stressed building technology in his influential *Histoire de l'architecture* (2 vols., 1899), which made lavish use of isometric drawings.
3. In margin: in Burgess's hand, "Renaissance renaissance."
4. The term "sentiment" as used by Burgess included the mood that a building's design conveyed, or the emotional effect that it invoked. Sentiment was not seen as having a uniform expression over time or place. It varied in terms of the purpose of the building as well as because of religious, economic, political and other factors.
5. Now the Victoria and Albert Museum.
6. On this proposal, see Spasoff, "Building on Social Power," 133.

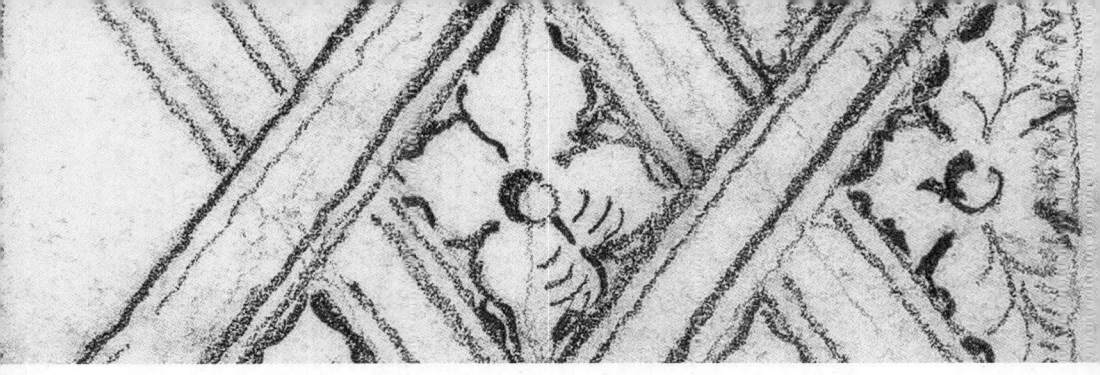

DOCUMENT 3

Architecture

IN 1912 the University of Alberta established an extension department with the aim of spreading the knowledge of the university to the whole province. While the University of Alberta was not alone in using such approaches, it was a practice that fit seamlessly with President Tory's ambition that the new university would be a provincial—not a local—centre of learning. Over the years, the extension services operated a lending library, offered workshops in such subjects as drama, lent slides (and later movies), and operated a radio station that broadcast educational programmes.

Another part of extension work was a lecture series by university professors in different parts of the province. Burgess participated in the lecture tour of 1913, and delivered this lecture to audiences in various small towns in southern Alberta. Burgess's use of historical precedents to demonstrate the importance of craftsmanship in architecture was typical of the justification of history's relevance for contemporary society and architecture. The study of architectural *history did not, however, operate in a vacuum. Given the belief that architecture was produced by its society and that architects only responded to the thinking of their civilisation, Burgess argued that the public needed to be educated about essential elements of architectural appreciation. This would help raise the intellectual tone of the society and encourage people to demand the improvement of architecture. Reflecting Anglo-Canadian viewpoints and attitudes of the time, Burgess's lecture was heavily slanted towards European precedents, or to buildings that had inspired European forms, as forming the essential references for understanding the meaning of architecture.*

Document 3 is a lecture delivered as part of the University of Alberta Department of Extension Lecture Tour, 1913, 71.213, file 93, UAA.[1]

To apply ourselves diligently to our business and to do it well is surely an admirable thing so long as that business is beneficial to ourselves or our neighbours, whether that business be the breaking of horses or the preaching of sermons. There is no necessity compelling us to do anything supremely well. We could all exist and get along somehow by just doing things middling well. Yet there is something within us which urges us to do somewhat better than "just well enough" and to admire the work that is well done. In fact, work done with thoroughness and intelligence always serves for more, or better, or for longer than work that is only done to serve the turn.

It is the feeling of satisfaction in work well done, especially if it is our own, that leads all skilful workers with their hands to be proud of their work, so proud that there is no pride more absolute than that of the craftsman in the work he has created. A man of another trade, or of no trade at all, may look at a big brick wall and think nothing more of it than that is very ugly. But if every brick is well and truly laid, the man that built it looks at it with a mighty satisfaction, and all who know good brickwork from bad will get great satisfaction from it. Line upon line the courses lie, true and straight horizontal, each brick in its place so that no joint comes immediately over a joint in the line below, but every one properly bonded and the whole knitted perfectly together. With good dappled bricks, each wrapped in its mortar bed, the colour is rich and mottled, and the man with an eye for colour is cheered by the sight of it. The great surface built up spot by spot with steady diligence seems to hum with industry so that a simple brick wall may be an example at one and the same time of many most excellent virtues. But you cannot see the beauty of a brick wall without knowledge and intelligence and a sense of the beauty of shapes and colours and an appreciation of human industry and the character that goes along with it.

It is of such virtues as these that architecture is built up, as are all the arts, for the poet is simply a man like the bricklayer who builds up beautiful thoughts line by line, well laid in their courses, well bonded together, line answering to line. To do things well, and better than well, so as no one else can do them so well, poets, painters and musicians have neglected everything else that seems tempting to other men, simply for the satisfaction and the pride they have had in their work. For I don't think that what posterity was going to do for these men was what spurred them on, but rather the joy they had of the works of their creation.

I am going to speak of more everyday things however—the industrial arts—for pride in these, excellence in these, though not a greater thing, is a more primary necessity in civilised communities. The value of having things well done around us is three-fold. It benefits the maker and it benefits the user and it benefits the whole community. To be intelligent and industrious in a trade, besides being a joy to the individual himself, ensures that a man has respect for the work of others, and that by him the world is going to be made better and not worse. If we are not willing to pay for good work, we may expect to remain an unskilful people lacking that character that only industry can bring.

The primary industrial art is the husbandman's. Through his skill we are fed and without being fed we can go no farther. Yet though first in order of the crafts, it is not for that reason the most valuable. Man shall not live by bread alone and year by year the produce of our harvests is totally consumed. Indeed, most of the works of men's labour, being on food and clothes, are thus consumed within the year they are produced or within a few years. But there exists a desire in men to produce something more permanent that shall not only last many years but that shall last from one generation to another. If it were not for this instinct or desire, we should have none of those great works made by our great-great-grandfathers and we should be tempted, however little we were actually accomplishing, to imagine that we surpass all the people that have gone before us in the earth, for these are the most striking and undeniable evidence we have of what our forefathers were capable of. Indeed, stories of wonderful people who lived long ago have sometimes come to be looked upon as false and idle tales until some day remains of ancient cities exhibiting their very buildings and the signs of their varied life have been dug up and have proved the old stories to be true. Thus it was with tales of Nineveh and Babylon and of the people over whom Minos was king in Crete.

We are constantly tempted to think we are far more clever and skilful than all people who went before us, and in many things, perhaps all the things that we are very keenly interested in, we may be so, but it is just as certain that the older peoples of the earth have had their enthusiasms about other things, just as we have about engineering and electioneering, and have, in those lines that they were enthusiastic about, far surpassed anything we are doing. The Greeks, for example, were a people very few in numbers and whose prosperous days lasted only a short time, yet they so far excelled us, and all other people who have ever been, in intellectual power, that their books are the primers of philosophy in every country of the world today. They achieved this pre-eminence over all men before or since by applying themselves to the simple great elementary problems of thought. It is interesting to see what evidence there exists as to what sort of men they were in the permanent work of their hands—in their architecture in fact. When we come to seek for their houses we find not a trace, and the reason is, that to leave themselves free to think of the great things, they spent little thought upon their daily wants. The simplest peasants have probably hardly equalled the Greek philosophers and poets in simplicity of life. The great philosopher, Socrates, used to harden himself in all ways that might make him a good soldier in case his services in battle should be needed. One of their greatest poets fought in the famous battle of Marathon. Their greatest buildings were temples of simple elementary form and of no imposing size, yet the skill and fine intelligence, the lovely material and the faultless workmanship employed in them command admiration. No forms are being more widely copied in America today than those which the Greeks developed 2,400 years ago.

The most famous building of the Greeks, the Parthenon, a temple of Minerva on the citadel hill of Athens, is typical of all.[2] A plain oblong building containing two rooms surrounded on the outside by massive and beautiful pillars which, along with simple beams and cornice which they carry, are designed with the most subtle sense of rhythm and harmony of form—with that quality which has been called "frozen music." The sculptures with which this temple was adorned have no superiors and they are not simply a few groups but a whole great and varied series. The material is the finest white marble, the blocks of stone from pillar to pillar (over fourteen feet long) are as long as the quarries could provide. The workmanship is so accurate that sometimes when stones have been chipped off near a joint, the break has not followed the joint, part of which has come away with the pieces of the adjoining stones still adhering together, and this in spite of the fact that they built without mortar. They are believed to have made these fine joints by rubbing the ends and the beds of the stones together to get them fitting perfectly. The delicacy of some of the curves introduced to give grace to this building are almost incredible, being in many cases hardly perceptible by the ordinary eye, but their existence and intention have been thoroughly proved by the most careful measurements. Whereas our masons work to about a quarter of an inch, the men who wrought this marble took account of the 100th part. Why did they take

Burgess's snap shot of the Parthenon, Athens. Not dated, ca. 1920s. (71.213–378, UAA.)

these pains? There can be no reasonable doubt that it was largely from pride of craftsmanship and because they rejoiced in their own fine intelligence and keen perceptions that could make good account of such delicate adjustments and because they were proud of the dainty finish the skill of their hands could give to tons of lovely marble. We are proud of our railways and the Greeks could not build railways. Yet, in their own way, they did do things which must have given them as real and deep satisfaction as making railways could have done, and whose beauty will be a wonder after our railways are superseded by flying machines and are merely traces of rust in the soil.

Let us look what remains to tell of the handiwork of another people, the old Romans. Rome grew from being a little city to be the conqueror and civiliser of the world. She made the nations hitherto unruly live by law. No nation, unless Britain, has done anything at all comparable in improving the condition of the peoples of the earth. The great deeds of a nation have generally a counterpart in the works of their daily life; diligence in their daily business and industry and intelligence in material works has trained them for higher work. What works did the Romans employ themselves on at home that maintained them in mental temper for their world-wide influence? We find that whilst they built many temples like the Greeks, for these old peoples were very religious according to their lights, yet they also built many other classes of buildings whose great shattered hulks soar over the little people that come from the world's end to gaze upon them.

One of the greatest enterprises undertaken in New York in recent years is the Pennsylvania Railroad Terminal, the grand hall of which—and it is a noble hall—copies the central apartment of a Roman thermal establishment, a unit of a group which was in its entirety a much grander affair than even the Pennsylvania Railroad Terminal.[3] These thermae or baths as they are sometimes called, were great popular clubs or places of resort for physical exercise and for entertainment of mind and body. Besides Turkish and swimming baths, there were all kinds of lecture rooms, libraries, lounging rooms, study rooms, walks, avenues of trees, running tracks and grand stands. Those known as the Thermae of Caracalla occupied about the space of twelve city blocks and there were a half dozen or more of these institutions in old Rome. No modern city provides so many or so great places to entertain its public. The Thermae of Caracalla we know were systematically repaired and put in good shape again 300 years after their building. Most of our buildings would need something more than repair after 300 years. These thermae were but a small part of the buildings for public entertainment in old Rome. Who has not heard of the Colosseum which could seat 50,000 spectators. This was their permanent circus. The place which they called their great circus, or Circus Maximus, was a chariot-race track with marble seats benched up around it to seat 380,000 spectators. The whole population of Edmonton and Calgary together, man, woman and child, would only make such a place look empty. Of the theatres, forums, basilicas, temples, triumphal arches and other buildings of Rome, I have not time to speak, but the city which could support so many and great and durable buildings must have had about ten times the energy of a place like New York, although the population was probably not at any time so great. When we try to realise the vigour of old Rome, we are reminded of Cassius' description of Julius Caesar

> He doth bestride the narrow world,
> Like a Colossus, and we petty men
> Walk under his huge legs and peep about
> To find ourselves dishonourable graves.

We are a great people and live in a great time, but let us remember there have been others.

There is a remarkable work of architecture in Constantinople, one of the most remarkable in the world, the Church of Ste. Sophia. With domes and minarets, it stands in the Turkish capital and is used as a Mohammedan mosque, but it was built as a Christian church. The remarkable thing about it is its splendid clear and open space singularly full of light and sunshine: 108 feet wide between the pillars, 268 feet long, [and] 185 feet high.

Besides this clear open space, there are great spaces beyond among the pillars and in the galleries above. There is a great central dome below which are half domes and below these are small half domes again, so that the roof appears to soar up dome above dome in a great cumulation of vaults. These vaults originally shone with gold mosaic surfaces on which religious subjects were depicted. The Mohammedans have whitewashed them over. The lower part of the church is panelled in the richest marbles and pillars of beautiful dark green mottled marble carry richly carved white marble arches.

It has always been, and still will be, a main problem of interest in all kinds of building—how to carry a roof or a road over a wide space or span. At the present day, the greatest examples of this are our great bridges, such as the Forth Bridge, and our great roofs, such as are seen over railway stations.[4] The material of which we have gained a great mastery is steel, and with its aid we do these works. The older peoples did not possess this skilfulness in steel but their works in stone, brick and concrete show as great an enterprise and as wonderful an ingenuity in their own way. The older works were more heavy and solid and therefore required proportionately a more immense labour in erecting, and many of them have of course lasted longer than we can expect our iron cobwebs to do. There is also a great satisfaction about this solidity, and we must needs feel just admiration for the courage of the men who could tackle and so well accomplish these massive and solid works.

The Greeks admired, as we all admire, the large stones of marble with which they were accustomed to build. To lay long lintels from pillar to pillar and from pillar to wall was the only way they used to make a solid ceiling, and their outside roofing was all of tiles of glistening marble from Paros, about two or three feet square. Some of their great lintels are over thirty feet long—most splendid stones. There are other ways of covering over wide spaces and one of these is by arching over—the arch stones supporting one another by all leaning together shoulder-to-shoulder and held in tight from spreading at the ends by a good weight of more stone. This is best done with small stones so that the turn of the arch is worked gradually round stone-by-stone. But the Greeks loved the largeness of their straight stones laid self-supporting with no sense of push or wish to spread, and they would have none of the arch. For this additional reason, there is always a quietness, severity, and restraint about Greek work. Just as in life they denied themselves the excitements of luxury, adopting plain living in order to have time and inclination for high thinking, so in the work of their hands we find them denying themselves such a useful expedient as the arch, which was well known among neighbouring nations, because they thought it too much of a makeshift for the most noble work.

The Romans used masses of concrete in the shape of rounded vaults. The walls to carry these concrete vaults had to be immensely thick, but they arranged them with great skill with wide openings in them so that one space opening to another gave a great spaciousness to halls, which had a considerable number of supports within their main outside enclosing walls. The work of constructing the great concrete vaults must have required a tremendous quantity and strength of wooden scaffolding or false work on account of the great weight and height. Careful investigations show that great ingenuity was exercised to economise this work. First of all, brick arching was set up upon wood scaffolding. These were not so very heavy, and when at the top they were rounded over, they became stronger than the wood scaffold. Then the concrete was gradually worked-up, resting largely upon these brick arches. The brick arches were left embedded in the concrete, reinforcing it until it had set firm, when, of course, the concrete in turn became stronger than the brick. There the brick arches may be found at the present day, a kind of concrete reinforced with brick instead of, as we make it, with steel.

The builders of Constantinople, whom we call Byzantines from Byzantium, an old name for the city, had not the natural material for making the concrete that was used at Rome, so they had to think of something else. They could get plenty of bricks but not readily a first class building stone. They were a wealthy and commercial people and could import the most beautiful marble by sea from all around the Mediterranean. Now people who build principally with bricks have got to use arches, for you cannot readily make bricks very big—they will not fire well, they would be underdone at the heart. So the arch is the natural resource. Because arches always have a push outwards, they need good heavy walls beside them to hold them in. It is the stones at the crown that push the side stones outwards. If you build a brick dome, there are few stones at the crown and many at the outside so there is less weight pushing and more weight to be pushed. A dome, therefore, stands firmer than the arch. The Byzantines found this out and their great buildings generally consist of a great central dome supported on half-domes with half-domes leaning against these again. At the outside of all are the walls, some straight, some curved like the half-domes, and inside the buildings are pillars, sometimes in straight lines, sometimes in semicircles, according to what they have to carry. The resulting arrangements are very ingenious and very beautiful. The brick surfaces are encrusted with mosaic where they are curved and with marble slabs where they are straight. The pillars are marble of the finest and largest blocks that the world could supply. This is the material way in which the wonderful and beautiful shapes of Ste. Sophia and other buildings of the same Byzantine family are accounted for. Whence came the enthusiasm and the desire to build this magnificent church, which those who have had the opportunity and the intelligence to study and to appreciate declare to be the finest building ever erected as an expression of a nation's praise and thanks to God? What they had to praise and thank God for that they felt so enthusiastic about it as all this, it is not my business tonight to tell you, that you may study in history. It is worth more attention than is usually given to it.

It may seem as if I were speaking of something foreign and far off in describing just how men did things in Constantinople 1,400 years ago, but the very largest cathedral that has been completed within the last many centuries—the Cathedral of Westminster in England (not Westminster Abbey) has been designed on very similar principles. We generally keep a bright lookout to see what our neighbours are doing so that we may do a little better. Our neighbours are not every day building vast buildings, and even at the present day, when we want to see the best done so far, we must

Burgess's sketch from a photograph of Greek pottery in the British museum. Not dated. (71.213–19, UAA)

often go back quite a way to find that best. In this manner, the builders of the Pennsylvania Railway Terminal had to go back to the thermae of ancient Rome, and the architect of the Westminster Cathedral looked around and saw Ste. Sophia still standing without an equal in her own manner, and that manner was the one that happened best to suit his purpose.[5]

I have spoken a good deal about how large stones are good for lintels and small stones for arches, and how bricks are naturally built in arches if you want to roof over wide spaces, for it is from the operations of building and other much humbler arts that beautiful forms are invented and developed. The Greeks did not allow themselves many luxuries, but one little weakness they had was for pottery. They loved to have terra cotta vases of beautiful forms and beautifully painted about their houses. They were exceedingly critical about the lines and curves of these pots and very subtle and delicate they made them so that Greek vases are of themselves a study which is a liberal education.[6] Amongst other subjects, they were fond of painting on these vases processions of men and women, warriors, and horsemen (to be a graceful horseman was a great ambition), and when we look at the great processional frieze of figures carved round the Parthenon, we find the noble attitudes of the men, the picturesque prancing of the horses, and all the things the humbler potters had been practising on for years enlarged and glorified in a great marble edition. The sculptor could never have produced so fine a thing had not many potters been diligent and eager in their search after beauty in their own art. Great virtue proceeds from handiwork thoroughly done, and as the work of the potters led up to the more grand and permanent works of Greek architecture, so I think that doing their big material work so well and thoroughly, discriminating with accuracy what was beautiful, searching out with severity what was truly grand if simple, was largely what enabled this people at a little later date to be the great thinkers and writers that they became.

The Gothic style of architecture is usually thought of as being the style of the pointed arch. So it is, but it is not the only style which is distinguished by the use of the pointed arch, for this is used also in a great number of the Mohammedan mosques of India and elsewhere. If we ask why the people of the middle ages who built the great Cathedrals built with pointed arches or with arches at all, we shall find that it was not simply because they liked the look of arches. [Rather], they were able to get plenty of good stones for building with, and they had not any great skill in devising machinery for lifting so many and such big stones as they would want for large buildings, and so they used small stones. When small stones are to be used for covering wide spaces, they must be built in the form of an arch. This accounts for the number of stone arches they used, especially when you consider that they had not skill in making steel-construction work.

The great majority of the buildings which were built in what are called the Middle Ages or between 1000 and 1500 A.D. are either churches or castles, a circumstance that shows very plainly that praying and fighting were two of the chief occupations of men in those days. Though not considered to be very companionable ideas now, to judge from the vast labour evidenced by the churches and castles, they performed both of these duties with great earnestness. In fact, they show that there was a third great occupation in men's lives. This was the erecting of great buildings, the means to fulfilling these two more important ends. The amount of work of this kind done is almost incredible. The population of England at the time of the Norman Conquest may have been about 2 million, perhaps about a quarter of that of Canada at the present day. Yet in the fifty years after the conquest, the quantity of solid stone buildings erected was enormous, even if we count only what is still standing 800 years after. How much of the work of our hands in Canada during the past 50 years will be standing 800 years hence? Yet these people produced, in addition to these lasting works, many smaller ones, for people were not altogether badly housed in Merry England. They were occupied also with cultivation; for the land was then self-supporting in this sense, not living on imported foods. More than this, those were days of great splendour and luxury, especially in dress and personal adornment, and there were many craftsmen skilled in the making of textile stuffs and in gold and silver work. It is therefore astonishing to see the amount and quality of their massive stonework still standing, and one wonders where they got the stone masons to execute the work. I believe they must have worked more than eight hours a day and applied their work very skilfully at that. The craftsmanship of the Gothic cathedrals is excellent and more than excellent. Workmen served long apprenticeships and had to pass severe tests for permission to become members of the trade guilds. They lived for their work alone in a way that modern life with its thousand and one distractions makes quite impossible.

One of the great ambitions of these strenuous builders was to construct fireproof buildings. Very early churches had often been constructed entirely of wood with the natural result that they were burned down time and again. So they began to build their more important churches in stone, but the roof was the great difficulty. It is very laborious and costly to build wide stone vaults. Strong temporary supports must be built up of wood and strong permanent supports and abutments of stone. It was the working out of the question of how to vault over a large building with stone in a skilful economical manner that led to the employment of a thousand beautiful forms, including the pointed arch, the vaulting ribs, pinnacles and buttresses that we see in the Gothic cathedrals. The gradual progress and evolution of this elaborate system of structure [is] an interesting chapter in architectural history. These builders succeeded so well that, in the finest examples, the roofs are, when you look up at them from inside, like beautiful parasols of stone with the ribs rising up from the top of the pillars and interlacing one with another towards the peak of the roof. A Gothic cathedral is a great tent of stone, carried high up upon tall pillars, between which, instead of walls, are great screens of stone bars with interspaces filled with splendidly coloured stained glass. No lantern has been invented which can give an idea of the splendid airy spaces which seem illuminated by the figures of prophets, martyrs and apostles of the church, shedding light from the high places where they stand rank upon rank above the living worshippers of today. The bigness of these buildings makes an impression upon one's senses that no picture can convey, and they are full of beautiful carved work in canopies over seats and niches and of elaborate memorials of the dead in ages past, and so richly and so fancifully carved and designed that they seem more like the work of fairies than of men.

This was the kind of work our forefathers spent their time on in those days when only a few learned men could read and write and which we call the "dark ages." I do not think we can altogether afford to despise them, even if we think we have discovered a hundred better ways of spending our time. If architecture is the chief voice that speaks to us from the dumb centuries, this is because these people were too busy doing beautiful work to tell us more about themselves than these works of their hands can most eloquently express.

About the great castles of that time—it would take too long to describe them. There was proportionately as much expended upon them as at the present day the great nations of Europe spend upon their battleships, [but] they were not scrapped every five or ten years. Many of them still stand in good repair in huge magnificence, so huge the first glance of a great castle takes away one's breath like the sudden sight of a precipice. All over England, France, Italy and other parts of Europe, more closely set than are the farms of Canada, there were churches and chapels, by far the greatest number being comparatively small, and some quite tiny chapels. On a Sunday morning the sound of their bells must have been heard literally in every part of the land. Every village in England has still its quaint old church, and some we even find in quite lonely places among the hills like those Kipling speaks of amongst the downs of Sussex—"Where little lost Down churches praise the Lord who made the Hill." So beautiful is the work of the Gothic builders that the more we study it, the more we admire it, and we come to wonder that men could ever give up working just that way, and [we] are tempted to think that men must at some time have degenerated and become incapable of doing so well as their fathers had done. But if we come down to the day's work in front of us, we shall soon see many reasons why things have changed. One of the important objects of these Gothic builders was to make fireproof buildings with only small building stones as their fireproof material. When we want to make fireproof buildings today, we use our wonderful Portland Cement concrete reinforced with steel and can make straight ceilings and floors which are very economical of space. It is only right that we should use our common sense and the good materials at our disposal.

It was not, however, the invention of new materials that caused people to change from the beautiful old Gothic manner of building. This was really brought about by a general change in ways of thinking and living. Much more began to be built to the order of private persons. Individuals were no longer so completely merged in the community. Instead of churches for common worship and castles for the protection of the community, individuals began to build palaces or large houses with gardens for their own pleasure. The Gothic buildings for common purposes were adorned with the workman's skill and it was the skilled craftsmen's ideas that supplied the pinnacles and tracery work that formed so large a part of their beauty. Private persons do not always love craftsmanship so exclusively as to want to have it as the only or principal thing about them. The study of old Roman and Greek books and thoughts at that time which we call the Renaissance turned men's thoughts to old Roman ways of building and adorning buildings, and so we find an introduction of pillars and lintels and other forms which many centuries before had been evolved and perfected in shape. People wanted to take an interest in other things than the craftsmanship which so exclusively occupied the attention of the Middle Ages. They applied these freshly rediscovered forms and arranged them according to general principles to produce effects of unity, dignity, restraint, grace, happiness, and other sentiments by which they now began to set great store. They thus escaped from what now seemed to them the confined limits of tradesmanly beauty and were free to roam in fields and pastures new in which they found many kinds of interest and delight. The passion for cathedral and castle building was supplanted, as our passion for "mechanics" may some day be supplanted.

If these few words succeed in giving a general idea of the change that took place at the Renaissance, that is all I can hope for. Many books have been written on the wonderful transformation then occasioned and many more will probably be written before we fully understand it. I can only speak of a few of the architectural results.

People had now ceased to have that exclusive interest in the service of the church and the army and the arts and crafts of daily life. They read books, they travelled and entertained one another for pleasure and accordingly they built fine houses in which were great libraries, picture rooms, and rooms for entertainments of many kinds. Around them they had grounds laid out for delight to the eye and for refreshment and exercise. In Italy many of these were in the cities, however, and instead of any grounds around [them], they had a fine pillared courtyard and there are many fine and stately houses of this type at the present day which were built 400 years ago. In France the fine Chateaux of the Loire country mansions surrounded by finely laid out gardens and woods and ponds and fountains are of the same period and are the outcome of the same revolutionised ideas about how to live and what sort of things to have about one and how to have them built and arranged to suit one's individual bent and pursuits.

In England we have the Elizabethan houses, the stately homes of England, with stately chambers, with their great oak or stone chimney pieces, their long galleries, their terrace walks and formal gardens. Long before this, very lovely houses had been built in England, but now they began to blossom out into a formal stateliness with finely shaped pillars and cornices, wide windows and round arched arcades. As time went on, this desire to be stately and dignified produced buildings of still greater formality and dignity, which at last increased to such an extent that life in such places must often have been rather a burden for those whose temperaments did not love the restraints of formality. Whether we are lovers of formality or not, we must admit however that these are beautiful buildings, that we should be the poorer without them, and that their existence does help us to realise how large and grand a thing human life may be. The Cathedral of St. Paul's in London is built in this stately Renaissance manner, as is also St. Peter's in Rome, and these also are among the great memorials of the past to us, telling us much—much that it is well worth our while to bear in mind of what our forefathers thought about and did and what size of men they were. Without such lasting work, these forefathers of ours would be out of sight and out of mind and we should be tempted to live in and for our little day alone.[7]

NOTES

1. Handwritten notes at top of page: "Combination of building trades in effort to serve varied ends. End and means in this case the means have great importance in themselves and modify the ends considerably. We must cut according to our cloth. History furnishes many examples."
2. The Parthenon was the temple of Athene Parthenos. Minerva was the Roman equivalent of Athena.
3. Constructed 1906–10 and designed by McKim, Mead and White. The building has been demolished.
4. The reference is to the cantilevered steel bridge, almost 8,300 feet long, built in 1890 across the Firth of Forth in Scotland.
5. Handwritten in margin: "New Law Courts, New York."
6. Handwritten in margin: "Chief Export."
7. Handwritten at end of lecture:
    "1. Architecture. The most wholesome and useful nucleus of the industrial arts
    2. Lasting monument of fine ideals and enthusiasms otherwise passing, incorporates them into traditions of the race. A means of holding the ground that civilisation has gained
    3. Incentive to being bigger."

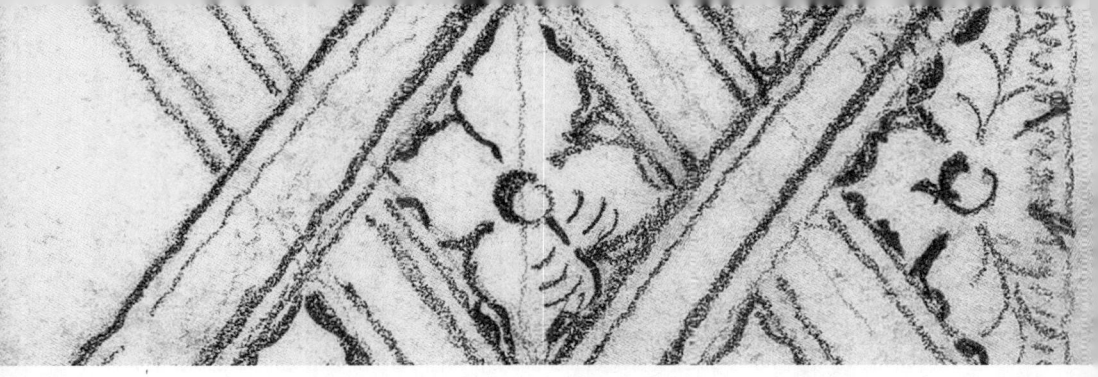

DOCUMENT 4

The Old House and the New

ARTS AND CRAFTS architects, like many observers, argued that as much care and thought needed to be placed on designing homes as public buildings. They commonly asserted that if homes were designed to serve people's cultural as well as daily needs, people's lives would be improved and made happier, the family would be strengthened and society would benefit. But the uniformity and lower standards of craftsmanship that industrialisation had supposedly brought worked against realising these hopes, as did the lack of professional design in house building. Domestic architecture was not a paying proposition for most architects, but Burgess's university position allowed him to work to educate the public about how to achieve better house design without the assistance of architects or other professionals.

As revealed in this talk, Burgess strongly supported the idea that a house was not necessarily a home. Burgess, like many of his contemporaries, argued that the design of a house should promote its role as a repository of social values *and traditions, as well as a place of comfort, retreat and family and social meaning. Similarly, the quality of craftsmanship in a house contributed to its social meaning by offering visual evidence of integrity and creativity. By such means, houses could become homes. This could be achieved without sacrificing the use of modern services such as electricity, plumbing and ventilation. In claiming that the "home" was a peculiarly English invention essential for achieving social stability and cohesion and for expressing important social values, Burgess was also asserting the superiority and legitimacy of British values in Canada.*

Document 4 is a paper read at Dr. Ferris's House, 1913,[1] 71.213, file 92, UAA.

ENGLISH-SPEAKING PEOPLE attach a very great importance to the word "home." They say there is no equivalent for it in any other language. And we congratulate ourselves on its creation. We feel that it embodies our idea of superlative value.

What is a home? It is a kind of a house. What kind of a house? If it is of so great a value, it is worthwhile to find out exactly what it is that makes a house a home—because times change and we are changed in them and it may be that our changing customs and circumstances are not now those around which the idea of home grew up. To preserve what is valuable in this beloved idea of home, it may be necessary to think well and carefully lest we lose it.

French people do not speak of home but they speak of the chez nous. And English-speaking people pass that expression lightly—perhaps thinking that, of course, home is ever so much better. The chez nous is however an expression worth thinking about. It is not a kind of house like our home; it is a kind of society—the society inside the house—the little human circle grouped within the walls of the home. The French think of house in terms of the human beings of which in their minds it exists. The English think of a home in terms of the rooms, the fireplaces, the doors, the windows, the tables and chairs, the clock, the teapot and perhaps the garden. These are the things of which the Englishman's home consists. Of course, we don't altogether disregard the family, but to us they are not the "chez nous," which is an idea as distinctly French as the home is English. An intense love for the material surroundings of our family life is a peculiarity of English-speaking people. It is embodied in the books of our writers, great and small, old and recent, and in our daily conversations. In fact, it is a tradition that flows in the English language.

We learn from this tradition to take delight in the material surroundings of our family life—a delight that is deep in our feelings. Whence did this arise, especially in the English-speaking peoples? I will attempt to account for it.

I do not suppose that the word [home] is really very old. It must have arisen amongst people who had something they could call their own and I suppose that before there were homes there were halls. In the Middle Ages the "hall" was the magic word that denoted happy days, and more particularly, happy long winter evenings, where games were played and where around the fire in the middle of the floor the talk was loud and free. Where at the long boards all the varied retainers of the manor sat at rest, and where at night all curled themselves up in the straw and rushes to sleep.

Gradually that early idea changed as men of less property acquired freedom and goods of their own. They who could not have "halls" could at least have hearths of their own, and around the hearth grew the "home" for Englishmen have always loved to gather around the fire. The period at which these humbler centres of human life developed into homes was one which has been called the working man's paradise—when craftsmen grew to be strong elements in social life and when they had their guilds and flourished in proportion as they developed skill of hand in the power of producing material things that were a joy to themselves in the making and the purchasers in the using. I quote the following from G.K. Chesterton's *Short History of England*:

Burgess's sketch of Loseley House, an Elizabethan house built by Sir Thomas More in 1562. (71.213–179 sketchbook, UAA)

The old Guilds insisted upon a high standard of craftsmanship which still astonishes the world in the corners of perishing buildings or the colours of broken glass. There is no artist or art critic who will not concede, however distant his own style from the Gothic school, that there was in this time a nameless but universal artistic touch in the moulding of the very tools of life. Accident has preserved the rudest sticks and stools and pots and pans which have suggestive shapes as if they were "possessed" not by devils but by elves. For they were, indeed, as compared with subsequent systems produced in the incredible fairyland of a free country.

This, I think, expresses something of the reason for the love of the Englishman for the material things of his house. The stones, the woodwork, the furniture and the utensils of these old houses had in them that magic delight which is given to work in which the workman had joyed to put his skill and thought and the peculiar humour of his individual mind. He shaped the chimney corner, the lattice window, the whole many gabled house and every thing in it so that it was all human and loveable by human beings and, accordingly, the human occupants loved it. This, I think, is where "home" began.

Times are changed and we are changed in them. But still, the word "home" has not lost its magic power. The realisation, in these old days awakened, that we could surround our lives with certain mere things that actually imparted happiness to our lives, lives on and we feel the value of the mere material things that please the eye, the ear, the mind that add to the cheerfulness of meals, to all the necessary acts of daily life in washing, dressing, going to rest at night, that make pleasant our occupations in housekeeping, gardening, reading, writing and music. Our idea of a home is a place peculiarly suited to give us pleasure in all those occupations and many others—in the conversation and entertainment of the family among themselves on all ordinary occasions, and with visitors on periodical occasions.

The old house was from economic reasons, apparently beyond our control, a more self-sustaining unit than the new—fewer things for daily consumption could be bought ready-made and therefore more had to be produced in the home. It was more of a little hive of manual industry. Relieved of some of this internal industry, the occupants of our homes tend more to external interests. People of a generation or two back lived more inside their homes and less outside. Attractions in shows and sports have multiplied. In those days there was, besides, much elaborate housekeeping, much handiwork in embroidery and other beautiful occupations. People read much to improve their minds and become well informed. Reading aloud was a common occupation and one that knit the family circle together. Now we wish to minimise the work of our hands and each one to follow separate work or recreation.

It is well to recognise that the times are changed and that we ourselves are also changed. It is not well, however, to spend valuable time in regretting the necessary fact for men live by and in change What we have to do is to see that what we do, we do with good exercise of our minds and good sentiment [so] that our homes are happy for all.

Let us look then at some of the larger facts that have changed our ideas in regard to the house and what adjustments we have made and are trying to make accordingly. Probably the greatest change from old times is in the largeness of our homes in proportion to the help available in keeping them. This is sometimes called the servant question. The old houses were complicated and required much labour to keep in that spotless condition that our grandmothers loved even more than we ourselves [do]. [While our grandmothers] may not have been able to give the scientific reasons for [this, it was because] labour was obtainable [then] and today it is not. This is perhaps not merely because there are fewer servants but also because there are more houses. In multiplying [the number of] houses we must try also to multiply homes. The consequence of this lack of assistance is naturally the demand for houses which entail less work in maintaining.

The next great point of difference between the new and the old is the more scientific and definite ideas that have been developed on the question of cleanness. I do not think we have any more appetite for cleanness than our ancestors, but we have more definite ideas as to what kind of cleanness we want and as to how to get it.

A third great point of difference in recent conditions is the comparatively mobile condition of society. Owing to facility in travel and new developments in industry, we move about more. Our dwelling places are less fixed and therefore tend to be of a less permanent construction and of less permanent occupation.[2]

There are no doubt many other points of change in modern life but these are four that are strongly influencing our ideas of house and home. They may be shortly named as the desire for 1) economy of house work, 2) hygienic conditions, 3) reduction of capital outlay, and 4) a more external life. I do not propose to discuss these questions farther. I think it must be granted that all bear strongly upon us and that they are resulting in changed ideas. Under these changed conditions then we have to build our houses.

In the matter of hygienic conditions we have come to realise, or at least to believe, that sunlight is a great controlling factor. We are becoming sun-worshippers, the only novelty about which is that we are doing so at the persuasion of science. We must get sunshine into our rooms. Yet here we are met by a curious difficulty. It has become the custom to lay out the streets of our towns north to south and east to west duly according to the points of the compass. Surely there is a mistake in this. The reason for this worship of sunlight is of course the knowledge that sunlight makes air circulate greatly and kills disease germs, moistens the air and, incidentally, by making dirt visible, causes its elimination.

A house is, at best, a compromise, but there should be a chance of sunlight in every room, even if it be only early morning or late evening. Besides the faulty setting of the house, this may be interfered with by verandahs so overshadowing windows as to shut out sunlight. Windows are mouths to drink in sunshine rays. I do not think it of first importance that they should be large. A comparatively small beam of sunshine or stream of fresh air will do good service. They are the mouths of the house—they are also the eyes to look out from. We do very well with small mouths and small eyes if we only open and close them at the proper time.

Another point in regard to hygiene that we have learned is its dependence upon water. In old-fashioned houses there was no water. People went out to the well and brought water in in pails. Now we realise that cleanness depends not only on the wholesomeness of the water itself but on the ease with which we can obtain it. It must be obtainable on each floor. Farther, as much of our house as possible has got to be cleanable. This has led to great changes in the shapes and materials of the parts of a house. The ideal is: whiteness, smoothness and hardness. These are the conditions of observing and getting rid of dirt. From this point of view the ideal house is a hard, smooth, white house. The forms of the various features of a house have undergone a simplification to meet this demand. Woodwork with its necessary chinks and corners is reduced, and where in older houses spiral and other quaintly-shaped stair balusters were delighted in, they now arouse the distressful feeling that they present a formidable array to dust and keep clean.

A problem in this line meets us in every house. This is the practice, which has its reasons, of running a baseboard around every room. The top of this, no matter how simple its form, presents a shelf for dust—small indeed in breadth but enormous in length if every wall in every room is measured up. In order to clean it of the dust which it inevitably gathers, all furniture must be moved out. A solution is

Many such apparently simple contrivances are still waiting the genius of the inventor. The difficulty is not so much in the contrivance as in the reduction of the cost.

In our Canadian houses probably the least economical portion of the house is the cellar. If, as is so often the case, it is of concrete, it is a costly construction and generally contains more space than is occupied in a way to justify its proportion of cost. The trouble, of course, is that it is not considered—whether truly or no, I am not convinced—suitable for bedrooms, and farther the untidy appearance of heating pipes and ducts makes it uninviting for the finer occupations.

Central in the cellar sits that fiery monster, the furnace—robbed indeed of some of his terrors when heated by gas. Yet I cannot place an absolute confidence in this expedient. What happens in case of a break in the gas main cutting off a line of houses? The coal bin is still necessary. Then also in the cellar must be a food store with its own decided demand for even temperature and good ventilation. After these two demands have been met, there are various ways of occupying a cellar. It is very usual, and I suppose convenient, to have a laundry. With some careful thought in planning the house, this may easily be much more conveniently arranged than is usually the case. It is too often casually crowded in as an afterthought. Conspicuously casual is the arrangement of many ropes on which to hang clothes. Some of these are, of course, winter requirements only, but a certain amount of permanent hanging apparatus should be provided in a suitable place. The idea of a row of one inch galvanised pipes arranged like a slatted shelf rising to the back instead of level appeals to me as convenient, suitable and orderly. I should like to have your opinions. The arrangements of washtubs, electric washer and ironing board in such a way as to economise

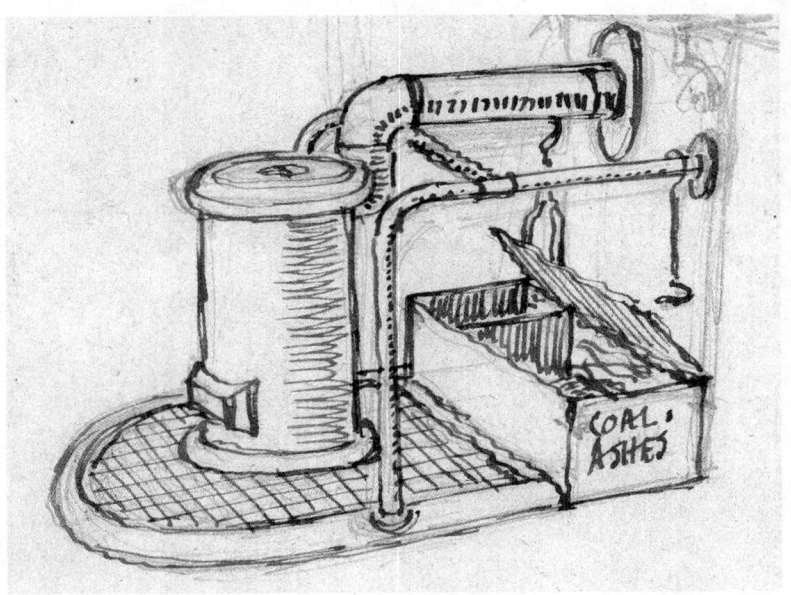

Burgess's undated ink drawing of a "fiery monster, the furnace." (71.213–193–2A UAA)

walking to and fro is I think important enough to warrant forethought. It can seldom result well from mere afterthought.

After these requirements have been met, there is still usually considerable space in the cellar and this is most commonly a general store place—very general indeed. If there is to be farther specifically utilised space in the cellar, my recommendation, subject to your criticism, is a cleaning-up lavatory convenient to the front and rear entrances of the house where one may get rid of dirty boots, wash-up very dirty hands after gardening, etc.—a place for all the extra out-of-door requirements, heavy coats, waterproof rubbers, gardening boots, with special provision for cleaning and polishing boots when muddied.

There still remains the general store of purposes too various to describe—a rather trying problem. Because of its very general purpose only, a general recommendation is to have around the walls as much hard strong slatted shelf as there is convenient space for. On this can be placed storm sashes

The Old House and the New   59

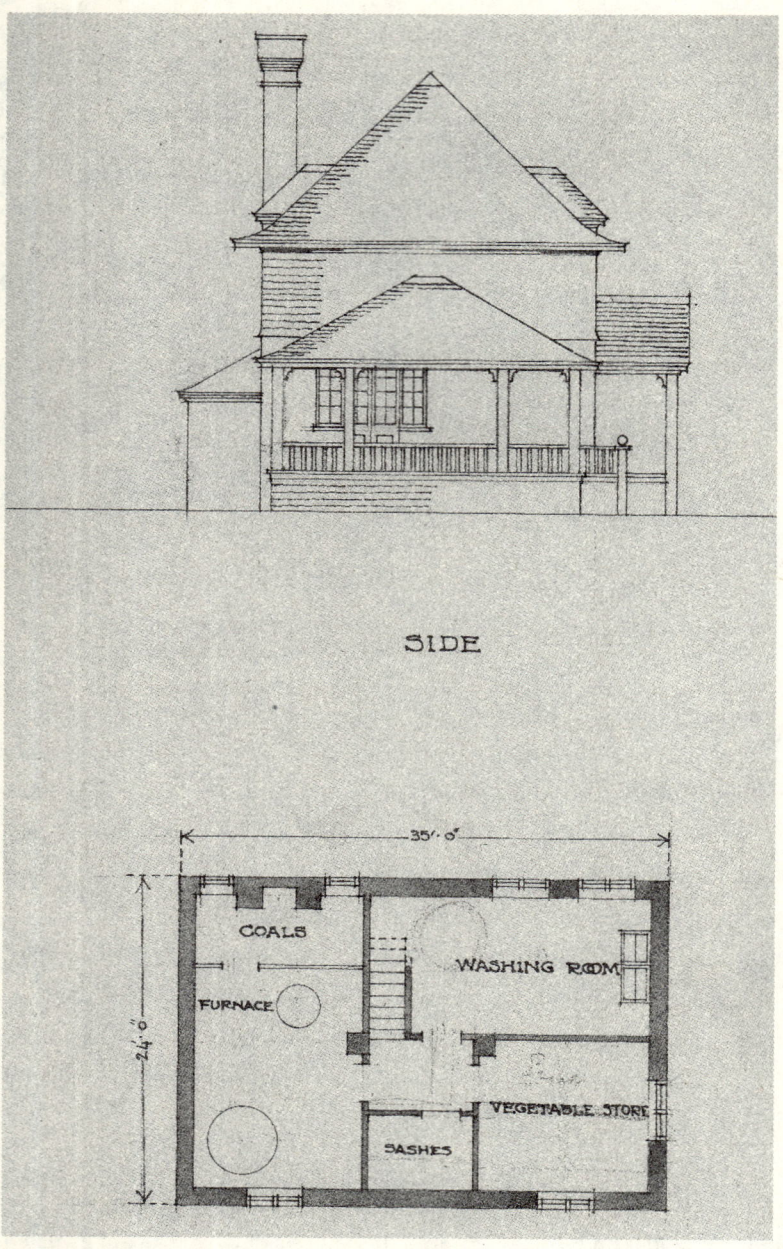

Burgess designed a series of houses for faculty at the University of Alberta in 1913 and lived in one of them until 1940. The relatively open layout on the main floor was then a popular innovation over closed plans in which rooms did not open one into the other.
(Type B House, 71.213–195, map case, UAA)

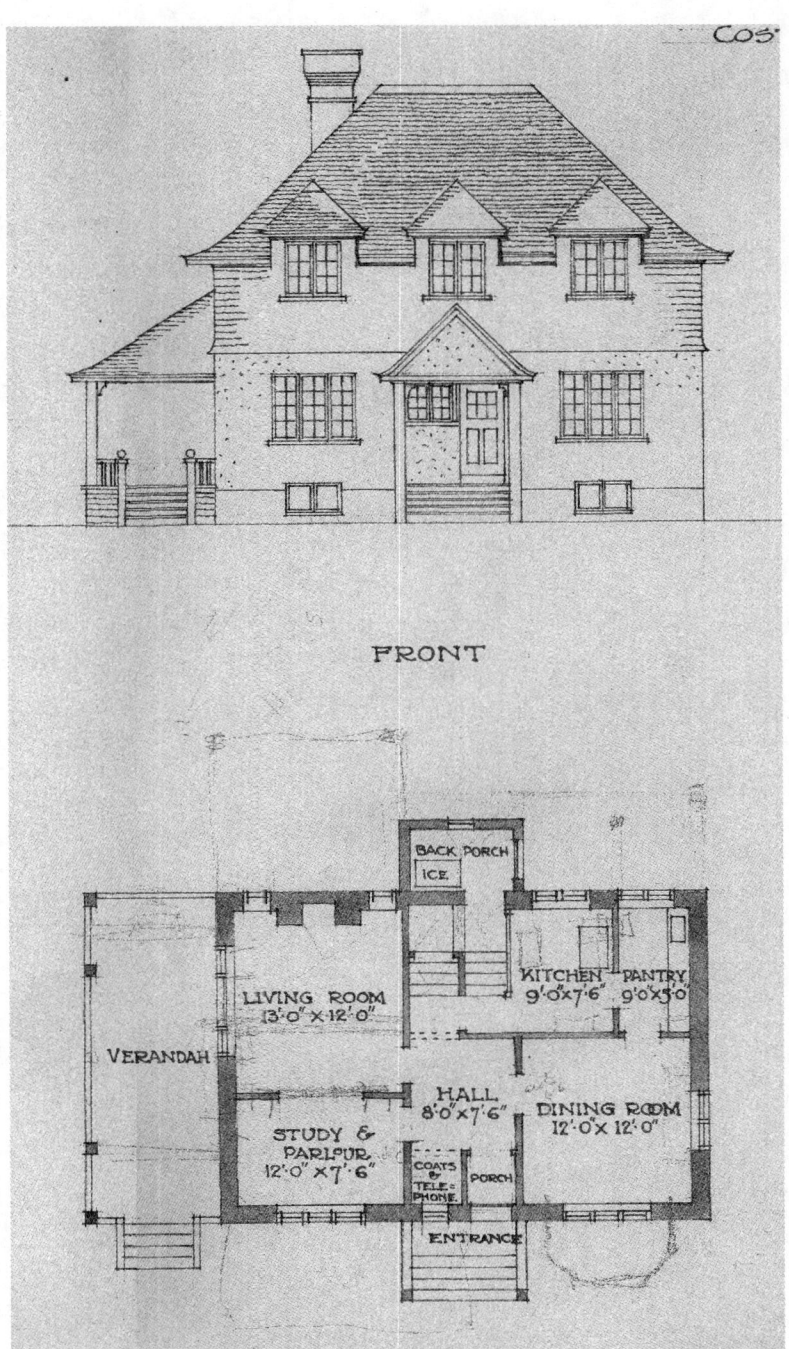

The Old House and New

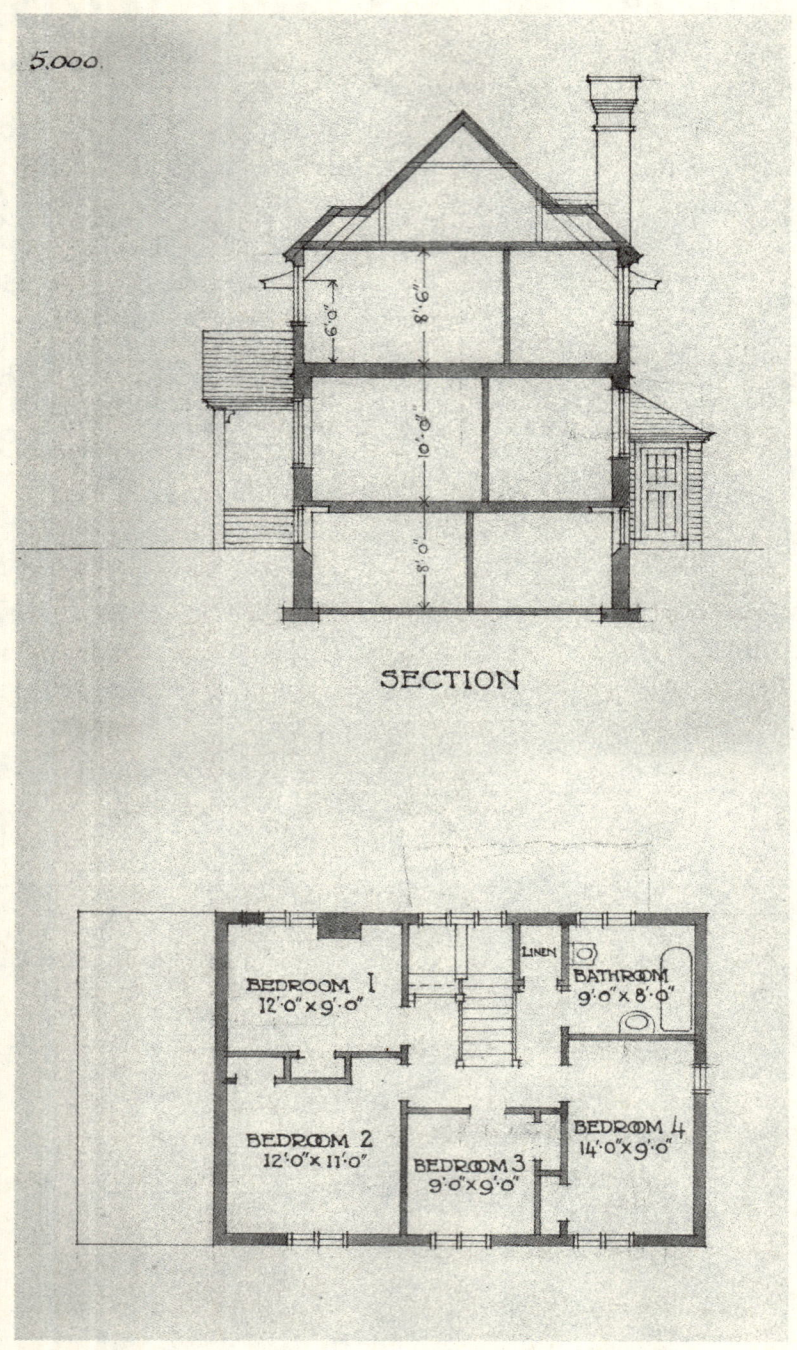

and fly screens and old boxes in which things are stored for very occasional use. Thus being on a shelf about eighteen inches above the floor, they are get-at-able and the floor can be kept clear and even clean without moving everything in the world.[3]

The distribution of the ground floor is the next consideration. Much of the virtue in this floor proceeds from the kitchen, just as in the cellar [where] the furnace is king. For though we know that "man shall not live by bread alone," yet we find that the quality of the words that proceed from the mouth of man is much controlled by the circumstances that attend what goes in. On account of the power of meat and drink to make our hearts glad, we must on the ground floor bow in reverence to the kitchen as we did to the furnace in the cellar.

So much has been said of kitchens, and you must all know so much more about them than I, that I feel I can only bow before you in this matter as if you were the kitchen itself. My remarks here must, therefore, be in the form of questions. I assume that a kitchen is a workshop. In workshops most of the work is done either standing or walking. Therefore, most of the appliances are of a height that suits an upright position. This should apply to the range, the sink, the cupboard top and the table, if any. Pots, dishes, etc., require lifting about. Should not this be done with a minimum of raising and lowering, especially when these utensils are full and heavy? Along with this, is there any reason for having a chair of the usual sitting height in the kitchen? Occasional rests are necessary. Are not these best obtained on a stool of the general type of an office stool, more or less high as may exactly suit the principal person concerned with appropriate foot rests and, of course, enamelled white? I find such a stool easy to get on and off for it means less change of elevation, less lifting and lowering, and the more erect position of the body makes the work easier. I think it is a healthier position for work. It is not without good reason that clerks and draughtsmen's stools and laboratory stools are made of this description and I have an idea that they would be serviceable for other purposes in the home, for children studying, for example, and even for such reading and writing as partake of the nature of active work. The material of the kitchen floor I find always a subject for discussion. Such discussions incline me to the opinion that a blue and white chequered linoleum of good thickness is the most approved. Is this right?

As regards the rest of the ground floor a principal change between old and new ideas is the newer demand for dining room and living room en suite with a wide doorway between. Indeed there is a general tendency to openness of view and circulation in houses. To compartment off each room—to be able to shut ourselves up in each division of the house—is not so much the aim as used to be the case. This leads to the suggestion that occasionally some economy might be effected in house building by the omission of certain doors altogether. For example, when the pantry is separate from the kitchen and is between that room and the dining room, it is often better to have no door between pantry and kitchen.

According to the special arrangements of a house, it will sometimes be found that the doorway sometimes exposes only a small portion of a room or hall, and that portion is quite pleasant to see. Is it not in many cases pleasanter when sitting in a room to feel that one is not boxed in by a door but has some pleasant peep beyond? Would not some light portable screen, Japanese or other, serve better and more agreeably than a door? Curtains and portières for doors in living rooms are probably more expensive than doors, but [they] have some advantages. They seem to me more appropriate for bedroom cupboards in which doors close up the place too much. If curtains on rings were used in this case, then we need not be tied down so much to the standard 6'6" x 2'6" entrance and the things inside would be more accessible.

Let us not go upstairs yet, however, [because] there still are some things down here I want to look at. Even if there is an overflow place in the cellar, and perhaps some in the bedrooms for coats and other out-of-door garments, we need cloak space near the entrance. My taste in this matter may not be entirely wholesome, but I do not think I really enjoy the view of an array of coats and hats hanging on hooks either on a wall or on a coat stand. I like a nook for them and I like the idea of this nook being at least so far screened with curtains that there is some mitigation of the display.

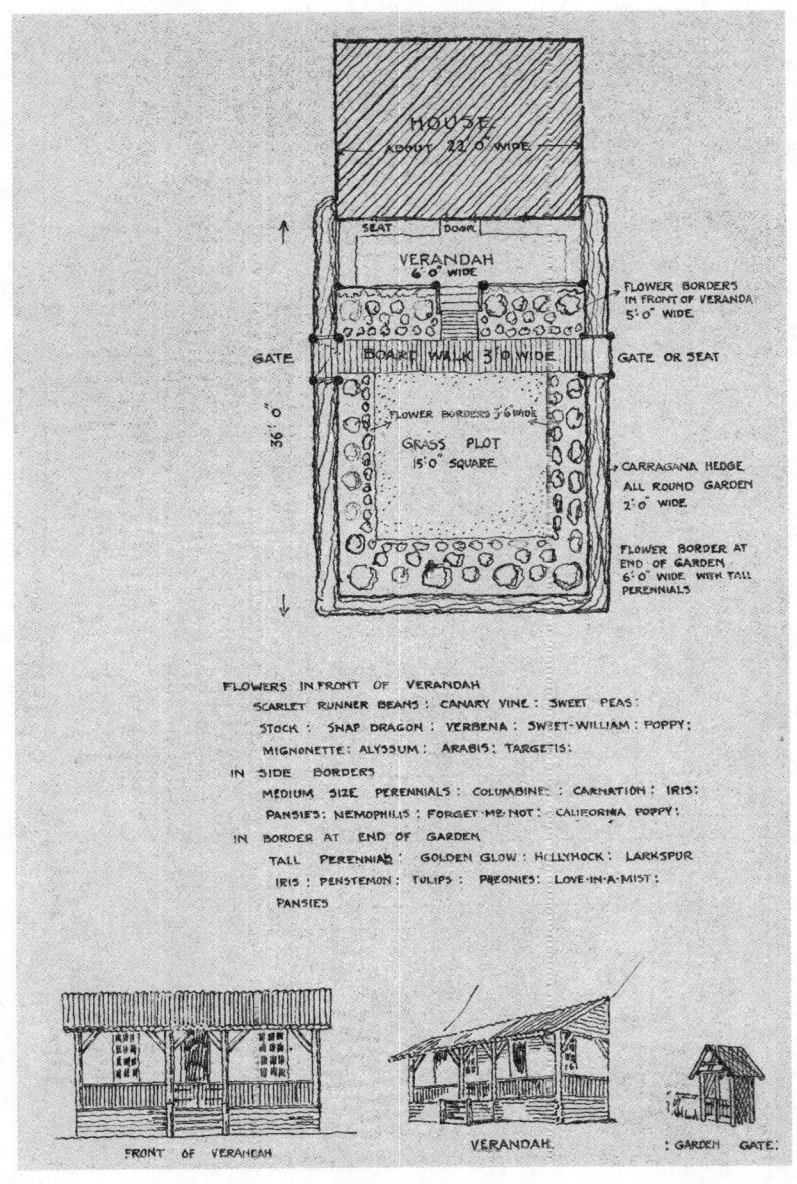

Burgess's plan for a verandah and garden, 1921. Location not identified. (71.213–240, UAA)

In our incomparable climate, a verandah is distinctly worth having and of a size, form and location that it is a real living room. Meals I think are nowhere so pleasant as in the open air. According to the latest "dicta" of science, to glass-in the verandah is to take a great part of its wholesomeness from it. If practicable, it should be placed in the best and most interesting outlook. If you can have a garden in front of it, let the garden grow as under the verandah's eye.

I have frequently heard it argued that the dining room is the least used and therefore the most costly luxury in the house. Therefore houses have been contrived with dining nooks close to, or even forming a part of the kitchen. This I do not agree with. The dining room is in many homes the most important room in the house for the reason that there are many families in which, owing to the nature of the occupation of the members of the family, the meals are the principal, and sometimes the only, occasions in which the family really meets all together.

In the old days, and more particularly in England, the family met around the fireside. There were times and conditions under which this was naturally and necessarily the case. This is not the case with us. The open fire is necessary only as an adjunct to the heating—a highly delightful and desirable luxury, but still a luxury, and being so can no longer take a central place in our life. With us the hearth must take second place to the board. So far as any part of the home is central to the very heart of our life, it is the dining table. Around the board, if anywhere, we must more than elsewhere learn to know and influence one another. This is our most sacred altar. Here in the breaking of our bread do we touch and handle things unseen.

These then are the most essential conditions of happiness. The conditions of happiness are fortunately not elaborate; indeed, simplicity is perhaps the chief part of their essence. Convenience in service is part of this simplicity. In this presence I will not venture farther on this sacred ground.

I believe it is a very usual arrangement that after supper the dining room becomes the children's place of study. It should be furnished accordingly.

Now let us go upstairs. The stair, with its steps and handrails, is a bold way of going up ten feet in two fine leaps and may well be a very picturesque feature and often is so. Sometimes it is so smothered by partitions endeavouring to eke out space for double purposes that it is unfortunately not so. I recommend to the attention of housekeepers the value of a certain amount of spaciousness in combined hall and stairway. I think it has an effect of welcome to the visitor from outside and of freedom and elbow room to the habitual occupants of a house. This openness and spaciousness is at times serviceable in preserving the plaster when furniture is transported up or down.

The upper floor is essentially the bedroom floor, yet here, as on the other floors, we find one dominant point in the bathroom. There is the water supply with all that implies in view of modern hygiene teaching. A matter of great general convenience in a bathroom is a real cupboard where extra towels, extra soap, etc., may be kept and everyone knows where to find them. The floor I like covered with linoleum.

Cupboards, or built-in cupboards as they are sometimes called, have come to be considered absolutely essential. In the old house, wardrobes were parts of the moveable furniture. The built-in cupboard is probably much the most costly as it means that the size of the house is usually increased considerably in order to provide them. In detail they very seldom are equal in contrivance and suitability to the old fashioned wardrobe. This, of course, is not necessarily so, but in practice it is so. I have already suggested that instead of the comparatively narrow door [on a built-in cupboard], the whole side ought to be open and the room screened by a curtain. It is, I think, worthwhile to provide a few simple but special arrangements inside the cupboard, as, for example, a low shelf so that boots and shoes [can] be kept up off the floor, and there should be a proper provision in bedrooms for the lighter operations of shoe polishing.

Parents are sometimes surprised and vexed that children, in growing up, like to spend a good deal of time in their bedrooms. I think it natural and wholesome and should be provided for. A bedroom for the young person should have conveniences for reading and writing. To be able to retire occasionally to solitary occupation is a necessary part of the human mental development. Too much of this may of course be a bad and unsociable thing, but the practice to some extent is an essential one. Of course, too long continuous occupation of any one room, and of a bedroom especially, must be guarded against for reasons of health. On the bedroom floor there should be proper provision for the special work done here. Provision for keeping every room clean is of course the first necessity. Then there is usually required a sewing room.

I have now taken a ramble all through the house, making such remarks as have occurred to me. Let me say a word about the difficulties the constructor meets. We struggle with the assemblage of numerous materials in our endeavour to preserve the warmth and to exclude the wind and the wet. It would seem no very difficult task, and not altogether beyond the wit of man, to discover one blessed material which should combine strength and plasticity with variety of colour and texture out of which we might simply create the structure of the house. Something that we could spread out in smooth surfaces like plaster, that would be equally suitable for floors and walls, that would weld together without cracks, that we could cast in flat slabs for doors and mould into steps and handrails and mantel shelves. This perfect material has not been invented and all our materials seem to have some grievous faults and habits. On the other hand, each material has a character of its own and requires a method of handling of its own, and probably the way of greatest interest and beauty is only to be attained through the imperfect things we have at our disposal.

As regards the beauty of our houses, one of the great difficulties is the multifariousness of our minor interests which tend to make us accumulate around ourselves so many things—a certain number of which may be beautiful or interesting in themselves, but which can have no permanent place in our material surroundings. Out of many pretty things, it is only possible to make a mess. One of our best hopes lies in the continual elimination of this messiness. Of too great simplicity we do not need in these days to have any fear. Let us be thankful that the garbage man has a strong back and let us make ample use of his priceless services.

To direct us in our thinking about houses that shall be homes, there are some golden rules. The most valuable things about a house are the people who use it, whose home it is. Their happiness and cheerfulness is ever the first consideration. The most interesting and valuable things about our rooms are the people in them—they should be treated as the background against which we see them. By a generous conception of these things alone can we build a "home."

NOTES

1. Dr. Ferris is not identified. Perhaps he was W.D. Ferris, who was a trustee of the Edmonton Public School board, 1905–08 and 1910.
2. In margin: "4. External life."
3. At bottom of page: "Carpenter or gardening shop, children's play room."

DOCUMENT 5

Hygiene in Architecture

SCIENTIFIC DISCOVERIES in the late nineteenth century about the spread of communicable disease had a profound influence not only on public health and medicine but on architecture. The work of various scientists, such as Pasteur, showed the importance of sanitation in preventing the spread of certain diseases. Such discoveries offered ways to control some of the greatest scourges of human life.

By the beginning of the twentieth century, it was thus widely accepted that the spread and occurrence of many diseases could be controlled by eliminating germs or controlling their spread. This knowledge became influential in architecture because it sparked demands that buildings needed to employ design elements that would encourage the availability of sunlight and fresh air to kill germs. So too, cleaning to eliminate germs became a high priority.

Burgess enunciated many of these principles in his 1913 talk, "The Old House and the New" (Document 4), but in this essay he provided a more *comprehensive application to architecture of the scientific theories that were reshaping architecture's expression and purpose. Indeed, when he wrote this article, all of his readers would have had fresh in their minds the flu epidemic of 1919, which only the year before had given a fearful demonstration of the power of communicable disease.*

Document 5 is a transcription of a typescript for publication in Alberta Association of Architects Yearbook, January 30, 1920, 71.213, file 95, UAA.[1]

THE HUMAN CREATURE instinctively delights in the sunlight and the breeze. All the knowledge that science accumulates confirms the rightness of this instinct and its value for the creature's health. Hygiene is the science of healthy living. This science is not new. Its broad principles have been well understood from immemorial time, and from the beginning all architects have desired to have their buildings healthy to live in. Sunlight and the circulation of air have always been recognised as the great means to this end; they still stand as the chief text of the hygienic preachers. The temples of the Greeks were built with their length running east and west, and the doorway to the east. Their rites were celebrated in the open air opposite the east front in the morning sunlight. Christian churches similarly were placed east and west, but with the entrance from the west. The worship being within the building, the worshippers thus faced the morning sunlight. The entrance most used in English churches was the south one, and this is often more important architecturally than the west door. It was on this sunny side of the church that people met before and after service; it was usually in the south porch that public notices were posted.

Whenever possible, the cloisters of monasteries were placed on the south side of the church, the only consideration that sometimes made them alter this arrangement was a hygienic one—the fact of water supply being on the north side. Great mediaeval houses requiring to be at the same time defensible, castles were built around courtyards which they completely enclosed. But it was realised that an enclosed courtyard meant more or less stagnant air and at the Renaissance, as soon as a more settled state of political affairs permitted the disregard of stringent defensive measures, great houses began to be built around three sides of a court only, leaving the south side open to the sun and embaying the sunshine. In civic planning of the present day this principle is recognised and carried further. It is realised that blocks entirely enclosing a central area are unhealthy and that openings at least should be provided at all four corners.

To take the fullest advantage of the beneficent action of sunlight, the long blocks forming the wards of hospitals should stand with their length north and south with windows west, south, and east to obtain the maximum of sunshine and of circulation of air. Modern hygiene has, however, thrown a clearer light on the subject of healthy conditions of living, has traced the invisible causes of the good influence of sunlight and air movements, and has in many ways reinforced our ability to combat sickness and ill health. The chief instrument in enabling us to obtain a clearer knowledge in these matters is the microscope, and the chief discoveries of the microscope tending towards better hygiene are the observation of the microbe and the structure of the human tissues. So important are these two discoveries that the study of each has been raised to the importance of a separate science: bacteriology and physiology. The discovery that disease is caused and spread by microscopic and, in some cases, by ultra microscopic living [organisms] is the foundation of modern hygiene as well as much of modern medical treatment. The purpose of modern hygiene is to eliminate the disease germ; that of modern treatment is to kill it or to strengthen the body to combat it. It has been determined that dirt, damp, [and] stagnation of air are favourable to these germs, that cleanliness, dryness and air circulation are unfavourable and therefore these are demanded by hygiene. It becomes, then, the duty of architects to see that in their building these conditions shall be insured.

Much of the bacteriologist's work consists in making experiments with materials and under conditions favourable to these enemies of mankind, the bacteria of disease, in order that he may determine their presence or absence in cases of sickness. Doctors send secretions from their patients to the bacteriologist at this university and from his report they ascertain the cause of sickness. Now the bacteriologist finds that he cannot get his cultures to succeed in sunlight or even in bright light. Sunlight kills the germs. It is the great germicide—hence, the great importance of getting sunlight into all our rooms. As you know, this is not always easy in practice. I have heard of one architect receiving instructions from a client as to his house. He specified about seventeen rooms, and all were to be in the south-east except one—the kitchen. We are, further, often tempted for the sake of external appearance to put windows looking north when they might be east and west. This can only be done at a cost of hygienic conditions and it will be well when we do these things to provide also some east and west light so that direct sunlight shall get into every possible room. I think it would be well on hygienic grounds that in civic planning all main streets should lie north and south so that all the main city blocks should get both east and west sunlight. I don't know whether this apparently important point is actually attended to in any great city, but the inconvenience of not attending to it is obvious in the fact that the north side of a shopping street is generally much more popular and valuable than the south side.

Sunlight is the great germ killer. It is also the enemy of dirt, damp and air stagnation, but within our buildings there can only be limited areas swept by direct sunlight. We must therefore use means of reinforcing and extending its influence. If not direct sunlight, at least as much light as possible must penetrate everywhere. From dust floating in the air and from other sources, dirt is liable to settle and accumulate in the comparative stillness of a building. Germs find a breeding place in dirt. Light exposes this dirt which when thus detected may be removed. Dark corners, dark passages, etc., are on this ground to be avoided. Our building should be penetrated with light. Again, in practice this is not always easy to obtain and we reinforce the sunlight with less beneficent artificial light, which if it does not kill the germs, at least shows up the dirt.

There are many other ways in which the architect may aid the occupier in combating dirt. He must provide the means of getting rid of dirt. In this there are broadly two methods—wet and dry—washing and dusting, water and the broom, or its modern development, the vacuum cleaner. Efficient water supply with its accompanying drainage is a great weapon in the warfare of hygiene; it is the means for getting rid of dirt, including germs. By efficient water supply in this connection is not meant simply the laying on of a sufficiently large supply pipe, but that water, hot and cold, must be readily available at every part of a building, both for washing the body and for cleaning the building. An awkward or difficult service means an inefficient service. Anyone who has had to make official inspections of premises knows that it is wise to see principally the cleaner's cupboards; if these are not clean, well supplied with their necessities and convenient for their purposes, all is not well and investigations and improvements are called for. In all large buildings a sufficiency of good cleaner's closets are a first necessity. These need not be large, they may be in odd corners unsuitable for other purposes, but it should be remembered that they are a vital necessity. They should be equipped for their purpose, they should themselves be convenient to clean, and if they have no window, they should have an artificial light in them. Water is a hygienic weapon; the objects and materials upon which it is to be used require consideration. Many materials do not lend themselves readily to cleaning with water, such as carpets and curtain stuffs. From the hygienic point of view, these should be eliminated or reduced to a minimum. Where a vacuum cleaner is available, the objection to textile materials is less. Of course, textile hangings are of high value for architectural effect, so that in many classes of buildings vacuum cleaning equipment is a hygienic necessity.

There are three qualities in materials that recommend themselves from a sanitary viewpoint: whiteness, smoothness and impermeability of surface.

Whiteness is a virtue for the reasons that a white surface in a good light shows up dirt better than any self colour and much better than mottled colouring. Black is probably next best in this respect and is sometimes used in linoleum for the floors of hospital wards. Plumbing fittings are, of course, generally made of white material; porcelain or enamelled iron, with this purpose of showing the dirt. Operating theatres in hospitals, dairies, bathrooms and lavatories aim at this idea of general whiteness and sometimes are very nearly all white. The lime whiting of stables is good from this point of view as well as for another reason. But colour is a lovely thing and we wish to enjoy it inside of our building as well as out. The desire to fulfill hygienic demands has, no doubt, done much to bring whiteness into modern buildings in the form of white tiles for floors and walls, white marble linings, white painted rooms. If we had everything white, however, in our buildings, it would probably prove too trying on our eyes and nerves and thereby produce another form of unhealthiness. It would seem necessary then to compromise with the demand for whiteness.

Whilst speaking of the matter of colour in relation to health, I may digress for a moment into the subject of poisonous colours. It has been found that arsenic is sometimes used in the preparation of some wall papers, especially though not exclusively, the green ones. This has been known to produce effects of poisoning on the occupiers. It is almost the only case in which the air of our rooms is liable to actual poisoning for the effects of air that is foul from any other cause are not [actually poisonous], as I shall endeavour to show later.

The second quality in materials called for by hygiene is smoothness. The object of this is that the surfaces of these materials may, in the first place, not easily lodge dirt and, in the second place, that these may be easily washed or brushed clean. Probably one of the ideal substances in common use in building operations, both as regards whiteness and smoothness, is plaster which rivals snow in whiteness and can be polished to a shining smoothness. In some countries a highly polished plaster surface is objectionable on account of the tendency for moisture in the air to condense upon it. This will take place when the air is full of moisture and the walls are cooler than the air of the room, so that the objection is liable to arise when a high degree of humidity is added to the air on entering a building. In schools and other institutions a sand-faced plaster is used to prevent scribbling on the walls, and there is probably no great hygienic objection to this for though dust will cling to this surface to some extent, it is easily brushed off. Plaster had a great advantage over wood as a finish from the fact that its smooth surface is, or ought to be, very continuous; that is to say that it is free from the many joints essential to woodwork. Its substance is also highly sanitary being chiefly lime, which is unfavourable to the life of germs. For this reason lime-whiting is highly useful in cow-stables, external lavatories, etc. In addition to the smoothness of its actual surface, plaster has the advantage that the forms in which it is used may all be made smooth. Internal corners of rooms may be rounded off, cornices may be covered and made accessible to cleaning. Probably in the future—wood being so high in price—plaster will be much more employed for internal moulded work as in internal window and door trim, and also for external work. Porcelain, as in plumbing fittings, enamelled iron, glazed tile, brick and terra cotta are ideal substances, both in point of whiteness and smoothness. They are, however, expensive whilst plaster is comparatively cheap.

Whilst woodwork can easily be made smooth and cleanable by enamel or varnish finish, it cannot so easily be made smooth in its general form on account of its necessarily much-jointed construction. In hospitals, panelless doors are demanded. As at present constructed, these are expensive and therefore not suited to moderately expensive structures such as ordinary dwelling houses. An inexpensive panelless door would, no doubt, be welcomed by hygienic authorities. Single panel doors approach their ideals and are quite practicable; they present only one ledge on which dust may gather. Skirting or baseboards, even when small, may almost be called a nuisance from the sanitary point of view. They quietly collect dust all the time, and being carried all round every room in a house, this amounts to a considerable quantity in the total. This dust is collected behind heavy furniture and in many places very difficult of access; it therefore presents a considerable problem to any housewife with ideas of scrupulous cleanliness. What seems to be required is some kind of floor laid in a plastic manner which can be finished with an edging turned up with a hollow quarter-round rising about six inches, or [by making] the walls and finishing flush with the wall plastering.[2] A satisfactory solution of this question would be a great step towards ideal hygienic buildings. [In any case], the shapes of all trim and woodwork are gradually being much modified to meet hygienic requirements. We have such things, for example, as simple stair balusters as housewives object to the labour of cleaning the older fashioned baluster forms. The closed string is enormously more difficult to keep clean than the open string, and further facilities in this direction are quite practicable. For instance, the use of a bottom rail on which to set the stair balusters would leave the majority of the treads free and easy to clean. Stairs would be more cheaply constructed and would be more easily cleaned if built without risers.

The vogue in mission furniture is probably a healthy thing in the eyes of the hygienists and of the housekeeper. However desirable dull finishes may be from an architectural point of view, there is no doubt that glossy surfaces are more easily cleaned.

I have already suggested that a floor with a continuous unjointed surface is the ideal one from our present point of consideration. Cement is too rough and gritty, or if smoothed and polished is too hard to live with. Substitutes, whether of magnesite composition, terrazzo or tile, are still too hard and are generally too liable to unsightly cracks. Hardwood and linoleum are, therefore, at present the most wholesome of practicable floors. Hardwood with a wax finish well maintained is probably in the end a cheaper floor than any softwood and is very satisfactory but for the joints. If these are sufficiently fine, they will probably become filled with wax and then the objection is the sharp angle at the baseboard quarter-round. Linoleum compares very closely with hardwood in hygienic quality and eliminates the chances of open joints. It also has the advantage of quietness and may be laid either on soft wood or cement. As most dirt tends to gravitate to the floor, its hygienic quality is naturally a most important one. Carpets and coverings on floors must be considered as dust traps and treated accordingly. The vacuum cleaner has done much to ensure their cleanliness. Carpets are expensive in any case, both in first cost and in the labour of cleaning, and I cannot help thinking that there is room for introduction of some more ideal flooring than we have at present: something that will be good enough in appearance to serve with rugs or carpets, something fairly silent under the feet, sufficiently tough to take the wear of boot-nails and metal castors. Indian rubber seems a perfect floor, but it is too expensive and has not a long life. Asphalt might be sufficiently comfortable but is particularly unattractive in appearance. Gypsum floors finished with oil are used in some countries, but I have no experience of them and should be glad to have some information as to the possibilities of this material.

The third requirement of hygiene in materials is impermeability, that is to say that they should be fairly impermeable to air or water so that germs may not be carried into their substance and there obtain an inaccessible lodgement. Hygienic materials should be easily washable and when wet should dry off quickly. This quality may be obtained in many materials, such as wood and cement by surface finishes, in terra cottas and brick by glazing. Sheet iron whether galvanised or enamelled answers this requirement well.

It must be disheartening to architects to find that hygienic science militates against so many cherished traditional beauties. It frowns upon colour and has no use for the classical forms with projecting ledges and filleted mouldings. The lovely ranges of acanthus foliage of the Corinthian capital are tabooed and the deep under-cuttings of Gothic work are anathema. It seems to ask of us to devise a new technique based on its requirements. In regard to materials, it seems to demand a hard smoothness which, except in the case of plaster, is generally accompanied by additional cost. Our old friend, woodwork, seems to have least favour. In forms, however, it asks for simplicity which should tend to reduction of cost. Perhaps some new material substitutes may be suggested. Asbestos board may have a future before it under a hygienic regime. Before the war it was to some extent displacing wood as being fireproof and unshrinkable. At present, its price has gone up even more than that of wood. Is it possible that some new substance may be invented which will be a general purpose material? Something like India rubber, mouldable into all shapes, capable of being plastered on in a continuous unjointed manner, strong enough for walls and floors, capable of all colours and textures, waterproof, fireproof? Where is the inherent impossibility of all of this?

Before leaving this question of hygienic materials and forms, let me refer to some matters of arrangement. The cellar is apt to be the most neglected part of a house, both in the building and in the occupation. There is not generally much smoothness or washability about it. In the interests of hygiene it should be dry and its floor cemented and well graded. This is quite often obviously intended, and quite as obviously not obtained through carelessness in execution [and] over-economy in labour and materials. As there are generally coals and ashes around here, there is more dust to be dealt with than elsewhere. This collects on heating and water pipes, on the rough sides of joists and on the tops of bearing beams. We cannot generally afford to finish cellars like living rooms, but a reasonable attention should be paid to them. Probably a fairly satisfactory compromise would be to lime-white them periodically and they might be prepared with that intention.

The kitchen is perhaps the room in which hygienic demands should receive most respectful attention. Cleanliness where food is prepared is highly important and should be made easy in order to be efficiently observed. The corners should not be made inaccessible by ranges, sinks or other fittings being jammed into them. It would be well if they could be made to stand empty always. In large kitchens the fittings should be clear of the wall sufficiently to admit of easy cleaning behind them. A good rule is to banish all woodwork from an ideal kitchen. Sinks are of iron; the cook's table is of steel; the baking is done on a marble slab; shelves should be of iron; cupboards and drawers there should be none. The presence of wood in a kitchen encourages the presence of vermin. These requirements do not apply to a small kitchen, and the kitchen ought to be small in a small house; the difficulty of cleaning [and the] difficulty of performing all necessary operations increases with its size. It may seem that too much emphasis is placed on the need to make everything cleanable. People have been accustomed to keep their houses clean in the past by a certain amount of wholesome hard work. If hard work is good for one, why do away with it? The chief reason, I suppose, is that, after all, the vast majority of people live in houses very far from being well fitted out in this manner. The well-to-do can look after themselves. The mass of human material, the most valuable material a country possesses, is not so well placed.

Take the case of a woman with five or six children whose husband is away from home working all day and the family income is too small to afford outside help. This woman has to purchase food, clothing and household utensils, cutlery, and table linen (if any). She has to clean and air the house, to dust and arrange the furniture (to say nothing here of the skirting boards), to keep up the fires, make up the beds and change the linen, [and] keep curtains and other household effects in good condition. She has to wash and dress her younger children—the older ones being at school—and she has, meanwhile, as her chief responsibility, the general upbringing of her children. Such a woman is surely amongst the hardest worked members of the community, and on the success of the efforts of such women the community depends for the tone and quality of the men the country produces. It may be true that to supply her with the hygienic possibilities discussed will only relieve her of a small part of her work. The question is: is this much not worth doing? It may be said that many of the demands of hygiene are costly and that they cannot be supplied on any accepted economic basis. The world is a good deal arranged upon the principle that to him that hath shall be given, and from him that hath not shall be taken away even that which he hath. This is a natural law that human laws might well be framed to correct. Human life is sustained by warring against natural forces and the life of the community is likewise a war against certain natural economic laws.

So far I have been speaking only of hygienic requirements as pointed out by the bacteriologist, the investigator of disease germs. The physiologist employs the microscope to investigate the tissues of the body and from his work we are taught some other points regarding healthy conditions for human life—amongst the more important of these are the action of the air upon the lungs and the air ducts and the skin of the body.

Disease germs are probably too numerous and have too much vitality ever to be eliminated from this earth, but a great deal can be done to strengthen the body so that its natural recuperative powers may successfully combat these and let them gain no hold on it. Statistics clearly show that the longest lived classes of men are those who have out-of-door occupations and this has been found to be due not as much to the fact of the air they breathe being so much more free from impurities as from the fact that they live in freer circulation of air. It is indeed really quite difficult to poison the air, even in a house. In the war the Germans demonstrated how the outside air might be poisoned for a short time in limited areas, but the operation was expensive to them in more ways than one. This kind of poisoning is not one that arises without *malice prepense*.

The stuffiness that develops in over-crowded unventilated rooms is sometimes attributed to the accumulation of CO_2. 1.5 percent of this ingredient is about the highest recorded by those who have made observations in overcrowded rooms—[this is] a very small proportion, and this gas is not a poison. It is generally stated in text books that the injurious effect of a stuffy atmosphere is due to the fact that the presence of even this percentage of CO_2 deprives the lungs of the amount of oxygen which this displaces. But in high altitudes, owing to the rarefied atmosphere, the lungs receive a very great deal smaller proportion of oxygen, still the effect is positively good. The fact is that the air in a room may have a large proportion of CO_2 and so long as the temperature is low, no inconvenience is felt, but if the temperature be raised, the usual effects of bad air—discomfort, drowsiness, headache and sickness—result. The reason for this is that in stagnant warmth and moisture, the body and lungs are unable to get rid of the heat they are constantly manufacturing in the usual way by radiation and evaporation and hence experience serious discomfort. Under these circumstances, even the revolution of a fan in the room will give some comfort as the movement of air over the skin will carry away heat and moisture.

The CO_2 in stuffy rooms is due to the excess of respired air and it is always accompanied by other exhalations, the nature of which does not appear to have been accurately examined scientifically. The presence of CO_2 is, however, an index that these exist. They probably vary very largely in their nature. It is these, and not the CO_2 itself, which is colourless and harmless, which cause the stuffiness and sickness. These exhalations seem to intensify the drowsy effect of the warm air and seem to have little effect on people when the air is cold. It follows from what has been said that even pure air, when very warm and quite stagnant, will cause this drowsiness because the body and breathing organs will not be able to get rid of the heat which they develop. They will suffer from "heat retention." An uncomfortable condition of the skin and lung passages, if long continued, will affect the nervous system and undermine the vitality of the whole body, rendering it much more liable to the attack of disease germs.

From these facts it will be seen that the circulation of the air is one of the most important requirements in buildings. To secure good health, our buildings must not only be easily kept clean, they must breathe freely. For buildings of large size, the designing of a ventilating system is usually undertaken by a ventilating engineer, but even in the first setting out of his plan, the architect must form some conception of the general requirements. Otherwise he may find that he will have to add three or four feet more to the width of his building to accommodate the ventilation ducts and may have to give up to ventilating requirements space that he fondly believed he could reserve for other purposes. After all, however, the majority of buildings erected, probably even a majority of those which architects design, are constructed without consultation with the ventilating engineer and with very little in the way of ventilation ducts to occupy appreciable space. It is therefore in the application of the principles of what is generally known as natural ventilation that an architect may secure the hygienic condition of his buildings.

Stagnant air is not only unwholesome for the human body, it is unwholesome for the materials of a house for dry rot and other moulds will only propagate in still air and dampness. A building is the better off being naturally well ventilated as well as being artificially well ventilated for somewhat similar reasons that a building should be naturally well lighted as well as well lighted artificially. The ordinary doors and windows of buildings are, of course, its natural breathing organs and in the summertime, if these be kept open sufficiently, nature will generally see to it that the buildings are ventilated except in very still hot weather when we know the benefit of mechanical contrivances such as electric fans. In extremely cold weather, on the other hand, such as we have been having lately, we are inclined to suffer from only too much circulation of air and proceed to stop up every accessible chink through which we find air entering. The greater part of the time, after all, we have some intermediate temperature and fairly still atmosphere. The question, then, is whether the majority of our naturally ventilated buildings are, under these circumstances, sufficiently wholesome. Probably the answer to this question is to be found in the statistics of tuberculosis which [run] quite high in this country.

In these circumstances, then, I think that architects could do much good by paying all possible attention to every matter of arrangement of plan and to the installation of many of comparatively simple devices for aiding a good natural ventilating system. Among the arrangements of plan which greatly aid wholesomeness of buildings in this respect are [that] passages should, as much as possible, have a door or a window at each end so that a current of air may be passed through at any or at all times. If the air of passages be not kept in circulation, there is little chance of the rooms opening off these passages being well ventilated, but if the air in the passage be good, then the opening of a room door and window will ensure a circulation of good air through the room. Similarly, every facility should be given for cross ventilation; by facility I do not mean merely possibility, but provision at least as likely to be made use of as not, and better if more easy to use than not to use. Whatever objections there may be to them in other respects, transom openings above doors are good things from a hygienic point of view and best if they have no sash, [and], therefore, remain permanently open. The CNR hotels have transom openings over bedroom doors with an opening and closing wood panel. This, of course, secures privacy, but glass has the hygienic advantage of ensuring light. A permanent opening secures both light and air.

Provisions such as I have mentioned provide lengthwise and crosswise circulation of air. Vertical circulation should also be ensured. Staircases are the natural main arteries for this and an architect can improve the circulation of air in a building by keeping in mind the air circulation when placing and devising the stairways. There should be free communication between these and the passages, and it will be well if at the head of staircases there be some outlet, even if it be only a small ventilator on the peak of a roof light.

With free air moving along passageways and rising through open stairways with some outlet at the top, air circulation through the whole building becomes something more than a bare possibility. Our buildings will be provided with breathing organs. The minor appliances for entry and exit of air are many and various. Most of us have a more or less wide acquaintance with a number of types of these. Probably what is most wanted in our Canadian buildings is the insistence on providing them as frequently as they ought to be provided. One difficulty is that in extremely cold weather they are apt to become not only unnecessary, but objectionable. We find our buildings difficult enough to keep warm and free from draughts in such weather as we have been recently experiencing. Doors and windows are the ventilating apparatus most easy to control effectively, and these must therefore be made so that they do not have to be hermetically sealed with cotton batting so as to prevent them being open whenever weather is mild enough to admit of it. I have no doubt that vertical outlets should be provided to a much greater extent than they are in all rooms that are much occupied. A three or four inch vertical pipe such as can easily be carried up in a partition would prove effective, even in a fairly large room, but in excessively cold weather this would require to be closed. The danger with all these smaller appliances is that once closed they remain closed and the cost of installation might better have been saved. Probably the most unhealthy house arrangement in anything like general practice in Canada is that in which a hot air furnace is used to warm a building without a direct fresh air inlet from outside. The occupants, in this case, live constantly in the recirculation of the same air. This arrangement is probably the cause of more tuberculosis than any other.

It would take a long time to discuss in detail the various merits and demerits of the minor contrivances for maintaining cleanliness and circulation of air. Many of these belong to the architect's province; there are also many which do not. I wish, principally, to point to the conclusion that a building in modern times has to be regarded more and more as if it were a living creature, a distinct organism requiring careful provision for the reception of food for its occupants, the cleanly preparation of that food, and the getting rid of waste products from whatever cause arising. Dirt and dust are among those products, and the quick and easy means of getting rid of these are of the greatest importance to health. Further, this creature, the building, must have an air circulation as an animal has a respiratory system. For its wholesomeness, it draws on the sunshine as do all living things. It demands, however, artificial conditions which it creates. The furnace may be said to be analogous to the heart with the heating pipes for arteries. If we keep this analogy in view in each of our buildings and through all the processes of getting these building designed, drawn, specified and erected, we shall have a good general guide towards establishing ideal conditions as far as concern hygiene in architecture.

NOTES

1. Published in the *Alberta Association of Architects Year Book, 1919–1920. Fourteenth Session* (Edmonton: 1920): 36–46. The text reprinted here is taken from the manuscript version. There are only a few editorial changes between the manuscript and published versions. The document has been reformatted and edited to press style.
2. On his idea of a hollow round shape between the floor and the wall, see the diagram in Document 4, "The Old House and the New." His second recommendation is basically that the trim around openings be made flush with the wall.

PART II

1921–1939

Overleaf: Cecil Burgess in 1919. *(71.213–274, UAA)*

DOCUMENT 6

Modern Architecture

FOR MUCH OF THE TWENTIETH CENTURY, the word modern was a catch phrase in European and North American society. But modernity is a difficult and often contradictory concept in architectural history. What did it mean to be a modern architect? What defines modern architecture and why? Is it possible to be modern and still be inspired by historical lessons and precedents? Do modern buildings have to look different than old buildings?

For Burgess the answer to these questions lay in his understanding that architecture was a social art that reflected social values and conditions. This presumed that architecture was in its essence a response to the needs of a particular time and place. Thus, as Burgess argued in this talk, modernity in architecture arose from the need for new types of buildings, the availability of new materials and new technology, and from new demands such as those for efficiency and hygiene. As well, new conditions such as city life and the steadily growing role of the state were also part of the rise of "modern" architecture. But

Burgess was also clear, as were many of his contemporaries, that these modern buildings could meet all these new functions without needing to look radically different than the buildings that had come before. Indeed, he argued that the inspiration of past architecture created connections over time that enriched a culture and gave it depth. Modernity was thus not a style—it was instead a response to the unique needs of a new age.

Document 6 is a talk to an unidentified audience. Not dated, ca. 1925, 71.213, file 85, UAA.

THERE IS A FAIRLY GENERAL IDEA that, in modern times at least, architecture is that art of which the general public has of all arts the least intimate knowledge; that many may have an intelligent idea of what goes to make beautiful music, or good novel writing, or an impressive drama or even a fine painting, but that no one who is not a professional architect need attempt to comprehend the mysteries of architecture. There may be some unimportant respect in which this is true, but it would be more strikingly true to say that there is no art which concerns all people high and low, rich and poor, so intimately, and there is no art the development and shaping of which is less in the hands of the professional practitioner. Architects no more create architecture than do politicians create politics or shape the destinies of nations. It is the people themselves who do that and it is not a bit less the people who make their own architecture.

In all the arts men express themselves, for our arts are the results of our enthusiasms about certain things. Whether in literature, music, painting, sculpture, oratory or architecture, art indicates what pursuits are occupying our minds, exciting our feelings and delighting our senses. [It also indicates] what quality of thought these pursuits give rise to, by what deep or superficial emotions we are drifted or compelled towards them, what degree of pleasure we derive from them, and with what intelligence we succeed in fulfilling our desires.

Architecture then as an art is one of the indications, and it is one of the greatest and surest indications, of what visions are chiefly stirring us to action, what motives are inspiring our lives, and what we at the present day are deriving our greatest pleasure from. It may be said, why should we go to architecture to learn these things—it seems an indirect and difficult way to learn them—when we might learn them by direct explanation. The answer to that is that to learn about anything there is no such thing as direct explanation. We must resort to some means such as spoken or written words, or photographs, or pictures, or poetry, or architecture, and of all such means, architecture presents the plainest evidence—evidence which meets us in every street, evidence that we cannot avoid or escape from if we would. It is so omnipresent that we are apt to overlook it. It is well to look at it then and to understand what it has to say.

Architecture is the human intelligence and sentiment that is built into buildings. However badly arranged or planned, or however ugly a building may be, it represents a certain amount of intelligence—an intelligence far above that of the lower animals for instance. Every building represents a certain amount of sentiment too, for it shows a desire to accomplish certain ends and an appetite for certain things, and such mental appetites are human sentiments.

What sort of people do our modern buildings show us to be? If we consider what sort of buildings we are erecting, we shall soon see how different are our pursuits from those of many of the peoples of other days. This fact is as clearly expressed in these buildings as in the letters that we write to the newspapers, the stories we are reading, the music we are listening to, or in the book and magazine illustrations we look at so eagerly and so quickly forget.

The most essential thing in a view of a modern city is the continuous rows of stores with high commodious office buildings over them and shop fronts with their multitudinous display of goods from all parts of the world. That corresponding buildings 200 or 300 years ago were on a much smaller scale only indicates that population, industry and luxury have greatly increased during the interval. But, if we consider Rome at the great period of the empire, we shall find that it was more populous than any but two or three cities of the present day, more richly supplied with all luxuries and with greater businesses transacting more important dealings. What kind of stores and offices would we find there? There is not sufficient evidence to tell with precision, but we know that the Romans had no glass for shop windows [and that] writing paper and all the processes and paraphernalia for making and duplicating letters and other documents were not the readily accessible affairs that they have now become. Consequently, goods had to be displayed without the protection of glass and locked up in windowless rooms at night, and business had to be transacted to a vastly greater extent than now by word of mouth. This was done in the open market or forum. Acres of the city of Rome were occupied by these forums, which were large open spaces surrounded by covered verandahs or marble pillars.

I must leave it to your imagination to picture how great a change has been impressed on our cities by simple circumstances like the invention of plate glass and writing paper. In matters of this kind, a people's architecture expresses very plainly their material wants and the resources which they are able to command to meet them. The fact that so much of modern architecture is taken up with the provision for the display of luxuries, and the accommodation of the businesses based on these luxuries, indicates how much of our effort at the present day is aroused by the appetite for such things as our stores display.

Take the record of architecture with regard to another aspect of life. How does architecture indicate that we differ from the ancient Romans in the matter of religion? We build many churches as they built many temples. A somewhat striking difference is that we build them chiefly in residential districts and they are apt to become disused when the districts around them change from residential to business quarters. In Rome, on the other hand, the temples were crowded around their forums and marketplaces. There were at least half-a-dozen great temples around the Forum Romanum, the original old market-square of Rome, and there were other temples in the immediate neighbourhood. They evidently connected religion very closely with their business. More remarkable still, however, is the fact that they did not look upon their temples as places in which to hold meetings. Their public religious rites, like their business generally, were carried out in the open air. This was partly no doubt a matter of climate, but it was still more a matter of public sentiment.

But past architecture is not now my subject. The instances I have given may serve to show that in architecture the modern conditions have created something vastly different from the works of former times. The product of modern architecture in mere number and variety of buildings exceeds anything that any past age has known. Of buildings that are either altogether modern in their nature or which have developed a type altogether modern, the following are a few examples: offices; stores; hotels; railway stations; governmental and departmental buildings due to modern development in the management of public affairs; public libraries, public baths; museums; picture galleries; fire brigade stations; police courts; law courts; prisons; factories; hospitals and post offices. Many of our teaching buildings are for purposes that in modern times have received great developments requiring highly specialised building such as science schools, including medical schools, technical schools, art schools and others. A mere list of such buildings is of itself a résumé of the life of our times and an index of the nature of our civilisation. This extraordinary change in our civilisation has, of course, largely been brought about by the application of mechanical inventions to increase production and to the facilities for the transportation of production as well as of the producers and users. The economic side of the question does not belong to my subject.

I intend to exhibit on the screen some examples of the typical works of modern architecture, [but] before doing so, I should like to point out certain characteristics which belong to these and which offer problems quite special to modern times.[1]

In the first place, a majority of our modern buildings offer complications of plan such as older architectures did not attempt. This is particularly observable in hotel buildings, club buildings, and in all governmental buildings whether belonging to government of the city, or the province, or the country. Some ancient Roman buildings had a great variety of halls and rooms. The mediaeval cathedrals had marvellously complex and wellbuilt structures, but nowhere in history have architects faced in either respect problems such as are common at the present day. In all classes of buildings, halls and rooms have to be provided of every ratio, length, breadth and height, of every variety of form, and for every variety of purpose. [All these must be] as intricately fitted into one another as the pieces of a Chinese puzzle, linked together by convenient passages and other connections, yet kept sufficiently apart for the degree of privacy each requires, and communication [must be] maintained through the whole organisation by means of hallways, corridors, lobbies, stairs and elevators.

The modern problem is farther complicated by the requirement of modern systems of water supply, drainage and plumbing, artificial systems of heating, ventilation and lighting [and] besides many minor arrangements such as telephones, elevators, dumb-waiters, chutes for letters or other purposes. The detail of many of these services becomes a matter for the engineer, but the provision for their accommodation such as will ensure efficient operation must be taken careful account of in the plans of the architect. Not only is this so, but the demand for precision of arrangement of all these things steadily increases. Everything must be as near to the user's hand as is physically possible. The steps a man has to take in his day's work are all numbered. All apparatus must fulfil its work with the utmost ease of manipulation. Not the least difficult part of the problem is that these things have all got to be accomplished with the most severe application of economy of space and of economy in installation and in operation. [Thus], the practical architect's function is largely that of a coordinator of trades.

Another important demand made of modern building in an everincreasing measure comes from the point of view of health. Modern medical science has discovered microbes in millions everywhere and has divided them into the sheep and the goats, and has called for the exclusion of the evil species from our dwellings and all our places of temporary sojourn. To combat these evil influences, more sunlight is demanded and our windows are enlarged and verandahs, sleeping porches and sun parlours are contrived. Scrupulous cleanliness is demanded and all materials that are white and hard and smooth are requisitioned so that dirt, if present, may be at once detected, and when detected, may be readily wiped out and in no case be permitted to penetrate the surface or permeate the substance. Ease of dusting must be considered. Sharp corners and crannies that can hold dirt must be eliminated and smooth round corners that can be easily cleaned off must be substituted wherever possible. Crumpled or elaborate forms must be straightened out, and every ledge that can be made to disappear must be banished. In fact, surface must be reduced to a minimum and, for such as remains, an equipment of vacuum pipe and hose must be provided. For floors, walls, and ceilings, new materials are being demanded and invented. White tiles, white cements, white enamels, white terra cotta and white glazed bricks help to fulfil the demand, and this not only for interior furnishings, but also for exterior facing of walls.

All this applies more especially to hospitals for the sake of giving the sick every chance of recovery. But the theory applies more or less in every building. In schools, for example, it is recognised that large numbers of very young people, whose health is liable to permanent injury if their conditions are in any respect unhealthy, are held long periods together in a manner that calls for careful consideration in every circumstance of their temporary habitation. Kitchens too require every precaution for scrupulous cleanliness, especially those of large institutions, to many of which any suspicion of the food served having been the cause of sickness would be fatal.

Thus we find the demand for sanitary conditions is accompanied by a definite call for the alteration or modification of shapes and surface materials, and for the adoption of light colour or absence of any colour. This call is subtly and surely affecting design in architecture. Yet it is likely to have certain definite limitations, for although we accept a number of these hygienic ideas into our houses—more or less according to our individual

The Alberta Government Administrative Building in Edmonton was a steel-framed structure. Opened in 1932, it served the needs of an increasingly complex provincial bureaucracy. (ND-3-5256b, GA)

The lobby of the Alberta Government Administrative Building used traditional materials to create an impressive and highly finished interior. (71.213-283, UAA)

temperaments—none of us is able [to adopt] all these things. The pitch of light and general whiteness required for ideal sanitary conditions is more intense than the nerves of most of us could stand as a habitual environment. The absence of colour is a deprivation that to most of us would seem hardly worth the cost. Hardness and smoothness of surface is a physical discomfort, [while] to all, the cost of providing the requirements suggested will be a matter of very serious consideration.[2]

Another source of change in modern architecture is the extraordinary development in available materials. In old days, people built in brick, wood or stone as these were available in their locality. Our increased ease in transportation brings the choice of these and others to our doors.[3] Glass, steel, concrete, reinforced concrete, hard terra cotta, porous terra cotta, gypsum block, and asbestos are a few of the materials available in general construction. For finishing floors, walls, and ceilings, their name is legion and their respective merits are advocated with a skill to deceive the angels.

One general tendency, beyond the sanitary, in the use of modern building materials is to economise space. You will readily understand that when large spaces have to be arched or vaulted over, much of the space between one floor and the one above is lost. Floors made with flat slabs as thin as possible are evidently the limit of economy in this respect, and this is effected by our system of steel and concrete construction to an extent never equalled in the past. The fact that it is now the aim to make all important buildings fireproof by this economical method of steel and concrete construction has also its effect on planning and on design. "With all your conveniences fireproof" is another instruction which adds to the intricate problem of modern building.[4]

When certain objections are stated in regard to the architecture of the day, let us remember the multitudinous and often conflicting demands it has to meet, the changing nature of these demands from day-to-day, and also the vast amount that it actually accomplishes. If it accomplishes its task imperfectly, it is because to accomplish such a task perfectly is, quite frankly, an impossibility. For a long time to come, we shall be striving to achieve things beyond our reach, but always making progress in the attempt.

Let us consider a few of the types of architectural works characteristic of the present day. As the steam engine in its various applications has done so much to revolutionise the social conditions and with them architecture, I may begin with railway stations which belong only to modern architecture. One of the most essential features of these—a hall roofed with simple glazing large enough to accommodate not merely a congregation of human beings but whole trains—offers a problem fairly simple in its programme, but on a scale large enough to tax the resources of the most skilful of modern engineers with all the advantage of modern applications of steel to structural purposes.

The Gare d'Orleans was built in about 1903 and at that time the principle of using electrical traction upon the railway lines was adopted within the city of Paris in order to avoid the bad effects of smoke in the city, not to mention in the stations themselves. More recently, this system has been adopted in New York. The Pennsylvania Railway Station, New York, is one of the most costly projects of this kind that has been undertaken on this continent. The waiting halls of these stations afford fine opportunities as places of interest; that at the Pennsylvania Railway Terminal is on the model of the lounge room of a Roman bath. In the Gare d'Orleans, the opportunity is taken to make an exhibition gallery for photographs of places of special picturesqueness and interest accessible by the Paris-Orleans line. The great artist, G.F. Watts, offered as a gift to the nation to paint great pictures to decorate the walls of Euston Station, London.

Closely connected with railway stations are those adjuncts of modern travel, the hotels often enough combined in one building with the stations. Of course hotels are a very old invention, but our railways have occasioned a type of building very different from anything of olden days. A modern railway hotel is a city of transients who, whether they like it or not, and whether they can properly speaking afford it or not, must be treated in magnificent style. They are provided with such dining halls, reading rooms, writing rooms, ball rooms, drawing rooms, boudoirs and smoking rooms as kings and queens have not in their palaces. The guests number many hundreds and every little need of each must be quickly provided. Hence the multiplication of elevators, call bells, telephones and every convenience of service. And as I have suggested, at the peril of the life of the whole grand institution, the kitchen arrangements and service must be above suspicion. The most essentially modern feature about a hotel, however, is its rotunda or lounge hall, which in favourable circumstances becomes a market or forum where men meet from all the earth either to exchange good cheer or to deliver their views to the world through the channel of the newspaper reporter. Amongst hotels themselves there are many specialisations. There are hotels specially adapted for tourists, like those in the Rockies; there are residential hotels which are apartment houses with services supplied; and commercial hotels and so on.

When our modern restless peoples do come to a comparatively settled state, one of their chief concerns is those offices in which is done the business fostered by machinery and railways. These office buildings are, as I have said, the most prominent objects in any modern city, and great is the effort and expense which is put into them. Much of this no doubt is mere advertising display, too much concentrated upon the hope thereby to increase [sale of] goods [rather than] to awaken much joy of any deeper kind. Yet mingled with this flagrant sumptuousness of which in our more reflective moments we are half ashamed, there is a good deal of sound reason and good sense.

The marbles, terra cottas, tiles, etc., that are so lavishly used keep things clean and wholesome and are in themselves fair to look upon. Offices are, of course, often highly specialised, and of these specific purposes, the banks are the most modern and most magnificent. The Bank of Montreal in Montreal claims to have the most magnificent banking hall in the world, whilst its neighbour, the Canadian Bank of Commerce, runs it fairly close. For these halls, the marble quarries of the continent are ransacked. Chiefly for the requirements of banks, the art of working in bronze has been revived and brought to a high pitch of technical perfection.

Whilst there are offices for special purposes, we have arrived at a wholesale way of designing and building offices. These are built with long corridors, with long galleries alongside, and the galleries may be divided up into rooms of greater or lesser length to suit the tenants. This unit system of planning is largely applied in those most remarkable developments of modern building, the skyscrapers. The sheer size of these buildings calls for their equipment with so many conveniences within their walls, for it is a long journey from the top of one to the top of another one just across the street. Some of them are said to be able to sustain their very considerable population for some days if their doors should be for that time closed for all exit or entrance.

The structure of these buildings is a matter of engineering rather than of architecture. Their chief defect as objects of delight to the eye is their liability to be mere fragments, well-finished indeed on one side or on two if they happen to stand at a corner. The other two or three sides are apt to be built with no more serious intention to appear well than are the packing cases to which Mr. H.G. Wells has likened the collection of New York skyscrapers. Packing cases indeed, which may conjure up to the imagination rare goods as their contents. As achievements, they are of the same nature, though perhaps hardly such complete and admirable triumphs, as are the great Atlantic liners of the present day. These liners themselves, as regards their internal design at least, might be fair to claim as examples of modern architecture. Floating palaces, as the common phrase expresses it.

The greatly increased density of population, itself resulting from increased capacity of production and transportation, has necessitated a great system of government and public service with corresponding buildings. Parliament buildings, municipal buildings, buildings for various departments of government, law courts, police stations, prisons (unfortunately), and fire stations. The larger of these buildings are striking examples of the complexity of modern planning. Post offices are a testimony to the tremendous exchange of correspondence and private transactions in small things. A glance at the chief post office of a modern large city impresses one with the power of the penny stamp.

The number of classes of public buildings continues steadily to increase. To preserve the health of our citizens under the artificial conditions of city life, we have athletic clubs with their gymnasiums and we have public swimming baths. The designing of halls entirely adapted to highly specialised ends like this results often in new and beautiful forms. To equip our people mentally for the problems of the day, we have schools of many kinds: museums, public schools, high schools, art schools, universities and technical schools. On the outstanding requirements of these as buildings I need say no more, but may I be permitted to say something about the bearing of the technical school upon architecture and upon the modern situation generally.

What are the real inducements to good building rather than bad, and to architecture rather than mere utilitarian building? If a man has horses or cows that he greatly values, he will take care to have his stables skilfully built of the most suitable materials so as to keep his animals in good health and good condition. If he is an enthusiast on the subject, he will do things a little better than merely well, out of sheer pride in his possessions. If a man values his wife or his children, he will naturally be still more desirous to have their house well-built and provided with all that will preserve their health and promote their well-being in every respect and aid them in being beautiful and pleasant. If he is an enthusiast on this subject, he will not be satisfied unless his home is a delight to them and to himself. If a man is proud of his city, he will want to see clean, healthy, cheerful streets and buildings. He will not be satisfied with poor materials and bad workmanship. Good materials and the right way of using them are the first things to be desired in all buildings public or private. They are the first essentials in all the arts. They are the starting point for all that civilisation clothes itself in, for all that adorns life.

To know and to make good materials and to learn and perform good workmanship is the first aim of technical education. There is in this country too little training in the trades, too little desire to be trained to produce good handiwork, too little of that joy in the highly skilled work of one's hands, which becomes to the honest craftsman a source of mental training and contentment. This state of things arises naturally enough in Alberta from the newness and rapidly developing condition of the province. Immigration provides us with a fair number of skilful artisans. But the children of these men generally want to make their living with their coats on in the less productive occupations of the middlemen of business. Hence, we seem always to remain dependent on the importation of the stranger in this matter, without making any endeavour to be self-supporting.

A technical school will be a great public benefit if it can be made to inspire respect for handiwork and promote the growth of a class of skilful artisans amongst the sons of the province for it will thereby be establishing one of the most profitable, employable, intelligent and enthusiastic classes of citizens, whose work will be a perpetual and valuable contribution to all the amenities of civilised life.

Let me conclude by again referring to what I said near the beginning of my remarks, that there is no art where development depends less upon the professional practitioner than that of architecture. All progress, and indeed each individual successful work, must spring from the peoples' love for their homes, their pride in their city and their country. If a people is without dignity, or delicacy, or vigour, or gaiety, or any other quality in its outlook upon home and country, it will be vain for the individual architect to work into his buildings a semblance of such qualities. Such an attempt would appear for what it is—a superficial make-believe. But if those qualities do exist in the people of a community, and they are enthusiastic about them, they will appear in their works if only there exist skilful workers to execute the work.

The function of the architect is simply to form an essential link in the process of translating the social aspirations of a people into visible forms. Architecture, towards which all trades and arts are contributory streams, is at the same time homage offered to our ideals in life and a material aid to their realisation and advance. It is a case of mutual reaction. By translating our abstract ideals into concrete form, we lay firmer hold upon them and rise upon them as on stepping stones to higher things. It is the end of architecture to give to the best we can think or feel in public or in private life a local habitation and thereby give them an express reality. By its aid, we not only think fine ideals, we bring them into our life of everyday. The simple means towards these fine ends is to cultivate the love and appropriate use of the beautiful materials that lie plentifully to our hands, the appreciation at its true high value of the skilled workman's hand and brain, and the application of these to the objects of our worthy pride.

LANTERN SLIDES, *Modern Architecture*

1. New Federal Capital, Canberra, Australia (1912)
2. Station, Washington, Plan
3. Station, Washington, Interior
4. Pennsylvania Railway Terminal [New York], Plan
5. Pennsylvania Railway Terminal [New York], Exterior
6. Pennsylvania Railway Terminal [New York], Waiting Hall
7. Pennsylvania Railway Terminal [New York], Concourse
8. Gare d'Orleans Railway Terminal [Paris], Interior
9. Vanderbilt Hotel, New York, plans
10. Vanderbilt Hotel, New York, view
11. Chateau Laurier [Hotel], Ottawa, plans
12. Chateau Laurier [Hotel], Ottawa, view
13. Royal Automobile Club, London, plan
14. Royal Automobile Club, London, section
15. Royal Automobile Club, London, view
16. Broadway, sky-scrapers
17. Woolworth Building, New York, view
18. Canadian Bank of Commerce, Montreal
19. Palais de Justice, Brussels
20. Parliament Building, Regina, plan
21. Parliament Building, Regina, view
22. Parliament Building, Winnipeg, plan
23. Parliament Building, Winnipeg, view
24. Municipal Offices, New York, view
25. Post Office, New York, view
26. Toronto General Hospital, view & block plan
27. Virchow Hospital, Berlin, plan
28. Virchow Hospital, Berlin, view in grounds
29. Operating Theatre, Dusseldorf, interior

30. Hammersmith Public Baths, interior of pool
31. National Gallery, London, Extension
32. Musée Galerie, Paris, Exterior
33. Opéra, Paris, front
34. Congressional Library, Washington, Plan
35. Congressional Library, Washington, view
36. Congressional Library, Washington, interior
37. Columbia University Library
38. King Edward VII School, Montreal, plans
39. King Edward VII School, Montreal, view
40. Britannia Royal Naval College, Dartmouth, plan
41. Britannia Royal Naval College, Dartmouth, view
42. Britannia Royal Naval College, Dartmouth, view
43. Toronto Technical School, plan

NOTES

1. See list of slides at end of the document.
2. Notation in text: "public health, city planning; city by-laws."
3. Hand written in margin: "leaded glass, window bars, plate glass, mirrors."
4. Presumably he is quoting a standard clause used in architectural specifications.

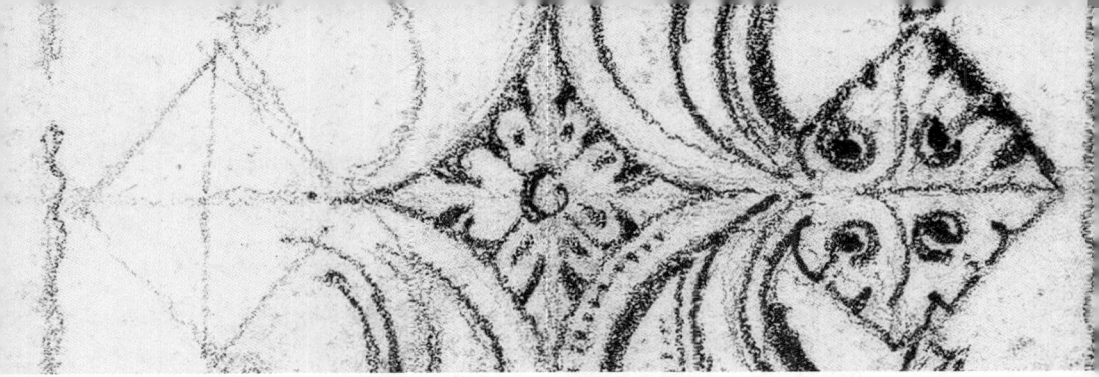

DOCUMENT 7

The Town

As Canadian cities grew rapidly in the late 1800s and early 1900s, the need for urban planning became apparent. The new understanding about the importance of hygiene and public health, combined with concerns about social order and stability in growing cities, led to various approaches and proposals to control or regulate urban growth. This task was not only administrative—it also involved the instilling of a new urban culture in popular thinking. Moreover, planning proponents were often divided on how to achieve the goal of more orderly, safe and efficient urban spaces and often became diverted by visions of grandeur in which the city became a space for monumental buildings and streets that expressed fantasies of civic power. Such imperial plans, like the one for Calgary that the English town planner Thomas Mawson published in 1914, were anachronistic before the ink had dried on them because of the immense costs of their implementation.

By World War I, urban planning began to move towards a more practical approach to making cities more functional. For critics such as Burgess, beauty (which was often expressed as picturesqueness and lacking in clutter) remained a practical goal of urban planning but could never be divorced from utility and efficiency. Nor could it be divorced from architecture, because both town planning and architecture were concerned with balancing expression, purpose and function with the use of materials and the social and economic needs of society.

Document 7 is a talk on Radio Station CKUA, June 4, 1928.
71.213, file 155, UAA.

LAST MONDAY I spoke about "The Home."[1] Today my subject is "The Town," not omitting to say something about the country too, for towns are, after all, only little spots in the country. It is of course the appearance of the town in which I am particularly interested, and more especially in the towns of our western Canadian provinces. We have in Canada some fine cities of which any country in the world might be proud—Quebec, Montreal, Ottawa, Winnipeg, Vancouver; but it is of our smaller towns I wish to speak. Have we the same reason to be proud of them? I think not. There is beginning to be felt an uneasiness about them. During the last sessions of the legislatures both of Saskatchewan and Alberta, acts were framed with a view to their improvement, and in British Columbia efforts are being made to make effective a recent Town Planning Act.

What is the matter with our towns then? Why should we want to make them better? How is this to be done? I read this in a paper published in Ottawa: "The new Alberta Town and Rural Planning Bill seems to be a legislative response to Premier Brownlee's vigorously expressed distress, after his European tour, at the debasement of the country-side in all directions by hideous advertising signs and by irresponsible building." Now town and country in Europe are on the whole much more beautiful than we see in our western provinces, but there are influences at work—"hideous advertising" and "irresponsible building"—which are threatening the beauty even of these, and we have the same influences at work in our own town and country, and we can much less afford to let them take hold here.

I said there is much more beauty in European towns. This is especially the case with the smaller and older ones, which in very many cases have a charm that, once seen, makes them linger in the memory so that they become a joy forever. Why is this? Some will say that it is their wonderful natural surroundings. Put one of our western towns in the same surroundings and you will find that it has no charm at all, it would only disfigure the surroundings. What is wrong then? Largely, "hideous advertisement" and "irresponsible building." It is not a question, remember, of these old world towns having more ornament about their buildings. They have very often *none at all* and almost always less than a quarter of what our towns have, and yet they are lovely and ours—well, just look at them.

Even the natural advantages are not all on the side of the old world towns—when you consider our soil and our climate. The artificial advantages are generally on the side of our own when you consider that they start on a fairly clean slate with no natural obstructions and are well served with road, rail and public utilities. Is it possible then for us to make our towns beauty spots, a delight to the eyes? I have no doubt at all that it is quite possible and that the principal thing needed is that we should really intend to make them so, but as a rule we don't do much serious intending of this sort.

We are apt to think that the principal object of towns is to increase and multiply and to furnish their people with bread and money. Why should we spend thought and perhaps even some money—there is really more thought than money needed—in having our towns delightful to look at and to live in? One reason amongst many is that these towns are the home towns of Canada's own native children. Their surroundings have a large share in the making of their minds. You might as well expect children brought up in careless untidy homes to be good housekeepers as expect

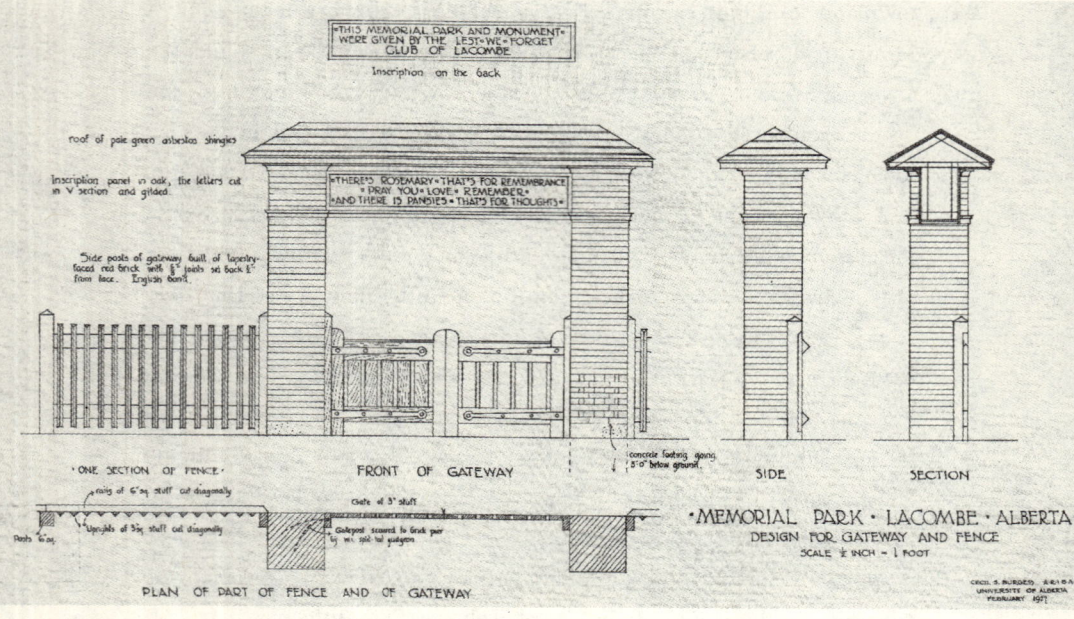

Burgess designed this entranceway to the town park in Lacombe, Alberta in 1927. The structure was apparently not built. (71.213-246, UAA)

them when brought up in unlovable towns to be good citizens. Look at your town and ask whether your children will have good reason in later life to look back on it with delight. Now what is really wrong with our towns and what is the way to go about making them better?

I shall first mention a few general points that would perhaps occur to anyone who sets about thinking upon this subject and that will apply about equally to all our small towns. After that, I shall say something as to how to go about getting things made better.

Every town has certain natural starting points from which to work in civic improvement. The planting of trees and the placing and arrangement of gardens, shrubs and flowers are great and inexpensive means toward making a better town. Every town should arrange its affairs so that proper provision for this should be made every year. There should be at least one street boulevarded for a certain distance, and every town should have at least one small park right in the town merely for rest and beauty's sake, even if it be but an acre or two fenced in, or better still, hedged in sufficiently to prevent it becoming a mere dog-run. This, in grass with trees around it and with a few seats, will be an asset to the town worth more than the money that is spent on it. It can be made much more of, for it can be made delightful in a score of ways with flowering shrubs, picturesque gateways, arbours and shady walks.

If you will imagine a group of towns competing as to which shall have the most pleasant town garden, you will realise that this is a subject of endless variety even in small spaces. Towns do compete against one another in baseball and hockey matches, and these are followed with much enthusiasm and do their part in keeping up mutual interest and good relationships. Competitions in town gardens would be of still greater and more permanent service, for each citizen every day, at least all summer time, would benefit by having his life made so much the more pleasant.

My next point is that every town has, or may have, a special business centre which we may call, even in a small town, the civic centre. Here should be the town hall, the fire hall, the bank, the principal hotel. It only requires a little less of our irresponsible building to give this a tidy, well regulated arrangement. Let me ask you to imagine this done and each important building fitting its place and put in a good setting. Will not this be to the advantage of each and to the advantage of the town? The way to manage this I shall come to later. I wish to mention one more very important point about all towns—their gateways—the railway station and the entrance to the town upon the principal roads that serve it.

As regards the railway station—the railways have already generally recognised their duty in this respect. Indeed, so well do they do this that in crossing our wide provinces by the greater lines, it is all too obvious that in 90 per cent of the towns where we stop the station garden alone absorbs the attention of the passenger who gets out to exercise his limbs and take in a fresh supply of ozone.[2] This is all to the credit of the railways. Now the station is the main gateway of the town, so that each of these towns has a good start-off. Why not play up to it? A little regulation each year would,

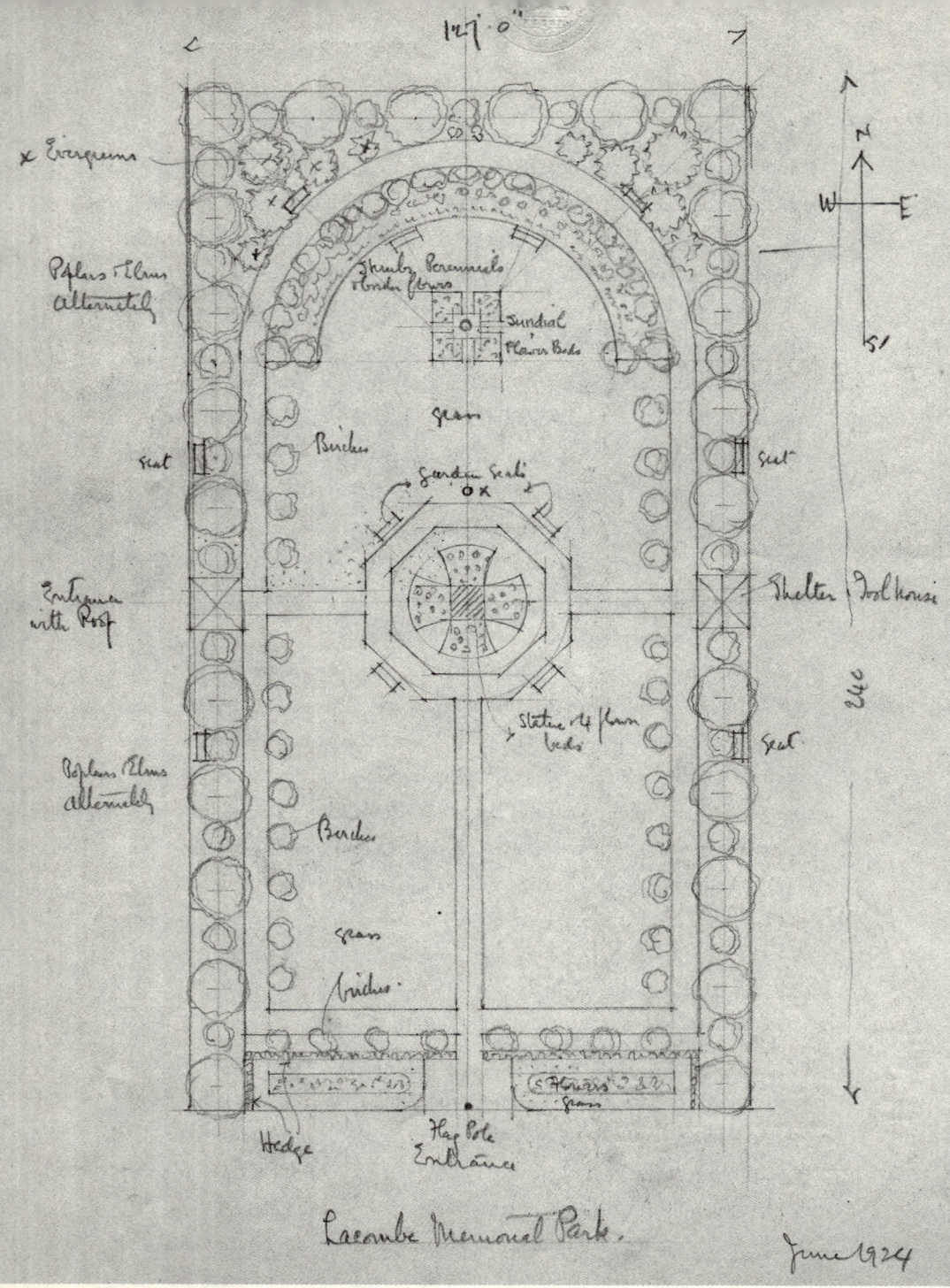

Burgess saw parks as centres for the development of civil society in urban areas of all types. His 1924 plan for a park in Lacombe was implemented by the town as part of its memorial for the dead of World War I. (71.213-193-3, UAA)

in a few years, make the whole view from the platform beyond the station garden something that would draw the weary passenger's eye with delight.

Perhaps if you think of the one to half-a-dozen towns with which you are most intimately acquainted with, their impossible jumble of scrappy irreconcilable buildings [would make you] inclined to think that what I am proposing may be a pretty ideal but quite impracticable in these particular cases. My answer is, first, that serious intention of doing better [is what is needed], and that is all there is to your "impracticable" theory. Second, the thing itself is not only practicable but not even very difficult nor very expensive; for even when buildings are hopelessly crude and ugly, trees and bushes judiciously planted may clothe and screen them in such a way as to create beauty out of ugliness. Third, that if these things were made a matter of civic interest and general discussion, building owners would soon, for their own interest and credit, co-operate in a scheme which they were convinced was a good one.

The railway station is the main gateway to the town. There are others on the main roads. You like the farmer-people to come in on certain days of the week. Have their entrances a cheering aspect? If they have not, then you are not as hospitable and welcoming as you should be. A good deal might be said about the tourists—always increasing in numbers—who pass through your town in cars. They and their impressions are worth thinking about, but as my time is short I feel that I can leave you to do all the thinking about this. I am really more concerned about the inhabitants.

Before I discuss the way to go about improving the town, I should like to say something about the streets and buildings themselves. I have already mentioned the importance of boulevarding and planting of trees and giving a natural setting to the buildings. Now in small towns most of the buildings are frame buildings and are painted. What colour should they be painted? There are some wrong ways of painting buildings and there are quite a number of right ways. I am going to make a suggestion which many will think surprising, perhaps disappointing, [and] some may even think it is wrong, but I have great confidence that it is right. I think that each town should have its own characteristic colour or combination of two harmonious colours, not too exclusively used of course, but so as to keep the place in harmony and be its characteristic. We are so individualistic that when a man occupying one of a group of houses considers what colour he shall paint his house, he generally decides to make it quite different from his neighbour's. I think, however good his intentions, his decision is quite wrong and that this is the source of much of the uncomfortable discord in colour in our towns. When houses are very much alike, distinguish them by minor differences. If your door is blue and your neighbour's is red, it is enough, there will be no chance of mistake. Another suggestion is that painting should be done to suit winter conditions. If houses look well in snow time when trees are bare, they will be all right in summer for nature is very kind in this respect, her painting is faultless in harmony.

The last and most distressing subject [is] those "hideous advertisements" that I mentioned. Advertising has become a real disease with us. It has its uses, its place, its proper forms, but it has ceased to recognise all these. Much of our advertising is of no use, goes quite out of its proper place, and takes forms that are an offence. I am persuaded that this disease is quite curable, and the cure lies in public opinion reasonably and firmly expressed. I have often walked along a town street taking note of the signs over the shops. That a people with any taste in colour and form—and we are a people with such taste—can commit such crimes is hard to understand. Not one in ten has the colour of its background; still fewer are harmonious with the building on which they are placed, and still fewer are made to fit the spaces they occupy. They project over the windows above and sprawl out in every way they should not. Now any sign maker knows better than that. These men have a pride in their work and a knowledge of simple harmonies. I know it is not their fault. As for the architects, I have seen some of my own buildings defiled with advertisements so that I feel sore that I wasted my time on them, and I had left suitable spaces for the signs too.

Look along the principal street of your town and I think you will agree that the way the signs are mishandled is the most disfiguring thing you will see. In the country, advertising signs are also a disease. But here I

In both city and town, Burgess decried the haphazard ways signs were placed on buildings. This example from Calgary in 1938 was typical of conditions throughout the country. (NA-3557-4, GA)

think the indications are more hopeful. Let me read what an English magazine says about some recent legislation concerning filling stations and gasoline advertisements. It says,

> At present, the Advertisement Regulation Acts do not touch advertisements dealing with the trade carried on in premises where they are exhibited. Consequently, filling stations are commonly plastered over with glaring signs and disorderly arrays of white globes. As the new amendment cannot come into action at once, petrol companies have still time to make a virtue of a necessity by voluntarily withdrawing the signs which every motorist condemns. A lead was given in 1924 by the Royal Auto Club, the Shell, Anglo-American Oil, British Petroleum and Dunlop companies agreeing to remove their road signs. Within the last few weeks, moreover, the Shell company has

The increased use of automobiles brought new commerce to the countryside. It also often brought cluttered and aggressive advertising such as on the Bowfort Service Station and Tea Room on the Calgary-Banff highway near Morley, Alberta. This photo was taken between 1930 and 1933. (NA–2555–3, GA)

decided to issue no more garage display signs and to withdraw the whole of its present advertisements, of which 500 have already been withdrawn. That is a far-sighted as well as a spirited action. Far more motorists will be induced to use a particular brand of spirit by a courteous reticence than are persuaded by an offensive display of signs. If the other big companies, the quality of whose spirit everybody knows, follow the lead, advertisement signs will soon be the token only of inferior substitutes.

This sentiment is the sure cure of the disease of offensive advertising.

Now I come to the point about what to do in order to improve our towns. I have said that the legislatures of British Columbia, Alberta and Saskatchewan have all been passing town planning acts. I will take the case of Alberta. Some years ago Alberta passed a Town Planning Act and it didn't seem to do the least bit of good.[3] So now another act has been passed called the Alberta Town and Rural Planning Bill. Will that also do no good? That depends entirely on you, the town resident. It has not come into force yet.

It shall come in force upon proclamation of the Lieutenant-Governor in Council. What does that mean? It means, I suppose, that if nobody seems anxious for it, its proclamation may be indefinitely delayed. What does the Act provide that would make anyone anxious to have it in force? It provides for the appointment of a Town and Rural Planning Advisory Board and this I think is the hopeful thing for this reason.

When any person or group of persons in any town becomes anxious to improve their town, there is always the question as to a scheme to follow. It may be proposed that a special town planner be called in to draw up a plan of improvements. This man, generally a stranger to the town, with no special interest in its financial capacities, prepares a plan which may contain excellent ideas, but they are beyond the financial capacity of the town to undertake seriously. The plan is paid for but the work is dropped. This is no imaginary case; it has often happened and, still oftener I suppose, the initial expense of engaging a town planner has prevented any steps at all being taken. Now if this [Town and Rural Planning] Advisory Board were appointed, towns would know where to go to for advice. The advisors would be sympathetic with their financial condition. Their own reputation would stand or fall by the practical results they could provide. The towns of the whole province would be under their care. They would adapt their advice to conditions with which it would be their business to acquaint themselves. This looks like a very hopeful procedure

Will this scheme work in practice? That depends on the public, that is to say, on whether the people in the towns have a real desire for improvement or not. The government is apparently prepared to do its part, and it is now up to the man in the street. My advice now is to "be the man in the street." Go out into the street of your own town. Take a walk all over it. Notice whether your bosom swells with pride at everything you see there; whether you can imagine anything better anywhere. This is the necessary first step and the one that counts most. It is quite an obvious and simple test of the excellence of your town. It is also the most severe test possible because it is measuring the real against the ideal. But do you really think that you or anyone else is going to get any farther forward without carrying out this simple test? I think not. But if everyone begins doing this with the government machinery all ready, as it is to help things on, do you think it will be long before things are made better? This is emphatically a matter where the opinion, and more that that, the desires and demands, of the man in the street is the thing that counts. On this depends whether the legislation that has been passed is to remain a dead letter or not. Opportunity is now knocking at the gates of the western towns. Will they rise to take it? Or do they really not care?

NOTES

1. "The Home" (71.213, file 141, UAA) was delivered May 28, 1928. It is not reprinted since it repeated many of the broad concepts in Document 4, "The Old House and the New."
2. Gardens at railway stations were a common feature of many small prairie towns. Maintained by the railway agent, the gardens were designed to create a pleasant environment for travelers and to promote knowledge of the fertility of the region (Ronald Rees, *New and Naked Land. Making the Prairies Home* (Saskatoon: Western Producer Prairie Books, 1988), 118–19, and Edwina von Bayer, *Rhetoric and Roses, A History of Canadian Gardening 1900–1930* (Markham: Fitzhenry and Whiteside, 1984), 14–33).
3. Burgess is referring to the 1913 Alberta town planning legislation by which towns were given wide power to plan in a number of important respects. All plans had to be approved by the provincial government. Regulations were not drafted until 1915 by which time the war was absorbing all energy and the real estate market had collapsed. Municipal financing problems of the early 1920s prevented any further attention to planning. For these reasons, the original legislation was a dead letter.

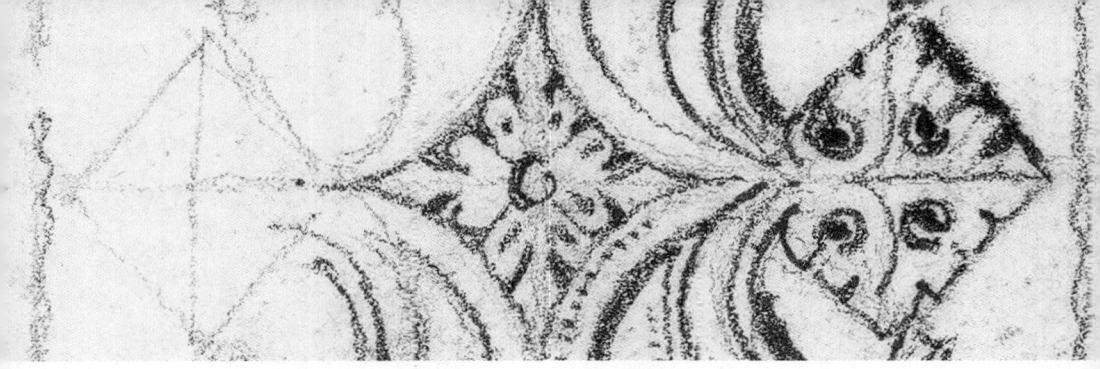

DOCUMENT 8

Civic Pride

BURGESS'S CONVICTION *that architecture arose from a society's needs and priorities led him to support the view that architecture reflected the culture and beliefs of the society that produced it. In part, the logic of this argument presumed that a society needed pride in itself and a consciousness of those things that were, in his words, of "real worth" because these values would be reflected in its buildings and streetscapes.*

In this talk, Burgess argued that great cities were made by effort and did not just happen. This was a conventional argument at the time—boards of trade and civic boosters everywhere in North America argued much the same in their claims that through collective effort towns could become cities, and middling cities could become great global centres. Burgess did not support such a crude equation, nor did he endorse the view common among business promoters that the best measure of the success of a city was the growth of population, industry and bank clearances. He did, nonetheless, draw from the same rhetorical tradition in his assertion that if people developed a collective responsibility for their environment and took pride in it, they would be striving to make their town or city the best and most beautiful that it could be.

*Document 8 is a talk on Radio Station CKUA, May 27, 1929.
71.213, file 156, UAA.*

I HAVE BEEN ASKED to talk on some subject in which I am interested and I have chosen civic pride, although I feel that some hard-working member of a town council would have a much better right to speak on this subject than I have. It is indeed on behalf of the many men who do work hard for the benefit of their towns and cities that I should like to make appeal.

I am sorry to say that my interest in civic pride does not arise from any great efforts I have made to practice it, but simply from the admiration which its results have aroused in me; for it has been my lot to travel fairly widely, to see many admirable cities and to hear and to read what the citizens of these cities have to say of them. Each has its own particular excellence and each has behind it a long story of struggle and varied fortunes. Every one of them has arisen from small and little considered beginnings and now [they] stand as a great inspiration and a joy to all who come from them and to all who visit them. What is this civic pride which has produced these fine results?

It is a peculiar thing about pride that it is both a vice and a virtue. It is a vice when it is a self-gratification over worthless matters. It is a virtue when it is a feeling of satisfaction over what is of real worth. And there is no place you can draw the line between the two for all objects of desire have some worth—it is only a matter of less and more. We say to one person, "do not be so proud" and to another, for goodness sake, "have a little pride." To have a "little pride" helps an individual to strike out for himself, to make efforts and to amount to something. In the little circle of the family, family pride leads its members to check one another up, to give mutual support to one another, and gives strength to each member greater than he could have alone. If we look on civic pride as an extension of the same principle, we can realise how it has come to build up mighty and famous cities. The principle of "each for all and all for each" is the same motive force as that which transforms a discordant helpless mob into a disciplined army fit to accomplish a great purpose. Here is a vast natural resource of greater potentiality than all our water powers if we could only direct it to its most advantageous ends.

Speaking, as I do, from Edmonton, Alberta, I have in mind more especially the small cities and towns of our western provinces for in western Canada we have no large cities except Winnipeg and Vancouver. I think it is true to say that all our towns are only at their small beginnings, a stage which, as I have said, all the great cities of the world have gone through—some of them many centuries ago. It is all the more important therefore that our towns should have a proper pride. I think it is quite fortunate that most of them have some pride and are not in that deplorable condition in which they would need to have to be asked to "have a little pride." Perhaps a stranger from some great old city might be amused at the boosting and whooping some of us make about our little tin-pot affairs. But in any case it is better to have ambitions and to make efforts than to have none, and I would respectfully invite the stranger to lend the help of his wider knowledge and superior experience. Many of them indeed do so with excellent effect.

In spite of a little cheerful boosting and whooping now and then, this tremendous natural resource, this wonderful motive force of civic pride, remains for the most part totally undeveloped and runs mostly to waste. It is more difficult to harness and direct than the Ghost River or the Spray Lakes.[1] There are two obvious reasons for this: first, it is difficult to realise the importance and the possibilities of it and, second, it is difficult to realise the exact points at which our individual efforts may be effectively applied. The fact is that it is not the individual effort that counts, it is the community effort. The part of the individual is co-operation. The inspiration that will effect this co-operation is civic pride.

The ways in which cities have shown their great ambitions are many and various. What concerns us is to set clearly before us what objects we most want to aim at, and to see what we can do about them. This is such a simple thing that every one can and ought to do it and to do it pretty constantly. It is so easy to neglect to do it that I am afraid most of us must plead guilty to the neglect. Suppose each of us were asked to write down clearly and simply, "What do you consider the points about life in your town which make it a good place to live in? What suggestions can you make to improve it and what are you personally doing to make things better?" Surely there is nothing unfair about these questions. Is it not up to everyone to ask them of himself, and to answer in his own way, for his own town? There is no town without some good citizens who, having asked themselves these questions, and answered them in their own way, are eagerly working for their city's good—often with little enough thanks. Do we back up these people and co-operate with them all we can?

The basis of civic pride must be interest in our town; interest in all the activities of all the people. So that if we are to develop any pride in the town, we must know what these activities are and we must interest ourselves intensely and practically in them. For that reason it is our business to take a look around and see what people are doing and how they are doing it, with a view to seeing how, by our interest and co-operation, we can help them to do it a little better.

What are the objects that we are to aim at? We wish to make our town a good one to live in. It is a great object of every town to see that business flourishes, that everyone is working and everyone is reaping a fair reward for his work. In order to get on to this prosperous basis and keep it when we get there, there are three prime necessities about a town. These are that its people should be healthy, happy and intelligent. Without these, a city cannot be a good place to live in—with them it cannot be a bad place. These three points can be put under one word "health": health of body, of sentiment, and of intellect. I don't think we shall go far wrong then if we start out by considering that health and all the things that relate to it should be the first consideration in our civic ambitions. This of course suggests a hundred practical matters—good water, good food, good drains, good housing, good habits, good clothing, good occupation, good recreation and good everything-about-the-place. On this first simple point there is enough material for practical thinking to keep every man, woman and child on the think for the rest of their lives.

Civic pride demands a certain amount of enthusiasm and there are many good things, especially those we find ourselves tolerably well supplied with, about which it would be pretty hard to rouse a general enthusiasm. We may like well enough to have good water but our enthusiasm about it is likely to be of a perfectly sober description. What are the things which our towns are likely to get a little roused-up about and which will make for health, happiness and intelligence?

I should think it will be at once agreed that the most valuable property pertaining to a city or town is its people. What pride and enthusiasm can we have or ought we to have in our townspeople? We are all accustomed to one form of enthusiasm of this sort—that about athletic sports. We have all local athletic teams who pay visits to neighbouring towns in friendly rivalry. Surely this tends to promote health, happiness and good sentiment and to maintain enthusiasm. It may be said that this is no very important part of a town's activities and is no great exhibition of civic pride; that a great deal of time is wasted in our day on sports that might be much better employed. There is some truth in this. Yet the basis of sport is so sound that I think it really quite an important matter. We are apt to think rather poorly or, what is just as bad, to think not at all about the other fellow in some other town, but when we have striven with him, even in a friendly manner, and he has shown himself no mean antagonist, we immediately do think of him in a fairly respectful way. Small affair though it may be, sport today forms a pretty keen rival to the League of Nations in fostering the peace of the world.

What is the relation of sport to civic pride? What should be the attitude of good citizens to it? I should say that they should see to it that their teams are their own boys and girls, their own men and women. Hireling teams can bring but little honour to a city. Further, it should be a matter of civic pride that our teams should "play the game" not merely to win but to show themselves "good sports." If these teams realise that their townsmen watch them keenly with that expectation, then they will live up to that expectation and will become such citizens as we can take pride in.

As regards the possible waste of time in sports, I wish to point out a certain truth in the charge. Skill in many of our sports involves a fine training of hand and eye, a careful and accurate analyses of movement and method acquired by long and painstaking practice. Imagine, if the many who devote themselves to this sort of thing should instead devote themselves with equal enthusiasm to something that would delight many others and even produce work that should be permanent. For example, if they applied this devotion to music, to painting, to sculpture, to literature, or even to humbler handicrafts, what a volume of admirable work would be produced. I venture to say that if the citizens of our comparatively small city could put this in practice for one generation they would make a name for themselves, not only throughout the world but for all time. It is because something like this once happened in them that the names of Athens and of Florence stand first and second in the world's scroll of fame. I do not point this out in the expectation that it will happen to us, but to support my contention that civic pride is a motive force of unimaginable potentiality.

If sports are after all a comparatively unimportant matter, what are the really important concerns of a town? As soon as a community is able to collect and to spend money in a corporate way, the first object to demand attention is the case of those who are unable or less able to look after themselves. Schools have to be provided for the children, hospitals for the sick and provision must be made for the old and for the poor. But a city does not exist merely to look after the poor and sick or even the schooling of children. Along with these there must be occupation and entertainment for the well and the strong and the grown up. Sickness and poverty are, we hope, abnormal. What do the normal citizens require, for if they do not get what they require, they are liable to become sick or abnormal too. The city is after all a place to grow up in, to keep well in, to enjoy life in.

The existence of any community depends absolutely on the work that its people do, whether industrial, commercial or professional, and if a city can produce work of special distinction, it is justly proud of it. The work of a community is the service of the community. We like to command cheap and efficient service. We shall not get it unless we can secure the facilities and conditions which alone will enable the workers to produce it. As pride may be a virtue or a vice, so work may be a blessing or a curse. It is a curse when its necessity is imposed on us under conditions that leave no room for self-respect. When treated with due consideration and respect it is a blessing. Work is the true sport of men, and the game must be played in the spirit of sport; by no means an easy matter under our competitive system.

The general good fellowship which is the first condition of civic pride would seem in theory to do away with any necessity for repression of ill-will. In practice it is always found that law and order must be preserved by means of some compulsion. Prevalence of misbehaviour will be a stain on the reputation of any city and a disease eating into the happiness and concord of city life. In modern days it is becoming more and more clearly recognised that discontent and crime have their causes, which have their reasonable and scientific treatments [and] that mere punishment and repression deal only superficially with the symptoms and do not remove the causes of the disease. It should be our pride and duty as citizens that we are protected in our enjoyment of life, not merely by the physical powers of the limbs of the law, but by goodwill and sound reason applied to all classes of our people. When a certain class of people for whom life is not too easy find that they are frankly praised for whatsoever good they do, and blamed only for the bad they do, there is an inducement created for them to tend toward the better. When they feel they get all the kicks and none of the halfpence, then they feel they are not admitted to the good company and form gangs of their own.

I do not know to what extent foreign elements collecting in certain localities are a danger in our western Canadian towns, but the cure for this is obvious—that is, to make them feel that they are "of us" by offering a welcome into our own enjoyments. There must be some halfway meeting, some approach from both sides. It would be hardly fair to leave it all to them. Seeing that these people have wholesome instincts and joys of their own, one must frankly admit their right to their own happiness. If, because of our different upbringing and circumstances, we cannot altogether share in their peculiar happinesses, we need not frown upon them. These will do neither us nor them any harm, they will tend to the common good and goodwill. We have to insist, it is true, upon the use of our language, for the lack of this divides a people and we cannot afford to permit so serious a cause of division. This is a sacrifice that we must ask of them.

Conditions of work, law, order, united interests and sentiment: these are all underlying necessities of good citizenship. What are some of the results that we may fairly expect to be built upon these foundations—that will make cities we can be proud of? A very great number of these may be said to be matters of "recreation."

At first this word "recreation" may sound too trivial. If we divide it in two and call it re-creation, it will perhaps sound even too grand. I have already said something about physical health. What I now mean to speak of is matters of mental health; the things that re-create, that feed and invigorate our minds, and I don't mean our intellects only, but our feelings and good sentiments; the things that make us broad-minded, that widen our interests, that keep our sentiments alive and active, that make us more human and sympathetic. There is a class of these things. What are they? What represents them in our cities?

Let us take one of them. I think it will be admitted that reading good literature is distinctly one of them. But reading is apt to be a lonesome rather than a social occupation. It becomes social when it takes the form of reading aloud to the common enjoyment of a number of people. Let us take another, music. This is almost essentially a social recreation. If we continue to make a list of them, we shall find that they may all be classed as "arts" and we must be prepared to find that there are not just five or six arts. There are at least a hundred, many of which have no special names. Their enjoyment, and their production, is not confined to a few so called artistic individuals. All people are artists in one way or another. Everything that can be done to make this earth, our home, more of a home and an enjoyable place is an art. There is an art in everything we do or make.

Amongst our young people there are those who are eager to be good speakers, good musicians, good singers. All such should be encouraged by citizens who wish their town to amount to anything. Encouragement does not mean the giving of prizes, though these may have their use. Public encouragement means intelligent interest, intelligent comment and keen criticism of the performance. Just as at a game every little point is appreciated and discussed, so must these things be discussed. No falseness of tone or sentiment should be allowed to pass without some attempt at correction. We wish to be proud of our cities' best products and therefore we must see to it that they will stand the criticism of the world.

All matters of public social entertainment and recreation come under this class of the arts. Our concerts, shows, lectures—all things that provide common thinking and enjoying. A town that does not provide well for its public in these matters cannot be building up a broad-minded widely-sympathetic citizenship. It is the duty of citizens not only to provide public social entertainment but continually to apply their fair frank comment and criticism, to hail what is good in them, to condemn what is silly or bad. We shall get what we deserve in this matter. Many of our shows are at present contemptible because we do not demand better. We can have perfect faith that our demand will create the supply. It is only necessary to be clear and to make clear what we really want. Our little western towns may be under a handicap in some of these matters. Let us "have a little pride" and make a little effort. We are going to be great and proud cities some day. The handicap is not so great as at first appears for the foundation of all the fine arts is common sense, honest work and good sentiment. These are denied to none. At least we can make it our business that their exercise is open to all.

This brings me to a subject in which we are rather obviously lacking—the appearance of our towns. To be good places to live in they ought to be beautiful. Many great cities are so. Ours are distinctly not so. We are, however, by no means alone in this practice. It is one of the great problems of modern life. All over the world it is being recognised that a great menace of general ugliness is threatening our civilisation. This problem is recognised and a machinery is being organised to meet it. When general feeling is aroused and people set themselves to tackle a problem, there is good hope it will be solved. Can we clothe modern civilisation with some degree of beauty, or must we go on making earth hideous? We spread the benefits of our civilisation amongst simple people who are living in the midst of beauty. These benefits seem for some time to have been steadily accomplished by the creation of ugliness so that we now speak of places outside of the range of civilisation as places of "unspoiled beauty." What can we do about it? Are we to let things go on, or are we to have a little pride and make some effort?

This brings me to the beginning of my subject and to the end of my time. I never could reach the end of my subject anyway for it is endless. It is up to all to carry it on. I shall endeavour however to carry on a little farther next Monday when my subject is "What our Cities Want."[2]

NOTES

1. The reference to Spray Lakes concerns the development of a hydro facility in Banff National Park in 1924. The project raised an outcry from environmentalists and led to the formation of The Canadian National Parks Association to protect the integrity of the national parks.
2. The talk was actually called "What Our Towns Want" (71.213, file 157, UAA). It is not reprinted here because it is somewhat repetitive to material in both Document 7, "The Town" and Document 9, "Relation of Architecture to Town Planning."

DOCUMENT 9

Relation of Architecture to Town Planning

IN 1929, Alberta implemented a new town planning act. This legislation created a framework in which communities could exercise control over the design and regulation of their physical environments. As a measure of its sincerity in viewing the legislation as a fresh start, the province hired a prominent Canadian town planner, Horace Seymour, as its Director of Town Planning to offer advice to local planning commissions on zoning and other aspects of town planning.

Burgess saw a direct connection between town planning and architecture. Even the best designed building would fail in its objectives if it was sited in a location where it could not properly show itself, or if it was obscured by incompatible development of adjacent buildings or by the clutter of advertising. While architects were inherently concerned with urban planning simply to make their buildings show themselves to the best advantage, the identity of architecture and town planning also arose because both aimed to create healthier and more efficient and expressive environments in which to live. Indeed, as Burgess argued in this 1930 talk, open space was architectural space because it framed and set off buildings. Moreover, the principles that Burgess employed in judging the merit of architectural design, such as purpose, variety and proportion, were the same ones that he applied to town plans. The difficulty was to apply such principles. Even if control over design could be implemented by a public authority, Burgess feared that it would produce a monotonous environment devoid of character and spark. Given these conditions, the only sure way to improve urban design was to use the new town planning legislation as a vehicle to encourage public involvement in demanding a better planned and designed environment in which to live.

Document 9 is a talk to an Unidentified Audience, Edmonton, not dated, ca. 1930, 71.213, file 87, UAA.

THE POPULAR IDEA is that town planning is architecture, and, after all, the popular idea is not altogether wrong. The conception of town planning put forward by the Director of Town Planning[1] may not seem to indicate this, but I may say at once—what I think must appeal to you—that all town planning without fine building is in vain. It would amount to building dreary, if in some respects, efficient towns.

I shall take the liberty of interpreting the word "architecture" very broadly so as to include the design of the open spaces as well as the buildings of a town. This is only right for in ancient and in modern towns all good town plans have in these respects been the work of architects. In what I have to say, I wish to begin by presenting the abstract aspect of the matter, then to show how the abstract principles operate in practice, and finally to deal with some actual examples.

The relationship of architecture to town planning is the relationship of an art to a science. Theoretical as it may seem, you will find it a thousand times worthwhile to form a clear conception of the relation between art and science. The want of such a conception is the source of endless muddle-headedness in everyday thought, or want of thought, and in everyday practical affairs. It is also a source of endless lack of sympathy and co-operation and, just most particularly in this matter of town planning, it is one of the causes of getting nowhere.

What is art and what is science? There is no real difficulty in being clear on this point. Science is the sphere of human knowledge. Art is the sphere of human action. The word "science" simply means "knowledge." You may qualify it by calling it systematised knowledge, but it still remains the faculty of "knowing." It has been sometimes said that science almost resolves itself into "measurement." Measurement of one kind or another is one way of acquiring knowledge. The statement that art is the sphere of human action may seem surprising to some of you who have not thought of it. But this is, very broadly indeed, but quite essentially, the sphere of art. Art is the human creative faculty—the faculty that out of nature's materials and forces creates, produces, and adjusts [materials and forces] to suit human demands.

You may take a distinction between applied science or art in its broadest meaning on the one hand, and what are called the fine arts, but both are engaged in the same purpose—fulfilling the demands of human beings—only the fine arts are applied more directly to fulfilling mental demands and appetites, a finer adjustment to finer appetites. The function of applied science is in general to put people into such circumstances that they can have their mental demands and appetites fulfilled—in other words that they may "enjoy life." But no definite line can be drawn where the creative activity of man becomes "fine." There is a gradation but no jump between applied science and the fine arts. The art of architecture is one of the most obvious examples of this.

What is the relation then between art and science? Science is the accumulation of knowledge; art is the application of knowledge to human physical, intellectual and emotional [demands]. Art is the use of knowledge. Art requires knowledge [and] has need of science in order to accomplish its work.

Town planning as it has been expounded by Mr. Seymour is the systematic acquisition of the knowledge necessary to design towns which shall satisfy human demands, physical and mental.[2] This systematic knowledge is very necessary as a basis on which to work. Hence the architect must welcome the town planner as one from whom he can get the information which will enable him to do effective work.

I have said that the function of art is to create or produce such things as will satisfy human demands and appetites. It is in fact to promote the enjoyment of life—not simply the healthy physical enjoyment of life, but also the mental enjoyment. Healthy minds are just as hungry for good mental food as healthy bodies for physical food. Hence the demand for what we call the fine arts—those that feed and nourish healthy emotions and sentiments.

I have been drawing as clearly as I can the distinction between the faculty of science, that of knowing, and the faculty of art, that of doing; but do not for a moment suppose that these exist in separate persons. No such monster exists as a pure scientist—one who knows and does not do, and still less possible is any such monster as a pure artist—one who does and knows nothing. We all possess both these faculties and we are responsible for making use of them. If the practical works we are severally engaged in are in some cases more constructive, more artistic and in other cases less so, we are all concerned in the result.

We are at present concerned with the making of towns. The engineer wishes to give efficiency to the civic services and the architect wishes to make the general appearance enjoyable. These are not conflicting ideas and every citizen is interested in them. Every citizen is bound to play some part in them, even if it be only the passive part of enjoying or suffering from the results as the case may be. Why is attention being called especially at this time to town planning? Is there anything specially wrong with our towns now more than at any other time? If so, what is the trouble and what are the problems we have to deal with in order to improve matters? [Thus] there are two questions: What is the matter? And what is the cure? I will not deal with these primary essentials which are not especially the business of an architect farther than to say that a town which has not an ample water supply and well-made roads is not likely to get much farther until these things are supplied.

Coming to the more specially architectural point—the buildings and general aspect of our towns—how do we stand? I find the following statement in an article in the *Journal of the Town Planning Institute of Canada*: "The new Alberta Town and Rural Planning Bill seems to be a response to Premier Brownlee's vigorously expressed distress, after his European tour, at the debasement of the country side in all directions by hideous advertising signs and by irresponsible building." I do not know whether the writer made a true guess, but it may very well be that he did. For, though historians are fond of telling us of the miserable conditions of the Middle Ages, the majority of European towns and villages were laid out for better or for worse in these wretched Middle Ages, and the plain staring fact is that these towns and villages are worth travelling thousands of miles to see, whilst ours are more often worth going a long way around not to see. Why is it that everything we do seems a blot on the landscape, whilst everything these allegedly wretched people did is a joy forever? That this is broadly speaking an undeniable fact I have no doubt. The causes are many—social and economical. I will not go into these for I cannot hope to change our whole social and economic conditions. Let us note this, however, that both our towns and countryside can be beautiful as these are beautiful—that we are in the process of brutalizing them and that brutal they will be and will remain unless we have the will and take the action that will make and keep them beautiful.

The Alberta Town Planning Act takes the whole countryside under its care, the whole of a great province. It is a mighty undertaking and in order to succeed it will require all the backing up it can get. I commend it specially to your support, for if you here do not support it, its chances are not going to be very strong. I am not without hope, for much is being accomplished elsewhere, notably in England where the mere rumour of legislation has already resulted in the voluntary withdrawal by large oil companies of many thousands of signs from the country and public competitions are being held for the improvement of filling stations.

To come to our cities, which are more especially the sphere of the architect. The obvious trouble is their *monotony*. This arises from the rapid extension over large areas of building schemes on which a minimum of thought has been expended. This minimum of thought results in space of undetermined size and form laid out in an even network to set chain measurements. Whilst occupied by small and humble dwellings these may not be striking disfigurements, but as these districts get more and more solidly built up, the monotony becomes oppressive. When this dismally monotonous scheme gets filled with the bustle of traffic, the whole expression of the place becomes a weariness to mortal flesh. Can this sort of thing be prevented? The only means I know of preventing it is to put a town planning act and a town planning scheme in operation as provided for by the Alberta Town Planning Act. Study the act and you will see how this operates.

On what principles should towns be laid out? The natural minimum-of-thought way is to lay out a simple gridiron of streets. It may occur to you at once that it would be a great relief to make the streets curve about. There is some truth in this, but I wish to warn you that this idea has its dangers and can in itself be [of] no use, for there is probably nothing more backboneless and wasteful than streets that meander about without reason or purpose. There are three chief stars in the designer's heaven; if he loses sight of any one of these he is hopelessly adrift. They are visible or appreciable purpose, order and proportion. Curving streets may be very beautiful, but there is no need to fly to [laying out] curves at once. If we do go to them, we shall need to look much more carefully to where this sort of thing is to end than we do with straight lines, which are at least more easily manageable. Let us consider first, then, for a little, what can be done with straight lines.

Up to a certain point the straight line for a street is a very satisfactory arrangement. It possesses in the highest degree the sense of order, and order is one of the designer's stars. If produced to infinity it will lose proportion—indeed much before infinity. There are limits to satisfaction in the length of a straight street; an endless vista is not desirable. Many of the straight streets in Calgary terminate with a plain view of a very plain bank of clay. These are some of the merits and defects of a straight street.

In the aforesaid minimum-of-thought gridiron plan the streets are not only straight, they are at right angles—again a very orderly idea and, up to a certain point, very serviceable. But if you continue your gridiron over a large area, you will find that your streets are serving their purpose poorly, for to get from corner to corner you have to go round two sides of a triangle. Broadway, New York, for this reason cuts diagonally through the general gridiron. It is the relieving feature of that city in more senses than one. Of course, this diagonal road idea results in obtuse and acute, or "flat-iron" corners, which with skill or a little sacrifice may be made a virtue of.

The gridiron has the farther defect that it takes no account of gradients. It is therefore quite unreasonable on a very uneven site, but not so unreasonable on level or practically level locations and, on our prairies, many towns have fairly level situations. There is another point worth noticing about a gridiron plan [and that] is its relation to points of the compass. The minimum-of-thought school of planning has very generally agreed that it is easiest to lay out the streets north and south and east to west. But it is not a great deal more difficult to lay out diagonally to the points of the compass, and then the buildings will all get sun on all four sides; there will be no due north side of the principal shopping street to monopolise the trade. This idea is subject to modification in relation to a strongly prevailing wind direction. Even then it will usually be better to design for wind breaks.

The fine orderliness of straight line planning is so great a virtue that it should not be lightly sacrificed. Let us look at some examples which illus-

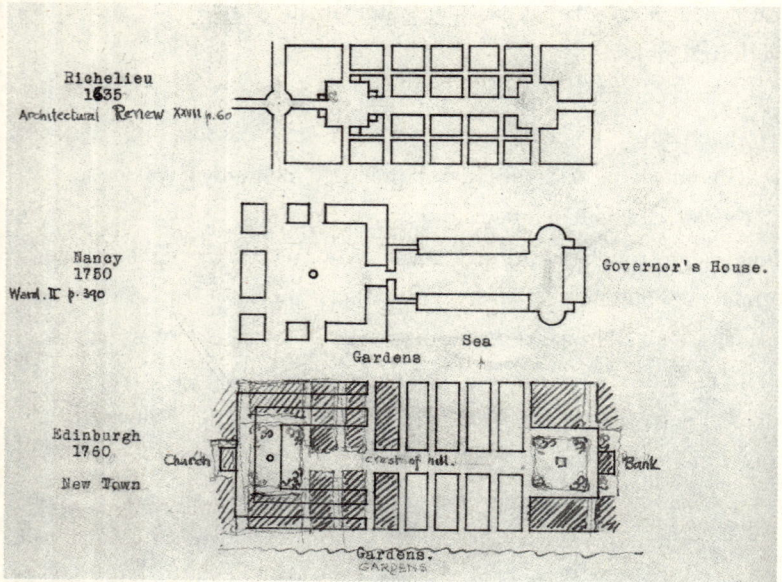

Burgess's sketch of city plans: Richelieu, Nancy and Edinburgh.

trate the relief and variety of which it is capable. *[see Burgess's sketch above of city plans: Richelieu, Nancy and Edinburgh.]* Such examples—of which many more might be pointed out—are far from exhausting the possibilities of relief and variety in straight line planning. These examples refer only to the horizontal plane and we can work in all three dimensions. There are, for example, the very beautiful expedients of bringing forward the ends of building blocks or recessing the centres. The recessing [of] the corners [opens] out street crossings into squares, thus opening the corners and avoiding blind turnings. *[see Burgess's sketch for street crossings, page 135.]* Another very fine means of relief and variety is the recessing of the upper part of the street facades, either wholly or at centres or at ends or both. In all great cities this is being done under compulsion of laws regulating the heights of buildings. This suggests the possibility or advisability of regulating architectural design; a question to which very serious dangers are attached and to which I shall return later.

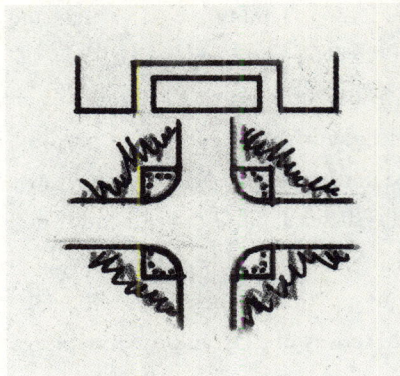

Burgess's sketch for street crossings.

Still adhering to the straight line plan, one important source of variation and relief is in the height of buildings. Whilst this has great possibilities of beauty, there is no source of variety which in practice is more abused. In plain fact, it is more commonly an occasion of disorderly and distressing appearance than of anything else. Yet in great crowded cities the first few tall buildings are generally hailed with delight. There is a perfectly good human instinct behind this. Such a building rising isolated and finely designed all round has the exhilarating effect of a great tower. If treated, as often happens, with one fine facade towards the street and mean brickwork and minimum-of-thought design on the other three sides, it is, of course, deplorable.

Probably the greatest and most beautiful source of architectural beauty in any plan, straight-lined or other, is the introduction of open spaces. Without these, streets become canyons, and fine architecture is lost. As the examples I have given illustrate, they are as easily provided in a straight-lined plan as in any other. If it be objected that it is uneconomical, it must be answered that open spaces are not lost spaces. They may serve perfectly utilitarian purposes such as the parking of cars. This will not prevent the planting of trees should those be wanted. Trees will not harm the cars, they will give them shade, and cars need not hurt the trees. But there are many instances in the old picturesque towns of Europe where there are great open spaces without trees, simply paved, which add immensely to the picturesqueness of the place and immensely relieve the traffic. In old days these were market places thronged with stalls on certain days of the week, but now they are frequently disused for that purpose, better accommodation being provided in the markets. Again in many cities we find squares not open to wheeled vehicles at all. Both in London and Paris there are many such [squares], and the restfulness they provide in the midst of busy cities is a matter of joy and thankfulness to the citizens.

There is no doubt that, for the purposes of play and exercise, large parks are more serviceable to a city, but for securing a general air of beauty and for setting buildings to advantage, a number of small open spaces is more valuable. The neglect of such provision where towns are small results in great expense later on when land that has been built over has to be purchased at a high cost.

So far I have said little of curved or winding streets. These are undoubtedly very picturesque elements in town planning. But, as I said, great care must be taken in laying out such streets. Of all curves that can be used, the circle is the surest of success from the designer's point of view because of all lines the circle is the most strongly suggestive of order—even more so than the straight line. Circles seldom occur in nature. They therefore are essentially a human idea. As applied to buildings, circles are costly, but when we can afford them, they may be most beautiful in effect.

When we look at old cities—mediaeval cities—we find the streets generally not straight, not in circular or any other known curves, but simply crooked, and they are incomparably picturesque. Would it be well to imitate them? I think it certainly would not. It would be just silly and would look just silly. Where does the difference come in? It is this—that we know and feel that these old world streets are crooked because they grew that way in accordance with the social and economic way of life that controlled their growth. If we simply imitate the old forms, we shall be creating something quite out of sympathy with our own conditions, and we shall be rubbing our sentiments the wrong way.

This principle may be illustrated in a simple way. You take a walk through the bush along the river bank. There you find a path which winds about among trees, dips suddenly down into hollows or rises up in places by steps. This seems delightful and perfectly satisfactory. It is according to the laws and conditions of the place. Lay out such a path in other circumstances and it will appear to be the work of a lunatic. Where then will it be reasonable to lay out curved roadways? There are I think four justifying circumstances, all involving appreciable purpose:

1. Where you have, on the flat, plenty of space and cost does not interfere, circles and segments of circles are justified from the variation they introduce and from the strong sense of order which they produce.
2. Where steep gradients will make straight roads up them inconvenient for traffic, it becomes the reasonable thing to curve the roads either to avoid the ascent altogether or to take it more gradually. A good case of this kind is shown on the plans of Vancouver.
3. It is often obviously reasonable to curve roads in order to shorten distance. In this function they may often be made to serve the purpose of diagonals even better than straight diagonal lines. In this connection it should be noticed that the end of a sharply diagonal street may often with advantage be curved to make a better junction with the main street.
4. When a fine natural feature, such as a river, a lake front, the sea front, suggests a road curvature to correspond, it would be a waste of opportunity not to take advantage of it. You may suppose that this is so obvious a case that no one would be so foolish as to do anything else. We have only to look across the river and see how the gridiron streets of Edmonton butt out on the head of the river bank. There you have a great object lesson in how a glorious opportunity may be thrown away. In fact, you have only to let loose a surveyor and furnish him with a chain and a minimum-of-thought and you will get this result every time; nature may do her best, but he will do his worst.

The rule with regard to curvature of streets then is that they should have a purpose and this purpose should be evident.

There arises in connection with the architecture of town planning the question of regulation of the forms of buildings. I think it must be obvious that a dictatorship as to what and how a citizen shall build is impractical for both social and economic reasons. Nevertheless, there is a proper sphere for regulations. It is reasonable to establish a line of front on which no buildings shall encroach. This regulation acts with salutary effect. It has been suggested that similar regulation should govern the height of buildings. [Although] this is a usual regulation, it produces little artistic effect, which in this case, means an orderly effect, because such regulations are merely limiting—they do not compel people to build up to the limit, and the general result is their irregularity. Suppose a regulation [states] that all buildings in certain streets should rise to a certain height above datum. I would grant that a certain orderliness would at length result, [because] when property values rose to a certain value, [property owners would be compelled] to come to that height in order to get full value out of their property. So far [so] good. Can regulation be applied as to type of design? This has often been done successfully, but I should think it highly inadvisable in young and growing cities. Perhaps the strongest objection to it is that in building design, as in other matters, progress is only made by free individual experiment and effort and a general decree against such free effort would be the death warrant of advance.

There exist, however, in all large cities building regulations which powerfully and beneficially affect architecture. For example, in central districts fireproof construction must be adopted. This ensures a substantial character of building without which there can be no fine architecture. Civic building regulations generally are in the interest of the safety and health of the public and usually react favourably upon architecture.

The *Alberta Town Planning Act* 1929 provides (Section 30.1) that the council of any municipality may make regulations (g) "controlling the architectural design, character and appearance of any or all buildings proposed to be erected in certain defined areas." Such power may be necessary to quash monstrosities, but it would not be well to use it in any highly critical spirit, and it should not be used without the security of strong popular support.

In all consideration and legislation regarding the improvement of our cities and country districts, there is a major consideration we can never afford to lose sight of. This is the popular attitude towards these things. There exists the usual force of inertia, the inclination to let things go their own way without applying any preventive. But, unfortunately, there exists today a strong positive inclination in the wrong way—the tendency to acclaim what is vulgarizing and brutalizing. There are many people whom I fear it will be impossible to persuade that the excitement produced by blatantly vulgar display is not the very essence of the zest of life. This is the source of more than half the degradation of our cities and has also taken a strong hold on many stretches of beautiful country.

If anyone here has even the slightest desire to improve the appearance of our towns and our countryside, I will ask him to begin his own personal practical observations by a simple series of tests. Go into any street or out in any part of the country. Close your eyes (figuratively I mean) for two minutes to clear your mind to obtain a fresh unbiased impression. Open them and ask yourself sincerely what is the impression. Be perfectly truthful to yourself, and if the impression is not delightful, ask yourself why, and what should be done about it. Are you entirely proud as a man and a Canadian of the scene? I think you will find that always in our towns and often in the country the thing that blights the view is most often what I will call diseased advertisement. There is a remarkably small proportion even of otherwise respectable store keepers who seem to have spent the minimum of decent thought on these. Scrutinize these a little carefully and you will find frontages and sometimes respectable frontages plastered with advertisement of such imbecility of disarray and uselessness that they seem to be the work of a lunatic. The people who do these things are neither lunatics nor imbeciles (difficult as it may be to believe this). Why then do they do it? If only they would cross the street and close their eyes in the way I suggested and then open them for a frank view of things as they are. I think [with] that seeing, they would see and be converted.

Back of any improvement in town and country there must come the simple process of opening our eyes and desiring better things. We shall get nowhere without this, and if only we can do this simple thing the possibilities for improvement are infinite. It is up to you.³

NOTES

1. Presumably Horace Seymour was in the audience.
2. Horace Seymour, 1882–1940, was one of the founders of modern Canadian planning. He worked at the Commission of Conservation with Thomas Adams, and later was resident engineer for the Vancouver Planning Commission, 1926–29, and the Alberta Director of Town Planning, 1929–32.
3. Typewritten note at end of manuscript: "The Council for the Preservation of Rural England has no powers of government or legislation behind it, but it has the will of the people—the power behind the throne greater than Parliament or King." Handwritten at end of manuscript: "City of Edmonton Zoning Plan."

DOCUMENT 10

Architecture as a Profession

THIS 1931 TALK was one in a series by university professors on careers as part of CKUA's Young People's Program.[1] By this time, university training had been firmly established as the only practical route to becoming an architect in Canada. Yet, as Burgess argued in this talk, architecture was not just about formal training—architecture was an art and an exercise of the individual's creative talent, but it was also a business that involved running an office, obtaining and working with clients, and dealing with the many technical issues associated with constructing buildings and using materials and services appropriately. Architecture was an interdisciplinary field, and the architect needed to draw on art, humanistic traditions, and pure and applied science to achieve its ends.

While the majority of architects in Canada were men, a number of women also practised in the field even though they faced discrimination. McGill University, for example, did not admit women to its architecture programme until 1939. In contrast, the University of Alberta admitted women to its architectural programme, but of the twenty-one graduates of the school, only three were women. Women architects, like all women, still faced severe barriers when practising architecture and often found themselves pushed to the margins of the profession. Burgess expressed no public objection to the admission of women to the university's architecture programme, but as this talk reveals, his persistent use of the male personal pronoun to describe potential architects likely spoke of his assumption that the profession was properly a male occupation.

Document 10 is a talk on Radio Station CKUA, April 27, 1931, 71.213, file 143, UAA.

I HAVE BEEN ASKED to speak about the profession of architecture in such a way that young people looking around for some occupation to take up may be able to form some idea as to whether this profession would suit them or whether they would suit this profession. These five points seem to me most important:

1. What is the nature of an architect's work?
2. How is the training for such work to be got?
3. What are the opportunities for obtaining work?
4. What natural qualifications should an architect possess?
5. What use and satisfaction is there in this profession?

1. *What work does an architect do?*

It is generally known that an architect makes a great many plans and other drawings. But it is necessary to realise that drawing is not the end and object of his work. Drawing is extremely useful to an architect, just as shorthand is very useful to a journalist, but only as one of several means he must employ to help him to his real object, which is to get good buildings built.

Why should a special profession be required to design buildings since it is evidently a building contractor's work to erect them? Buildings are costly articles. Their cost is not reckoned in hundreds of dollars but in thousands and in hundreds of thousands of dollars. They therefore require much and most careful consideration beforehand. A builder has to engage many workers, to organise and instruct them for work, to keep them fully employed and to provide them with regular payment. He has to purchase materials, to see that these are good and that they are delivered at the work in proper time and duly paid for. He has to lay out his work so that it shall go forward systematically, and to supply tools and machinery required in the operations, besides many other things necessary to building. All these are works of a nature so different from the careful arranging and designing of a building and all its parts to suit the occupiers that the builder has a right to expect that when he starts work he will have full and exact information in his hands about everything that is wanted.[2] This information it is the architect's business to collect, to set out in drawings and descriptions, and to supply to the builder. There is plenty of work for both architect and builder on any building of importance. The one man's work naturally supplements that of the other.

The architect's first work then is the making of a carefully and skilfully arranged design showing the form of the building and all its parts to scale and of the required cost. This requires considerable time and generally many consultations. He follows this up by writing a full description, called the specifications, of all the materials and the methods of doing all the work. This may run into hundreds of items. He has then to get prices from various builders and to arrange a contract with one of these. It is his duty to see that whilst this contract is fair to the builder, it will insure the building owner's interests in every respect. The work is then begun. The architect visits it frequently to see that his instructions are being understood and carried out. He makes further drawings,

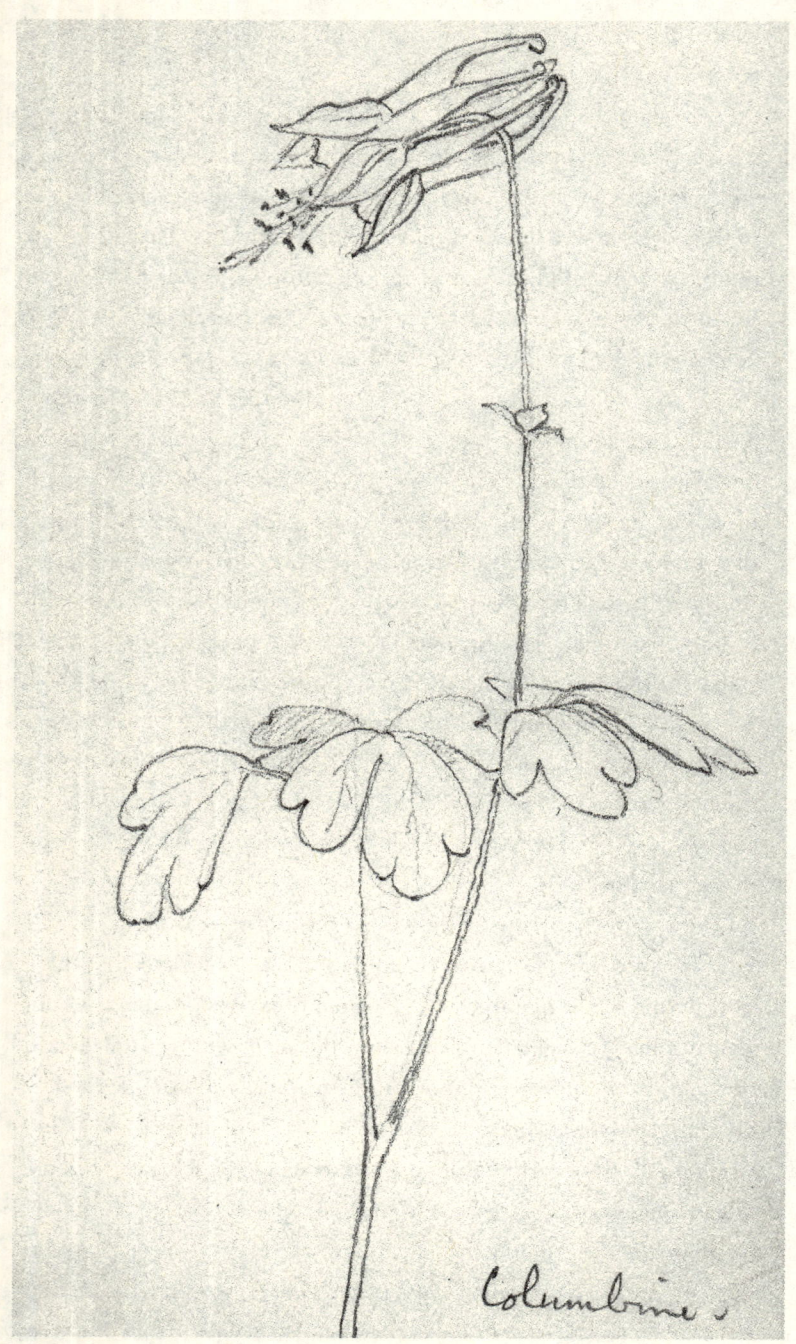

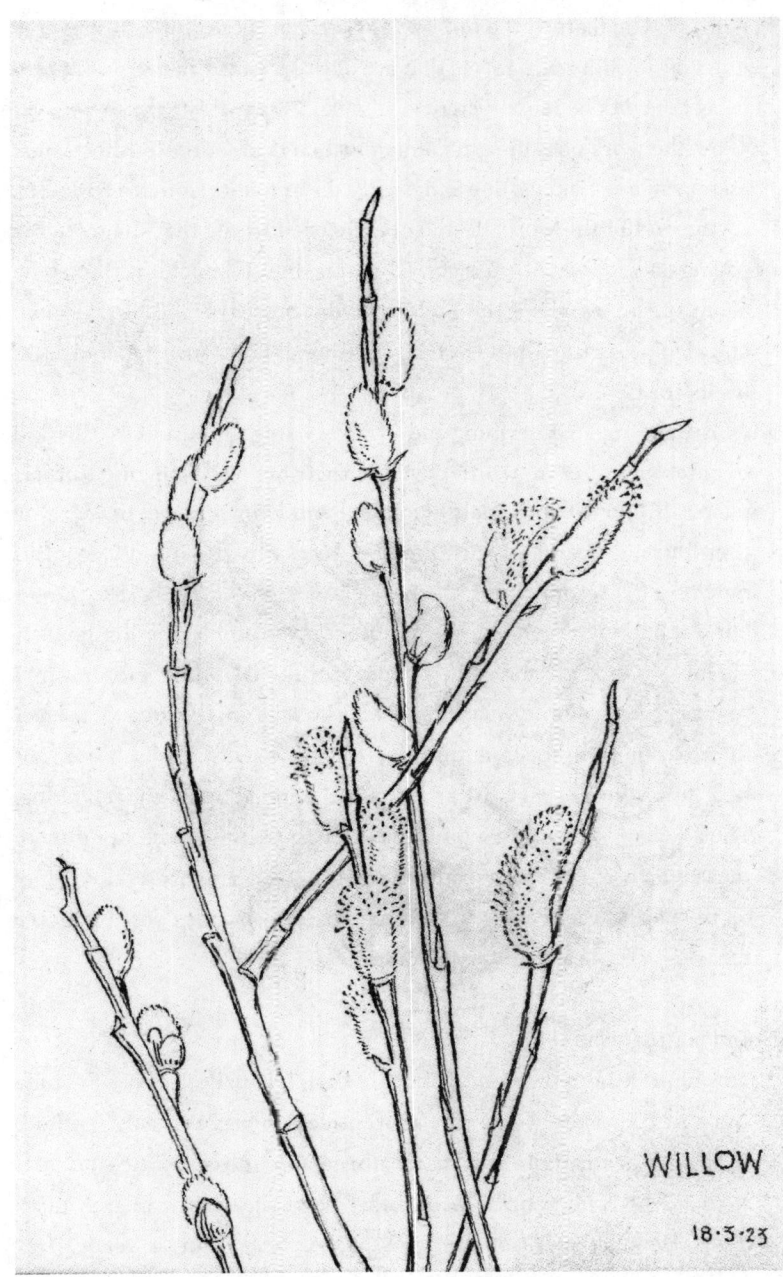

Sketching of all sorts was an important skill for an architect. Burgess drew these sketches from nature for his own pleasure in the 1920s. *(71.213–181 sketchbook (Columbine), UAA; 71.213–188 sketchbook (Pussy Willows), UAA)*

many of which are at the full size of portions of the work, to show the exact dimensions and forms that are desired. Any difficulties likely to delay the work he must overcome at once.

As the work goes on, payments must be made. The architect must ascertain how much is due and certify the amounts from time to time. At the end of the work all must be checked to see that the owner is paying only for what he has got. In all this, the architect is acting as the agent of the owner of the building, who must trust to his skill and knowledge to make the wisest expenditure of his money and look after his interests.

In drawing, in describing and in supervising his buildings, the skill of an architect is shown in devising their best adjustments to their purposes, in ensuring health, comfort and convenience, in securing their durability and all with the best economy. It naturally requires much thought, sometimes much ingenuity, to secure all these things, but on the top of them all, the architect must supply one thing more. He must give a fine and sightly appearance to the whole building and to every part. In other matters he may collect much valuable special information from the building owner and other specialists, but in this he is himself the specialist and this will depend upon himself alone. The good appearance of a building is a great satisfaction, not only to those who use it but also to all who see it. It is therefore a public duty on the part of the architect to provide it. It also adds considerably to the commercial value of the building.[3]

2. *Training in Architecture.*

This must be both theoretical and practical. It is to be got both by study and by experience. Formerly, apprenticeship was the only method. Today in Canada there are practically no apprentices in architecture. No boy who is quite untrained can be worth any pay in an architect's office. He must learn something, especially something of ready practical drawing elsewhere. Courses in architecture, which occupy four or five sessions, are given in most Canadian universities. Technical schools give courses in drawing which may be sufficient to make a boy helpful in an office and thus give him a start. Office work, by itself, cannot give a complete training, so whether at further technical school or at a university or by himself at home, the rising architect has much to study. In a general way the subjects of which he must get a systematic and working knowledge are these:

1. The properties and uses of materials employed in buildings.
2. The methods of constructing all parts of ordinary buildings.
3. The stresses in structures and how to handle them.
4. The requirements of building contracts and the laws in regard to buildings.
5. The principles of heating, ventilation, hygiene and sanitation and the methods of putting these principles in practice.
6. An acquaintance with the best existing architecture, whether of the present or of past times.
7. The principles of design in building and decoration and how to apply them in actual work.

It is usual for a young architect to work for several years as a draughtsman for architects in practice. If he succeeds in making himself useful with a firm that has a very extensive and varied practice, he may learn a great deal in a single office and it may be worth his while to remain there a number of years. If his lot be to work for a man or a firm whose practice is small, or limited to a special class of work, he will find it better education to gain wider experience by moving on from one office to another and, indeed, from one city to another. If in doing this he should have to sacrifice something in salary and something in personal comfort, he must remember that variety of experience will be of high value to him.

3. *Opportunities concerning the openings and general prospects for work as a young architect.*

Just as in other professions, such as law or medicine, there is no regular beaten highway into the realm of architectural practice. Each man has to blaze a trail for himself and the going is sometimes rough.

A look over the field in which architects operate will be some guide as to the direction in which the effort to get work must be made. Large cities are the most favourable location for architects and small ones—even when busy, active and growing—are generally poor ones. The principle of this may be illustrated in this way: a salesman took up the selling of fine shirts. He knew many little bustling towns where the people were running about in sloppy shirts all out at the elbows. These, he thought, are the places that are most in need of my goods. Soon, however, he found out that this idea was all wrong. These small-town people had no use for fine shirts. To sell fine shirts, you must go where fine shirts are already worn and appreciated. To get work in architecture to do, you must go where good architecture is known and appreciated. In the smaller struggling towns, the architect's services are grudged and their work is not appreciated. In the larger centres, the value of good buildings is realised and people demand them. They therefore require architects.

To build up a practice, an architect must be an active member of an active public whose service he makes his business. A practice can hardly be built up on buildings for purely private purposes such as houses or residences. The young architect must therefore consider what sorts of buildings are required in the everyday life of a city. I shall enumerate some of these classes of buildings:

Buildings for Business: Stores, office buildings, banks, hotels, restaurants, warehouses, factories, garages.
Institutional Buildings: Schools, colleges, museums, art galleries, churches, church halls, libraries, hospitals, clubs.
Buildings for Recreation: Concert halls, theatres, athletic clubs, swimming baths, dance halls.

Public Buildings: Legislative buildings, city halls, community halls and meeting places of many kinds.

Buildings for Common Residence: Apartment houses, convalescent homes, YMCA and YWCA buildings.[4]

That is a partial list, but it may be taken to represent the field of opportunity for architectural practice. Of the requirements of several of these classes, the architect should have some intimate knowledge. His knowledge of the principles of planning and design will help him in any or all of them.

I think it will now be plain that for an architect to work up a practice he must himself take an active interest in quite a number of those matters that are of general interest to his fellow citizens, making himself helpful and acceptable. In this way only can he become known and so be looked to for professional assistance when occasion arises.[5]

I have said that a practice can seldom be built upon private residential work. I shall further explain the reason. It might be enough to say that in actual fact only about 5 percent of residential buildings are designed by architects. In addition to this, these buildings are relatively small in cost, and small works alone will not yield a living to an architect, though it is part of his duty to undertake them when offered and they *are* quite worthwhile when taken along with larger work. For example, the smallest commission that professional etiquette allows or on which a living can be made is 5 percent of the total cost of the work. Even this seems large to people whose schemes of buildings are small and they are unwilling to pay more. Suppose then an architect to be carrying out fifteen different works and that their total value is $100,000. His receipts will be $5,000. At first this may seem not too bad; but if he is looking after fifteen works, he will probably have more than one hundred rather long interviews with the owners of these fifteen buildings and a great deal of his time will be taken up outside of his office altogether. Clearly he will require a good draughtsman and a stenographer.

To these, and for his office, rent and expenses, he will probably have to pay about $3,500 a year, leaving him about $1,500 for himself. For this return he will be kept pretty hard at work, and still harder to get fifteen new works each year.

On the other hand, if he should have just two or three works whose total value is $200,000, he will require no greater out-of-pocket expenses, he will have more time to study his work carefully and to look out for more, and his return from his business will be about $7,000. This is probably more than the average architect makes. In these hard times few make so much.

4. *What qualifications should one have for success in the profession of architecture?*

This is pretty well indicated by what I have said on the other points. As regards drawing, given a fair skill of fingers and the will to use them, the draughting required by an architect is not hard to learn, much easier indeed than many other parts of the profession.

The really important qualifications for an architect are a sense of order and proportion with an endless patience. His work consists in taking a multitude of practical requirements and unwearily weaving each and all together, giving each its right place and right space so as to produce a whole plan, orderly and proportionate.[6] He must also have some personal interest in form, colour and texture so that he will be inclined to study these things and use them in his work.

5. *I now reach my last point—what is the use of an architect's work and what satisfaction does he get out of it?*

The use is of course the service of his fellow citizens—the material and the mental satisfaction that his work gives to them. That end, if he attains it, is use and satisfaction enough for most men.

In addition to this, there is a satisfaction that the architect finds in the midst of his work. He is always working towards the making and producing something tangible and that of itself is a source of delight.

His thoughts are continually being materialised into things necessary, important, visible and beautiful for the public service. This is the exercise of the creative faculty, which is itself that incentive that impels all artists to keep on doing their work in spite of all apparent discouragement.

If the sort of work I have described as the work of an architect has an appeal to a young man, he may take up architecture with a chance of success and satisfaction, but if it does not, he had better think of something else.[7]

NOTES

1. *Report of the Department of Extension for the Year Ending March 31, 1931*, 5–6.
2. In contemporary terminology, one meaning of the term "the builder" was a general contractor. By 1931, when this talk was delivered, general contractors had become an accepted part of the building industry. Prior to this point, general contractors were only used on the largest projects. In Burgess's practice, there is no record of a general contractor being retained in 1913–14 for Pembina Hall, his first large project in Alberta, although one was hired for the Arts Building in 1915. After World War I, the use of general contractors became more general in Canada. A general contractor from Winnipeg was employed for construction of the Medical Building at the University of Alberta (1921) and for the Natural Resources Building (1929–31).
3. Hand-written on back of page 3 of the manuscript: "Draughtsmen's employment. The sporadic nature of an architect's work. Preparatory work postponed or abandoned. Slack periods extending over years as in 1930—architecture first to feel the slump and last to recover from it."
4. Handwritten in manuscript: "Buildings for the Country: work."
5. Hand-written on back of page 5 of the manuscript: "The architect must be an active member of society—must be something and amount to something as an individual personality—not just bury himself and lose himself with his head down over a draughting board in an office."
6. Hand-written on back of page 7 of the manuscript: "The complexity of a plan—medical building." The reference is to the Medical Building at the University of Alberta. Designed by Nobbs and Hyde, Burgess acted as supervising architect. Opening in 1921, it was the first specialised science building at the university
7. Hand-written on back of page 7 of the manuscript: "In the future architects will probably be called on to take a wider view of the environment of the works they carry out; both the physical surroundings of buildings—as groups of buildings and as parts of the

whole surrounding scheme of buildings. This relates architecture to town planning. Architects will also need to relate their buildings to the whole scheme of social and civic life. To look on them as instruments to make the life of individuals more happy and convenient, not only as separate individuals or institutions, but as these related to community life."

DOCUMENT 11

Appreciation of Architecture, Lecture 1

Architecture and the Arts

IN HIS FOUR-PART LECTURE *on architecture at the Edmonton Museum of Arts (of which Parts 1 and 4 are reprinted in this collection), Burgess grappled with the challenge that Modernism posed for contemporary architecture. Architectural Modernism presumed that the first task of architecture was the design of efficient buildings to produce hygienic, functional buildings. It also called upon architects to use fully the new materials and construction methods that had been developed as part of the industrialisation of western societies. Such architecture cast aside historical forms and styles in favour of undecorated functional structures.*

Such views posed a radical challenge for architects such as Burgess who had been trained and had practised their craft within a different theoretical and historical framework. For Burgess, architecture represented human triumph over the chaos of nature, and he was confident that architecture was an art (indeed sometimes a fine art) as well as an applied science. This art, he contended, was based on broad criteria that could be ranked in their importance. As he enunciated them, these criteria were, from least important to most important: workmanship, display of materials, utility, the visual appearance of stability, composition and, of highest importance, emotion (or what he also called sentiment). Buildings that best met these criteria, he argued, were ones that could be said to have architectural merit. The Modernist rejection of many of these criteria thus posed, for Burgess as well as for many of his contemporaries, a challenge to the basic rules used to judge the merit of architecture.

Document 11 is Lecture 1 of a Four-Part Series of Talks for the Edmonton Museum of Arts, delivered in the Medical Building, University of Alberta, October 27, 1932,[1] 71.213, file 99, UAA.

Introduction

It has very often occurred to me that architecture is a subject so important to the general public that it is very desirable that its aims and services ought to be placed and kept much more prominently before the public than is actually the case. There are certain difficulties in the way of presenting the case for architecture. On the one hand, the scope of the subject is so wide and its elements so complex that it is difficult to make a concentrated statement of it that shall be easily intelligible, and, on the other hand, it is always difficult to find artists, whose usual means of expression involves no words, to undertake any popular verbal expression of the principles, claims and aims of their art. It has been said that if the message of a painting could be expressed in words, it would not need to be painted. In fact, it just cannot be expressed in words. So in architecture. Architectural qualities just cannot be expressed in words. The works of architecture speak for themselves in their own language, and that is untranslatable into the language of words.

These difficulties were fully present in my mind when Mrs. Bowman[2] invited me to undertake to give four lectures on this subject under the auspices of the Edmonton Museum of Arts. Yet I accepted because I thought something of the kind ought certainly to be done, and since I had the opportunity, I ought to make the bold attempt. I fear it was a case, "fools rush in where angels fear to tread." There is, however, very seldom a fair opportunity for an architect to lay any kind of exposition of his art before the public. An architect should be grateful to the Edmonton Museum of Arts for furnishing such an opportunity. If my effort shall prove a feeble one, perhaps it may serve as a challenge to others more capable than myself to show a better way.

I suppose it is proper that a lecturer should preface his remarks by apologies to his hearers for his deficiencies. Apologies however are apt to be tiresome to both parties. I shall confine myself to an apology for my ignorance of the subject. I think, however, that an artist is privileged to fill up the gaps in his knowledge by the help of his imagination. The dreadful fact is that there are many of the buildings of which I shall speak which I have not even seen, but I have imagined them with such assistance as I could find. As to why I have not seen them all; I shall not explain that; I shall leave that gap for your imagination to fill.

Appreciation of Architecture: Architecture and the Arts

The title of this course of four lectures is the Appreciation of Architecture and my purpose is to take a look at architecture, past and present, discussing its value to, and claims upon, the citizen of today. There is, of course, a great deal in works of architecture that is highly technical so that for its practice the systematic and intimate study of a wide range of subjects is necessary. Nevertheless, architecture is very specially the affair of the community at large. Of all the arts, this is most especially the community art, the one which is always and necessarily exposed to the view of the community. It is always, or ought to be always, intended for their appreciation and service.

But much more even than this is architecture the community art. It arises directly out of the wants of the community and therefore it expresses their desires. The community is responsible for its forms. The professional architect may make many adjustments, but the general purpose and form of his works depend upon the demands and requirements of the community. In general, a community gets the architecture it deserves, just as peoples get the governments they deserve. Take a look around you then and see for yourselves what your merits in this way are. This is your business, professional architects are merely your interpreters to put your aspirations into being when requested to do so. Since over 90 percent of building is carried out without the employment of professional architects—to save expense and to reduce employment—it is vain to blame the professional architects if the general result appears somewhat less than ideal.

It has been said that law is more than lawyers. Law is a great and serviceable power. It is not brought into the service of man nor into that of a community by lawyers. It is primarily the business of the community. Lawyers are doubtless of great service in giving it system and definition, even in administering it [and] keeping it in good operation. But law will not flourish if a community is not intensely interested in making it flourish. Respect for law, backed up by practical enthusiasm for law, is the necessary condition for having a law-abiding country and, of course, behind these lies the great motive of self-respect and social pride, supported by intelligence.

Just so architecture is greater than architects and is a great service to the community. Sir Christopher Wren says, "*Architecture has its political uses; public buildings being the ornament of a country; it establishes a Nation, draws people and commerce; makes the people love their native country, which passion is the great original of all great actions in a Commonwealth.*" High claims indeed, which however may be made also for law and other services. There is enough truth in this fine statement to be worth much reflection. Architecture cannot, however, be drawn into the service of a community by architects. It is the business of the whole community. Architects have their function in shaping the examples of it. But architecture cannot flourish unless the community has the interest and practical enthusiasm to make it flourish. Behind this, as in law, lie the same great motives of civic self-respect and pride, supported by intelligence. Because architecture is in this sense pre-eminently the community art, I think it is a very proper subject for popular lectures. My intention in this little course of lectures then is to talk about those aspects of architecture which it is well that all good citizens should have information about so that they may bring their ideas to bear upon it and do something towards its better establishment.

In this course of lectures I propose to follow the programme as laid down and which has been advertised. In the first and present lecture on architecture as an art I propose to discuss the nature and purpose of art in general and the principles which govern it. In the second lecture on our architectural heritage, I shall review the greater works of architecture, showing how they embody great human sentiments which they have made a permanent and valuable human possession. In the third lecture on the yesterday of architecture, I wish to lead up to the present day by reviewing the more immediate past of architecture in order to show how we have arrived at our present position. In the final lecture, I shall try to put before you present-day views with regard to architecture and the aims and practice of present-day architecture. In connection with each of these lectures, I shall exhibit a certain number of slides so as to give visible demonstration of the points I may verbally explain.[3]

It is of first importance to know what is to be aimed at—to have clear ideas as to what is good and what is bad in architecture; what it is possible to do about it; whether it is going to cost some effort and expense, and if so, what purpose it is going to serve. In other words, is it worth while to have good architecture, or is it a fad of a few over-refined people who would spend other folk's money merely for the satisfaction of a few who perhaps can afford to purchase their own satisfaction for themselves—if not in this way, then in some other way.

To answer this question, I wish to discuss for a little the place and purpose of art in general—for architecture, whilst it is something besides being a fine art, lays its strongest claim to our attention as being a fine art. Discussions as to the arts and fine arts are apt to become somewhat vague and bewildering, so I wish at the start—at the risk of taking a limited view of the question—to lay down some very plain and reasonable statements to which I can refer throughout as necessary and easily applicable standards about all art and about architecture in particular.

Nature of Art

First, let us try to agree on the question *what is art?* and in deciding what art is, let us get a clear and reasonable idea about the purpose of art and agree upon the question, what is art for? After that it should become plain how we are to judge of its quality, whether bad or good, and whether it is worth having. My intention being to make only plain and reasonable statements on which all can agree, I will not attempt elaborately safe-guarded definitions but only such broad general statements as shall give the general sense of things.

First then, what is art? I find a broad statement which I think contains the general sense of this question in a sentence of Sir Francis Bacon's, *"Art is the shaping of the shows of things to the desires of the mind."* This simple statement seems to me to cover fairly completely the object of what we call the "fine arts." It would cover what are sometimes called useful or utilitarian arts also if we added to it in some such way as this: "art is the shaping of things to our physical needs and to the desires of our mind." For the sake of architecture, I want to include our physical needs as well as our mental desires because architecture partakes both of utilitarian and of fine art.[4]

The shaping of things, or the shaping of the shows of things, is the essential thing about all arts high or humble. Art is that function of the human being which makes or shapes. Art is not only creative, it is *the creative faculty* of man. We human beings are dropped into this world of nature and here we have to proceed to sustain our existence with the aid of the materials that we find supplied in nature. If we proceed to adjust these materials to our service, if we cut down trees and collect the logs, if we gather stones and pile them up to provide shelter, we are exercising our creative faculty and our work is a work of art in its broadest sense. If we shape our shelters so as to give us mental satisfaction, if we shape the shows of these things to the desires of our minds, this operation is "art" in the more special sense in which the word is commonly applied and understood. All the arts are of this same nature. Music is the adjustment of sounds—air vibrations if you like—to our mental satisfaction; poetry is the adjustment of words to a similar end. Dance is the arrangement of human figures in movement; painting is the application of colour in the creation of something that the mind desires.

This statement of the nature, the sphere and the purpose of art is surely simple and clear. It is the creative faculty, the faculty of making things. Its purpose in its humbler sphere is the making of things to meet our physical requirements; in the higher sphere, which is more generally recognised as that of art, things are made that give satisfaction to the mind. I think this statement will be found reasonable and sufficient for my purpose: *"Art is the shaping of the shows of things to the desires of the mind."*

Morality
Morality or ethics is our guide in conduct whereby we make justice, mercy and truth prevail. It has evidently nothing to do with the making of material things.

Science
Science is, broadly, knowledge or the knowing about things. More specifically, it is the acquaintance with the varieties, properties and qualities of the materials and with the forces of nature. When science is applied to practical things, it is departing from its essential function of knowing. Applied science is creative. It enters the sphere of art and makes things for our physical requirements. It thus belongs to the class of utilitarian art and it may go farther, for if it satisfies our minds in a fuller degree, it will enter the sphere of the fine arts. Architecture itself is to a very large extent

applied science. In fact, the application of science, of knowledge about things, is necessary to all arts in a greater or less degree.

Desires

Let us consider a little more particularly what *desires* the mind has that *can* be satisfied by the shaping of the shows of things. For evidently, our minds find satisfaction in many things that have nothing to do with the shapes of material things. I have referred to ethics and science; these are human faculties that are concerned with quite other things than the shaping of material things. There may be many other faculties of the mind, but I take these to illustrate the special position of art. The exercise of all our faculties is necessary to living. Art, the faculty of making things, will evidently not advance very far without making use of science—the knowledge of nature's forces and materials—and it will not satisfy the desires of the mind if its productions conflict with morality. There are intimate and inseparable relations between the various human faculties, yet we can distinguish a special sphere for that faculty that creates material things and which we may call "art" generally, and which we call "fine art" when it satisfies certain mental desires. What then are the mental desires involved in the operations of art; of the creative faculty?

I am going to take six examples of mental desires or appetites which find satisfaction in the shapes of the material things which men produce, and [I] intend to illustrate these further by slides.

1. *Workmanship*. First, there is the act of production itself. Men's hands are marvellous instruments capable of producing wonderful effects. Skill of hand is itself a quality that affords a great mental satisfaction, so much so that one might fill many hours in considering this little part of the subject alone. Let us consider it sufficiently to appreciate its importance in art—in the shaping of the shows of things. Skill of hand, which in its relation to architecture we call craftsmanship, is capable of producing such exciting and wonderful results that there is often even a danger of its being overestimated. It should, however, be recognised

that the ambition to excel in skill of hand is a very universal and wholesome ambition and the mere observation of it gives a great and legitimate delight to the mind. This delight is so deeply ingrained in human nature that we do not seem able to live without it. People whose daily work has nothing to do with the making of things will occupy a considerable part of their spare time in playing or viewing games of skill such as tennis, golf, shooting, etc. I do not need to enlarge upon the fascination of skill of hand in the realm of sports. The persistent way in which men occupied, and often very closely occupied, with work of an intellectual nature will nevertheless take up some manual hobby or sport with great earnestness suggests that the normal human being requires a proportion of skilled manual work to preserve balance and sanity of mind.

In architecture and the other arts, skill of hand is at least as legitimate an object of admiration. I think I should be speaking truth if I say that in the greatest works it is always present in abundance and is always a source of genuine satisfaction and that we have a right to look for it. On the other hand, it must clearly not usurp the whole field. We look for much besides this. This is particularly felt amongst modern painters. Skill in imitative representation is to many people easily acquired, and it may be true that many paintings have little else to present for the satisfaction of our mental desires. This has led some of our painters to the conclusion that they had better either do without it, or at any rate, force it back out of notice. Hence we get some results that revolt those of us who are ingenuous enough to take a quite wholesome and proper delight in skill of workmanship, or in technique as it is sometimes called. I wish to maintain, however, that skilled workmanship is a basic element in all art and in architecture in particular; that we have a right to expect it, that one fair criterion that we shall properly apply to all work is to ask what physical skill it displayed. It is true that many fine works of art are inferior in skill of workmanship. We have to pardon this in them, it is not of itself a virtue, and we do not pardon it except when the work has other positive qualities that give the mind such satisfaction as redeems the defect.

I think it is not out of place in speaking of the "appreciation of architecture" to point out the social and economic value to any society of having a large body of its citizens skilled hand-workers. From my own personal acquaintance with skilled artisans, I can vouch for the fine character and intelligence of this class as a whole. A man who is master of a handicraft is naturally one whose general intelligence is keenly alive. The honest pride in the making of things, in exercising the creative faculty, even on this technical side alone, is a genuine source of human happiness. There are many branches of craftsmanship outside the field of architecture, but since in most settled countries the building trades have a larger payroll [and] employ a larger number of men than any other occupation, there is here alone good reason why architecture should flourish. This is a subsidiary way, but a really important way, in which "architecture establishes a nation."

2. *Display of Materials.* The next element of mental satisfaction that I wish to mention is that derived from the qualities of materials. In the making of things, we have at our disposal the materials that nature supplies. These in many cases are of themselves full of delight, as we say, "to our eyes," [but] really, of course, to our minds through our eyes. These are matters sometimes of colour, sometimes of texture, sometimes of form, and sometimes of capacity for service. That we should take delight in these qualities of the materials we make use of in our buildings is as natural as that we should take delight in natural scenery, in landscapes and cloud effects. It is all part of the same instinct.

These two sources of delight that enter into architecture (and many other arts) are elementary. They are not those of highest value, but they are primary and essential. They are easily detected, and if you wish to appraise the value of a work of architecture, they are qualities that you have a right to expect, though their absence does not necessarily preclude the presence of still more valuable qualities.[5]

3. *Utility.* A third important "desire of the mind" to which architecture responds is the fulfilment of human use or convenience. If from a shape-

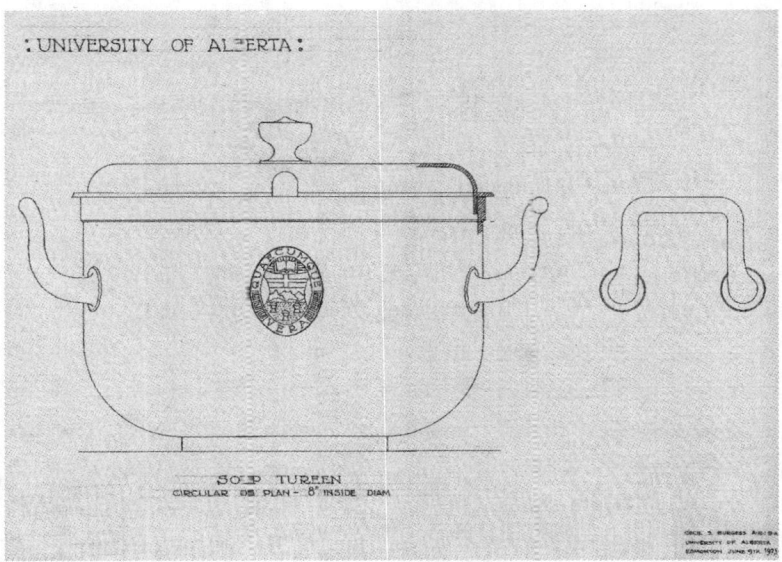

Burgess's design for a soup tureen for the University of Alberta demonstrated his contention that a circular form was naturally beautiful and "if you wish it to stand firmly you will depart so far from the hemisphere as to add a foot, and the probable effect will be a farther mental satisfaction." This tureen (minus the lid) is now used as the University Cup, a University of Alberta award for research and teaching. (71.213–209, Map Case UAA)

less mass of clay you shape a bowl which will hold water, you have adjusted it to a useful human purpose. The form you give it depends on the function you wish it to fulfil. You will most naturally make it circular or even hemispherical, giving it a geometrical form even if that does not add to its usefulness. This you do from another desire of the mind, orderliness, which I shall discuss later.

These two elements of design do not conflict. Your bowl may be a geometrical form, say a hemisphere, but if you wish it to stand firmly, you will depart so far from the hemisphere as to add a foot, and the probable effect will be a farther mental satisfaction. This element of the reasonable fulfilment of convenience is particularly to be noticed at the present time as there is today a strong effort in architectural criticism to give importance to what is called "functionalism." It has become quite a "slogan" which has produced some remarkable results in recent work. If it has been pushed too far, it is because it has sometimes been accepted as the only element of mental satisfaction in a building. That it is, however, a legitimate and necessary desire, I think there can be no manner of doubt.

That a building or any other work of men's hands should be so formed as to perform the useful functions for which it is made is eminently reasonable. If it does not do so, it will not certainly be shaped to the desires of the mind. There may be cases in which the performance of a certain function controls all other considerations of form, colour and texture, in which there is no room to introduce any other consideration of design, but such cases must be rare in architectural work. They are not uncommon in the case of tools and implements and in what we call objects of utility. These will generally be found to develop forms of a peculiar interest as, for example, motor cars, ships, locomotives, bridges. The functionalist school claims that architecture is liable only to the same laws as these objects, but so far, architecture has persisted in clothing itself in farther and higher qualities.

4. *Stability*. A fourth element of satisfaction to be found in architecture is that which arises from the control of structure, thus harnessing nature's forces to the service of men. We appreciate the quality of stability. This is a peculiarly or specially architectural quality. For this is the "static art" and makes an appeal through the eye to the mind by satisfying the appetite for stability. There is a justifiable pride in controlling the forces of nature in employing them in such a way that they shall serve good human physical convenience and mental ambition. I can only point out a few of the many ways in which this is done.

The old Egyptians, I am sure, derived a vast enjoyment in removing huge stones and raising them into place in their mighty works. The only force of nature which they employed in their structures was that of the direct vertical force of gravitation. That is to say, they did not build arches in which inclined and horizontal forces are brought into play. By confining themselves to this simple scheme of forces, they ensured stability and they farther emphasised this impression of stability by the inward slope of their walls and the tapering forms of the pyramid, which is the very type of stability. [By rejecting the arch] the Greeks similarly safeguarded the idea of stability by simplicity of construction. They also preserved the idea of an inward tapering form in their buildings. In many other ways, they subtly gave value to the impression of stability, so that if the pyramid is the type of stability, the Greek temple is the finest exposition of static excellence. A great part of the splendid effect of Roman and of Mediaeval buildings arises from the obvious mastering of a more complex statical problem—the harnessing to human service of the forces involved in the arch and the vault. At great heights, solid vaults are not only sustained, but their side thrusts are skilfully resisted by counterpoises which keep the mass in equilibrium.

A very different show of things will satisfy our demand for stability when other materials than stone are employed such as wood or steel. When a tough, instead of a brittle, material is used, a wider spacing is obviously demanded by reason, and a totally different scheme of proportions, an entirely slenderer type, will be structurally right. I have not time to go into all that is involved in this, I can only call attention to it. There is, however, an important consideration that I wish to emphasise (since architecture is essentially a visible art): the appeal is directly to the eye, thence to the mind. There must, therefore, be a visible stability. It is not enough that we have some written or other guarantee of unseen means of securing stability. The great buildings are visibly stable and frequently their architects have taken special farther means to give visibility to this stability.

A simple example will make plain what I mean. We naturally feel that the ends of a wall, whether it be merely an isolated wall or the façade of a building, must be specially strongly built. In architectural buildings this is generally a corner where two walls meet from two directions. This very fact makes it a point of strength, but you will often see built up [at] such a corner a line of specially projecting corner stones, sometimes rough-faced to give an appearance of rugged strength. This is not a necessary feature, it is introduced merely to give the eye an assurance or expression of strength. The architect has felt some necessity for this device quite apart from any real structural need. [When] this expedient is carried farther, it suggests other applications of the principle. Instead of mere projecting lines of stones up and down the corners of a façade, suppose that a considerable portion of the end of the building, say enough to include one window, is made to project somewhat and in such a way that a series of windows one above the other is included in the projecting part. It is evident, I think, that such projections at the ends of a building will give a satisfactory appearance of stability to a long façade and, if the façade be a very long one, another perhaps even more important one, in the exact centre of its length, will add to the appearance of stability.[6] Remember that architecture is especially the static art, that art is the shaping of the "*shows*" of things to the desires of the mind, and you will realise something of the appropriateness of these devices.

Now similarly consider the horizontal direction of a building. It is naturally composed of layers or courses laid down in succession one upon another. Scientific principles require that the lower courses shall be wider, especially near the ground, to sustain the weight of those above. A spreading base may or may not be actually necessary, but will satisfy the demand of the eye and mind for *visible* stability. Similarly, specially strong courses at intervals will give additional strength and are often employed merely for their effect of appearance of stability. The head of a wall normally requires some special protection, hence is derived the cornice, which gives emphasis to the upward termination of a wall. An emphatic and often splendid crown to a façade was employed in the Greek order of building and became a great means of expression among the architects of the Renaissance period. It may often even be fitly described as their crowning glory. Perhaps some of this effect is due to the feeling of structural service rendered by the wall in upholding aloft a feature of magnificence and special interest. That which is strong should obviously carry something proportioned to its strength.

All this indicates that in architecture there exists a principle of visible and apparent law, corresponding though dissimilar, to the principle that gives beauty to nature's creations. The principle of growth of structure in a tree or plant is one of its chief elements of beauty. Animals have each their peculiar beauty of a different order from that of plants, but here again, [it is] largely dependent on the manner in which their structure is designed and arranged and the manner in which they grow. The tree and the flower attain their beauty obeying and displaying the laws of nature that shape them, and all lovely things in mountain stream or sky are shaped to the last pebble, or ripple, or wisp of cloud by ever operating laws and forces of nature and owe their beauty to the operation of, and display of, these laws.

Buildings cannot and do not imitate plants or animals, rivers or mountains, but they have their own essential principles of structure and development. Similarly, they owe an important part—though by no means the whole of their beauty—to their expression of these principles. This element of their beauty I may call their static excellence. Though I have gone to nature for an analogy, it implies no imitation of anything in nature. It is a man-created principle and a specially architectonic quality. The desire for visible static excellence is thus a desire of the mind which we may expect to be satisfied by the art of architecture.

5. *Composition.* As the next desire of the mind, next in ascending scale, I shall take that of "order" or "composition." This is a very large element in the effect of works of architecture, though it is well to remember that in requiring this we have not yet reached the highest desires of the mind, the highest demands that are made of a work of art. This is the part of architecture in which the individual, the professional architect, plays most part and contributes his special skill. Perhaps because of this, the meaning of the word "composition" in relation to architecture, sculpture and painting is apt to remain a vague and mysterious matter in the minds of the average layman. The operation of designing or composing may require high skill, or the power to produce it may be

the result of much thought and experience and imagination, but its nature is simple enough and should be clearly understood. It is simply the *arrangement and proportioning* of the parts of the work to the best effect. The word composition as applied to a picture or to a work of architecture has the same sense as when we apply it to a work of literature. It is the "order," or arrangement, in which the theme is presented. "Order" is the basis of all artistic composition [and] such high orderliness as will best satisfy the mind is the aim of the designer.

The human mind strongly desires orderliness. In relation to human needs, bodily and mental, wild nature presents a chaos, and the work of civilisation, that is to say the work of adding value and power and joy to human life, consists largely in bringing nature's chaos into such order as the human creature can make ready use of. When we begin to shape the shows of things to the desires of the mind, we apply to them principles of order. Thus we say that order is the basis of composition.

It is worth while noticing what we mean by order, this great principle of design, which, being the base upon which composition is built, holds such sway in all the arts. It has its essential basis upon geometrical form. You know that if you push a number of objects into a straight line, or a circle, or a square, rectangle, ellipse, or any other geometrical form, you have created an order. You have done a stupendous work, you have created order out of chaos, and, in doing so, you have displayed the conquest of the human mind over matter. You have satisfied a desire of the mind, you have made matter express a human impulse and satisfy a human emotion.

It has appeared to many a hard saying that geometrical ideas have a very large share in producing beauty in works of art. Many fine artists have kicked against it, [and] some have denied it altogether, so maybe it is not true. I wish, therefore, to give some illustration of the case for it. The Greeks appear to have had no doubts at all about the value of geometrical ideas of form and proportion and schemes of proportion in architecture and sculpture. Ictinus, the architect of the Parthenon, wrote a work on architecture which has unfortunately been lost, but all

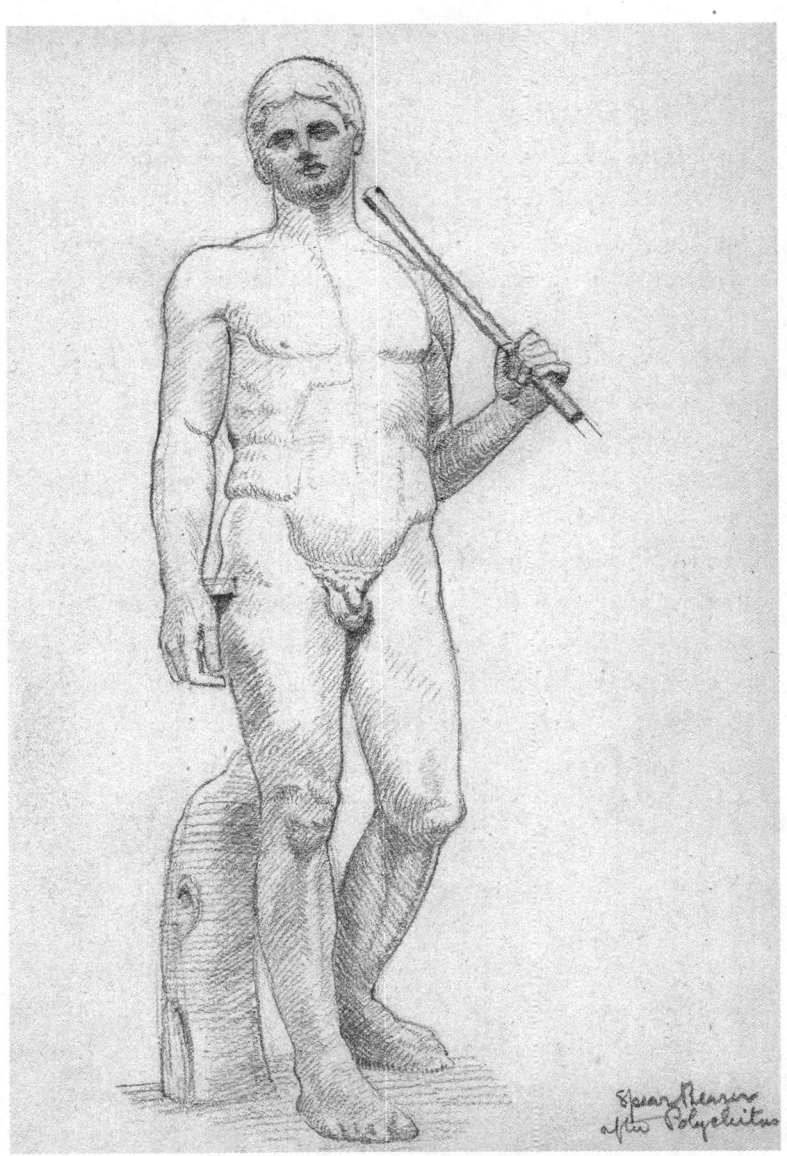

Polycleitus's sculpture of the Spear Bearer (or Spearman) has been lost and knowledge of it survives only through Roman copies. Burgess probably based this sketch on a photograph. (71.213–189–010, sketchbook, UAA)

references to this, and to the theories of others of the ancient Greeks about architecture, seem to show that they pinned their faith firmly to the essential value of geometrical form and to geometrical and arithmetical ideas in architecture. By "proportion they meant a definite prearranged relation of measured quantities."[7] Polycleitus, the famous sculptor of the golden age of Greek sculpture, wrote a book called *The Canon*, and made his fine figure known as the Doryphorus, or Spearman, to illustrate it. The head of this figure was one-seventh of the total height, and all the other parts had definite ratios. Moreover, a saying of his is preserved: "success in art is attained by exactness in a multitude of arithmetical proportions." Greek artists seem to have agreed to such a theory, and although it was ill-founded, yet the myth led them on—that is, they set about discovering perfection—and we "know what wonders they accomplished in consequence." Here Lethaby, who was a fine and sensitive artist, says, "this theory was ill founded, yet what wonders it accomplished." I think he does not anywhere explain wherein the theory was wrong. I suppose he thought there was something quite obviously wrong about it, as many others have thought. It seems a pity we could not discover some more wrong theories that would have such wonderfully right results.

In the same article of Lethaby's from which I have quoted, he goes on to show what a great modern, Sir Christopher Wren, considered to be the essential elements of architectural design. This time, Lethaby expresses no disapproval, he is commending Wren's dicta: "there are two causes of beauty," Wren says, natural and customary. Nature is from geometry, consisting in uniformity, that is, equality and proportion. Customary beauty is begotten by use, as familiarity breeds a love to things not in themselves lovely. Here lies the great occasion of errors, but always the true test is natural or geometrical beauty. (The customary source of beauty, you see, is here eliminated, and the natural or geometrical beauty—these words are used as synonyms—is left as the only source of beauty.) "Geometrical figures," he continues, "are naturally more beautiful than irregular ones; the square, the circle are most beautiful; next the parallelogram and the oval. There are only two beautiful positions of straight lines, perpendicular and horizontal; this is from Nature and consequently necessity, no other than upright being firm." Surely in these statements Sir Christopher Wren comes perilously near [to] endorsing the wrong theories of the ancient Greeks, and yet his works are noble examples of architecture.

I have a suspicion that there must have been at least a pretty large grain of truth in the Greek theory and that the strong objections that are felt towards it arise from the conception that this theory of the geometrical source of beauty in art represents, or was intended to represent, the whole content of works of art. But these abstract ideas were being applied to material concrete objects. Even if Greek sculptures far transcended all nature's examples of the human figure, they were based upon the human figure and must have derived some valuable quality from that fact, besides what they have derived from geometrical ideas. In their architecture, we shall find that in applying their abstract geometrical ideas to the concrete matter of architecture, they made certain subtle compromises which are the supreme triumph of their art. They made strict geometry bend to what [were claims] of their own that must be recognised.

The important point about all this, however, is the fact that all our ideas of order are based on geometrical forms and all our ideas of proportion are based upon geometrical ratios. Order and proportion are universally admitted to be the high essentials in the beauty of art generally, and of architecture in particular. If we can say that a building exhibits no sense of order or proportion, we have indeed condemned it!

6. *Emotion*. This brings me to the final element in architectural, as in all artistic endeavour, the element of human emotion. It is perhaps not obvious that architecture can express emotion. Emotion seems to imply some kind of movement, whereas architects must always take the greatest care that their buildings shall not move, whatever may happen to them. It is evident, however, that buildings do at least express

moods. Some are grave [or] severe, others gay, others quietly companionable. Some, I regret to say, are aggressive and repellent. They express the human qualities, the character, of times and peoples. The great buildings of Greece express a perfect mental balance, the poise of those who have attained a mastery. The mediaeval buildings stir one like stories of bold adventures, they make one hold one's breath to see what stout hearts men have borne, what courage and daring they have shown. The buildings of the seventeenth century bespeak the urbanity, the self-satisfaction of people who have arrived, have attained an orderly way of life in which many people are living satisfactorily together. This emotional element in architecture is expressed by means of the other elements that I have mentioned working together:

Craftsmanship—the magic of human hands
Materials—the beauty of nature's materials
Utility
Static Excellence
Composition—the masterly ordering of form to function, to stability, to complete harmony.

Perhaps the most dominant, the most characteristic, and the most general emotion expressed in architecture is the feeling of mastery over the disorder of nature. Of all the arts, architecture demands the most effort, the greatest co-operation of men and minds, the greatest collaboration of skilled hands, the fulfilment of the most multifarious requirements by the most varied means. The successful co-ordination of all these, the production of a simple unity comprising so large a complexity, arouses a feeling of pride in common achievement. This feeling pertains of course to any great effort to satisfy even the purely physical (as distinguished from mental) demands—the construction of a great bridge, for example.

When the many labours [and] varieties of skill involved in a building have achieved, through the imposition upon them of a simplicity and

Modernist ideas that became current in the interwar years dismissed decorative details such as the ones Burgess sketched at Lincoln Cathedral just after World War I. Burgess defended such decoration as contributing to the shaping of "the shows of things to the desires of our minds." *(71.213–182–6 sketchbook, UAA)*

unity, a proportion of parts and control of lines and forms that appeals to the mind so that the mere physical service or utility of the building appears to be a minor consideration, the work takes its place as preeminently a work of high value, of "fine art." In such works, it is usual to say that they have "dignity," and amongst professional architects the dignity of a building has become the most general touchstone of its architectural value. Fine architecture is generally recognised as adding dignity to civic life. Its presence or absence in a city is considered a criterion of the civic pride, the civic self-respect of its citizens.

Each building, each type of building, must express and impress an emotion that is individual to it. This individuality, of course, must be influenced by [the] special human convenience or purpose that it serves. It ought not only to serve that purpose, but to look as if it served that purpose, if that purpose is one in which the community or the individual may take a just pride—that is to say, if it responds to a wholesome appetite of the mind. Thus a library should look like a resort for literary enjoyment, rather than a storage place for books or even accommodation for readers. A city hall should speak of civic control and order, rather than a mere convenience for collecting taxes. I have an idea that a house ought to express the qualities we associate with "home." But as we shall see later, there is at the present day a very lively advocacy for its looking like a "machine to live in."

If we can make our buildings in accordance with the principles that I have reviewed and can clothe them with the sentiments belonging to our ideals of life and of living, we shall have shaped the shows of these things to the desires of our minds.

NOTES

1. The series was delivered between October 27 and November 18, 1932. Lectures 1 and 4 are reprinted here. In the two lectures not reprinted, Burgess applied the concepts developed in Lecture 1. Thus, in Lecture 2 ("Our Architectural Heritage," UAA 71.213,

file 100) he recapped the ideas presented in Lecture 1, discussed the value of history and then applied to specific examples the six criteria (workmanship, display of materials, utility, stability, composition, and emotion) for judging architectural merit. In outlining this canon, he discussed the Great Pyramid at Ghiza; the Temple at Karnak; the Parthenon, Athens; Roman Halls (using the example of the Pantheon, Rome), Ste. Sophia, Istanbul; Medieval cathedrals and the Taj Mahal, Agra. In Lecture 3 ("The Yesterday of Architecture," 71.213, file 101, UAA), he looked at architectural movements, styles and forms, discussing specifically Italian Renaissance palaces; Tudor houses; Elizabethan Antics; the Adams style; Gothic revival, and Georgian architecture. Overall, the emphasis in Lecture 3 was on the way that architectural style reflected social conditions and thinking.

2. The Edmonton Museum of Arts was established in 1924. Mrs. David Bowman was one of the founders of the gallery and went on to be an energetic volunteer at the gallery.
3. The list of slides Burgess used in this lecture series has survived only for Lecture 4.
4. Hand-written notation in manuscript: "Complete however as it stands because the fulfilment of physical needs is as much a desire of the mind as any other desire."
5. Hand-written in margin: "Examples: grain of wood; marble; brick; bronze; wrought iron; combinations and contrasts."
6. Note in text: "See [University of Alberta] Arts Building."
7. Note in text: "Lethaby 69." The reference and the following material in this paragraph is to W.R. Lethaby, *Form and Civilization. Collected Papers on Art and Labour* (London: Oxford University Press, 1922), 69–70.

DOCUMENT 12

Appreciation of Architecture, Lecture 4

Architecture To-Day

IN HIS CONCLUDING LECTURE at the Edmonton Museum of Arts, Burgess asked his audience to assess the meaning of the new Modernist architecture that was appearing in Europe and North America. As revealed in the buildings that he chose to discuss and his commentary on the slides that he showed during his lecture, Burgess often welcomed new materials and methods if they were serviceable. He also recognised that the needs of architecture had changed in the face of urbanism, industrialisation and scientific developments. Like many architects of his generation, he sought a compromise between the new building forms and the architectural traditions that he valued. As part of his effort to understand Modernist architecture, he tried to analyse the social forces that had given rise to Modernism and found an answer in the new demands arising from modern science (especially the health sciences), new *applications of materials, and new cultural patterns such as the desire for speed and efficiency. Not all of these forces were, to his mind, beneficial, but more importantly he worried that Modernism involved a rejection of architecture's role as a public and social art. Burgess nonetheless identified in this lecture a number of buildings that he thought successfully reached a compromise between Modernism and traditional demands. He also suggested that some of these buildings (albeit only the most conservative) also offered new approaches and use of materials that were consistent with the spirit of the times.*

Document 12 is Lecture 4 of a Four-Part Series of Talks for the Edmonton Museum of Arts, delivered in the Medical Building, University of Alberta, November 18, 1932, 71.213, file 102, UAA.[1]

FROM WHAT I HAVE SAID in previous lectures, the responsibility of the architecture of today lies not so much with the professional architects of today as with the society of today. The general social conditions [and] the prevailing sentiments of today are the great determining factors, but these it is not my business here to discuss in any detail. I wish rather to look at the architecture that is being produced and to describe the influences that are bearing directly upon it.

Hand versus Machine

In my first lecture on architecture as an art, I pointed out that one of the primary considerations in making things is the ability to manipulate nature's materials, the skill of human hands to shape things to the desires of the mind. I pointed out that the architecture of the Middle Ages displays the greatest triumphs of sheer handicraft. This is the mainstay of the beauty of mediaeval art. The mediaeval cathedrals, churches and, at the close of this period, the Tudor houses, are triumphs of workmanly beauty. Ruskin and

William Morris raised loud protest against the decay in modern times of the failure to maintain this hand-made element of beauty. It is still a subject of lament and justly so. The value of handicraft is immense. It is also a source of moral strength in the workman and in society. A class which has the opportunity to keep itself occupied with the work of its hands will be not only serviceably and intelligently occupied, it will be contented and happy. How desirable economically and socially would it be to have the majority of our citizens so occupied. All the interest that is taken today in handicrafts societies and their exhibitions is based on the realisation of these great facts.

The cause of the arts and crafts appears, however, to be commercially hopeless. In our precious wealth-pursuing age, they do not "pay." They are there with their offer of beauty and of contentment of life, but they are neglected—starved out by the machine-made products—by the competition of mass production against which they have not a chance. It ought to be clearly understood that the ability of the human hand, that magic power to evoke the charm of beauty, has not died, it lives today and it never shall die. It is submerged beneath competing powers.

On the other hand, the machine is here and it is not essentially a monstrous enemy of humanity—though in some cases it does appear so. Machines are invented to help humanity, even to alleviate its labours and to make its conditions happier. That they have done so has by some been categorically, emphatically, sometimes passionately denied. It has been said that not one human lot has been relieved, not one human being has been made happier by the introduction of machinery. This indictment is a terrible one and a formidable array of evidence can be produced in its support. I cannot think, however, that it is essentially true, or at least that [it] is always to remain true. The machine is produced by human reason with a reasonable purpose. If its products are not directly the work of the wonderful human hand, they are certainly still the products of the human mind and are capable of giving useful (or utilitarian) service and mental delight. The slab door (such as you see in this room, and still more beautifully done in our Arts Building, sometimes called a hospital door) is an example of a machine-made product which supports this statement. Its purpose is to help in providing hygienic conditions, a prominent modern demand, and this it effectively does. It also has a delightful quality to the eye, displaying the beauty of the natural grain of wood more effectively than any other form of wood construction.

Similar claims may be made for plywood generally, an essentially machine-made product.[2] There is a very large range of machine-made products in which the element of delight to the eye is neither neglected nor absent. It is truly, however, a harder job in producing machine-made work to attain superiority to handmade products than is generally realised. I am inclined to say that they very seldom do so. Their chief virtue is their mass production. This ought to mean that they are available for the benefit of a large proportion of people and perhaps this is a fact. I hope so, and I think it is so.

Materials

The next and still elementary point to which I called attention as an important element in architecture is the employment and display of the beauty of materials derived from nature—though maybe altered in some cases for better service by the art of man. There is certainly today a much larger range of these available through research of many kinds. Of all that may be called "new materials," however, no great proportion is essential to architecture, which has always served itself with the commonest and most widespread products of nature. Stones of greater or less preciousness are the materials the mountains are made of. Clay from which bricks are baked underlies the flat country generally. Wood is produced from trees. Even cement, which in its present form may be considered a new material, consists essentially of lime and clay, two of the commonest natural elements—and so with plaster. These are the main materials of the architect as they were 6,000 years ago.

Yet today there is an increasing demand for what may be classed as new material. Cement, especially in combination with small stones and steel as ferro-concrete or reinforced concrete, [is] demanded for the sake of safety against fire where, in floor and roof construction at least, it is economical and in some cases it has the advantage of rapidity in construction. This is the *material* that is having the most effect in demands for altered architectural forms.[3] Modern applications of metal and, in many cases, new alloys have had their influence chiefly in the mechanical accessories of architecture, the conveyance of steam, water, etc., and in fittings, sanitary apparatus, taps, hardware, etc. Chromium plate, stainless steel and various alloys are also being used more and more extensively for the sheathing of surfaces, external and internal.

Utility[4]

In considering the influence new materials are having, we have to consider the social demands which these fulfil. The modern demand that is having the greatest influence in bringing new materials into service of architecture is, I think, that of improved hygiene. This has itself been caused largely by the more congested manner of modern life, crowded as it is becoming into large cities. Medical science has been chiefly instrumental in voicing the demand.

I am inclined to think that modern ideas of hygiene have influenced, and are still influencing, the forms used in architecture more than any other motive, more even than any more highly scientific methods of structure. The demands of hygiene may be classed, I think, under two headings: increased cleanliness and better air.

To meet the demand for cleanliness requires the exclusion or ready elimination of dirt. This in turn does, of course, imply ample water supply, but so far as architectural appearance is affected, it demands more whiteness (or alternatively blackness), hardness and smoothness. Whiteness, or at any rate relative lightness of tone, is asked for so that dirt may be the more readily seen and marked down for destruction. Blackness is sometimes substituted with the same aim. Hardness, or at any rate impermeability of surface, is asked for so that dirt may not get beyond the surface and may be readily removed without doing injury to the surface. Smoothness goes with cleanability and, of course, implies a general simplification of architectural form.

Architecture today in consequence of these demands employs a great deal more of light-coloured (or black) porcelain as in sanitary ware, tiles, [and] white metal. (The spire-formed tops of some recent skyscrapers have been sheathed in bright metal).[5] Our interiors have become generally lighter in tone. The approved mediaeval lining for a room was oak panelling, now it is plaster. What was in old days considered a beautiful, restful tone would now be considered gloomy, though the older was the much more interesting to the eye. Perhaps the more brilliant key of light in our rooms may account for our more restless, less stable, temperaments. Lightness of tone has a farther hygienic value in that it is economical of light by absorbing less and therefore saves our eyesight.

The smoothness of form now demanded tends to eliminate all the intricate forms invented in past ages. The moulded panels, even on doors, tends to elimination of intricate form as in hospital doors and elsewhere. Panelling of all sorts tends to be driven from our walls. Hollow round corners are made and similar junctions between floors and walls, and ceilings and walls, [are now used]. All the paraphernalia of the classic orders—the joy and infinite resource of our learned and cultured eighteenth century ancestors with their cornices, carved friezes, moulded architraves, elaborate capitals and bases—are sins against modern ideas of hygiene. The logical end of all this is complete bareness of form and complete absence of colour. Shall we endure all this, or shall we risk the death that lurks in a shade of colour or a kink of surface?

This may seem amusing to you, but it is a serious matter for the poor architect. He is driven from his old beloved resources with the prospect of utter bareness before him. There are some rays of hope. In colour, concessions are made—we cannot live either healthily or happily in a blaze of whiteness, and there is much joy even in light tones of colour. If public health demands uniform smoothness, it would be dangerous to life on floors on which we cannot walk safely without slipping. On walls and other surfaces, public health would deny us the pleasure we may derive from varying textures; but for a long time to come the actual cost of complete smoothness will be a practical bar to living up to this, though it seems there will be continuous pressure towards it. As regards the entire simplification of form which is the ultimate aim of the ideal of smoothness, the point is a very serious one for the architect; and architects are in fact having a hard time endeavouring to meet the point, though it has not perhaps yet begun to concern the general public very seriously.

It is not only hygienic requirements that today are demanding a simplification of architectural forms. The classical orders of pillars upon a support, and themselves supporting a superstructure, have in the past commanded so much admiration and respect that they for a long while became customary. Long familiarity begot an affection for them so that for a long period they were a general demand. This is a historical fact. I have pointed out what an important and reasonable part they play in such buildings as St. Paul's Cathedral.[6] But this affection has now become loosened. It has begun to be felt that whilst they were an excellent stock in trade, they had come to exercise an undue domination in design. As internal decorative motifs, their somewhat intricate forms are objected to on hygienic grounds. Externally, their right to monopolise the scene is challenged, and the more so, probably mostly, because they are expensive to build. It is in fact widely demanded that architecture shall do without these well-accustomed building features. This does not, of course, imply that the principles of order, proportion, harmony and rhythm—especially as applied to essential structure and the utilitarian features of buildings such as distinguished from the said columns, bases, entablatures and cornices, etc.—are in any way challenged or excluded. But the best of principles cannot exist in visible form without some concrete members wherein they may be exhibited. The familiar members of the old orders are not necessary parts of modern structures. What then is to replace them? The columns may be replaced by rectangular piers, and plain wall surfaces may to some extent be relieved by projecting wall strips which are often structurally necessary. If we must have visible variations of form to satisfy the demands of the eye, what better, or other, forms can we give them than those that the wisdom of past ages devised? Above all, the magnificent and beautiful cornices that have been the outcome of so much fine thought and refined by so much care—what is to become of these? How are we to form any satisfactory visible crowning glory to our buildings wanting these? This, I think, states one important problem with which architecture is wrestling in experiment, with what success, you may judge from some examples of recent work.

The paraphernalia, the stock in trade, the staple material features that lay to the architect's hand in all that the Renaissance period had derived from the ancients, or built up for themselves from suggestions derived from ancient work, had a great interest for the eye. What interest can be supplied to take their place? I think we have not yet built up a sufficient supply of ready resources, but we have some at our command. In variety of material we are probably better off than any previous age. Bricks are now readily manipulated to every variety of texture and colour. Many other materials are brought into use for superficial clothing of our buildings: tile, glass, plywood and varieties of stucco, even new uses of metal, bright or otherwise. These may all be exploited in themselves and in their combinations and may be of great service in supplying interest to our work. In some cases, they are quite cheap and economical to use, in others so expensive that they must of necessity be reserved as special luxuries. Most of them affect the flat surface only and supply no new motif as to general form. Their value is in the flat, and not at all for supplying relief or form in three dimensions.

Painting [and Sculpture]
In many designs now appearing, architects, while still fulfilling the demand for general flatness and freedom from conventional classic features, endeavour to reinstate interest of appearance by bands, vertical or horizontal, or by spots of sculpture. This may seem an expensive resort and not to be quite faithful to the smoothness idea. Ingenuity may overcome much of the expense. It need not be open to the charge of not being of our time or for our time. Sculptural relief need not be of the superb sculptural skill of the Panathenaic Frieze of the Parthenon to produce an interesting textural effect. It may be little more than pattern-work. This resource is a

valuable one which is capable of more exploiting than it has yet undergone. The degree of relief to be obtained in this way, however, is not at most very great, though it may be fairly telling, especially if emphasised by colour.[7]

The possibility of resort to sculpture and to colour opens up a large and important question. In the great works which form our great heritage in architecture, there always appeared a close and apparently natural alliance of the works of architecture, of sculpture and of painting. Egyptian temples were painted and sculptured and works of sculpture stood around in great profusion. Greek temples were highly enriched with sculpture and they had certain brilliant touches of colour. Mediaeval cathedrals were vast fields for sculpture, much painting was employed on them, though most of this has disappeared. The windows were themselves paintings in transparent and living colour.

Modern buildings, by comparison, offer meagre opportunity for either sculpture or painting. The feeling is that these, even when employed, are merely added and are not inherently necessary to the idea and design. Why is this? It is not that architects have any objection to sculpture and painting. It is because the public has lost the appetite for this very desirable food for the mind, perhaps through not having experience of the enjoyment it affords. When I suggest that this is desirable, I mean that it would give a tremendous satisfaction if we could get it. Lay aside for a moment your probable mental reaction as to what it would cost. Forget for a minute, if that be possible, the existence of taxes and bank balances or deficits and all that sort of thing and, "Just Suppose."

Suppose we had on our walls in homes, in schools, in public libraries, in hospitals, even in universities, just quite generally, pictures. I don't mean pictures in gilt frames and glass hung up in odd places by strings and wires and wall hooks, but paintings in suitable hygienic light tones, if you like, and in such key of colour as really looked as if they belonged to their place, as if that is what ought to be there, and painted on the walls and forming part of the walls, not out-of-place excrescences and not pictures of things totally external to our lives, but of things that we feel are of ourselves, of our lives, of the things that make us what we are, of subjects that make us feel happier and better. In our homes these might be [like] windows from which there looks into us our own Alberta in its loveliest moods. Our mild and matchless gold of autumn on poplar and birch, our mountains pillaring our perfect sky, our skies that fill our two eyes full, our rivers and lakes with their high and wooded banks, our prairies, our winter, our summer. And are there not incidents in our history that are great and significant that are fit to live and reign in our minds, to keep in visible form before our eyes in our public buildings. Our painting should summarise and symbolise the things that really matter to us and that we love. I am a militant believer that one great function of painting is to teach, to inspire, and to gladden the heart of man. I believe our school room walls should be made to teach the essential lessons of good life, the beauty of good sentiment. There are many such lessons that can be painted with the charm that comes home to us in painting and that cannot be spoken.

We are probably far from any such condition of the use of sculpture and painting as I have sketched. But so far from the general idea being impossible, I believe it to be necessary, ultimately inevitable, if painting and sculpture are to enter our life, and perfectly practicable. Such things have been done before, and we shall live to do them better than ever before. Meanwhile, I believe you will all agree that the position of painting, and therewith the position of painters, is pretty nearly impossible. The work of the painter has no fit or acknowledged place in our social life. Consider how such work is handled. Painters work in isolation and in an atmosphere of forced and unhealthy individualism—or class isolation—and they paint their hearts out in their pictures. To give their work a chance of being even seen by their fellow men, they have to frame them in gold frames so as to emphasise their isolation from all other human things and to get them placed in public exhibitions, which I may suitably call pictorial prize fights. In a gamble, compared with which putting money on horses looks like a sound investment, they may have the luck to exchange these pictures for much needed money. The fate of these lucky pictures is to be hung on the walls of billiard rooms and smoking rooms of "moneyed" individuals whose appreciation of them may be great. But is all this a fitting way and end for painting? Is it any wonder that painters are often brain-sick and full of delirious fancies and ideals? The wonder is that painting survives; it would not do so if it did not have a charmed life. Perhaps some might question the technical ability of our painters to fill the situation I [have] sketched. To me, this suggestion is a sort of blasphemy against humanity and has no basis in fact. Our painters possess about ten times the necessary technical skill. They spend most of their time raising their technical skill to fantastic heights, many of them have more skill of hand than professional jugglers. We don't require all that, though it might all be used. What painters need is a popular enthusiasm to demand the kind of satisfaction that painting can give. Remember that law is greater than lawyers, architecture than architects, and just so, painting is greater than painters and is the business of the public, without whom they labour in vain.

This may appear to be a digression, but I feel that architecture is in many ways being robbed of human interest and, not least so, in its almost entire divorce from sculpture and painting. Whilst free sculpture and easel painting will always occupy an important place, these, by proclaiming themselves "free," proclaim themselves out of relation to architecture and they isolate themselves from many other important relationships to life. Created in isolation, they must be contemplated in isolation. The great *Last Supper* by Leonardo da Vinci was not thus isolated. It was made for its time and for its place, a part of the life of the refectory where it is placed, and still it is for all time, and the world can show no greater painting. The sculptures of the Parthenon have the same quality and the world can show no greater sculpture. But a great painting by Rembrandt or Velasquez is a very different matter. You cannot hang these anywhere where they will be thus in place. They cannot belong to any place. They ought to be put each in a separate room and should normally be kept covered up, to be contemplated from time to time by themselves and for themselves. Paintings vary greatly in their capacity for being related to surroundings. It has been remarked (by the Dean of Windsor, I think) that Canaletto's paintings have of late years greatly appreciated in value so that prices are being paid for them comparable to those given for works by Velasquez. No one would claim that Canaletto as a painter is on the same plane as Velasquez. The reason for the high prices is that people are finding that, as objects to take their places in drawing rooms, Canaletto's paintings are delightful, whereas Velasquez, as I have suggested, just won't belong there. Now Canaletto's paintings were not made for the places for which they are being purchased. Is it not reasonable to suppose that, with less skill than even Canaletto's, paintings could be produced for given places that would look more delightful than his—paintings that would have definite relationships to their place, to our time, to our interests and to *us*.

Functionalism

Claiming to supply a solution to the problems of modern architecture, there has arisen the school of "functionalism," more properly it should be called "utilitarianism." We hear a great deal from "functionalists," more in theory than in practice, and though some good results can be shown from their teaching, yet many of the results are hardly inspired or inspiring. This is not a school with any very fully developed or systematic code of doctrine; most of its teaching consists in a number of dogmatic statements—more or less consistent. In general, however, the functionalist say [that because] the conventional features of classic derivation have ceased to be the expression of the actual structure of a building, or to respond in any way to the convenience of use and service of the building, they must be absolutely banished. Form must only be dictated by convenience of use. Further, through the use of modern materials and the exploitation of these by scientific methods of structure, forms due *to requirements of structure* must give way to convenience of use. So that convenience of use, that is to say, utility, is left to us as the one controlling element of form.

Let us look at a few of the logical consequences of this theory so as to appreciate its meaning. The thoroughgoing functionalist shrinks from none of these consequences. We have hitherto been strongly inclined to arrange windows in tiers, one above the other so that those above will be exactly central over those below. This has commended itself to us, first because it was tidy and orderly—a geometrical reason, [and] second, because this arrangement lent itself well to good and economical construction—loads were concentrated regularly and carried directly to the ground, [satisfying] a demand for visible static quality. The functionalist says our reasons are insufficient. The least claim of convenience is sufficient to justify the windows being placed without any regard to our fanciful geometric order, and with our complete modern scientific control over structure, all the alleged difficulties of structure may be easily overcome, even if by invisible devices.

They farther point out that whereas we have hitherto imagined it necessary to make the corners of our buildings points where strength should reasonably be concentrated and [emphasised] for visible appeal, we can now easily secure sufficient strength anywhere. [Thus], we should place our windows at the corners of our rooms where they will light the rooms most efficiently, the light naturally sweeping along the walls and leaving no unlighted corners. If an important and necessary-looking corner post interferes in any degree with convenience, it must be removed [and] a system of cantilevers can be contrived so that its work may be accomplished without its interference. This is a plea for more liberty, and unfortunately an opportunity for license. These men are all for more thorough economic use for all constructed work, and will have roofs flat so that these also may serve practical human convenience.

Any projections from a wall surface in any way of cornices—as they generally serve no utilitarian end—must be abolished and the same fate awaits anything whose only excuse is that of ornament. All this will leave us rather a featureless, plain-faced, generally rectangular block, and we may regret its general resemblance to a packing case. If we say that this is not beautiful, the functionalist will say that it is beautiful, and anyway, it is all the beauty you can get in architecture, all you have any right to get. He will assure you that the only source of beauty in such work is efficient service; perhaps he will refer you to certain bridges which seem to derive their beauty from this principle, and, quite certainly, he will point proudly to the beauty of the modern motor car. If you produce some picture of an

Burgess showed a slide of LeCorbusier's Villa La Roche at Auteuil (built in 1923) as an example of functional architecture. The house now serves as the offices and archives of the Fondation Corbusier. (Architectural Review LXI, January-June 1927, p. 3.)

old-fashioned coach and claim for it a higher degree of beauty, he will say that it too depends mainly for its beauty on lines which were contrived for service only.

The point, however, is by no means so well taken as the functionalist imagines, as designers of motor cars are well aware. One motor car differs from another in glory. We at once realise that some have greater beauty than others. We say they are better designed. To what is this due? [It is] not by any means [due] entirely to their mechanical efficiency, but to their more thoroughly designed lines. The simpler geometrical forms of straight lines, squares and circles may perforce have given place to more subtle lines, to elliptical parabolic or cycloid forms, but the geometric idea of order is still the foundation of its beauty. Even if the designer be unaware of this, he has felt its compelling power.

Not all functionalists are prepared to carry their argument to the extreme logic of their position. In practice, those examples of their work that compromise least appear to me to be the most offensive. Some professional architects, however, have accepted the argument as having a high degree of rightness and have achieved some degree of success. We are assured by this school that if we do not like the results of their arguments, the fault is certainly not with either their arguments or their works, but lies in ourselves—that we have become so much the slaves of customary work that nothing else appears right to our jaundiced eyes, [and] that in time the goodness and beauty inherent in their work will triumph and be accepted as the only true beauty.

It seems to me that whilst the theories of the functionalists are right and form a right and necessary element in architecture, they simply do not cover the whole situation. Art is the shaping of the shows of things to the desires of the mind, and the mind has desires much more numerous, more extensive, and of a higher order than any the functionalists endeavour to satisfy. By the functionalists, a building is conceived of as a machine to live in. This is one of their most emphatic axioms, and sums up their whole case. A building is a machine to live in. Is this an adequate, a satisfying conception? I think there underlies the definition an inadequate conception of the meaning of living, and an exaggerated idea of the value of mechanical contrivance. I prefer to think of a building as something liveable and loveable, and to think of living as much more than the operating of machines and man as something more than a machine-tender. As for what is loveable, you may of course love your motor car, or any other machine you like, but the mind's desires—even in the meagre list of six which I set out in my first lecture—are more to be loved than smooth-running wheels and the apt adjustment of an implement to certain clearly defined physical uses.

In my first lecture I suggested six desires of the mind which I considered that buildings more especially may be shaped to satisfy: skill in work, beauty of material, utility, the show of static excellence, high orderliness and sentiment. Of all these, the functionalist chooses to place utility first, and merely to permit skill of work and beauty of material as necessary evils, the rest nowhere. This seems to me an inadequate view of the proportion of values.

Jazz

I must now refer to another influence which threatens to introduce a disturbing element into architecture. I shall be correct I think in calling it the jazz element. It arises probably from the sheer desire for novelty. At the best, it exhibits itself in the use of violently striking forms and colours sometimes definitely barbaric and with distinct resemblances in many cases to well-known barbaric forms and patterns. At its worst, it makes a bold endeavour simply to run contrary to all systems of acknowledged order. It is difficult for ordinary law-abiding people, or even for any one accustomed to render a reason for his actions, to execute work of this essentially lawless character. Yet there apparently are to be found ingenious persons who set themselves seriously to work on it. Its object is to startle or hypnotise. It is essentially, therefore, a modern method of advertising and its serviceableness to humanity begins and ends there. It is not surprising, perhaps, in this age of loud and blatant advertisement, that it achieves a certain amount of commercial success. It has, however, no place in architecture. Those who practice it are only showing off, they are not teaching or inspiring. Such work may have a power to distract the mind from other and better things, but it cannot satisfy the desires of healthy minds.[8]

Skyscrapers[9]

I wish now to take up the solution to modern problems that architects are producing along this line. And first, because as I shall show, the very nature of the case has almost of itself offered something in the way of solution, I shall take up the question of tall buildings, commonly called skyscrapers. It is curious and interesting to note that in modern times, that is, since the fifteenth century, the Italians produced the initial solution to modern architecture of the beautiful straight facaded building; France gave us the great wide spread building punctuated with corner and intermediate projections; and England produced the group with an important central mass supported by minor outlying masses.[10] America's contribution is the building whose height greatly exceeds its breadth. This type, the tall building,

The Woolworth Building, New York. (Photo by Donald Wetherell)

is so far confined to America, being deliberately excluded by building regulations from other countries, with the possible exception of Canada where the present tendency is to admit them under certain conditions.

The form of the skyscraper is one of the most striking in recent architecture. Towers, of course, are from of old, but the tower for human occupation is a response to certain modern conditions of life and is the result of modern methods of construction, especially structural steel. It was for long the attempt of American architects to apply the usual Renaissance features to these buildings. Strenuous efforts were made to give them horizontality of design and composition, and to cap them with the classical crowning features by constructing cornices appropriate to their great scale by building these cornices up with structural steel sheathed with galvanised steel or with copper sheet. More recently, however, it has been recognised that this was a laborious and difficult operation, often of doubtful success or value, and their tower-like masses and the essential verticality of their structure naturally suggested the application of the principles of design for which there was excellent precedent in the mediaeval church towers in which no classical cornices were applied. The Woolworth building in New York and many others were actually made mediaeval in their details generally. Even these mediaeval dressings were found to be unessential. The very tall proportions accentuated by the recurring vertical lines, which the method of construction required or suggested, gave an essential interest to their outlines. Intakes at certain levels could be made to supply an interest of proportional parts, and, finally, the tall central tower with its well-proportioned divisional reductions could be set upon spreading masses at the base to produce forms of great contrast and interest of outline. This, at the same time, goes a long way towards meeting hygienic demands and giving "stability." In the case of these buildings, the problem seems to be at least well on the way to varied solutions without the aid of so much of conventional ornament as to have any prominence in their general lines. A diagram will show how the skyscraper is carved into interesting form by the application of modern building regulations made in the interest of hygiene.[11]

But the future of the skyscraper itself is by no means assured. It fails to meet certain modern requirements, more especially that highly essential one of public hygiene. This point is probably best brought home by the statement that by reason of the great height of buildings in New York, more than a million people—more nearly two million—get no direct sunlight either in their dwellings or in their places of work. I have, however, [later] shown how this objection is capable of being fairly met.[12] Farther, the increase of high buildings in great cities has led to such congestion of population in certain centres that traffic problems are reaching a point of despair. Finally, the high building has not clearly justified itself economically. It may eventually do so, but during the present depression it is said that all have become disastrous commercially, being "all vacant above the twentieth story." Frequently no view [of the building is] possible except from sea or lake.

Unless we accept the skyscraper as the real solution of ideal city building, we must still consider the building of more moderate height, and the blocks of buildings of greater length than height, to form the bulk of buildings of the future. The problem is to inspire these with interest under the pressure of [the] demand for smoothness and the general flatness that is the necessary result if this demand still remains.

In those cities which forbid the skyscraper—and most great cities in the world definitely do so—there are regulations which require that, for hygienic reasons, buildings which rise above a certain height at the street line may be carried still higher only on condition that the higher stories are set back a certain distance from those beneath. This regulation made for hygienic reasons has resulted in an added interest of form and a field for exercise of proportion. Since the terraced-type of building thus evolved can without offence to any ideas of hygiene or serviceableness be provided with balconies, which almost of necessity introduce an element of interest, this again supplies the architect with a valuable resource.[13]

Having dealt with certain exceptional classes of buildings, I will now take up some more normal types and first, I will deal with Swedish architecture. This deserves a foremost place in the architecture of today for the

Ragnar Östberg's Stadshus, Stockholm. (Architectural Review LV, January-June 1924, p. 1.)

reason that it is the result of a real popular enthusiasm for architecture. Public buildings in Sweden may be said to respond to William Morris's fine dictum that art should be carried on by the people, for the people, a joy to the maker and the user.

Swedish Architecture

1. *The Stadshus at Stockholm*

    The Stadshus at Stockholm by Ragnar Östberg is one of the most typical examples of Swedish architecture. It sits with two fronts facing upon the water, the long terrace front is shown in the photograph. The main portions of the walls are of deep red brick, the pillars of the arcade are of granite, the smaller decorations at some of the windows and the delicate work of the balcony are of marble. The cupolas of wood (though Östberg wanted to have granite) are touched with gold. The roof is of vivid green copper, each copper plate of which was a gift of a citizen.

The great glory of the place is the Banqueting Hall, Östberg's Golden Hall. It is of splendid dimensions 137 x 42 and 41 feet high and the effect is said to be "no less than majestic." The windows along the side are set in deep semicircular niches with very beautiful effect. (The windows in St. Paul's, London are similarly set.) The sole decoration of the walls is gold-glass mosaic which has a cool yellow or even greenish tint. The colossal mosaic figure on the centre of the end wall represents Stockholm, "The Queen of Mälar," receiving tributes from east and west. The mosaic walls are enriched with patterns and figures of the mythical and historical heroes of Sweden. The ceiling beams are of concrete of the natural colour enriched with geometrical patterns painted in crimson red. These patterns form longitudinal lines in the ceiling. The floor is of cool-grey Kölmarden marble sufficiently smooth to take reflections from the golden walls and from the furniture.

2. *The Concert House, Stockholm*

[In] the Concert House at Stockholm by Ivar Tengbom, the walls of this building are finished in stucco, blue-grey in colour. The pillars are sixteen-sided and their colour is raw umber slightly tinged with purple. The general design is, of course, derived originally from Greece. The later Greek work tended to become more and more slender in its proportions. Here the attenuation is carried much farther, presumably in logical accord with the greater tensile strength of reinforced concrete. These proportions may offend eyes accustomed to the transcendent beauty of the ancient work. It may, however, be conceded that this building appears to belong to its place and surroundings, whereas a strict copy of the classic colonnade with its cosmopolitan air would not appear truly Swedish.

[In the] interior of the Great Concert Hall, the attenuated columns reappear. The actual ceiling of this hall is a smooth curve which passes clear over the cornice and disappears behind it so as to detach the general structure of the rest of the hall and give it the illusion of an out-of-doors theatre. This open-air effect is carried on beyond the pillars of the fixed scene. This permanent scene is in forced perspective, appearing deep whilst really not far from upright. The panels are an open-work grille to admit the sound of the organ which is placed beyond the visible end wall. Since the main ceiling of the hall passes clear above the top cornice, the main artificial lighting of the hall is placed back beyond this cornice, out of sight of the audience who receive the light only by reflection from the ceiling. The fronts of the galleries are covered with stretched cloth with hand-worked Swedish embroidery, the background of the lower fronts being darker, the upper, lighter in tone.

Within the Concert House there is a second smaller concert hall besides a splendid entrance hall, crush halls and other rooms in the decoration of which all the finest artistic workmanship of Sweden was enrolled, including sculpture by Karl Milles. Yet the effect everywhere may be described as that of rich simplicity.

The keynote of Swedish architecture is the desire to make Swedish life happier, and surely no art could have a healthier root. It may fail to charm us as seen here in photograph. The ways of it are Swedish and unfamiliar to us. The traditions these people love and express are not our traditions, but all the more on that account it is appropriate and right in its own place.

Buildings in England

1. *Imperial Chemical House*

    At the north end of Lambeth Bridge facing the Thames, London, by Sir Frank Baines (opened February 22, 1929). This may be considered a typical conservative modern London office building, containing, as many of these now do, recreation rooms and restaurant for the accommodation of the employees in the many offices in the buildings. In this case, there is a gymnasium and squash courts in the basement. An office building being thus approximated to a club.

Building regulations required the setback of the upper stories, though it is hard to see why they should since the building has the whole width of the Thames opposite to it. This regulation, however, has added to the interest of the appearance of the building. The architect has evidently not been so austere a modernist as to feel impelled to exclude the use of the classic orders. The material is all stone, including the roofing material. The ground storey is of polished grey granite—for cleanness. The building is eighty feet high to the first cornice line and fifty feet above that, one hundred and thirty feet in all, about the legal limit.

2. *Broadcasting House*

At the head of Regents Street, London, by G. Val Myer. As in the case of the Offices of the Underground (to be next shown), the orders and all belonging to them are excluded, there being neither cornice nor column anywhere. This building was completed in the present year.

3. *The Head Offices of the Underground Railway*

In Westminster, London, by Adams Holden and Pearson (1929). This building is, clearly, shaped in accordance with the modern demands and needs that I have called attention to. The ancient scheme of orders and their accessories have disappeared. From the hygienic regulations demanding setbacks to various distances at different levels, a considerable degree of interest has been derived—making a virtue out of necessity. The extreme severity of the building is hardly felt, on account of the vigorous stepped masses.[14]

[With the] fireplace in the Chairman's Room, you will see that the same spirit of severity has been, I think, successfully carried out in the interior. Projections are reduced to a minimum. Beautiful material supplies the chief interest—in this case a light grey (Subiac) and black (Belgian) marble. The clock is of gold lacquer.

The Head Office of the Underground Railway, London. (Architectural Review LXVI, no. 396, November 1929, p. 229.)

4. *The New Royal Horticultural Hall*[15]

In London, England by East and Robertson (1928). This is an exhibition hall intended for flower shows. The whole form as you may easily realise is controlled by a structural expedient. The great parabolic curve of the roof, seventy feet in span, is a feat of modern economical engineering. Not having myself seen this hall, I shall give you an appreciation of it in the words of an enthusiastic admirer, Mr. P. Morton Shand:

> The first glimpse of the great hall is one of the most thrilling which the interior of any modern building has to offer—unlimited light and air seem to have been joyously captured in that splendidly luminous and intrepid vault. Involuntarily one takes a deep exhilarating breath on entering it as when after just turning to enjoy the view on reaching the summit of a mountain. Concrete has been taught to smile. There is a complete absence of grimness and the sense of roughly conglomerated or ponderous bulk. The eye takes up delightedly the soft felicity of contrast between the iron grey ribs, offset and mellowed by the silvery brickwork on each side (on the lower part of the walls and not well seen in the photograph) and the glowing ochre of the acoustic plaster (on the ceilings and upper part of the walls).[16]

The line of square chequered panels under the lower windows form part of the scheme of warming and ventilating which is said to be excellent. The panels themselves, simple as they are, are finely decorative.

5. *Ideal House*

At Great Marlborough Street, London, by Gordon Jeeves and Raymond Hood (1929). In this building, the traditional classical elements are dispensed with. The hygienic demand for cleanability is met. The intake at the top is probably due to building bylaw requirements in the interest of light and air. Instead of white, black has been used as about equally good for exposing the presence of dirt. The lack of the classical features has left the building bare and this bareness has been relieved by colour.

The Royal Horticultural Hall, London. Burgess used this image in his 1932 lecture on architecture at the Edmonton Museum of Art. (Architectural Review LXV, no. 386, January 1929, p. 25.)

Resort has been made to the use and display of the beautiful materials available for modern use. These give the building a definite preciousness of appearance which of itself is an excellent quality.

The main wall surfaces are of black Swedish granite five inches thick facing a concrete structure. The frames of the doors and of the windows are finished with twenty-two carat double English gold leaf. The other windows have frames and sash bars in white. The ornamental

This is the photo of Ideal House, London, that Burgess showed in his 1932 architecture lecture at the Edmonton Museum of Art. (Architectural Review LXV, no. 391, June 1929, p. 290.)

framing around the doors and windows of the ground storey are of cast bronze inlaid with enamel in yellow, gold, orange, green and red.

This building has naturally called forth a number of criticisms. I shall mention some:

— The walls being of polished black granite and the windows being naturally of polished glass, the building is apt to appear, according to the light, either all black or all a grey sheen. In other words, the contrast between window and wall is apt to disappear.

— Next, the building is aggressively self-assertive, having no relation to its neighbours and this of set purpose for "advertisement value." I could wish that modern advertisement took no worse form than this.

6. *Daily Express Building*

At Fleet Street at corner of Shoe Lane, London by Herbert Ellis and Clarke. This building is constructed of reinforced concrete and faced with specially toughened, polished black glass. A space between the concrete and the glass is filled with pumice-concrete for insulation. The plates of black glass are fixed in place with strips of silver white metal (Bermabright). The window frames are all of metal. The glazing on one floor at least is of ultraviolet-ray glass. The rail running around the building at the fourth storey is a track from which a cradle may be hung for the purpose of washing down the building. A reasonable system of static design is observed in the broad window's vertical bands. That ideas of hygiene and of the display of fine materials govern the design is obvious. It may be said that such a building as this is erected largely for advertising purposes. This method of advertising may here be compared with others or some of its neighbours.

7. *RIBA Premises*

In London. Not yet built.

— Premiated design, G. Grey Warnum.[17]

— Third premiated design, Percy Thomas and Frank Prestwich, sculptured frieze aiding proportional division as well as texture.

8. *High and Over [Ashmole House]*

In Amersham, Bucks, England, by Amyas Connell. This typically modernist house was built by Bernard Ashmole, Professor of Archaeology at the University of London. The architect Amyas Connell had won a Rome

Daily Express Building, London. (Architectural Review LXXII, no. 431, October 1932, p. 221.)

Scholarship for the study of classical architecture and was working in the British School at Rome when Professor Ashmole first met him. The plans were passed "with extreme reluctance" by the local authorities whose duty it was to preserve the character of the countryside in the matter of new buildings.

The owner says it "was built with three main objectives: to take advantage of the scanty English sunshine; to enjoy to the full the magnificent view across and up the valley of the Misbourne; and to conform to the immediate contours." It is built of reinforced concrete stuccoed on the outside. On the whole, it is the nearest approach to the so-called functionalist type of building that I could find worthy of calling to your attention. It is, however, far from being uncompromisingly utilitarian. The interior is, I think, much more interesting than the exterior.

[In] the living room, the walls are plastered and sprayed with jade-green cellulose (sometimes in this country known as Duco), a paint which sets with a particularly glossy and hard finish which makes it suitable for motor cars. The corners and small trim around the doors are of chromium-plated steel. The steel doors are cellulosed silver and glazed. Indirect lighting comes through the flat ceiling panels.

The whole building definitely aims to supply the wants of a family with healthy appetites for work and play, and for the enjoyment of light and life, of beautiful material within and of the fine outlook upon a beautiful country without. To these ends no expense of thought or money is spared. All that modern science can suggest for the accomplishment of these aims has been taken advantage of, and all that does not contribute to these aims has been sacrificed so that the total effect outside and inside is one of simplicity. In the inside a rich simplicity, but externally somewhat impoverished.

That enthusiasm for the use of unusual materials can be carried to fantastic extremes may be judged from the following quotation from an appreciative criticism of a building which is perhaps not so extreme as the appreciation itself.

> Enter the long hall and you suffer a sea change. From the walls of silver lead sprayed with aquamarine lacquer and the semi octagonal ceiling arch of silvered fluted glass, the light reflects with a subaqueous sheen deepened and made more Atlantean by the polished black Induroleum of the floor. Here is Marvell's "green thought in a green shade." The smooth, textureless surfaces give the light a gloss, a lustre, a still liquidity, which is at once strange, restful and leaves the clean lines of the hall unsoftened from their geometrical conciseness. The transparency of the planes, far from deliquescing their containing lines, serves all the more to accentuate their straight delicacy and firm articulation, and little could be more refreshing than the spider-web intersections of the plate-glass junctures in the mansard ceiling. This rests on a narrow ledge of gold fluted glass supported by plate-glass dentils at its lateral ends, and again the vitric edge has an acute firmness unbelied by the apparent lightness of the material. This combination of certain line and transparent plane has all the clarity and lightness of a washed pen-drawing,

and so forth for a page or two. All this seems to me "journalese" of quite a brain-sick order.[18]

9. *Stratford Theatre*
Elizabeth Scott [architect]. This building has not, I believe, met with much popular approval. Let me quote to you the estimate of Mr. Christopher Hussey, a wise critic, strongly inclined to favour all fresh endeavour:

> The main masses, logical expressions of the plan which dictated them, form by themselves an interesting composition of simple forms, which the architect has let to speak for themselves. Irrelevant ornament has been eliminated altogether—when one considers

the amount of fustian and false sentiment that the name of Shakespeare can be made to invoke, one cannot be too thankful that a design so honest and courageous as Miss Scott's was selected.

But I think that the building just falls short of complete success. Simple as its main masses are and honestly dealt with, the whole is made rather restless by frequent variations of scale. And Miss Scott seems not to have been quite clear whether the elevations were to be symmetrically balanced or not. The main masses are quite regular, but the lower portions surrounding them seem anxious to deny the fact. On the river front the levels change frequently and, in accordance with her belief in honesty being the best policy, Miss Scott has let them have their own way. A little coaxing, a little give and take, a little more tact, and I think the whole could have been given greater distinction. Nevertheless, a problem of the utmost difficulty has been solved with considerable ability, and Stratford can invite the world to a theatre surpassed by none in efficiency and inspired by much that is best in contemporary English architecture.

I think it would be fair to sum this up by saying that utilitarian qualities have usurped too high a place in the work.

10. *Roman Catholic Cathedral, Liverpool*
Perspective View. The [largest] building of all times. Of a greater area than St. Peter's at Rome and of greater height. The view was published in September 1930, the line drawings in April 1932.

— In this view the main arch over the entrance appears insufficiently abutted. The contrast between brick and stone appears rather unpleasant; the choice of the brick and of the stone would make this a beautiful element of interest and colour.
— Apparently many very large windows on the upper stage of the main walls.

— The base of the dome and its general form insufficiently abutted by the eight relatively small buttress masses.
— The main masses slope inward in the manner, though more delicately, than the Egyptian pylon.
— The great dome, 168 feet in diameter, is not massively abutted on the four diagonals.
— The parabolic line of structure is more evident and is emphasised by the sloping lines of the main masses.
— The general air is almost austere but relieved by the two steeples with cheerful tops and by the trim around the windows at wide intervals.

Expensive Buildings

The buildings which we may call the most up-to-date, that set themselves to take advantage of all that modern science and modern manufacturers have made available and that modern thought has suggested as most beneficial, are necessarily costly and therefore are produced by and for either wealthy individuals or wealthy companies. Is this high-cost building in accord with modern social ideals—with what some years ago we rather proudly spoke of as democratic ideals? Is it justifiable? Is it wise?

When society is in a very primitive condition, wealth is equally distributed because there is nothing to distribute. If society progresses at all there is bound to come a time when individuals, by greater industry, strength or ingenuity, produce something more than their neighbours. Wealth is then unequally distributed, but there is more of it. The richer individuals have not made society poorer, but richer. When they proceed to spend their riches they distribute them so that every individual is richer, though if the richer people are few and the poorer are many, the general rise may be imperceptible.

As society advances and becomes more complex, many methods of creating wealth arise. All occupations that tend to increase the production of desirable things or that tend to increase the health, happiness, peaceableness or intelligence of the community do their share in the production of wealth. The general improvement is brought about by pioneers of all kinds. The first advances in society are made by strength, by skill, by diligence. All such advances require some special power. In our own relatively advanced civilisation, much of this special power is in the form of accumulated wealth which is thus one of the forms of strength by which pioneer advances may be made. The spending of this wealth ensures that it belongs to society; generally, it is part of the common wealth. No matter in whose hands it is, its expenditure is *distributing* wealth from the richer to the poorer.

Those people who introduce these new materials and methods of doing things do so at a great cost. Naturally the first introduction of anything new is costly—there being no general demand for it. In these high-cost buildings, these new ideas are put to the test of experiment. These people are pioneers in the use of new materials and expedients, some of which will not prove ultimately satisfactory, but there is good hope that many of them, possibly most of them, will give the satisfaction that is expected. The most beneficial, the most desirable, of these new things will no doubt gradually come into more general demand and increased supply will reduce their cost and so bring many of the best into general use. In what other way could this be done? How is this sort of pioneering to be done? By the rich or in some kind of socialistic way? I know of no approach to this question from the socialist side. On the other hand, I know of no valid objection to the rich doing it, nor to there being rich people to do it.

The fact that one man is rich does not make his neighbours poorer, it makes them richer. The fact that a minority is rich does not make the majority poorer, it makes them richer. That all should be equally rich together is obviously impossible. It would mean that all enjoyed the same things (whereas tastes differ), and I suppose that all should work equally profitably through equal durations of time. It would involve the equal proportioning of imponderable values and incommensurate things, which, as Euclid says, is absurd.

Now as regards the advisability of putting expense into buildings rather than into other things, I read in the current number of the *Architectural*

Journal (R.I.B.A. October) "It is significant that the Building Industry has during the last thirty years or so grown, almost imperceptibly, to be the largest directly employing industry in the country (the United Kingdom). It has become the industry upon which almost every other form of industry depends for, in some part the investment of its capital and, in some instances, the greater portion of its capital. In the creation and stabilisation of national wealth it is pre-eminently the most fundamental industry of the country." In other words, it is second to none as a means of distributing wealth.

[Conclusion]

I have now passed in review the great buildings of the past and have shown you what efforts are being made in the present to make some contribution. With these efforts I have every sympathy and have hope that we also shall be able to make some worthwhile addition to the resources of architecture. The architects of the Middle Ages did so when they showed how great and inspiring work could be produced by the magic skill of the human hand. The Renaissance architects made another valuable contribution when they showed how the wall itself, apart from any screen of columns, could be a living and expressive thing. We still learn the great fundamental lessons from the architecture of Greece and Rome as almost all the buildings of first class importance testify. Of all buildings of the past, the greatest inspiration still comes from that broken building on the rocky crag of Athens—the Parthenon.

Such then is the work of architecture and it is, as I have said, the business of the public in which the professional architect can only play a secondary though essential part. When we consider the danger to our cities of a deadly monotony due to the continuous multiplication of buildings over endless acres, you will realise that a more general survey and control of these things is necessary than can be exercised by any individual. Beautiful buildings are essential to beautiful cities, but beautiful buildings may easily lose their effect in promiscuous and ill-ordered surroundings. Therefore, it is of the utmost importance to the architecture of the future that [if] our cities should not grow rankly and promiscuously, there must be a general control and direction over the development of cities themselves. Cities are not made, they rather grow, but over this growth the modern science of town planning is capable of exercising great and beneficial control. To establish scientific town planning in a city is, I firmly believe, the only hope to save our modern cities from a deplorable condition of confusion and ugliness and, incidentally, to give architecture a chance to tell with any value.

To return now to the point from which I started. What is Art? "The shaping of the shows of things to the desires of the mind." What is the sphere of art? Whatsoever we do or make is the subject of art. If we try to spread more truthful ideas as to the nature and relative values of the affairs of life, if we endeavour to preach the gospel of love of man to man, or of justice to all, or of the tempering of justice with mercy, the motives that impel us belong to the sphere of morality, but the means we take belong to the sphere of art. We shall not succeed in our efforts unless we apply in practice the principles of order and proportion and apply these principles to build up in a stable manner institutions and practices out of the elements that we find useful for this building. We distinguish a sphere of morality as something apart from art—apart from the creative faculty. But morality cannot act upon life without art. Nor, on the other hand, can art if divorced from morality attain its end, the satisfying of the desires of the mind, for the healthy mind desires the satisfaction of the moral sense. It will not be satisfied with hatred, with falsehood, with injustice, or cruelty.

Again, science is the acquisition of the knowledge of the materials and the forces of nature. If knowledge is to acquire any force, to have any wide sphere, study must be proceeded with, with system and classification. Thus again, the application of the principles of order and proportion are called in. Art is the tool which we must employ to establish science. The application of science to the service of man is an affair of art—the creative faculty. Here again, art has need of science, without knowledge of the materials and forces of nature art can do nothing. The more knowledge art has, the greater its power. To run counter to science can never satisfy the desires of the mind. To employ science to the limit of our powers is itself a great mental satisfaction.

In all the dealings that men have with men in whatsoever sphere—in conversation in its widest sense—the turning or mixing together of men with men, the appreciation of order and proportion, and the due employment of the means at our disposal, which vary according to the nature of these dealings, is an art—the greatest art of all—the art of living for which our moral sense is the motive, knowledge the guiding power. Art is the doing of work well that is to the satisfaction of the mind, of the whole being. As law is greater than lawyers, architecture is greater than architects, so art is greater than artists. It is the human creative faculty, a talent to be put to common use, not to be hidden away in a napkin.

We have been studying the small part of the sphere of art which we call architecture—the housing of men in their occupations with efficiency and happiness. We have seen some of the satisfaction that is within the sphere of this particular art to give. These satisfactions range from the slightest pleasure to the eye through the exercise of our several mental faculties to heights of great sentiment. I do not claim for architecture the highest place amongst the arts. It must always work with solid and relatively intractable materials. It cannot soar as music on vibrations of the air, nor can it raise the mind to the ecstatic heights that are within the reach of poetry, literature and painting. It must lay many a humble utilitarian duty upon itself. But all the more for that, it is especially the community art, the common art. Its feet must always be upon the ground and its strength must be to stand still. The conditions by which it is bound compel sobriety and sanity. It is not apt to be blown about by every wind of doctrine. It is essentially part of man's home on earth, the home not only of his body but of his mind, the environment from which all the other arts emanate and in the midst of which they must take their setting. Architects fondly speak of her as the mistress art because to them all other arts appear as the handmaids of architecture. Painting, poetry, song or story must find their most fitting home here. These are not her rivals, but each another jewel in her crown. Happiest in serving them all, her honour is exalted by her services.

By the application of the simple tests that I have suggested, one may go far in the appreciation of architecture. The aims of architecture today are in their broad lines the same as ever and the same as of all the arts.

— We still demand skill in the production of work
— The adequate employment and display of the materials at our disposal
— Good service for utilitarian ends
— Stability of appearance
— Order, high orderliness, conspicuous order and then fine sentiment governing all will ensure good architecture.

LANTERN SLIDES—*Appreciation of Architecture*[19]

1. Head Offices Underground. *Architectural Review* LXVI, plate III, p. 226.
2. Chimney Piece, Head Offices Underground, *Architectural Review* LXVI, p. 239.
3. Stockholm, Stadshus, West front, *Architectural Review* LV, p. 5.
4. Stockholm, Stadshus, The Golden Hall, *Architectural Review* LV, p. 7.
5. Concert House [Stockholm], main front, *Architectural Review* LXV, p. 185.
6. Concert House [Stockholm], interior, *Architectural Review* LXV, p. 190.
7. Horticultural Hall London, *Architectural Review* LXV, p. 25.
8. Ideal House London, *Architectural Review* LXV, plate III, p. 290.
9. Daily Express Building, *Architectural Review* LXXII, July plate II, p. 4.
10. High and Over, exterior, *Country Life,* September 19, 1931, p. 302.
11. High and Over, interior, *Country Life,* September 19, 1931, p. 305.
12. Broadcasting House, *Country Life,* May 2, 1932, p. 596.
13. Stratford on Avon Theatre N.E., *Country Life,* April 23, 1932, p. 464.
14. Stratford on Avon Theatre, E., *Country Life,* April 23, 1932, p. 465.
15. Canadian Bank of Commerce, Toronto, Cutting.
16. Walnut St. Garage Building, Philadelphia, Cutting.
17. Bau Ingenieur, p. 6 bottom, illustration 5. Nicolai Claude Datmund.
18. New R.I.B.A., *Journal,* R.I.B.A., May 14, 1932, frontispiece.
19. New R.I.B.A., *Journal,* R.I.B.A., May 14, 1932, p. 577, lower left.
20. Roman Catholic Cathedral, Liverpool from West, *Country Life,* September 30, 1930, p. 335.
21. Roman Catholic Cathedral, Liverpool, West elevation, *Country Life,* September, 1932, p. 490.
22. School Amsterdam, *Architectural Review,* March 1932, p. 106, fig. 1.

23. Roman Catholic Church, Prague exterior (by Joseph Gocau), *Architectural Review* LXIX, p. 152, fig. 2.
24. Roman Catholic Church, Prague interior, *Architectural Review* LXIX, p. 152, fig. 3.
25. Church at Montmagny, *Journal*, R.I.B.A., 1927, p. 323.
26. House at Auteuil by LeCorbusier (Jenneret), *Architectural Review* LXI, p. 3, upper only.
27. Los Angeles Public Library *Architectural Review* LXVI, p. 27.

NOTES

1. In the original manuscript, slides used in the talk were listed in the text by number. These numbers have been omitted because there is no correlation between these notations and the extant list of slides.
2. Hand-written in margin: "explain."
3. Hand-written in margin: "Large unobstructed floor spaces/high buildings/rapid because slight construction."
4. Hand-written in margin: "multifarious types of buildings—all affected by similar modern ideas."
5. Burgess may have been alluding to the Chrysler Building, New York, which had opened two years earlier.
6. In Lecture 3 (not printed), Burgess had noted the centrality of classical columns in Wren's design. Burgess had also noted that not all of these columns were structurally necessary but defended their use as "concrete form and features by means of which play and proportions, rhythms [and] harmonies can be made, and since in themselves they display the law of structural beauty, they have a special appropriateness" ("The Appreciation of Architecture, Lecture 3, The Yesterday of Architecture," 71.213, file 101, UAA).
7. Hand-written in margin: "Explain later re: RIBA [Royal Institute of British Architects] building."
8. Hand-written in margin: "Structuralist and Functionalist work slides." These slides are not identified in the text or in the list of slides. Presumably, one of them was Le Corbusier's La Roche House at Auteuil.
9. Hand-written in text: "Stability/Structuralism. A more important matter is that of modern pioneering with new structural methods—much on the basis of mediaeval development of new forms of stone construction but now in structural steel and in reinforced concrete."
10. Burgess had discussed these various building forms and styles in Lecture 3 (not reprinted).
11. The diagram is not part of the manuscript. In the margin is written "Ferris." This presumably refers to an article by Hugh Ferris on the set back provisions of the New

12. York building bylaw (Hugh Ferris, "And the Zoning Laws of New York," *Architectural Review* 58 (November 1925): 174–77).
12. See also lecture on town planning, "Land Coverage. Insolation: Building Heights" (not dated, ca. 1939, 71.213, file 65, UAA) which draws on the theories of Walter Gropius (specifically an article in the RIBA *Journal* (1934): 692), on recommended spacing and setbacks for tall buildings.
13. Hand-written in text to introduce unidentified slides: "Other structuralist buildings in reinforced concrete. Functionalist Buildings/Materialist."
14. Hand-written in margin: "Epstein's 'Night and Day.'" This reference concerns two sculptures above the doors of the building. The sculptor was Jacob Epstein, who created two nude figures—one male and one female. There was public outcry, and to mollify his critics, Epstein reduced the size of the penis on the one figure. Apparently, the female figure did not cause equivalent concern. Other sculpture on the building by Eric Gill and Henry Moore was less controversial. For contemporary illustrations of this building and the sculptures used by Burgess in this lecture, see Walter Bayer, "Sense and Sensibility: The New Head Offices of the Underground Railway, Westminster, London," *Architectural Review* 57 (November 1929): 225–41.
15. This section is preceded by a heading, "The Central Public Library, Los Angeles by Goodhue." There is no text in the manuscript. One slide illustrating this building is listed.
16. The source for this is P. Morton Shand, "Salute to Adventurers. The New Royal Horticultural Hall. Designed by Easton and Robertson," *Architectural Review* 65 (January-June 1929): 17–31.
17. Hand-written in margin, "set back."
18. Hand-written in text: "Article Finella A.R. LXVI p. 265." The reference is "Finella: A House for Mansfield D. Forbes, Raymond McGrath Architect," *Architectural Review* 66 (December 1929): 265–72.
19. The Appreciation of Architecture, Lecture 4. 71.213, file 102, UAA.

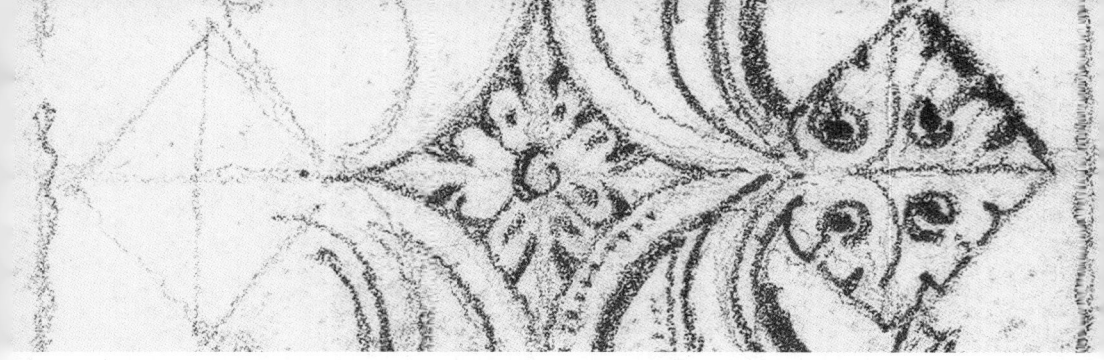

DOCUMENT 13

Recent Domestic Architecture

THE CHANGES that Modernism brought in use of materials and its assertion that function was a primary architectural value did not persuade Burgess to substantially change his views about domestic architecture. As he had asserted in his 1913 talk (Document 4), domestic architecture needed to meet people's day-to-day needs and to serve as a conduit for tradition and meaning. Rather than mimicking the ethos of a machine, house design needed to respond to actual social, not theoretical, needs. Important among these needs was the comfort and shelter of the family within an affordable environment. Thus, while he saw the new construction materials favoured by Modernists as adaptable to the traditional home, he was less certain that their demand for efficiency should be the primary objective of design.

Burgess was not unique in seeing the traditional house as offering a bulwark against the rapid social and technological change of the interwar years. It was often contended that the changes brought by such things as movies, radio and *public entertainment threatened social stability and the familiar lines of authority among men, women and children. Indeed, in his 1927 report to the Alberta government, the Calgary lawyer, Gerald Pelton, had asserted that the home needed to be strengthened to control social change and prevent juvenile delinquency.*[1] *Burgess only partly endorsed this type of thinking. Indeed, he often welcomed greater community activity as a way of building a better society. Nonetheless, he did strongly agree with popular sentiments that the home was a central social institution and argued that domestic architecture could play a central part in strengthening the family as a social institution.*

Document 13 is a talk on Radio Station CKUA, November 2, 1932, 71.213, file 145, UAA.

AT THIS HOUR last week, I spoke on the subject "Modern Architecture" generally.[2] My subject this week is "Recent Domestic Architecture" particularly. Last week I said that the aim of architecture is to serve the public by housing it in its public and private life, in its work, and in its recreation and to do so in such a manner that this work and recreation may be carried on both efficiently and happily. Evidently, domestic architecture too must provide for both work and recreation for there is always work as well as recreation carried on in our private houses.

Ideas of how to live our private lives are changing, and have changed a good deal recently. Different people have different ideas about this matter and the circumstances of different people require varied ways of living. There is not now such a general uniform idea about how to live our private lives as was once the case. The problem of recent domestic architecture has therefore become correspondingly varied and complicated. The most general difference, I suppose, is that we are no longer so fixed in one place as formerly. Travelling has become easier and many of us are com-pelled to travel far in seeking occupation. Jobs do not come to us, we go to them. Not often now do sons occupy the homes in which their grandfathers or even their father lived, and indeed people seldom live in the same home for a great many years. Naturally, we cannot attach the same kind of importance to a home that once was attached to it, nor can the home be regarded with such a strong affection as once belonged to it.

Again, our lives become much more public than formerly. We go out more for our entertainment, to concerts, to shows, to meetings of many kinds such as social or sporting clubs. Old people speak with regret of the days when the family around the fireside worked at homely tasks whilst one member read the latest wonder produced by the mind of Dickens, Scott, Carlyle, Ruskin and other magicians. These things and a hundred others may well be regretted but we have to face the facts and to make the best of our own times which, after all, may have their own virtues. We have to recognise the fact that our homes are not lived in so much nor in the same way as those of past times.

A house used to mean the same thing as a home. It does not necessarily mean a home any more, for a home was a place to be occupied by parents and children, and when these children grew up, again in succession parents and children in turn occupied it. Nowadays, young people much more commonly go out into the world in a single independent way. We have a large floating population of single persons, and since families are generally smaller now and leave their homes sooner, we have a larger population of couples living without their children.

All this has led necessarily to changes in recent domestic architecture and to housing schemes of various kinds. Yet I do not wish to speak as if the single family house were quite a thing of the past. It certainly is not so. A run around the residential quarters of any city will quickly show that it still maintains a numerical majority and therefore I shall first discuss the single house which is not only still the most popular, but in its general form and arrangements has not in the whole altered a great deal in more than a hundred years. Let us compare this kind of house, which I shall call the old house, though many of them are new, with what I shall call the modernist house, though these are few and far between.

The old house, or old type of house, is still being generally built, but of course with what we call all modern conveniences, which are quite easily incorporated in the old form without making any general difference of appearance. There are certain very good reasons why the old type of house retains its place. The principal reason is that it is now nearly 400 years since builders learned how to use all the common building materials in the manner best suited for houses, that is to say, stone, brick, lumber and plaster. These builders at that time worked everything by hand, and that is the best way to develop the possibilities for use and beauty of these common materials, and they brought the use of these things to the greatest perfection. Since that time we have learned little more about how to handle these things, except expeditious mechanical methods of production and erection, and these have not increased but rather diminished the beauty of the work. The old builders thoroughly solved the practical serviceable use of the common materials.[3]

If you want evidence of the truth of this statement, I will point out that at least 50 percent of the most expensive and beautiful new homes that have been built in the last fifteen years in Canada, in the United States and in England have been built in the manner of the houses built in England about 400 years ago. If you say that the recent houses have all modern conveniences, I will reply that hundreds of the old houses I speak of still exist, and they have been supplied with all modern conveniences and this fact has not disturbed their appearance a little bit.

What I have been saying refers only to the general form of the house. In details some changes have taken place and are likely to take place. In my talk last week I explained how our ideas of hygiene and healthy living conditions had made all our interior forms simpler; fewer ledges, corners and projections to catch dirt and facilitate cleaning; lighter colours to show up dirt where it exists and to conserve more light so that we may reduce our electric lighting bills and preserve our eyesight. Hence, we tend to abolish the beautiful wood panelling on our walls and substitute plaster and lighter schemes of colour. This all applies to houses even more than to most other buildings. Our ways of living in our houses also demand more economy of cost and efficiency of service. We are more particular in the arrangement of the rooms; to have our kitchens not too large, not too small and properly arranged, to "save steps," as we say. We take care to have our dining rooms close to our kitchens for ease and efficiency of service. Speaking of this, there is an expedient which may claim to be modern—the dining nook—which has been introduced and tried out in various ways—sometimes as part of the kitchen, sometimes as part of the dining room, sometimes ensconced between the two. Sometimes people will have a dining nook just because they think it looks nice or because it is fashionable. You will realise that such things all depend on how you are living your life. I imagine the most serviceable dining nook is the one in a house where there is a number of small children of school age. Then with a nook in the kitchen, the children may be packed in there and conveniently fed straight off the stove, so to speak, and so happily despatched in time for school.

This is one little example [of] a number of the problems of the modern house. We have now to think of the various occupations of the various members of a family and see that all are as fairly met as the purse of the owner can accomplish. I cannot now investigate these, but I will suggest to you this happy occupation. Just think that you are going to build a house for those whom you are living with or wish to live with. Think of what is the usual routine of life and ideas about living of each, and see that each can follow it out with convenience and pleasure. Then consider the special occupations of all so far as those are carried out in the house; their privacy, their companionships, their entertainments alone or with invited company, their study, their play or other recreations. Try to plan a house to meet all these requirements and you will realise the problem of modern domestic architecture.

From this sketch of requirements, you will admit that some members of the family, or some of their wants, are apt to be neglected. This may suggest an answer to the question, why do some people leave home?

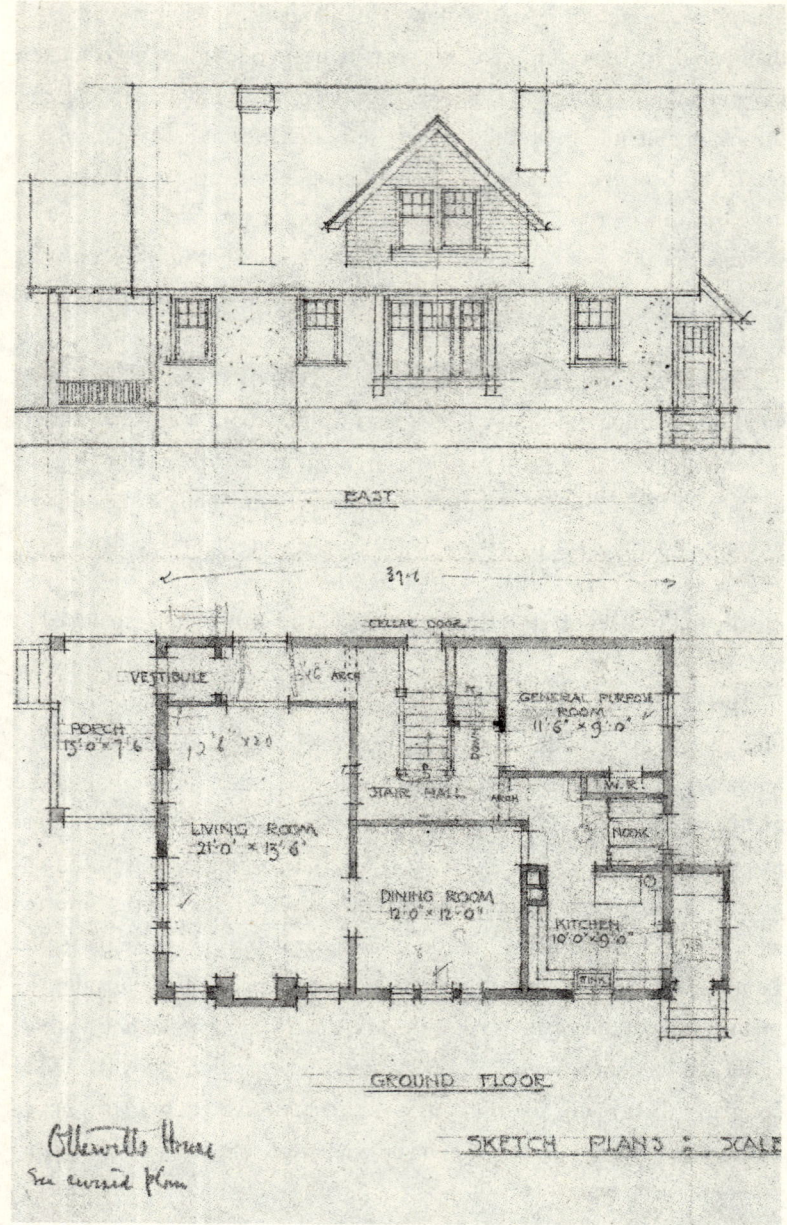

Burgess's sketch plans for a house for A.E. Ottewell in Edmonton featured a kitchen nook. Not dated, ca. 1925–1935. (71.213-165, UAA)

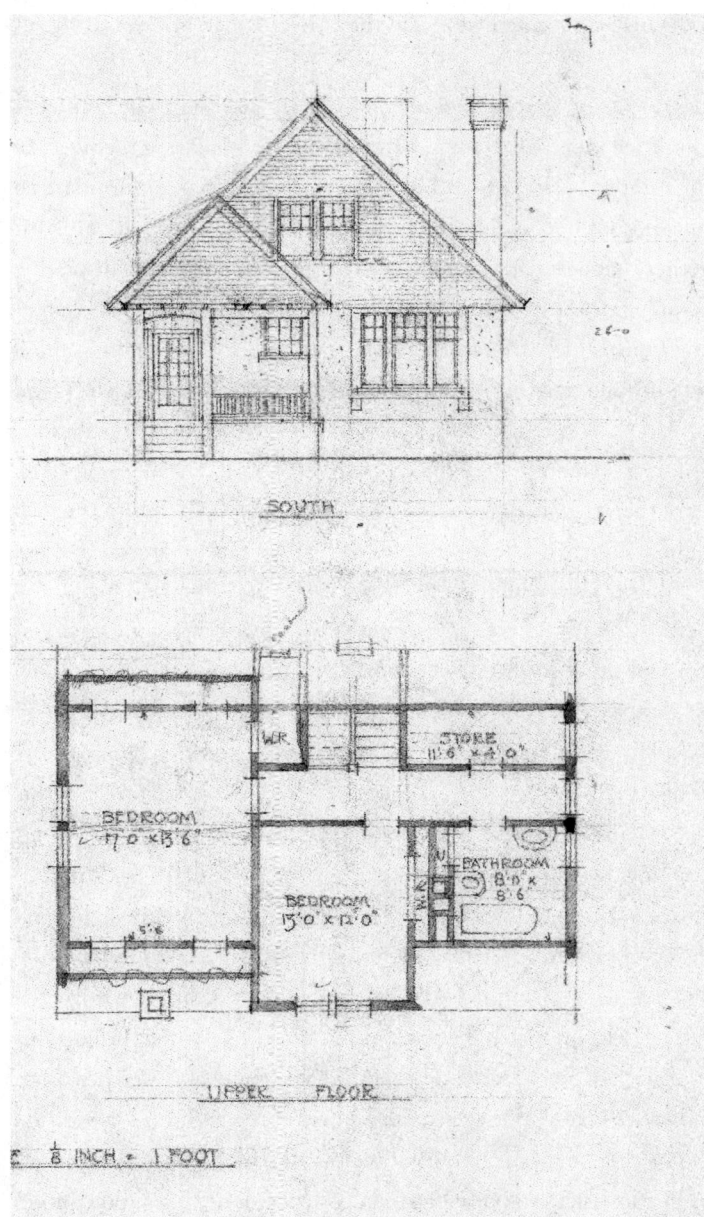

Perhaps the others monopolise it and they are crowded out; it is difficult to suit all.

As regards the general conditions of life in the house, perhaps the greatest improvements that are being made are in insulating the walls so that heat is not so easily lost and in making the internal air circulate so that rooms do not become stuffy. Good insulation reduces the bills for fuel, whether that be coal, gas or electricity, and new and better insulating materials are constantly coming upon the market. The very usual system of heating houses by warm air has of late years been put upon a much more scientific and satisfactory basis by the introduction of a forced system of air circulation. This is a most valuable improvement, a minor revolution.

So far I have said nothing of the "modernist" house. I have simply been speaking of the gradual changes that have been incorporated in the "old house." The modernist house endeavours to reject old material and old ways of doing things whenever new materials and new ways of doing things can be found to take their place. Now there are a great many of these, many of them good and well worth adopting. Yet, thorough-going modernist houses are really very rare, and the reason is that they are very costly. In addition to this, the majority of people, besides being rather poor, are also conservative and do not greatly like the appearance of this new type. I shall try to describe some of the modernist characteristics, explaining why these are adopted.

Reinforced concrete, being a new and highly serviceable structural material, is employed for walls and floors and roof. The walls are therefore smooth-faced, generally finished with stucco. In accordance with the modern desire for simplicity, there are as few cornices or other projections as possible so that the windows are plain rectangular holes. Quite often the windows are placed at the extreme corners of the building—a position in which it would be difficult to have them with older building materials and ways of construction, but which can easily be done, if you don't mind the cost, with the help of reinforced concrete. Windows thus placed in the corners of rooms allow the light to sweep the walls in such a way that no dark corners are left.

The roof of the modernist house is flat. This eliminates all waste space, of which there must always be some in a peaked roof. It also allows the roof to be made use of in various ways. To the conservative taste, this gives the appearance of bareness, as if the house were roofless. Never mind, says the modernist, this is efficiency and sound reason, and these are surely the best guides. This flat roof may or may not be very useful, but if you want it, you will have to pay for it, for no efficient flat roof suitable for much wear and tear has yet been invented that is cheaper than the ordinary peaked roof.

In the interior, the floors may be covered with rubber, in sheets or in rubber tiles, for this meets requirements of easy cleanability and quietness. The walls of rooms must similarly be smooth and cleanable and, as an ideal way of attaining this, they may be plastered and then surfaced with coloured cellulose colouring. Cellulose may be described as a superpaint, hard, glossy, [and] resistant to water or heat; for these reasons it is used for motor cars. Any projecting corners of rooms, such as may occur at fireplaces, and also the plain trim around doors, are made of chromium-plated steel, bright and stainless. The doors also may be of stainless metal or lacquered copper. Window frames also, to be up-to-date, should be of stainless chromium-plated steel.

The modernist house has, however, a number of alternative interior wall treatments. Since natural wood in the new form of plywood is now supplied in large sheets, modernist rooms are sometimes finished entirely in sheets of plywood, of mahogany, rosewood or other very beautiful materials. Many other materials are also used for wall and ceiling surfaces, such as parchment or lacquered silver or gold leaf. To be in keeping with these things, the furniture of modernist rooms employs the new alloys of metal for table tops and legs and for the chairs; the present favourite type of chairs being those framed up of metal tube [bent] to the shapes required.

You will see from these examples that really modernistic domestic architecture is an expensive business and the people who employ it must be looked upon as pioneers. The results of this pioneering may not always please everybody, and sometimes not even be beautiful, but they are giving modern materials and modern inventions a chance to show what can be done with them. Some of them will be found very satisfactory. These will be produced in greater quantity and so become cheaper and thus pass into the service of people of moderate means.

There is just one warning about all this that I should suggest. Many enthusiastic modernists of today have got into their heads the idea that a house is a machine to live in and nothing more. Now I think a house is something more. We may like a machine but we cannot love it. A home should be loveable and it must be something more than an efficient machine if it is to be that.

I have left little time to speak of other types of residences. Community houses, group houses, or apartment houses are more and more required by our modern comparatively nomadic ways of life. There is no doubt of the economy of living in a flat for people who live singly or in twos, and as I have pointed out, these have come to form a much larger proportion of our population than formerly. A great deal is being done to improve the convenience of this class of building.

There is another type of building to which more attention might very well be given. I mean places of summer residence. It is a growing and a good and wholesome custom for individuals or families to leave town for several months of the year. This ought to be made easier and the provisions in housing should be made better. But this is a large subject and I cannot include discussion of it in this talks. So now I must stop.

NOTES

1. Wetherell and Kmet, *Useful Pleasures*, 44.
2. Not reprinted because it largely duplicates material in other lectures, including Document 12, "Appreciation of Architecture, Lecture 4."
3. Notation on manuscript: "5 minutes." This suggests a rather rapid pace of delivery.

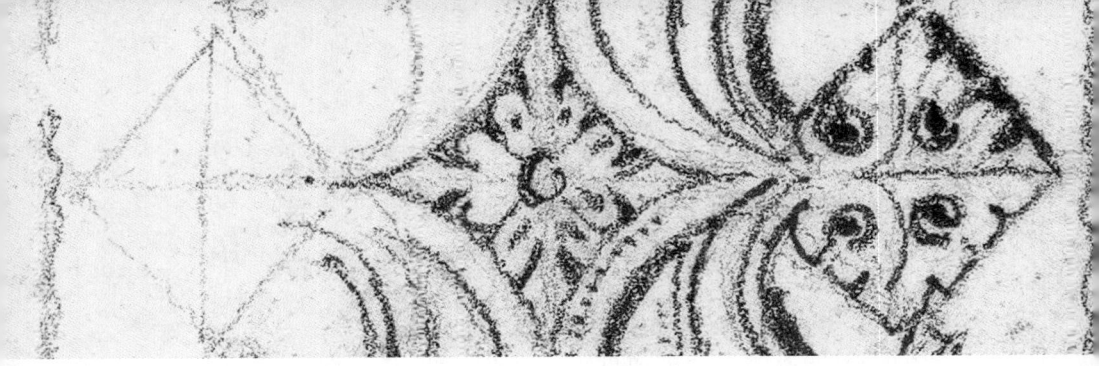

DOCUMENT 14

City Improvement

THE HOPES THAT HAD BEEN RAISED by Alberta's 1929 town planning legislation were seriously challenged in the early 1930s because of the Depression. Horace Seymour, the provincial director of town planning, was fired in 1932 to save money. Many communities also retreated from the controversies and expense that went along with urban planning and dealt instead with the more immediate challenges of the Depression. Even so, planning initiatives continued in some places. Edmonton, for example, had established a town planning commission in 1929 and it continued to operate throughout the 1930s. Made up of elected and appointed members, the board was not a professional body, although some of its members, such as Burgess, had more than passing familiarity with planning issues and procedures. As a member of this body, Burgess assisted in the early 1930s in developing a zoning bylaw and a traffic plan for the city. These plans were seen as basic building blocks for guiding future development.

By the mid 1930s, however, the limits of such voluntary approaches to planning were becoming apparent. Planning remained an important activity, Burgess contended, because rapid growth over the past three decades and business priorities had made many urban environments inefficient and ugly. Urban planning could solve this mess, although not all at once. For many critics, it was becoming clear that effective planning needed to be professionalised in order to implement approaches that would be dynamic, responsive to social needs, and long range and incremental in their outlook and approach. These needs were met by new planning methods, such as City Planning Procedure.

Document 14 is a speech to the Men's Faculty Club, November 23, 1935, 71.213, file 133, UAA.

I HAVE OFTEN BEEN ASTONISHED and sometimes ashamed of my own appalling ignorance of many of the activities and institutions that are being carried on around me. Even if these do not quite directly affect me, yet I realise that I share immense indirect benefits from them in common with society in general.

How frequently it happens, for example, that one receives a circular letter from some philanthropic society. One reads this through and is impressed as to its services to some class of people. It seems very good and necessary and deserving of support. The letter ends with a humble request for a subscription. We look at the upper left hand corner and see a list of persons who act as sponsors for the work. They are good and responsible persons and we take the risk and fork out a dollar. And that is that. It is all these people ask for, and it is all they generally get, and I imagine rightly or wrongly that they are very thankful indeed to get it. But there is so much of this sort of thing that I am impressed with the amount of human service that is carried on by unpretentious people of whose actual anxieties and painstaking efforts we know very little.

I am not going to appeal for any dollars, but it occurs to me that the problem of city improvement is one of which few people know the workings. Much good work is being done on the subject, yet how it is proceeded with, few are at all aware. It is in the hope—perhaps I ought to say fear—that some here might be as ignorant of the matter as I find myself about most other matters that I am venturing to say something about it here.

I really know very little about the subject. I have collected a few ideas and facts together in the hope that these may interest you. If they do, we have as a guest with us tonight a man who knows all about the subject—one of those whose painstaking efforts have done great services to this city in the matter of city improvement and in many other lines.[1] He can correct any glaring mistakes I may make and throw light on any phase that I may leave in obscurity.

I have made the title of this talk "City Improvement," rather than the more familiar one of "Town Planning," as being more appropriate to the view which I wish to take of the subject. This subject is one that is, naturally, of interest to all who live in cities, and it is one to which a very considerable amount of thought has been given of recent years. The fact that modern cities, if not subject to continuous and intelligent control, tend to develop disagreeable conditions of life is obvious and calls for attention and correction. Perhaps the most obvious direction in which our cities tend to fail is in the matter of appearance. Most of our cities are either on the whole or, at any rate, in parts offensive to the sight. In other directions also they tend to develop undesirable conditions, as, for example, in becoming overcrowded, congested and unhealthy. In order to correct this continuous tendency, it is necessary to consider somewhat carefully what occasions it. As regards the appearance of a city, it is noteworthy that some cities, and still more small towns, have a reputation for their beauty. This may arise in some cases and in some degree from the natural site on which they stand, but a town built amidst the most beautiful surroundings is frequently the reverse of beautiful.

In travelling through the older countries of the world, it not infrequently happens that the traveller feels impelled to deviate from a direct course in order to see some old town remarkable for what is called its "unspoiled" appearance. Because it remains pretty much as it was built in the Middle Ages, it is worth going out of our way to see. A good many modern towns are worth going several miles out of our way in order not to see them. In the majority of these old towns, it is certainly not the natural setting of the towns that attracts us but the towns themselves. Nor was it because these places enjoyed greater facilities for beautification that they became beautiful. They were much more restricted than we are in this respect. In general, for safety's sake, they had to build in a closely packed, congested manner and they could not allow themselves the luxury of large open spaces or other opportunities for the planting of trees or the making of public gardens.

The difference between these old towns and our own is caused no doubt by the difference in conditions of life and the structure of society. Since the cure for our troubles is not likely to consist in a return to the conditions of the Middle Ages, I do not wish to enquire farther at present into the causes of those differences, but merely to point [out] the fact that our modern social conditions seem to tend naturally to produce unsatisfactory physical conditions in our cities and that some special means must be taken to improve them. City improvement is definitely one of our modern problems. This problem is being attacked not without some success. Certain definite lines of action have been very generally agreed upon. I wish to outline some of these and to point out that, for their success, all citizens should have some comprehension of them in order that they may have the public support upon which their success necessarily depends.

What are the causes of the imperfections of our cities? Some of these are superficial and some underlying or fundamental. Amongst the superficial, I may mention the cheapness and temporary nature of much of the building and the display of obtrusive and disagreeable advertisement. I think it will be true to say that if prosperity continues and increases these tend in the course of time to be eliminated. The better businesses tend to improve the quality of their advertising. It is the poor struggling place of business that plasters its facade with advertisements and it is the natural ambition of a thriving business to erect more sightly buildings and avoid defacing them with advertisements. Nevertheless, I will not deny that some judicious measures may at times be applied to speed up this natural tendency.

The chief underlying or basic cause of city imperfections is that lack of orderliness in its component parts; the haphazard way in which incongruous things are jumbled together. The reason for this is that cities are not developed under any prescribed plan. Hence we may find congestion of traffic and congestion of buildings at one part; vacant, neglected gaps occurring even in central locations; workshops—and these sometimes noisy and more or less noisome—occurring in the midst of residential districts; streets wide where they should be narrow and narrow where they should be wide; important buildings in out-of-the-way places and buildings that should be-out-of-the way placed so as to attract the attention of all; residents or workers overcrowded to the detriment of their health and insufficiently provided with sanitary conveniences; sometimes long journeys to make to get from one place to another at no great distance apart; gradients that inconvenience and delay transportation; buildings that amount to so much kindling adjacent to valuable properties; [and] industries scattered in various sections that would be more efficiently carried on adjacent to one another. These are a few of the evils that not only may arise, but that have arisen in almost all towns that have undergone any fairly rapid growth.

One is tempted at once to say to all this that towns ought to be planned from the beginning and regularly developed. In reality, however, it would be about as reasonable to say that a child should plan out the course of its future life on the day that it is born or have it planned for it. For towns are born and grow, or sometimes they are born and do not grow. The probabilities regarding the child's life admit of infinitely more certainty than that of a town. Of course this is not always so; cities like Washington or Canberra have been planned beforehand with more or less success. The Garden City at Letchworth is a case in which a complete town has been planned in its general lines and it may, I think, be said to be a complete success. Desirable as the Garden City method is, and urgent as has been the demand for more of the same result, Letchworth and its sister Welwyn are to date, so far as I know, the only really successful experiments along these lines. I may call these "synthetic" cities and I grant that there are good hopes that more in the future may be created along these lines. In the meantime, it is necessary to consider more natural growths.

When once a town has really started to grow with some hope of farther increase, it is at once found that bad developments have already taken place, and it may enter the minds of some of its more thoughtful citizens that something ought to be done to correct these. Should they attempt to do anything of this sort, difficulties become at once apparent, and these difficulties appear so insufferable that these same citizens are inclined to come too speedily to the conclusion that it is too late; that the task should have been undertaken sooner. I am going to point out, farther on, what measures should be taken, but I wish at this point to indicate that no matter at what time a scheme of city improvement may be proposed, one of the first feelings that would be roused amongst good citizens is that it is a thousand pities this thing was not thought of earlier. It should be realised that in the earlier stages of a city's growth, it is generally impossible to rouse any kind of enthusiasm for a scheme of improvement. The mess a city gets itself into is the most effective, and perhaps only effective, spur to adopt measures of improvement.

This brings us to the source and cause of misgrowth. This is the ambition of those who own property in the town to make the most profit out of what they own—in itself a highly laudable and proper desire and often a sheer necessity. If you own a property and wish to build and operate a store, you will, naturally, if you have the means and the necessary business abilities and opportunities, use every inch of the ground for this purpose; and so with a workshop or other occupation. If you own a property and find you can profitably build dwellings upon it, you will be tempted to build as many of these as you can put upon it with fair hopes of selling or renting them. In certain localities the *shopkeeper* in the city is by common consent accorded the right fully to occupy his property with building. But if *residences* are too crowded, they become unhealthy and the community assumes the right to limit the activity of the man who will act injuriously to the community in overcrowding his property. In the case of the workshop, if this property is in the midst of residences, it is considered a nuisance. But in small communities it is only a minor nuisance to the few, and the business carried on by a good workshop is a very beneficial one to the community at large, so the offence is overlooked. In order that any business may grow up in a small community, it is felt that as few restrictions as possible must be placed upon the use that a man makes of his property. There are many reasons why in small towns artificial restrictions cannot practically be applied. There comes a time in a city's growth, [however], when they must in the common interest be introduced, and probably it is only possible to introduce them by degrees. It will be noticed, however, that effective control can only be exercised by limitation of private use of property in the interests of the community, and that so far as an existing town is concerned, such limitations must cause some disturbance of existing conditions. (Incidentally, I may point out here that in the case of a growing city it usually goes on taking in outlying property and that in such properties new limitation or regulations are more easily imposed since there will be little or no existing building conditions to disturb.)

The problem of the modern "town planner," as he is called, is then to consider the city that has already grown to a considerable extent and to undertake its improvement in a systematic way. Until about twenty-five years ago, what seems to us now a rather naive but perfectly natural line of approach was adopted. The fathers of the city decided that the city had got itself into a thorough mess and that something should really be done about it. They therefore called in a town planner to study their case and make his expert recommendations. The town planner arrived and in due course, for a suitable fee, supplied the city with a plan of itself as it ought to be. This plan was often drawn with great knowledge and skill, it was often much praised and admired, and later, [it] found its way into a pigeonhole from which it never again emerged. This was done in hundreds of cities. It is perhaps safe to say that the more entirely comprehensive was the plan, the less chance it had of ever being seriously put in practice. Some cities that only wanted a special district re-planned carried out their schemes, and generally, I believe, [did so] with conspicuous success. Chicago and Los Angeles were amongst these. The reason for this general failure was, of course, that every step in the carrying out of these plans meant the buying out of private interests, and any land that it was necessary to purchase in carrying out the scheme was suddenly and very properly found to be of enormous value, as it always is in cases of compulsory expropriation.

Since that time another approach to city improvement has been developed with greater success. This is officially known—not very correctly, I think—as "City Planning Procedure." By the year 1928 this procedure had been adopted by 400 cities in the United States and its enthusiastic supporters claim that no city that has adopted it has ever thought of going back on it. The reason for this continued adherence is, of course, that, although in comparison with the idealistic town planner's method it appeared to its first promoters like a new revelation, it is after all only the systematic application of accepted principles of law and order concentrated upon the particular case of city improvement.

That it did appear like a new revelation may be illustrated by the case of Vancouver. There, a number of enterprising citizens formed a society for the purposes of securing some radical improvement in the layout of their city. Individual members travelled about observing what had been done in the way of improvement in the United States cities and some, at least, were impressed with the excellent work carried out by a certain firm of town planners, Messrs. Harland Bartholomew and Associates of St. Louis. They at length advertised widely for competitive designs for a new city plan. A number of plans were received, but from the firm referred to, Harland Bartholomew, only a telegram to this effect, "Not interested in plans of the kind you ask for, would be glad to offer our usual services at the usual fees." This led to closer enquiries as to the "usual services," which were simply the adoption of the "City Planning Procedure," and finally to the engagement of that firm and the adoption of that method.

What is the "City Planning Procedure"? I shall describe it by following out the steps of procedure in the order in which they are generally taken. The first step is to prepare what is called the "basic plan" or plans. This involves a certain amount of tabulated statistics, but it is the plan that is the essential thing. As this plan contains much information, it involves a considerable amount of work, but the information is, in any well conducted city, already available on their records. The work is tedious rather than difficult. In its complete form, so much information is condensed upon the plan that it may require separating out as many as a dozen or more copies of the plan.

The nature of this plan is interesting and important. Its purpose is to supply a visual record of the physical assets of the city and of the distribution of its population in relation to these. It is necessarily a very gay affair for it shows and distinguishes by means of colour and by every conceivable conspicuous device such matters as the streets—which are paved, which are gravelled, and which are dirt roads. The water, sewage, gas, electric supplies and all their branches [are also shown]. The width of streets must be indicated—whether they are 2-way, 4-way, 6-way and so on. The streetcar service must be shown. All parks and recreation grounds, schools and other institutions [are also distinguished]. All individual lots must be indicated and show their ownership, whether private or civic. The nature of buildings, whether frame or solid building, [are shown]. The population must be indicated *in its residential distribution*, one dot for each person or one dot for fifty persons.

This plan is valuable as conveying its information at a glance. Any particular problem may be elucidated by special copies. For example, a special plan may be made to show the schools, and in relation to each school, the pupils attending that school. Concentric circles around a school will show how many pupils are within one-quarter mile, half-mile and so on. Similarly, with the [street] car service, there may be shown the number of cars traversing each part of the system, the number and distribution of population that is farther than half-a-mile from a car line, the number of people which certain car services minister to, etc. It will be of importance not only to know, but to have a visible picture of the parks and playgrounds of a city and to what proportion of the population these are practically available and what proportion have no such facilities.

These plans are necessarily on a large scale. Their first presentation in a city council chamber is usually a revelation even to those who know their city well. To many questions as to the desirability of certain services, they furnish a complete answer without a word being said. If City Planning Procedure has gone no farther than the development of this method of visibly portraying a city's assets, it would still be of enormous value.

If a professional city planner has been engaged, as in the case of Vancouver, he will be expected to carry his basic plans farther to include definite suggestions for the improvements immediately to be made, or to be recommended and determined upon as ultimate objects to be carried out as opportunity offers or as necessity compels.

There are, however, apart from special schemes—involving re-laying out of a subdivision—certain general abuses or defects to which all cities are liable, and these require special treatment and special farther City Planning Procedure. According to the necessity of the particular city concerned, the next step may be either a major streets plan or a zoning plan. I shall suppose that it is the major streets plan.

The streets of most of our cities have not generally developed [haphazardly], although in many cities of the Old Country or of Europe it would sometimes appear so. It generally happens in these old cities that the lines of the main streets continue those of the principal roads leading from the country and from other cities into the centre of the town, towards which they radiate. They are useful in forming short-cuts between distant parts of the cities. The arrangement has the advantage of furnishing the city with an important central point or area. It has unfortunately on this continent been too much the custom to rely on a general layout of streets on a simple rectangular or gridiron plan, probably in the supposition that this was a scientific arrangement. From this custom has arisen a number of unhappy results. It has provided no main focus in a city—every rectangle being equal to every other each to each. It has provided a complete series of long vistas with nothing to be seen at the end of them—roads with no appearance of leading to anywhere. It has lengthened all journeys by always leading the journeyer around two sides of a triangle. It has disregarded natural gradients with the result that in some cases streets are intolerably steep. Farther, it has developed cities of depressing monotony. It is true that these gridiron plans have frequently started upon the basis of a main street of extra width and sometimes two principal cross streets of greater width than all others. But it is quite frequently found that natural developments have been such that the greatest amount of traffic is not that which flows through those particular streets, or that in any case a number of streets have become too narrow for the traffic that has come to use them whilst others are needlessly wide.

Here then is a specific problem for City Planning Procedure. The base plan will show the width of streets and the number of car services at each point. It will be necessary to take the count of the number of vehicles passing the busiest points at the busiest times and the proportion of vehicles that approach these points from the various tributary streets. In these traffic counts boy scouts have in many cases served their city well. To improve the traffic conditions it may be necessary to widen certain streets or parts of streets. Arrangements may be made for diverting traffic of tributary streets to less congested junctions. Or it may be necessary to lay out new streets altogether. In any case, it is well to consider the problem of city street traffic as a whole and all together and with adequate information. Obviously, if radical changes are found to be essential, it will be well that these be planned and arranged for some years ahead of the time when they have to be carried out. Compulsory expropriations call for high compensations whereas, if time is allowed, opportunities for favourable purchase terms almost certainly occur in many cases, and a city has generally opportunities for offering site owners advantageous changes on good terms to both parties which will materially relieve city expenses, especially in providing opportunity of purchase by exchange of property instead of by cash payment.

I do not propose at this time to go into the principles which govern a city planner in arranging and re-arranging the major streets of the city farther than to point out that experience gathered from many efforts in this direction has suggested a number of valuable rules to be observed: that industrial traffic should be as far as may be separated from shopping, office or tourist traffic, and that very busy centres should be provided with by-passes to relieve them of unnecessary traffic. Various such like considerations must be taken into account.

I wish next to refer to the problem of city zoning—a most important element in all city improvement. The term "zoning" in this connection is not entirely self-explanatory. It means the allocation of the various classes of buildings of a city in suitable districts. Thus, certain districts will be utilised for residential purposes only, others will be commercial, light industrial or heavy industrial and so on.

At first sight this may seem to be the most impossible undertaking, yet there is probably no sphere in which City Planning Procedure has been of greater practical service. A glance at the base plan will show that the town has grown up—all towns do—regardless of any system in the matter of distribution of residential occupations. But the base plan also shows exactly how many defects of this kind exist and where they exist. Clearly, to arrive at any orderly system many occupiers must be disturbed in their occupation. Opposition may be expected. But the benefit to the community is obvious and in a great many cases *benefits will arise also for the disturbed occupations.*

The division of a city into appropriate zones involves some laborious investigation and much well-weighed judgment. In this again the accumulated experience of the application of City Planning Procedure in many cities has suggested methods of operation which ease the task and point the means of overcoming difficulties and ways of applying inducements and, if necessary, gentle compulsion. An instance may be given to illustrate the actual working of a zoning scheme. A certain district is zoned as "residential" but there already is a store or other occupation—there may be several—in the midst of the district. The occupant of this store is not disturbed, it is simply marked on the plan as a "non-conforming use." Now, non-conforming uses are liable, according to legislation, to which I shall refer later, to certain restrictions as to farther extensions, and when the existing non-conforming use lapses it cannot be reinstituted. In case of the premises being destroyed by fire, the non-conforming use lapses. It has been found in practice that non-conforming uses do tend to lapse (more quickly than might be expected) owing to the common chance that happens to all. Other causes tend to eliminate non-conforming uses. City Planning Procedure provides, usually at suitable corners, "local business districts". Now the isolated store becomes less favourably placed for business than the store at the local business centre—where shoppers may kill two or three birds with one stone. He will therefore find it to his advantage to move there. Should the city, as not infrequently happens, own some lots at a local business centre, the city has an opportunity of effecting an exchange on good terms so far as the storekeeper is concerned, or with little or no cash outlay on the part of the city. Should the storekeeper simply make his own arrangements about moving, it will be found that, now that the district is ensured against non-conforming uses, the value of the residential lots is improved. This improved value of property is one of the great levers that works in favour of the zoning scheme. It will be seen that it operates very strongly in certain zones. For example, if a good "heavy industrial district" is located in an area near the railway, then railway facilities will be cheaply provided to industries in that district and not elsewhere. Industries will naturally gravitate towards that area.

Amongst the valuable data that experience has provided are such things as the extent of shopping frontage appropriate to a given number of inhabitants. The town planner will adjust the available frontage in a commercial district accordingly. One might go on to discuss the parks and playgrounds system of a city, but from what I have said it will be seen that this also is subject to systematic examination and adjustment as to type and distribution. These naturally vary according to local facilities and the demands or requirements of the public. Sites unfavourable for any other purpose have frequently been converted to excellent park spaces. [Another] matter that will always demand special attention is a suitable civic centre. Of this, each community is liable to develop its own particular ideal. In its creation, its consideration had better be undertaken at an early date to allow time for gradual rather than enforced sudden acquisition of property. Its location is naturally central and there property is expensive.

Now it must have occurred to most of you that in order to carry out such improvements as I have been speaking about, municipal or other local authorities must exercise very considerable authority and that they must therefore be endowed with some special legal powers and must farther set up a certain special organisation or machinery, if you like to call it, so in order to operate a City Planning Procedure. And this is so. This part of the procedure has also been evolved or systematised in the last quarter of a century. For various reasons, town planning legislation in Canada has followed the lead of that in the U.S.A. This will be found to be the right and natural course since social and other conditions are fairly similar in these two countries and differ from those in older countries in a way that renders the methods of these older countries inadvisable and indeed inapplicable on this continent.

In the province of Alberta, a number of statutes were passed at various times relating to town planning and the preservation of natural beauty. These were amended and consolidated and superseded in the *Town Planning Act of 1929*.[2] (Farther amended by an amendment act of 1934). This act then of 1929 is based on what is now generally understood amongst professional town planners on this continent as City Planning Procedure as I have been describing it. The nature of the act is well set forth in a note which was attached to the bill but which does not form part of it. This says: this bill re-enacts the provisions of the town planning and preservation of natural beauty act and replaces the town planning act which was passed in 1913 by provisions which are *suggested by experience in carrying out town planning schemes in recent years* (i.e., Town Planning Procedure). Part II is designed to enable a municipality *to formulate a general plan of development* of the land within its boundaries, which cannot be departed from unless such plan is amended in the manner therein provided (ensuring [against] vacillating policies). Part III empowers a municipality *to enact zoning by-laws*. Part IV provides for a more effective control of subdivisions and affords a means of ensuring that *land shall not be subdivided in such a way as to cause inconvenience and difficulty in future development*.[3] Part V provides for the appointment of the necessary *officials to administer the Act* and supervise town planning.

This *Town Planning Act* of Alberta differs from a typical town planning act in that it makes provision for the preservation of the natural beauty of the province and calls for the appointment of a Town and Rural Planning Advisory Board under a Director of Town Planning. So far as it refers to cities and other localities, it "permits" local authorities, including city councils, to appoint "Town Planning Commissions."[4] The Town Planning Commission's work consists in

(a) acting in an *advisory capacity* in matters pertaining to town planning;
(b) preparing and carrying into effect a town planning scheme;
(c) preparing and administering a zoning by-law.

The city council delegates "powers" to the commission to do these three things, but of course does not delegate the power of raising money or expropriating land. It is an advisory committee giving advice to the city council. The council may or may not ask the commission's advice, but the commission may give its advice whether specifically asked for or not. It has the power of originating, formulating and submitting advice to the council. It may ask for funds for specific purposes but of course cannot command them.

The preparation of a basic plan of course requires money and this must be voted by the council. If a very active campaign involving considerable alterations of existing conditions is to be undertaken, it will be advisable to appoint a (permanent) professional town planner. This is highly advisable in any large city. For smaller towns, occasional expert advice may be sufficient. A permanent professional town planner is in a position to be of immense service in a great city.

In the actual operation of City Planning Procedure, the most continuous work of a town planning commission is the operation of the zoning plan and the zoning bylaws, which they must prepare in relation to the zoning plan. The zoning plan cannot be made fixed for all time. Natural changes in the growth of the city demand some modification, but all modifications must be recommended by the commission, approved by the council, and finally be ratified by the Minister of Public Works. They cannot be made at the mere whim or by the personal influence of any single individual. There is ample provision in the statutes for the approval of the public, for all action to be taken has to be duly advertised, objections being invited and heard, and there is full provision for appeal in cases where undue hardship might be imposed or in case of improper administration.

I have tried to give an outline showing [of what] modern Town Planning Procedure on this continent consists. It has been adopted by, I believe, more than 1,000 cities and it has been claimed that no city, having adopted it, has ever forsaken it. Wherein lies the strength of this movement which in definite form is not more than 25 years old? I shall try to summarise the sources of this strength.

1. It sets an *end to the casual uncontrolled development* which is the fruitful source of the disorder, inefficiency, unhealthiness and general degradation of cities.
2. It serves the obvious *interests of the community* in advancing the healthy and enjoyable conditions of life of all classes of citizens.
3. It equally tends to produce improved appearances and monetary values of property. Every year brings some improvement, not perhaps very noticeable from year to year, but [it is] steadily cumulative so that over a period of years notable assets can be pointed to.
4. Its provision for *gradual application* is a means of improvement that avoids great and sudden changes and disturbances. Individuals

pass away relatively quickly. The city takes its time and awaits the opportunities that time and chance afford to a *steady policy*. It looks to effecting changes by a *method of city development* rather than to a revolutionary change of actual conditions.

5. The *incidence of cost* in obtaining possession and use of land required for civic purposes is spread [out] and the actual amount is materially reduced.

6. Where private interests are for the moment adversely affected, it makes very clear that neighbouring interests are favourably affected—a considerable element in reconciling the individual to what can frequently be turned to the interest of the individual himself, and compensation may often be given to the individual by exchange without cash outlay.

On the general working of the plan, it may be said that restrictions to individual action—which are essential in all laws—ensure general community benefit, and surely that is the ideal of legislation.

It may have occurred to some of you that there is one great question which seriously affects the appearance, the efficiency and the health of our cities that I have barely touched. This is the housing question. The Town Planning Procedure that I have been outlining is not sufficient of itself to cope entirely with this problem—for it is a problem. Nevertheless, it does have its application in the enforcement of zoning and zoning by-laws. Its effect in this way is salutary but chiefly restrictive, and something more than restriction is needed to ensure good housing for all. Some idea of the magnitude of this problem may be conveyed by the following statements: In England and Wales an official review of the housing situation in 1931 found that there were then in these countries 1,421,000 more dwellings than there had been in 1921—ten years previously. It was farther calculated that 1,700,000 additional houses must be built by 1941 to furnish sufficient standard accommodation. Of these, up to 1934 (October 1st) 800,000 had been built. That is to say that nearly half the program had been completed in the past three years out of the ten. According to the report of the Ministry of Health of 1934, about 700,000 working class families had definitely improved their living accommodation in the course of one year. Critics of the official view call for higher standards and lower rents rather than greater numbers of dwellings. The provision of funds is naturally a question that asks for solution.

These statements may indicate the fact that the solution of the housing problem is calling forth very considerable effort. What is the spur or motive that occasions the effort? It did not primarily arise from a desire for more beautiful cities nor even for greater efficiency in civic operation. I think its origin can be clearly traced to efforts towards public health, to improvements in modern medical science, to the devotion of members of the medical profession and to the consequent appreciation by the public of healthy and sanitary conditions. Public sentiment, indifferent enough to other things, has been genuinely aroused in this direction and people have been led seriously to think and to take active measures on no small scale starting from this basis. Besides benefits to health, numerous incidental results have come into view—improved appearances for example—but others too, such as facilities for recreation.

Cities, in taking stock of their various assets, find it desirable to possess more and better industries. Many industries, many workers; but workers are not likely to be either numerous or efficient where accommodation for them is too limited or quite unattractive. It will often be remunerative for a municipality to provide working class accommodation at small direct profit to itself in view of the advantageous position which it may thereby achieve. This is no doubt one of the underlying reasons why we find a number of cities, such as Leeds, launching immense building schemes covering many acres of ground with dwellings for hundreds of people of moderate incomes. Those schemes are well laid out, on a large scale, with playground spaces and open lawns, and trees on which the occupants may look out and which provide a very picturesque and agreeable setting to the buildings, which are themselves substantially constructed and well provided for a healthy and comfortable life.

Another incidental benefit arises from these building schemes. Many men are employed in the actual building operations. The variety of materials used by the building trades and the necessary purchases and transportation have ramifications that extend far beyond the municipality. Indeed, all round the world business is more or less stirred up. Since these advantages are found to accrue, it is not surprising that money to carry out such operations is forthcoming at a low rate of interest. Builders are obtaining money for them at from 3¼ to 3⅝ percent. In Alberta, 5 percent of doubtful collectability is proving no incentive under the *Dominion Housing Act*.

It may seem surprising that, being an architect, I have said little or nothing of the place or effect of architecture in a discussion of civic improvement. Architecture is the flower of building. Even in amateur efforts at gardening, you may have observed that in order to have flowers at all, you must dig, and seed, and plant, and water, and tend, and prune. Similar preliminary operations are necessary in city improvement before you can have fine civic architecture. On the other hand, you may produce a physically healthy and an efficient city without good architecture. This would be a dreary and unhappy efficiency. Good civic control provides opportunity for architecture, and architects there are in plenty at present who may be said without exaggeration to be literally dying for want of the opportunity. Even if you may have no eye or appetite for this fine flower of cities, it may be well to remember that without the flower you can never have the fruit, which is, in a word, civilisation.[5]

It is precisely the great value of a good Town Planning Procedure that it alone can give a good basis for not only good architecture but for the improvement of cities in many ways. The civil engineer may then effectively apply his skill in improved types of roadways and bridges, the landscape gardener may exercise his art with real efficiency in the handling of parks, gardens and boulevards—a modern means of making cities desirable to live in that was practically denied to the builders of mediaeval cities. In addition to these, the enterprise of various trades in the production and employment of improved building materials is engaged to real advantage.

Without a proper general procedure, all these efforts are discouraged and when employed are displayed with little effect.

The actual effort of the conscious recognition of good procedure is making itself felt in all the cities in which it has been adopted. The most hopeful element is the evidence that a genuine pride in cities is thereby encouraged amongst the citizens of these cities. They begin to be zealous for the orderliness of fine appearance of their surroundings. When once civic pride of this sort is aroused, success is ensured.

In the City of Edmonton we have at present not too many citizens who are inspired with the desire to promote its efficiency, health and beauty as a city; but we have a Town Planning Commission and we have had since 1929 a city council which has backed it up loyally. I am hopeful that if this continues, sufficient improvements will be established—and these are steadily, if somewhat slowly, being established. I am hopeful that at a certain stage this will come to be generally recognised and sufficient civic pride developed to ensure rapid and steady development and continuation along these lines until this city shall become one of which its citizens may feel proud when they travel abroad through other cities. This is, I fear, hardly the case at present.

Some of you can remember with delight the cities from which you came. Surely you shall wish then that your children shall be able to say:

> Surely in toil and fray
> Under an alien sky
> Comfort it is to say
> "Of no mean city am I."

NOTES

1. In margin: "Mr. Milton Martin." Martin was the Chair of the Edmonton Town Planning Commission.
2. *An Act to consolidate and amend the Statutes relating to Town Planning and the Preservation of Natural Beauty*, Statutes of Alberta, 1929, Chapter 49. The official short citation was *The Town Planning Act, 1929*.
3. In margin: "explain."
4. In margin: "See Act re: Compulsory Powers, 1929–37(3)."
5. In margin: "or culture."

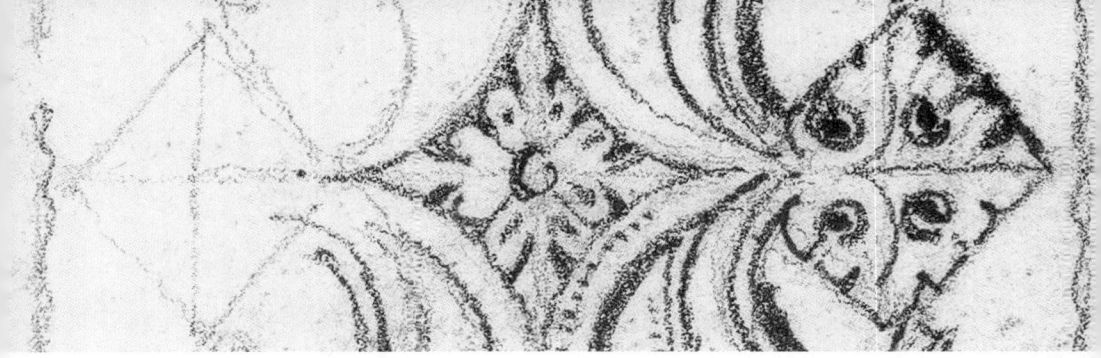

DOCUMENT 15

Garden Cities

THE GARDEN CITY CONCEPT, which was developed in England by Ebenezer Howard, remained an attractive model for urban planning throughout the twentieth century. Planned with green spaces and open areas, Garden Cities were not, however, designed as suburbs of existing large cities, but as new towns with self-sustaining economic activities. This approach was widely admired as a solution to the various problems created by the growth of massive urban conglomerations because it promised to decentralise urban growth; something that the steady expansion of suburban areas tied to the city did not offer. In essence, Garden City concepts offered the powerful dream of starting urban development afresh.

This model was applied widely in the 1930s, but as Burgess noted in this lecture at the University of Alberta, many of the North American applications of the theory were merely well designed suburban areas, not the new towns that the original Garden City concept had advocated. Radburn, New Jersey, designed by Clarence Stein, for example, was only a suburban area—albeit one of fine design—that was dependent on nearby larger urban centres such as New York City. Stein would go on to design many other similar suburban areas, as well as some new towns, including Kitimat, British Columbia. Built for Alcan, construction began on Kitimat in 1951.

Document 15 was Lecture 15 in Burgess's Town Planning Course at the University of Alberta, not dated, ca. 1939–40, 71.213, file 168, UAA.[1]

THE EXPRESSION "Garden City" has a strong appeal to the imagination of many. It suggests everyone sitting under his own vine and his own fig tree or whatever may be the local equivalent. To some, it may be only a potato patch. On the other hand, there are no doubt many less happily constituted persons to whom none of these are objects of allurement.

Theoretically, there is no reason why one city should not satisfy all sorts. Those who wish or require a garden may have an individual house and ground, and those who do not may live in a multiple dwelling on the tenth floor if they like that better. The active life of a city with its varying and sometimes rival ambitions and private ambitions is bound to create pressures which, in many unforeseen ways, upset the balance and harmony of the various parts. This is the very natural result of a vigorous community life. But there can be no doubt that, in cities as they are, the result has been many undesirable conditions. It is not the aim of town planning to produce model cities that will be perfect "machines for life" and will remain "just so" forever. Towns must be, and continue to be, flexible and ready to admit all changes that are good of human aspirations. The aim of town planning must be to be forever adjusting cities, keeping in view the basic needs of human life and seeing to it that these are never swamped by elements that interfere with them.

The value of a city, as compared with a small town, is the many-sided environment which it offers. A town, which is essentially a collection of workers' houses around one or several factories, cannot be reckoned a city. A city must have large intellectual and spiritual as well as material interests in order to fulfill its functions as a forwarder of human progress. Even in a small town, the intellectual and moral standards must be maintained and kept in healthy and flourishing condition.

The overgrowth and congestion of our great metropolises calls for some cure. There would seem to be two alternatives; either to disentangle the great cities from their present confusion, or to start new cities on a plan that admits of such control as to avoid the occurrence of desperate deterioration. The situation practically calls for both sorts of effort, and both are being put more or less in practice.

To relieve the congestion of a great city, the most immediate means which all great cities adopt is to spread themselves in continuity over the adjoining country. This is clearly showing itself to be an inadequate solution. The creation of "suburbia" or "dormitory quarters" intensifies the congestion of the centre. Many fine residential suburbs have been built on the outskirts of cities. Hampstead Garden City, so called, and Golders Green on the north of London are good examples. But these are merely "residential districts" of the city, most of whose residents make the rather long and not too inviting journey into town and out again daily. They are beautifully laid out and are delightful places to live in for those who have retired from business. Another stage is made by the "satellite town," which is again not a separate town, but essentially a residential suburb placed entirely in the country several miles from the town. In all countries of the world experiments are being made with these two types. At the best they are safeguarded by green belts of country to preserve conditions of health and to limit the size of the district. One of the most recent examples, and one that has received much publicity, is that known by the name of "Greenbelt."

Greenbelt is a town in Maryland, twelve miles from the centre of the city of Washington D.C. There are other similar projects known as Greenbrook,

Greenhills [and] Greendale, all being carried out, not under the Federal Housing Authority, but by the Federal Resettlement Administration. Besides these, there are many somewhat similar schemes in various parts of the United States.

Other countries are doing similar work, [but] Greenbelt may be taken to be a good type, though each is different and many may be even better. The procedure is to purchase the ground, lay out the town, provide water, sewage and roads, and to build, say 1,300 dwellings, increasing this later to 3,000 and finally 5,000. These are low rental dwellings for families who earn from $1,000 to $2,000 per annum. Rentals are on the basis of one-fifth of the family income, i.e. from $16.00 to $33.30 per month. The federal authorities manage the affairs of the town until it shall be able to manage them for itself under a city council. The people remain, however, renters, so that strict control may be preserved over the properties. Practically all are commuters, their work is in the city of Washington and mostly in the employment of the federal government. "To the city worker it offers a home in healthy country surroundings, yet within easy reach of his job. To the small farmer living in the Greenbelt area it offers better facilities and a steady market within a few hundred yards of his own fields." The fact that the people work in the city puts this in the class of satellite towns; it is not properly a "garden city."

Some of the aims in the laying out of such a satellite town are worth noting. The houses here are mostly "row houses." Six in a row is commonest, but they range from four to ten. The contours of the ground suggested a crescent form, with streets following the form of a crescent. It thus approximates the "spider web" type of street layout, as do a great many of such developments. Wythenshawe, a district of somewhat similar purpose near Manchester in England, has, by exception, a hexagonal street system. At Greenbelt, the houses all face on minor service roads of light and narrow type, with a continuous strip of grass along the house fronts.

The spaces at the rear of the houses are not subdivided, so that there are no private greens. The houses are, as it were, set in a part common to all, with footpaths for general use. There are thus three grades of roadways; main traffic roads, light service roads and footpaths. The footpaths cross traffic roads by underpasses, so that people may walk from one part of the town to another without encountering vehicular traffic. This is especially serviceable in the case of children going to school. There is a town centre in which are placed a public school, gymnasium, swimming pool, theatre, community hall and a shopping or business centre. This town centre can be reached without crossing traffic roads by means of the underpasses. The lack of private gardens is to some extent compensated by allotment gardens in the greenbelt. Many of the people have motor cars, but this is not essential for there is good bus service to the city. The project has now 3,000 dwellings and is fully occupied. The people have a local newspaper supported on advertising. There are local clubs for many purposes. Various church denominations flourish. There is no high school in the town. One in the neighbourhood serves the town and surrounding district. There is a very active public spirit.

The purpose of the "satellite town" is set forth in a Federal Resettlement Administration publication. "The significance of a greenbelt town extends far beyond its own boundaries. Every growing metropolis should, if it is wisely planned, develop a chain of similar suburban communities around its borders. They would offer an opportunity for orderly efficient expansion. Their greenbelts, linked together, would form continuous open spaces around a city, protecting it and each suburb from overcrowding and sprawling, haphazard, suburban developments and encroaching industries." This envisages a great metropolis as a planet with a planetary system of satellite towns around it. The theory is attractive, but it does not seem suited of itself to reduce the already unwieldy size of overgrown cities. It does afford a means of relieving congested conditions.

The "Garden City" proper faces the problem of the wider distribution of towns with the view of reducing the tendencies toward overgrown towns. By far the best known example is that of Letchworth in Hertfordshire in England. Thirteen miles from Letchworth is Welwyn, another garden city with the same aims. I know no others of quite this class; "A garden city is a town planned for healthy living and industry, of a size no larger than is necessary for a full social life, the town being surrounded by an agricultural belt, and the whole of the land owned by, or on behalf of, the community." (C.B. Purdom).[2]

Ebenezer Howard of England began agitating in favour of the idea of the Garden City about 1898. He published a little work called *Tomorrow*, later published under the title of *The Garden City*.[3] Howard realised the interdependence of country and city. A surrounding agricultural belt would serve to provide food for the town and, in addition, would prevent the total extinction of all ideas of the basis of life upon nature in the minds of the townsmen. He says; "town and country must be married, and, out of this new union will spring a new hope, a new life, a new civilisation." Howard's town was not a mere suburb; it was a complete social unit. It was to be a place for work as well as for residence, and whilst it was to be a place for work, it was not to be dominated by the idea of work or any other specialty, but [was] to be a place for a good all round healthy life. Mumford says of Howard that he was "the first thinker about cities who had a sound sociological conception of the dynamics of urban growth."[4]

Letchworth was founded in 1903. A joint stock company called First Garden City Ltd. bought 3,818 acres of land thirty-two miles from London at £40 per acre. This was served by two existing lines of railway. Water supply and sewage drainage were installed; gas and electrical plants were erected. Roads were laid out and a town plan prepared with a suitable distribution of commercial, industrial and residential districts. Buildings were erected for administrative purposes, etc. Otherwise, the company did no building. They leased lots on a 99 or 999 years' ground rental. Houses were built by private persons who might be aided by building societies or local authorities. All buildings were subject permanently to the company's regulations, but not to their design or dictation. The company advertised their scheme and attracted shopkeepers and factories to the town. A limit to the size of the town was set at a population of 35,000. There are probably about 20,000 there now. The company limited its profits to 5 percent on their investment. For some years they did not earn this, but they gradually got on to a steady paying basis. A comparatively small part of the capital was expended on buildings.

An important point about Letchworth is that it does pay dividends. The affairs of the citizens are managed by themselves except [for] the care of town planning, which is, of course, considerable. The ground rents pay for the maintenance of roads, sewage, electrical, gas and water supply. The company takes care to introduce a diversity of trades so that a depression in one or two of these shall not seriously affect the prosperity of the town. By 1925 over 60 industrial companies were established in the town. The schools and police are under the county authority. The urban district council looks after the cleaning and lighting of the streets, the fire brigade, refuse collection, open spaces, and public health services.

There is nothing spectacular about the appearance of Letchworth. This naturally arises from the fact that each owner builds as he pleases, within the regulations, which are liberal. It can be claimed, however, that the health of the town is excellent, that there are no slums, no poverty, and no inferior living or working conditions. The place is free from smoke. In summer time the cottagers' gardens are smothered in flowers, especially roses, of which they are particularly proud. The site was, of course, chosen primarily as being a good centre for distributing manufactured goods.

Reed and Ogg in "New Homes for Old" say; "After Letchworth had been in existence for 35 years a survey showed that 'insured' workers (that is, all industrial workers) lost only half as many working days through sickness as insured workers in other English industrial towns, and the death rate for all England was 50 percent higher, the infant mortality rate 84 percent higher, and the tuberculosis rate 100 percent higher than at Letchworth. Welwyn Garden City is likewise a going town!"[5]

Letchworth having proved successful, another garden city was started at Welwyn, about thirteen miles from Letchworth. Although on a smaller area, this was planned for 50,000 inhabitants. Though Ebenezer Howard was also the moving spirit in its establishment, it is the work of a separate company called Welwyn Garden City Ltd. It is twenty miles from London.

This company operates very much as a limited dividend company would operate under the Canadian National Housing Act. It borrows money from the state at 5 percent, loans being negotiated from time to time as required. The amount of the loan is limited to 75 percent of the value of the property.

When these two projects were started, the motor car, the telephone and the use of electrical power in factories were only in their infancy. Their development has greatly aided these towns. They both struggled rather slowly at first, but they operate today as justifications of advanced town planning.

As between the satellite town and the independent garden city, there is a radical difference. The satellite town is an extension of the metropolis. The garden city belongs to "regional planning." It takes a larger view of the whole situation and offers some basis for national "land use." Though the relative merits are sometimes discussed to the disparagement of one or the other, it must be realised that each does service and that they set out to fulfill purposes that are quite different the one from the other. Both have effected much good in improving living conditions.

An important experiment often referred to is that at Radburn, New Jersey.[6] This is twelve miles from Times Square, New York, and midway between the towns of Paterson and Hackensack. It consists of 1,200 acres and is expected, when fully completed, to house 25,000 people and to cost $60,000,000. Though at present a "greenbelt" is included in the area, it is not proposed to protect this indefinitely. It is intended to attract industries to the town. In this respect it is a "garden city," but many of the people will be commuters to New York and elsewhere. The cost of houses ranges from $7,500 to $8,500 as against from $2,500 and up at Letchworth. It is therefore not a low cost housing project. The general arrangement of the streets is excellent and the architecture is strictly controlled. Much economy has been effected by reducing the number of main roads and servicing by light roads and footpaths as was done later at Greenbelt.

This project may be said to be half-way between a satellite town and a garden city. It is being carried out by the "City Housing Corporation," a company which limits its profits to 6 percent. Whilst the project is often referred to as being a great advance, so far, in garden city or, indeed, in town planning, superiority may be claimed for Letchworth on three main points:

1. At Letchworth the land remains under a general ownership which ensures permanent public control. At Radburn, the lots are sold outright, though the deeds of sale contain restricting clauses and all are subject to zoning bylaws.
2. Radburn does not propose to have a permanent surrounding greenbelt.
3. The cost of housing at Radburn is about three times that at Letchworth.

There is an important class of towns which may or may not be garden cities—the company town. In a democratic country the idea of a town being owned by a private industrial company may sound highly undesirable and contrary to the broad principles of modern social development. The company town cannot be disregarded on such grounds. The following points may be considered:

1. Many industries, from their dangerous or other objectionable nature, are excluded from cities. A separate community becomes a necessity.
2. Many large industries are tied to an isolated situation on account of the fact that only there do they find the means or materials for their industry. This may be a matter of necessity or of rational economy. Examples are mining towns, paper mills, etc.
3. The ease with which electrical power for driving machinery may be transmitted encourages the establishment of large industries in out-of-town localities where they escape and relieve the congestion of cities.
4. The isolated company town exists under provincial laws which may regulate their conduct advantageously to the workers.

As a matter of accomplished fact, many such company towns have proved very beneficial, not only to their own occupants, but also to the welfare and wealth of the country. Pioneering in this respect has been done by such firms as Cadbury at Bournemouth and Lever Brothers at Port Sunlight. Indeed, such pioneers have been leaders to call attention to the benefits to be derived from providing humane conditions for working people and have been the chief inspirers of the public with sound ideas in regard to town planning. Thousands of experiments have been made in company towns; some good, some bad. Those that have been well conducted have been loyally supported by the workers and have been a good source of profit and benefit to all concerned. Prerequisites, however, are a business of sufficient size and stability to support the scheme, and a reasonable prospect of permanence. Whilst the land may be owned by the industrial company, the financing and managing of the town may be handled by a separate organisation. There is a considerable variety of ways in which this may be arranged.

NOTES

1. On top of first page: "References: Town of Lens, Saskatchewan, *Town Planning Journal*, Canada, September 1921, p. 1; Mariemont, Cincinnati, *Town Planning Journal*, Canada, May 1923, p. 1; Plan of Radburn, *Town Planning Journal*, Canada, August 1928, p. 107."
2. The reference is likely to C.B. Purdom, *The Garden City. An Intimate Account of the Foundation and Development at Letchworth* (London: n.p., 1913).
3. The full title of Ebenezer Howard's 1898 book was *Tomorrow: A Peaceful Path to Real Reform*. In 1902 it was revised and issued under the new title, *Garden Cities of Tomorrow*.
4. In *The Culture of Cities* (London: Secker and Warburg, 1946) (first published 1938), 397–98.
5. William Reed and Elizabeth Ogg, *New Homes for Old. Public Housing in Europe and America* (New York: Foreign Policy Association, n.d. (ca. 1940)).
6. Designed by Clarence Stein. The Radburn plan was highly influential in Canadian suburban development after World War II.

PART III

1940–1946

Overleaf: Cecil Burgess in 1940. (71.213–266, UAA)

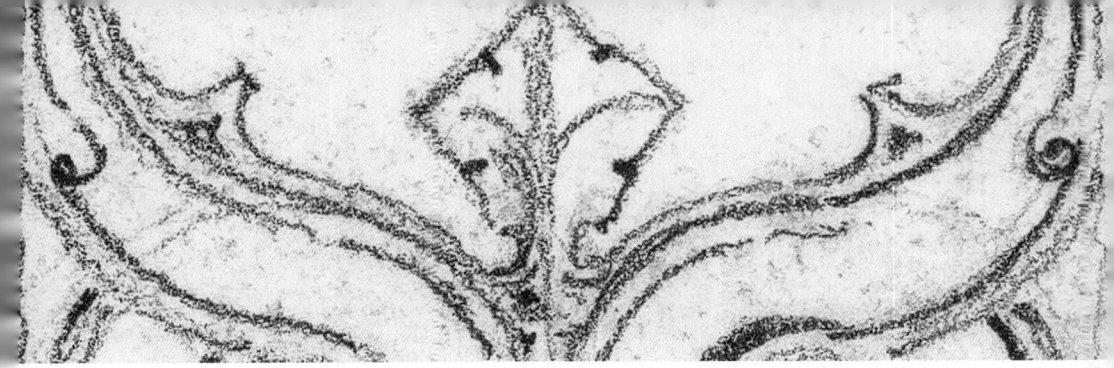

DOCUMENT 16

Home Building Exhibition

THE DEPRESSION *of the 1930s had a double pronged effect on housing: it caused a slow down in house construction and householders often could not afford to maintain their houses. With this legacy, it was not surprising that the sudden increase in demand for housing during World War II created a housing crisis in many Canadian cities, including those in Alberta. Increased housing supply was encouraged by various policies, including relaxing zoning and building bylaws in order to bring new housing onto the market. Construction of new houses was also a priority, but rising prices and the diversion of materials to war needs ensured that accessibility to housing remained limited for many people. As a result the federal government brought in rent control in Calgary in late 1940, and in the next year extended it to other cities in the province.*

In this talk, Burgess pointed to a number of popular theories about how costs could be reduced while maintaining principles of good design. At the same time, he reiterated several recurring themes in his thinking about house layout and design, most notably that the primary principle governed house design was to meet the demonstrated social and personal needs of the occupants.

Document 16 is a talk given in the McLeod Building, Edmonton, not dated, ca. 1940,[2] 71.213, file 83, UAA.[1]

THERE ARE MANY considerations in building a house; probably the most important is cost. Supposing you know how much you can spend and that you can get the accommodation you want, there is still a crowd of considerations.

The site ties you down to a number of these—you cannot place your house corner-wise to the compass to get sunlight in every room. You have a north side and this may be to the street. It should never be forgotten that sunlight is the most valuable article that enters into a house because it kills germs and causes a gentle circulation of air. Make your house to catch the sunlight. A verandah is a most pleasant place, but do not let it shut out the greater part of the sunlight. It is hard to avoid this on a narrow site facing south; the only thing to do then is to keep the verandah as narrow as will give proper service and as high as circumstances will allow. This is a matter of cheerfulness and health [and] it must not be disregarded.

It is not important that windows should be large. Large windows are cold and expensive in first cost and in heating charges. A comparatively small beam of sunshine or stream of fresh air will do a lot of good. Windows are mouths to drink in sunshine and air. They are also eyes from which to look out. People with small mouths and small eyes can manage very well if they open and close them at the proper time.

It is worth while spending a little extra care and expense on good walls. Air spaces and substances which stop the wind secure warmth. Boarding [and] paper [over] studs and framing secure these well so that frame houses may very well compare with brick for warmth. The point to make sure of is that there are no leakages in the construction. Such leakages are most liable to occur at the junction of the ground floor with the cellar wall [and] around the windows and at the eaves of the roof. This last is less important than the two others except in bungalows. Ground floor joists should be embedded in the wall or filled in between with good bricking and the siding should lap well down over the top of the wall. Windows should be placed in position first and the walls made close to them. Building paper and, if possible, clapboarding should overlap as far as possible on the window frame. In arranging a house [for warmth], I think it quite a mistake to have the front door entering the living room without any porch. All these points refer to leakages through which cold air enters and our money leaks into the coal cellar.

What is it that makes the planning of a house seem a difficult and complicated problem? There are so many plans of houses that we may say that no two are alike. This partly is because no two persons approve of the same way of arranging their way of living. There is, however, one perfect plan. This is the single room. It only suits very small families, but for them it is perfect because everything is conveniently at hand without going out at one door and in at another to reach it. With a window in each wall, it is the perfectly lighted and ventilated house. The only possible objection to it is that some people are cranky enough to require privacy for certain operations: cooking, dining, reading, sleeping, washing, etc.

We try to get this privacy by building partitions around ourselves and the neatest way we have invented to do this screening-off is with stud partitions covered with boards or plaster. Simple people are content to dine in their kitchens; we are so particular that we must be free from the sight and smell of cooking when we eat. People one degree less simple are satisfied to sit in their dining rooms, but we must have our living rooms. Some are content to read and smoke in their living rooms, others must have a den and so goes on the complication of our civilised life. Meanwhile, we are making our houses larger, more costly and more complicated; more difficult to clean and to keep well sunned and ventilated. If you are going to build, keep these facts in mind. Realise well what it is you are paying for, and see that you get it if you do pay for it. If your dining room is unpleasant to dine in, your living room unpleasant to live in, and your den unsuitable for reading and smoking, you'll have paid for something you did not get. You will have paid in money and you have paid in air, sunlight, work and other things.

A great deal is said about saving steps in a kitchen. It is very sensible to have everything handy in a kitchen, which is a sort of little factory. As to the exact arrangement of a kitchen, there are differences of opinion which perhaps do not amount to a very great deal. It is not those small points of difference that matter very much. If you are not going to eat your meals in a kitchen and it is exclusively a cooking place, then let it be small and you will have few steps to reach any part of it.[3] Only doors of [the] room and cupboards must not clash with one another nor interfere with work, and you must be able to stand or to sit exactly in the places where you need to stand or sit in doing kitchen work. I think a kitchen could possibly be arranged so conveniently and so well that a cook could sit on a revolving stool and do all the work.[4] This would, in my opinion, be to reduce a theory to an absurdity, for a certain number of steps are good for any one, even a cook.

In regard to bedrooms, I should not provide any bedroom without sufficient and suitable places for bed, bureau and a wardrobe. Across the window is not a suitable place for a bed, and personally I much prefer that the head of the bed be in shade, not directly opposite a window. In a bathroom too, the bath should not be directly across a window.

Speaking of windows, I think it is a common mistake to put the sills of windows too low. This, I know, is done with the idea that one should be able to sit well within the room and have a good view of the ground outside, but there are only one or two rooms in a house where this is any object. In bedrooms, bathrooms, kitchens and, in many cases, also in living rooms, windows placed fairly high up in the wall give a chance of far more convenient arrangement of furniture and equipment.[5] Further, windows thus placed give a more beautiful and efficient lighting and are more healthy. They illuminate the ceiling and the ceiling reflects light into every part of the room, a light that is much more pleasant and restful to the eyes than one that strikes them from a lower level. High-placed windows are healthy, for if they open close to the ceiling, the room is more thoroughly ventilated. The door opens to the floor and the window to the ceiling, and the whole air of the room is stirred. High-placed electric lamps are efficient and good from a lighting point of view for similar reasons. Pendants are vulgar luxuries.

As regards doors, quite a little economy is sometimes made by leaving out a door. This is worth considering. If a door is omitted and a curtain substituted, there is no economy, for a good curtain is more expensive than a door. To the landlord, however, it will be cheaper for he pays for the door but not the curtain. There are some cases in which it is better to have neither door nor curtain, as between a kitchen and a china pantry. You do not want to close up either one from the other for the sake of privacy.[6]

Another little economy might, I think, very well be made in regard to many doors in a house. Out of ten doors commonly used, only one needs a lock and key at all. Yet all are generally provided therewith, and they are generally provided with very poor ones, nominally cheap but far too dear for all the use they are, which in most cases is no use at all. The old fashioned thumb latch is better, but I am afraid a good thumb latch is at the present day about as dear as the ordinary lock and handle, and not much better. I wish to suggest what I think would prove a really satisfactory and economical arrangement. Namely, that doors should be fitted with a simple grasp handle and held closed simply by a Bales catch or a bullet catch. These are now made with a good projection of spring and the cost is only a few cents. Whatever is the best way of doing it, [it] is quite time for us to give up the nasty and troublesome system of turning handles which periodically drop off and of locks and keys which are never used and are not worth the money paid for them. When doors have to be locked, get a real lock, and when a little barrel bolt will serve the purpose—as it often will—cut out the lock.

The floor is the hardest worked part of a house and it also requires most work to be put upon it. Almost all the dirt in a house gravitates to the floor and, in addition to this, a good deal of dirt inevitably is carried directly on to it. If you are going to take pleasure in the cleanness of your house, you will not grudge to spend something on the most efficient door-mats and scrapers, placed not only where they may be used, but where they will be used. If you like, you may put them out of sight when the snow has paved our streets so that no marble on earth can rival them, but have them well in view when the black soil asserts his supremacy.

This, of course, is not enough [because] the floors themselves must be easy to clean. Although it does not look a very difficult thing to invent, yet the perfect floor has not been invented. The perfect floor will have no cracks in it, it will be laid like cement, but it will be smooth, a pleasant colour, no dust will rub up off its surface, and it will be soft and pleasant to walk on. The best practical floor in common use is the hardwood tongued and grooved floor. Even that is costly, but the cost is made worthwhile by the saving in labour of cleaning [and] in the wholesomeness and beauty of the floor. Linoleum and rubber mat flooring, even when laid on soft wood floor, are more expensive than hardwood. They give, however, great satisfaction in kitchens and bathrooms. They approach fairly nearly to the requirements of an ideal floor in having practically no cracks. Painting softwood floors gives them a smoother surface [that is] easier to clean. In a cellar, it is probably better to have a dirt floor than to have a bad cement floor. Cheap cement floors become in a few years an eyesore and a heart break. The best of cement floors are never clean. The more you take the dust off, the more there remains. If, however, a cement floor is made good enough to be painted with floor paint, one has the satisfaction of real cleanness.

The science of health has made great changes in architects' ideas in regard to houses. This chiefly arises from the three ideas that are insisted on for ideal health conditions in matters of construction: whiteness, smoothness and impermeability of surface. Whiteness [is necessary] to show up dirt, smoothness to allow of dry cleaning, imperviousness to allow of good cleaning and to prevent dirt and germs soaking into the substance of [the] material of construction. In ordinary houses we cannot go all the way towards these ideals, but we do so in those places where dirt has to be handled: kitchen sinks and sanitary appliances generally.

Whilst these ideals [for hygiene] in some directions make for cost, in others they make for cheapness. We simplify the shapes of things. Square balusters on stairs, for example, and a general absence of cornices and projecting ledges. The kalsomining of rooms, which around this city so largely takes the place of wall papering, is, I think, a much more beautiful and wholesome method of finish. When we have doors and other woodwork of fir, it is more beautiful stained than painted and it is cheaper in first cost and in maintenance.[7]

NOTES

1. The audience and the reason for this talk are not known.
2. Following his retirement from the University of Alberta, Burgess located his office, as well as a town planning consulting firm, in the McLeod Building, a downtown Edmonton landmark that opened in 1915.
3. Note in margin: "In some houses a kitchen is separate in order that the cook may be kept separate."
4. A recurring theme in twentieth century kitchen design was the idea of the kitchen as a factory, an idea that Burgess had long endorsed. Thus, it was argued, kitchens should be as small as possible to encourage efficient production (Wetherell and Kmet, *Homes in Alberta*, 85–87, 201–04).
5. Note in margin: "piano."
6. Note in margin: "doors in amateur plans—amateur versus professional plans."
7. Notes in point form at end of page: "Rough cast probably worthwhile from maintenance point of view; Japanese the cleanest houses; 1. Houses for the private lives of occupants; 2. Houses for entertainment and show-off; That it does not pay an architect to build houses; The Blue Print idea."

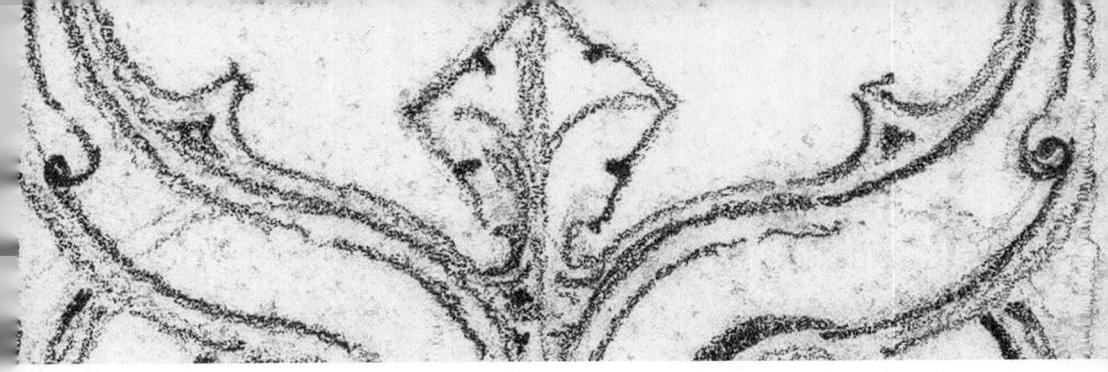

DOCUMENT 17

The New Town Planning
1. Scope and Purpose of Town Planning

As demonstrated by his involvement with Edmonton's town planning commission, Burgess was concerned to influence the shape of Edmonton's urban fabric. He was also committed to public education about town planning, and in 1941 he published a series of articles in the Edmonton Bulletin to inform the public about town planning principles and objectives. The series of sixteen articles was published in the Saturday edition. Only the introductory article is reprinted here.

The series included articles about zoning, slum clearance, Swedish and British low-cost housing projects, and, among others, garden city planning. Overall, the series offered a summary of contemporary thinking about urban planning and was linked by the theme that successful town planning needed to be practical. As Burgess argued—with obvious reference to Modernist principles—urban places, like buildings, had to be treated as living things, not as rigid machines, in order to best meet the needs of their residents.

Document 17 is Article 1 in a Series of Articles Published Weekly in the Edmonton *Bulletin, May 10, 1941,*[1] *71.213, file 168, UAA.*

DURING THE LAST THIRTY YEARS a revolution has taken place in ideas about the purposes and methods of town planning. Thirty years ago the work of the town planner was chiefly directed to making towns more beautiful to look at. In the meanwhile the whole outlook has changed. Whilst a beautiful city is still the ultimate aim, it has been realised that cities are in urgent need primarily of many improvements which must be made on the way to that final ideal and there has steadily been developed, and is still developing, a systematic method of procedure for the improvement of towns. In the new view, town planning is, at root, a social question. It consists essentially in the arrangement of a town to meet the social requirements of the citizens. The town planner has to ask himself, and his fellow citizens, such questions as these: Are our people adequately housed? Can they with convenience and enjoyment move about to the various parts of the town to which their affairs call them? Is the buying and selling carried on with ease and satisfaction to the buyers and sellers? Are there proper facilities for all the kinds of industries and occupations practiced in the city? Are services, public and individual, conveniently arranged for? [Are the arrangements for transportation into and out from the city of goods and persons as suitable as they can be made?] Are conditions for all people at home, at work or at recreation such as to give satisfaction, to ensure health and to supply the needs of mind and body? Are there facilities readily accessible for education, for bodily and mental recreation and for religious purposes? A city will not give mental satisfaction unless it is at the same time beautiful. Its beauty should be its crowning glory, but not a mere façade behind which lurks inefficiency, disease or distress.

From the above enumeration, it will be appreciated that modern town planning has in front of it a very wide and difficult program which, if approached piecemeal, is not likely to be advanced very much. The realisation of the size and scope of this program has resulted in what is known as "Town Planning Procedure," a system of attacking the problem which is methodical and scientific and which it is proposed in these articles to explain in outline.

The needs, wishes and ambitions of the citizens must be the motive power behind any advance in town planning. If we have good laws, it is because we are a law-loving people, not because we have good lawyers, though these are essential to the development and working of any system of laws. Just in the same way, if we are to have a well planned city in the new sense of town planning, it must arise from our having good citizens intent on the betterment of the conditions of their fellow citizens and on the promotion of better social life. The town planner's function is to put these intentions into such practical form as will steadily and progressively work towards general improvement.

Town planning has, in some quarters, attained the position of an important social movement. Both in Britain and in the United States this has been greatly stirred by the war. In Britain especially, on account of the density of the population, it has been realised that town planning is only part of a larger subject, "regional planning," that is to say the allotting of all "land use" in a reasonable and efficient manner. In all industrial countries there is a strong tendency to the vacation or under-population of the country and to the over-population and congestion of towns. The British Ministry of Reconstruction is strenuously at work surveying this condition, which is a great evil both for the country and for the cities, and is devising means to rectify it after the war. But even here, in western Canada, the same evils have taken root and require to be watched and corrected. Western Canada has not been [entirely] neglectful in the matter. Vancouver has a town planning commission established on comprehensive lines with extensive plans for the future. Edmonton and Calgary have also commissions on somewhat similar lines. So far as I know, these are the only Canadian cities which have such comprehensive arrangements for methodical procedure. Other cities, such as Ottawa, may have produced more spectacular effects, but they are operating on more piecemeal methods which do not face the whole problem. The methodical procedure which I wish to explain later does not consist in a general tearing down and rebuilding, but in the institution of plans and bylaws which, in process of time, tend steadily to all round betterment of conditions. It necessarily consists largely in the unscramblement of the chaos into which cities get themselves by unconsidered and undirected growth. Modern town planning might well be described as the art of city improvement, and town planners have come to look upon their work as the "culture" of cities, which must be treated, not as machines, which do not grow, but as growing things such as plants or trees. The tree has its own nature which cannot be changed. It has its own method of growth. It spreads out according to the law of its nature. Cities are growing things when considered as social developments. Nature produces trees, but a man skilled in tree culture may direct the growth of a tree and cultivate a tree of much more service to his needs than he will find in undirected nature. He will apply many methods of cultivating, fertilising, protecting from injury and disease, [and] pruning, etc. Similarly, by applying methods proper to the case, the town planner practises town culture which has become an art based on collected knowledge and requiring, back of these, a sound philosophy of social life. This implies careful study and the mastery of a complex technique as well as a vision of the social good such as make the profession of town planner a necessity in modern city life.

NOTE

1. The text reprinted here was transcribed from the manuscript version. Text in square brackets in this reprinted text indicates material that appears in the manuscript but not in the version printed in the newspaper.

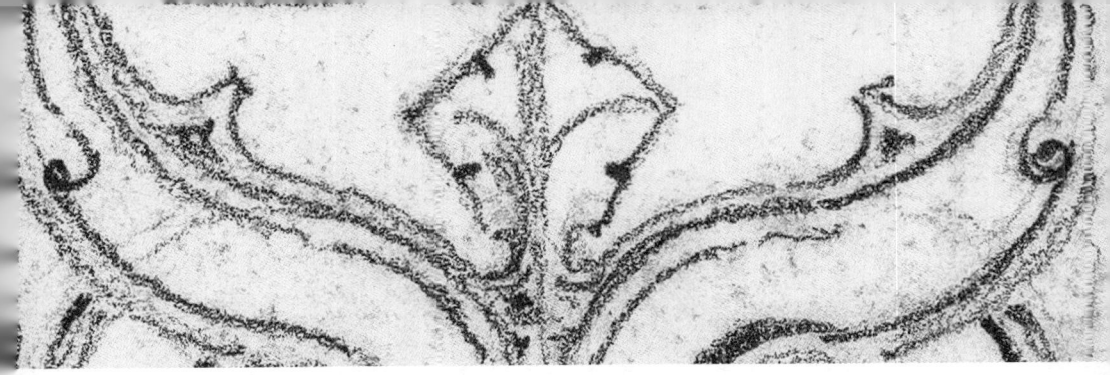

DOCUMENT 18

Housing Present and Prospective

WORLD WAR II was not only about military engagements. To be sure, they were always central in Canadian minds, but worries about employment, housing and social problems that peace would bring also concerned many people. In Alberta, this concern would be expressed in 1943 in the work of the Postwar Reconstruction Committee that made recommendations on postwar economic and social development. On the national stage, the federal Committee on Postwar Reconstruction conducted similar investigations between 1941 and 1944.

This 1941 talk by Burgess was another reflection of such concern about postwar Canada. But like many others who thought about these issues, Burgess's talk expressed a confidence that current and future social issues could be managed by forward-looking empirical research. Only through such sociological understanding could solutions be found to the problems that beset the country during the war and which would likely only grow in importance once the war was over.

Burgess's talk also revealed particular concerns about the nature of housing. Burgess, reflecting conventional Canadian thinking, believed that the single family dwelling offered the best housing from a social standpoint. In contrast, apartments were suitable for specialised housing needs (such as single people), but not for families with children. In other words, "homes" could not be made in apartments. The problem was that housing located on its own plot of land was too costly for many Canadians, and many people assumed that housing affordability would be a central issue in postwar adjustment. Burgess believed that one solution to this problem was co-operative housing models that could be financed with mortgages under the National Housing Act.

Document 18 is a speech to the Women's University Club, Macdonald Hotel, December 1, 1941, 71.213, file 136, UAA.

I AM TOLD that this Club is interesting itself in problems arising out of the present world crisis and facing us for the future. Housing problems being amongst these, I have been asked to say something about housing in relation to the future.

In Britain, in Canada and in the U.S.A., when these countries began to organise industry on a war footing, we forthwith began to hear of many serious strikes in manufacturing industries. There were various alleged reasons for these strikes but, undoubtedly, the main purpose behind all was to raise the wages of workers in these industries. The nation's emergency was the workers' opportunity. Was this a criminal lack of patriotism, treason to the cause of freedom? Let us examine the workers' economic position in relation to this subject of housing.

Before the war—in 1938—there were in Canada 541,427 wage earners in manufacturing industries alone, and their average annual earnings were $956.00, a little less than $80.00 per month. As this is an average amount, it may be said that about half of these people were earning rather more than that amount but, on the other hand, there are many industries, notably the great building industry, which are not included in these figures. The point is that a vast number of people do not earn more than $80.00 a month and these people are not negligible members of society. They are absolutely essential to our economy, both in peace and in war, and are indeed the foundation on which society stands, without whom that standard of living in which we feel some satisfaction cannot exist. It is of national interest to know what standard of living these people themselves enjoy, for, as their strikes suggest, they do not appear to be quite satisfied with it. I take it that these strikes are a protest against it and an appeal for its improvement. In Britain the strikes have ceased. The situation is too grave. The strikes have ceased in consideration of certain promises that unsatisfactory conditions will be improved. Definite steps are being taken to ensure that they shall be improved. Lord Reith's Commission is in charge of the plans that are to be framed and put into execution. It is busily occupied with the first stage that is necessary in any such great operation. That first stage is that of a wide and searching enquiry into and diagnosis of existing conditions and an examination of troubles that exist, with suggestions of practicable solutions. This is what in this country is called the fact-finding stage. Let us try to do a little elementary fact-finding on a small scale.

What is the family budget of a man who gets $80.00 a month? It is sometimes said that one-fifth of a family income may be spent on rent. This is only a rough approximation and may be far from true in many cases, but let us assume it for the moment. In this case it will be $16.00. When our worker goes house hunting with the help of his wife, he has to look out for something at this price. It is interesting to know what he can get for that money. Owned housing should cost about 5 percent less, which would be about $15.25 per month or $9.00 less per year, and this is worth considering when means are small. He must, however, pause to make some farther calculation. If he is to pay $16.00 per month for shelter, that will leave him $64.00 for all other necessary expenses—food, clothing, heat and light.

Consider this man, not simply as an individual but as the representative of a class, which, as I have said, is essential to our community and all its standards of living. Should that class be treated as self-perpetuating? By this I mean should we look on the class as one in which the members marry and have sufficient number of children so that their numbers do not diminish, in which case, the class would [not] have to be continuously recuperated from some other class. No doubt this process of dying out and being recuperated from the country has gone on in our great cities to an enormous extent. Writers who deal in statistics state that no city on this continent of over 100,000 population is self-perpetuating in this sense, and these same statisticians go on to say that this process cannot continue very much longer because the country population is by this and for other reasons being steadily depleted.

I am therefore going to assume that our worker has a wife and two children under 16 years of age. How do they make out on $16.00 for rent and $64.00 for everything else? Applying a moderate standard of living, they will require $30.00 for food, $35.00 for individual expenses and $30.00 for general or overhead expenses; a total of $95.00 per month, which is more than our friend's entire income. You may well ask where do I get these figures. You know a great deal more about housekeeping than I do. I am merely working with statistics made out by other people and base my figures partly on Dr. Eular's report on Edmonton of 1938, well known to some of you, and [printed] in the *Labour Gazette*.[1] This is not the occasion to go into all the details. I may explain that under "individual expenses," I have included clothing, care of health, recreation, transportation, and under "general expenses," I have put fuel and light, current housekeeping, education and savings or insurance. Food I have placed quite separately. This list of items is a familiar one to students of household economy. Perhaps no two estimates will agree as to the exact proportion of any one item. To the best of my judgement, the figures are very moderate and the items are all essential. I have put food at $30.00 for four persons for a month, which is exactly $1.00 per day for four persons or 25¢ per day per person. That is not riotous living. Perhaps some may be tempted to say that it can't be done. Notice that my figures suppose an expenditure of a total of $111.00 per month. If this implies a moderate standard of living, how do a million or more people manage on a total of $80.00 a month? Obviously, by adopting a lower standard of living. There is no use saying that it can't be done when we know that it is being done all around us all the time.

Let us now consider this expression "standard of living" as applied to housing. What is a fair standard of housing? I don't mean an ideal above practical accomplishment, but a standard which we can wish for [everyone] with at least some faint hope of obtaining. What would we like all people to have? A standard that will be compatible with health and happiness. What is a good house and what does it cost? I wish to draw an ideal picture, but without sheer extravagance.

First I shall consider the basement. A basement is not essential but I shall suppose one because, from a working man's point of view, it has several very good uses. Warmth comes best and most economically from a basement. It is a security against dampness and so ensures the endurance of the building. Boys are apt to carry on the whittling of sticks or other instinctive operations involving mess which it is well to keep out of the living rooms. A working man wants a place where he can "saw wood" in various senses for he does most of the maintenance of the house himself. There may be a laundry in the basement for this will disencumber the kitchen which is going to be quite small. Here the girls of the family will be free to learn and to practice the useful and necessary occupation of washing and ironing. To people of low incomes, it is an economy to store boxes and other odd things which come in useful for repairs. More may be said, but let us go to the ground floor. This might be in one room serving as kitchen, dining room and general living room and perhaps even as sleeping room. Our means might force us to this, but let us suppose a division, not forgetting that any division costs money. On the principle then,

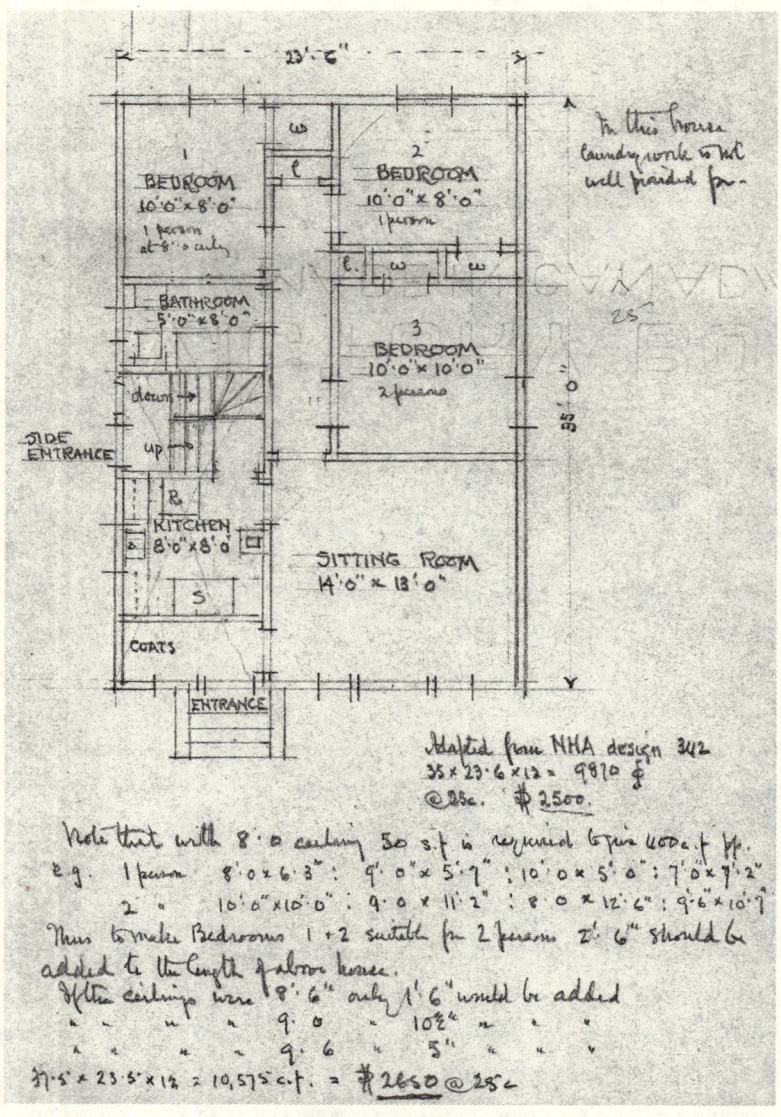

In one of the many housing plans Burgess sketched, he adapted a design from the National Housing Authority's plan book for a three-bedroom cottage. Not dated, ca. 1940. (71.213–165, UAA)

of a place for everything and everything in its place, there will be a separate small kitchen. Next, should there be a dining room apart from the general living room? I shall suppose that there will be so, for, though it may seem an expensive luxury to have a special room only for eating in, yet in this case it is going to be otherwise serviceable. The children will use this for study and play, whilst the parents or those who do not wish to play may be in the living room at their own occupations or conversations. Having set this high standard for the ground floor, what shall we have upstairs where the bedrooms and bathroom are placed. As the bedrooms have got to be small, it will not be well to have more than two persons in each room. If the family consists of the two parents and two boys and two girls, this means three bedrooms. Three bedrooms will still be required if the family consists of two parents and one boy and one girl.

Before we build this somewhat luxurious house, we must consider what it will cost. Since it is going to be a fully modern house with hot and cold [water], warm air heating and all conveniences, the cost will be a shock to you. So I shall postpone that matter till I have discussed the site.

It has been said with much truth that the environment is half the home. At this point the objection may be raised that I am going entirely on the wrong lines because cheaper and better accommodation can be provided in a flat or apartment in which the house-keeping is much easier. A lot of people are saying just that. This is where the value of the environment is evident. I have heard and read much discussion on the question of houses and flats and have come to a conclusion that may be quite simply expressed. The individual house and the apartment are both social necessities, but for quite different purposes. Apartments are excellent accommodation for grown-ups but they are quite wrong for the bringing-up of children. For these they can be no real home. In planning for the future, it is of the greatest importance to ensure a good standard of provision for children, for they constitute one-third of the population. They are the citizens of the future. The welfare of the future demands that their welfare be safeguarded. No child should be brought up in an apartment; it is not fair. It is true that good children are frequently so brought up, but this depends on the special character of their parents and on the special attention they can pay to their children. Even bright though these children may be, they suffer not only in general physical constitution but also in general mental constitution, for they lack the natural outlook upon life that is absorbed by the home-bred child. Parents too, who live in apartments as tenants, lack the attitude towards good citizenship of those who own their own dwellings. Finally, no type of dwelling deteriorates so quickly and surely as the apartment. It might almost be said that *where there are no apartments there can be no slums.*

A good deal of discussion has taken place in regard to the most suitable size of site for the homes of people of low incomes. This frequently centres round a statement made, now many years ago, by one of the wisest and most experienced of town planners—Sir Raymond Unwin.[2] I shall quote his words:

> with the narrow frontages usually adopted for small cottages, it is possible, under existing bylaws, to crowd as many as 50 houses or more to the acre. There can be no doubt that this number is altogether excessive for reasonable health or comfort; it provides for no garden ground, only a small backyard attached to each cottage...One may safely say that, according to circumstances, the desirable number would be between ten and twenty houses to the acre, and in this case, I refer to the net measurement of the building land, excluding roads....Twelve houses to the net acre of building land, excluding all roads has been proved to be about the right number to give gardens of sufficient size to be of commercial value to the tenants.

By commercial value, Unwin explains that such a garden makes an appreciable contribution to the larder.

You may get an idea of how much ground one-twelfth of an acre means if you can visualise the size of that most frequent site in this city that has a 33 foot frontage and a depth of 132 feet, which is exactly one-tenth of an acre. If you cut off 22 feet from the rear, making the depth 110 feet, you then have one-twelfth of an acre, the size that Unwin recommends. The bylaws of Edmonton actually require more than this as a minimum.

The facilities for family life are certainly not complete without consideration for the wider environment. The family should have access to community services, for shopping, education, recreation, [and] meetings. Smaller children should be provided for by playgrounds where they may be safe and under supervision. Farther playgrounds and parks are needed for various kinds of exercise and recreation. Schools, libraries, museums and other exhibition places should be safely accessible. Underpasses of traffic routes are sometimes provided in modern housing suburbs. Lewis Mumford suggests that a child's education is not complete without opportunity to watch men working at a variety of trades.[3] This suggests that some trades should be permitted and encouraged as part of each residential district. There is a real value in the suggestion.

In paying all this attention to the individual family dwelling, I am assuming that family life is the essential basis of community life and therefore of civil life, that is, of civilised life. The method of carrying on "life" in a home must be facilitated by the arrangement of the rooms and equipment. To the basic requirements of food, clothing, shelter, warmth, etc., must be added the still more important needs of civilised life; privacy, recreation, hygiene, education, rest, etc. This means that the family must have facilities for preparing and serving meals, for play and study, for removal of wastes, for personal cleanliness and sound sleep. Education is not to be understood in terms of the mere reading of books. Learning to cook, to wash and iron, to carry on hobbies, singing, the practice of music, using the radio, the telephone, conversation with friends; all these things and many more are parts of civilised education, and the home should provide for them. The plan of a house should be arranged with all these things in view.

Now let us return to the cost of the small three-bedroom house that represents a modest standard of living according to modern ideas. The site may cost $200. The building $3,000. Incidentals, say $100.

Of course this is quite beyond the means of our $80 a month wage earner, but we shall come back to him later. Meanwhile, when one considers building a house, it is usual for the prospective builder to have collected a sum of money [for the down payment] and to borrow the rest to be paid back by instalments. Let us suppose in this case that $800 has been collected (The National Housing Act [NHA] required only 10 percent or $380). Let us also suppose that $3,000 can be borrowed at 5 percent. This is optimistic but the NHA actually advanced money at 4 percent including repayment or amortisation, which meant that after paying for 36 years the interest and original debt was cleared off. If the arrangement that I have supposed were successfully made and the house built, how much is the owner going to have to pay every year for his house? This will be: interest on $3000 @ 5 percent = $150. Taxes @ 50 mills = $95. Insurance @ 30 cents per 100 = $10.50. Maintenance and repairs at about 4 percent = $140.50. Total, $396 per year or $33 per month.

If this house [is to] be rented, the owner will expect to get at least a clear 5 percent on his investment. This will be $190.00 per year. To get this he will fix the rent at $48.00 or $50.00 per month. On the other hand, if the owner lives in his own house and is a handy man, he will do much of the repairs himself and may do these for about $45.00. In that case he will be living in his own house for $25.00 a month.

Now to return to our wage earner. There are millions of people to whom the building of a home like this is not even a dream. How do they manage, for they do continue to exist? The answer is that they throw overboard all the so-called standards of living. These don't mean a thing to them. They don't have a basement. They don't have central heating. They don't have plumbing. They don't limit themselves to two in a room, nor do they stick at sleeping in the living room or any room. They do not pay 50 mills. They don't borrow money at 5 percent or any percentage. They don't make a contract with a builder who must charge for his services. They build their own houses with their own hands. They build where the taxes are 20 mills because there is no water supply and there is no sewerage system. When they build, their wives help, their boys help, their girls help, sometimes their friends help You may see crowds of these houses on the outskirts of all our cities. Often they don't look very nice; but if any of us have said that they should not be allowed, may God forgive us. For these are the truest homes in all our beloved land. These are the homes of heroes, the homes that heroes come from, the homes that heroes are prepared to fight for. The people who build these houses are full of energy and initiative, they are ingenious, handy and capable men and women. Their standard of living is very low. Their standard of life is high. They love their homes, they love their land, they love one another. But they sometimes feel that their life is hard and they sometimes strike for higher pay.

What then is likely to be done in the matter of housing after the war? The great defect in our communities is the lack of adequate housing for wage earners. It is said that these are better provided for in totalitarian countries. Our ideals are higher—their performance is better. Whatever may be done for these people after the war, we may be sure that if they get the chance they will do most of it for themselves for that is their nature. In them there resides more than in others the home-building instinct. If we have any regard for justice, we shall not stand in the way of their just aspirations and obvious needs.

We are told that our standards of living generally will be seriously impaired after, and perhaps long before, the war is over. Is the standard of living of the wage earner also to be lowered? I should be inclined to think that they will have something to say about this. There will be a shortage of many things that we associate with our high standard of living. The want of those things which may properly be called luxuries will not do us much harm; it may even be a benefit. But we must be prepared to do without a number of things that have become dear to us. For some time a greater proportion of production will be applied in raising the standard of [living to a level that is] just and desirable. It is necessary to the carrying on of our civilisation, which under past conditions was becoming self-strangulating.

How many of us will feel inclined to volunteer to lower our own standard of living for the sake of the large majority of others? There will be no call for volunteers. There may even be all-out conscription. What sort of change is really called for? Some speak of having to make great sacrifices and as if this were something to make us tremble. I believe that there is nothing at all to be afraid of. After the war all those who are left will, generally speaking, have two hands to work with. The earth will still be here to yield her increase as of old and, with increase of skill, even more abundantly than ever. Food, shelter and clothing we shall not lack though we may have to say goodbye to many of the frills. We may be the better for that. If we face the future with courage and good-will, then, though the standard of living may go down, the standard of life shall surely go up. What is sacrifice when it is made to put our friends on their feet? It is not a sorrow but a joy. We have only to realise that the true standard to follow is not that of living but the standard of life and to advance that standard.

NOTES

1. Euler was Minister of Trade and Commerce. The reference cited by Burgess could not be located in the *Labour Gazette*. A copy of a typescript of the report that Burgess refers to, "Family Living Expenditures in Canada, Edmonton Alberta" (Dominion Bureau of Statistics, Cost of Living Report for Year Ending September 1938), is in 71.213, file 165, UAA.
2. Sir Raymond Unwin was an English architect and town planner. He designed Letchworth, the Garden City, near London. He wrote *Town Planning in Practice* (1909).
3. Lewis Mumford was an American writer on technology, literary criticism, urban development and, among others, town planning. A prolific author, his work includes the Renewal of Life series, which was published between 1934 and 1951, and included *Technics and Civilization* (1934) and *The Culture of Cities* (1938).
4. The growth of low income suburbs outside the cities remained a notable feature in both Calgary and Edmonton well after World War II. In the economic boom after 1947, it became a sufficiently serious problem by the 1950s that it was the subject of a royal commission, the Royal Commission on the Metropolitan Development of Calgary and Edmonton, which reported in 1957.

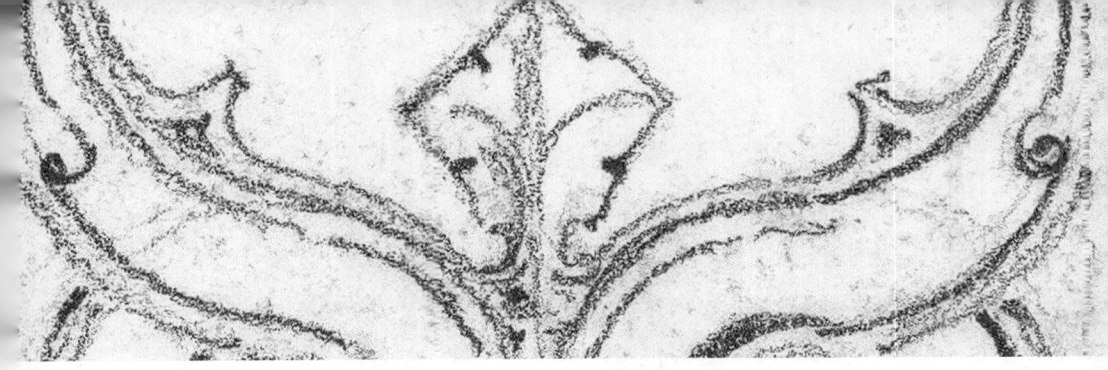

DOCUMENT 19

What Zoning Does For Edmonton

BY THE MID 1940S, the voluntary approach to city planning still held sway in Edmonton, and the Edmonton Town Planning Commission, staffed with volunteers, continued to oversee planning efforts in the city. The zoning bylaw that the commission had devised in 1933 remained the basis for Edmonton land use regulations. This bylaw also mandated provisions for residential districts such as the allowable set back of buildings from the street and height and distance between buildings. But its most distinctive contribution to the city's future was its provision for public parks. As a result of the zoning bylaw, extensive park lands were reserved in the river valley, in some of the ravines that cut through the city, and in residential neighbourhoods. In many cases, land was reserved for parks well before development took place, allowing park development to be incorporated easily into future growth.

The zoning bylaw gave Edmonton guidelines for development that were a model in Canada at the time. But growth of the city, new approaches to planning, and especially wartime growth made its provisions increasingly out of date by the mid 1940s. So too, the voluntary approach to planning was becoming increasingly difficult to manage because of local politics. Thus, by the late 1940s, Edmonton began creating new professional agencies to regulate growth and provide public services. A Parks and Recreation Commission was created in 1947 and trained recreational consultants were employed to offer public services in city parks. In the late 1940s, Edmonton further revamped its approaches to planning by hiring a full-time professional town planner, bringing to an end the era of voluntary approaches to urban planning.

Document 19 is a radio talk for the Federation of Community Leagues on CKUA, November 15, 1943, (Broadcast Repeated June 7, 1944), 71.213, file 163, UAA.

As a member of the Edmonton Town Planning Commission and Chairman of the Zoning Committee of that Commission, I have been asked to explain what zoning does for the good of the city.

Zoning means the apportioning of various districts of a city for special purposes so that, for example, stores or manufacturing industries shall not be permitted in the midst of a residential district or zone. This arrangement involves restrictions on the use to which an owner may put his land and therefore it requires legal authority for its enforcement. The city of Edmonton has obtained this authority by adopting the *Town Planning Act* of 1929 and has proceeded to zone the city, prescribing where industries, stores, apartment buildings, etc., may or may not be built. It took about three years to decide the use that should be made of every parcel of land in the city, to make the bylaws which should regulate the different types of zones and buildings and to get the approval and authority of the city council. Of this time, a year was given to its consideration by the city council, during which time it was open for any one to examine the map that shows the zones and the bylaw that describes the restrictions and to make any recommendations [and] to raise any objections.

It is easy to understand the general purpose and intention of zoning and the necessity for it. Before zoning can be introduced, a city has to get itself into a mess that causes annoyance to a great number of its citizens. They then say, "why is this mess allowed?" The work of zoning is really the disentangling of a mess. It is natural to suppose that zoning could be introduced before a city is built, or at least before it has got itself into a mess. This just cannot be done. A city must grow to a certain size before it is a mess, before it is evident how it is going to grow, before it knows whether it is going to grow at all. It is like a field where you must allow the weeds to come up with the crops and do the weeding afterwards. Not only that, but it is like a field in which the crops have got themselves mixed up with one another and you must select the parts which have the best promise for each kind of crop, and weed out the others from that, thus separating the different crops. In a city, those uses which have got into inappropriate places cannot simply be ordered to move out. They represent the means of living to some persons, perhaps to many persons, and must be treated with justice and consideration. The zoner therefore leaves them where they are, but he calls them "nonconforming uses." This means that certain restrictions are laid upon them by law. If such a building should be destroyed by fire or other agency, or if its nonconforming use ceases through failure of the business or other cause, then that nonconforming use is extinguished and the property must therefore be used in conformity with the zoning bylaws. There is another method by which a nonconforming use may be removed. The city may offer to the nonconforming user a lot owned by itself, in a proper zone, in exchange for his. This method might, and ought to be used much more than it is, if only it were more widely realised that it can be done. The city will willingly do it. It is of advantage to both parties.

Zoning goes much farther than the mere segregation of the uses of land. Just where a certain class of building may be built, and where not, can now be ascertained at a glance from the district map of the city prepared by the zoning committee. The zoning bylaw farther prescribes the restrictions which must be observed in the erection of buildings. Thus, in residential districts, the fronts of buildings must be set back twenty feet from the street line, the sides of buildings 10 percent of the width of the frontage, the rear of the building twenty-five feet back from the centre of the rear lane. Heights of buildings are also regulated. In business districts, on the other hand, there is no restriction on the extent of the building on the property. Buildings here extend to the street line and to the sides of the property and also to the rear line, with certain provisions for loading and unloading vehicles. Such restrictions are made not for individual interests, but for the protection of neighbours, for the health and convenience of the community, and for the appearance of the neighbourhood.

The bases of most of the restrictions imposed are the tendencies that people have shown by their usual practice to be convenient and desirable. Such a requirement, for example, as setting back of houses twenty feet from the street line is made because it is usual for people to set their houses back about that amount. It is frequently complained that in many of our streets the houses are set too close together. The bylaw requires the building to be set back from the side of the property 10 percent of the width of the lot. With 33 foot lots, this is 3'4," leaving 6'8" between houses. This leaves just 26'4" for the width of the house. This is a fairly severe limitation. It might be desirable to leave fifteen feet between houses, but that would leave only eighteen feet for the width of the house, which is quite too little. The trouble arises from the lots being so commonly only thirty-three feet wide. They were so laid out before zoning was introduced. The [Edmonton] Town Planning Commission has recommended that, so far as practicable, lot widths shall be altered to forty feet in width. This can only be done in a limited number of cases.

The general effect of zoning, then, is to sort out the purposes for which city land may be used by different groups of users. There is always some natural tendency for similar occupations to group together. It is natural for heavy industries to be together near railways so that they may have ready access to means of transportation. It is of advantage for retail stores to be grouped together so that customers are saved many footsteps in making varied purchases. It is the business of the zoner to note all such reasonable tendencies and to base his zoning upon them. To get uses together or in suitable groups in a town where they have become scattered is to restore the natural advantages which they have lost by getting themselves into a mess. Few, if any, other cities of Canada have adopted a system for zoning so full and detailed as that of Edmonton. We have parks, four types of residential districts, three of business districts, two of industrial and one agricultural. The most exclusive of these are the residential districts, for whilst business or industry may not build in residential districts, residences may be built in any district.

By far the largest portion of any city is occupied by residences, generally much more than one-half. Since business is carried on for the purpose of living, and not living for the purpose of business, this may be considered not only the biggest part of the city, but also the most important. Residential districts therefore require the greatest consideration. They consist not only of blocks of houses surrounded by gardens, but must be provided with a number of things necessary in carrying on everyday life. There must be in the neighbourhood a local business district where minor daily purchases or services may be readily obtained. There must be permitted schools, churches, perhaps a library or a hospital, and certainly parks for recreation of various kinds. Very important from this point of view is the community league, which may give a focus of social interests to a district and requires some property for its purposes.[1] The larger a city becomes, the cohesion of interest amongst its people weakens. It becomes too large a unit to maintain a civic spirit. This can only be remedied by local communities, and it is remarkable that in Edmonton this seems to be instinctively recognised, for the two dozen or so of community leagues that have automatically sprung up in the city fairly well covers its entire extent. Some of these, it is true, have as yet a small and struggling existence, but they are there and merit the support of all good citizens for their potentiality for good is very great. If these do not look out for and promote the needs and amenities of their districts, they can hardly expect others even to know what these are.

The policy of the city in regard to these leagues is liberal. They are very willing to lease land for sports and other community purposes at the nominal rent of one dollar a year, giving ten years security in the use of the property. They also give assistance in the making of skating rinks. This is a wise policy calculated to create civic spirit, for even a small skating rink fosters social interest and generally leads to other sports such as tennis, bowling, curling, etc., and to the erection of club houses which can be used for other social purposes and may serve as meeting places for a variety of clubs and associations and for musical or other interests.

So much for the organisation and theory of zoning in Edmonton. Does it work smoothly and with success and benefit? It might do worse or it might do better. There is a certain amount of evasion. No laws can be made so perfectly that misguided ingenuity will not find ways around them, and no inspection short of strict watch over every individual can wholly combat evasion. But on the whole, we are a law-abiding people and the zoning bylaws are, on the whole, loyally accepted. There is one respect, however, in which these laws are at present under severe pressure. The preamble to our bylaws sets forth as amongst their purposes "preventing the overcrowding of land" and "avoiding undue concentration of population." Now, both the federal government and the city council are pressing for more housing accommodation for a great influx of population.[2] People are being urged to subdivide single family residences into apartments for as many families as can be crowded into the space. This is in fact *calling for* congestion of population. Apartments may be built in their proper place for excellent purposes, but such a call as is now being made threatens to invade our safeguarded single-family residential districts by a dangerous element. For a crowded apartment is a future slum. This is the one and only seed from which the slum grows in due course. They are a menace to healthy conditions of life, especially to the lives of children, and once established they are as difficult to get rid of as dandelions from a lawn. This may seem an exaggeration to those who are unacquainted with the natural history of the slum, but it is a matter of general observation and experience.

It is reasonable to ask, in view of post war reconstruction, whether zoning is capable of farther beneficial expansion. That will depend on the powers that may be given to it and also on the persons that would exercise those powers. At present the town planning commission and, of course, its zoning committee are entirely composed of *voluntary* workers, of citizens at large, not of experts trained in town planning.[3] The time these people can spare from their private business is strictly limited. They are purely an *advisory body*, and, as such, are not in a position to propose, initiate, and guide any new or expensive schemes. They may have excellent ideas on many of the subjects involved, but they naturally feel themselves bound to work within the framework that has so far been set for development; for example, the thirty-three foot lot or the existing layout of streets and drains and subdivisions generally. If they proposed bold departures from custom, they would involve themselves in working out details that only an *expert* could successfully handle. No radical changes ought to be ventured upon except by a trained professional town planner. I have no doubt that such a man could suggest many great and practicable improvements and it seems to me likely that, in the hoped for period of reconstruction, all cities must, if they are materially to improve their conditions, employ town planners. These will require to be men with a knowledge of the business needs of the city, its trade and industry, [and] its social conditions and aspirations. A town planner would require to have ready access to all the records and statistics of the city and to work in full and continuous co-operation with all other departments of civic work, including, of course, the city council. Such a town planner would prove to be a great co-ordinator of all the work of the city because of his necessary co-operation with all departments. As a necessary part of his training is in design, he would also make his city more beautiful.

No such training is given in Canada today and so there are no trained town planners in Canada.[4] If substantial progress is to be made in the reconditioning of our cities, we must train and employ the men who can do the work.

NOTES

1. The first community league was established in Jasper Place, a suburb of Edmonton in 1917. The idea spread quickly in Edmonton, and in 1921 the Federation of Community Leagues was established to create a focus and give stability to the movement. By 1924, there were 20 leagues in the city. The movement developed in the context of several decades of thinking in North America about playgrounds and neighbourhood community organisation, but it reached its earliest fullest expression in Canada in Edmonton.
2. As a wartime measure, the federal government in 1942 overrode local zoning bylaws in Canada in order to bring more housing onto the market. In places such as Edmonton, where housing shortages were very severe, the override allowed the development of much marginal housing in the form of conversions of nonresidential buildings such as garages into houses and the subdivision of houses into suites.
3. Burgess was for many years the chair of the Edmonton Town Planning Commission zoning committee.
4. The first school of urban planning in Canada was established at McGill in 1947. It was largely staffed with British planners. Central [now Canada] Mortgage and Housing Corporation was an important force in the establishment of this school (Interview by author with Howard and Mary Spence Sales, Vancouver, 2002).

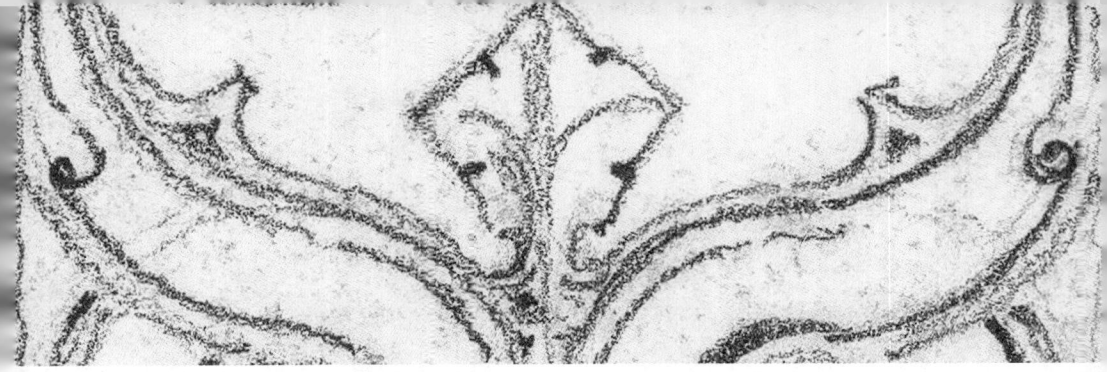

DOCUMENT 20

Improvement of Business Street Fronts

A Study of the Most Common Defects, With a View to Their Correction, in Special Reference to Jasper Avenue, Edmonton, 101st to 106th Streets, March 15, 1946.

THERE IS TODAY *a common belief that the historical fabric and character of Canadian cities was lost as a result of the large scale adoption of Modernist architecture and the commercialisation and huge expansion of cities after World War II. This, however, represents only one interpretation. As revealed in Burgess's 1946 description of Jasper Avenue, then Edmonton's central business district, such pressure existed well before the postwar boom. Rampant commercial development was not only a postwar vice, but an inherent part of the economic and social life of Canadian cities.*

Burgess believed that human motivation lay behind all design. He held that an age could be judged by its architecture and the common expression that arose from people living and working together. Consequently, he argued that good design, as he defined it, arose from a society that valued harmony, personal restraint, decorous behaviour and a sense of community and neighbourliness. This formed the basis for his critique of the appearance of Jasper Avenue, where he suggested that the greatest barrier to good design arose from the expression of popular attitudes towards property and public taste and the public's acceptance of the legitimacy of unrestrained commercial activity.

The motivation of the city of Edmonton planning department in commissioning this study is unclear, although seemingly the department saw the cacophony of the street as something that reflected poorly on the city. Despite this, the city did almost nothing in the future to control development or advertising along Jasper Avenue. The street is no longer the important focus for Edmonton's civic or commercial life that it once was.

Document 20 is a study commissioned by the City of Edmonton Planning Department, March 15, 1946,[1] 71.213, file 171, UAA.

THE FOLLOWING GENERAL STUDY is made with a view to a future examination of the particular district [above] named, in order that certain principles may be established to form a basis for consistent criticisms and recommendations in regard to that district. It should be frankly admitted that the laying down of principles and rules for work of an aesthetic nature can never have an absolute authority. In art, more than in any other sphere, the exception proves the rule. A certain number, though only a small number, of cases occur where the rules proposed in this study are contradicted, and yet a good effect has been produced. In the great mass of work represented in an ordinary business frontage, however, it may be fairly claimed that the observance of the recommendations here made would produce a vast improvement. It may be farther claimed that only those acquainted with and accustomed to regulate their work by rational principles can have the skill and the right to overrule them upon fit occasion. Such people as these are not likely to raise objection to an endeavour to elucidate the rational principles that habitually govern good work.

**Recommendations for the Improvement of Business Frontages.
Jasper Avenue, Edmonton, From 101st to 106th Streets**

The frontages of the business streets of modern cities commonly present an appearance of disorder in which individual interests struggle somewhat vainly to assert themselves with complete disregard to general interests, resulting in a chaos of ugliness. Jasper Avenue is no exception, it is merely typical of many. A careful examination of the causes of this distressing condition will show that much of it is needless and can be remedied by attention to some simple corrections which, in many cases, involve no great expense, and in some will eliminate useless expenditures.

It would be quite possible to create a vast improvement by enacting and enforcing three or four simple city regulations. But our people resent control by bylaws which interfere with them in everyday matters that concern their individual personal actions. The alternative is that each should impose on himself such regulations as will appeal to his own good sense and be to his own credit and to the public good. In the matter of improving our street frontages, this attitude could produce very great improvements. It requires, however, some clear knowledge as to what particular things it is well to do and what to avoid doing. This can be arrived at only by careful consideration of the faults that cause our present appearance of mess and disorder, and of the means for remedying these faults. It is here proposed to note and examine in detail each of the common faults and to suggest good remedies. First, however, it will be serviceable to make some observations of the general condition of our street frontages.

If we first look at the general scene to distinguish its better elements, we note those that command the most respect are such businesses as banks, trust, and insurance companies. These observe a restrained decency and respectability. Amongst retail stores, the more efficient and successful rely on the same qualities expressed in a different way appropriate to the carrying on of their business. The smaller, less efficient and less prosperous the store, the more its owner is tempted to bedizen it and to offend against appearances in order to attract attention. This may, indeed, attract attention, but it does not therefore necessarily attract customers. It may actually repel those who take any keen pleasure in good appearances, and will certainly do so in time if the drift continues. When one small store tries to outbid its neighbours by violent advertising devices, others feel compelled to resort to similar methods, and the total result becomes an offensive medley in which none secures any predominance, and the value of advertising—which is great when it is good and efficient—is entirely lost in the general confusion. In this confusion one store modest enough to distinguish itself by good-mannered simplicity and appropriateness of self-presentation will alone recommend itself above the others. It will be well for a small storekeeper to realise that there is a certain kind of homelike intimate charm possible and appropriate to small things that cannot belong to bigger things and that he should endeavour after the qualities of neatness and tidiness appropriate to his situation. By each one observing this, a whole neighbourhood may become an attraction to customers who otherwise betake themselves to where order and efficiency are better observed.

In order the better to analyse in some detail the faults of which correction is required, it will be well to consider in order: (a) the buildings, (b) advertising signs, (c) certain accessories.

The Buildings

In regard to the buildings along our business streets, it is perhaps too common to imagine that the distressing appearance of these streets is due chiefly to faults in the design of these. On the contrary, one of the chief sources of the trouble is the disregard of the essential structural and decorative features of these buildings, which are too frequently smothered and obscured by shoddy and trivial matter. It must be recognised that the substance and the features of a building have a dominating value in the general appearance. It is a good principle to permit the building to show its figure and features, however simple, even if it be merely honest building unadorned. Yet it does sometimes happen that business buildings, either through positively bad original design or owing to the defacement of thoughtlessly added changes, do display glaring faults. Of these faults, some may still be retrieved by simple means.

One of the most common faults in store buildings is an irritating and unnecessary irregularity in height. This arises from an entire disregard of adjoining premises, the absence of neighbourly consideration. This sin of disregarding neighbours will be shown in various parts of this study to vitiate the appearance of our streets in many ways. If no attempt is to be made to correct this, good general effects are hopeless. This does not mean that all should be alike, but rather that all must co-operate in reasonable relationships with one another. Regularity of height does not imply that all are the same height—for example:

1. A regular line of higher and lower fronts alternating may make a definite decorative effect.
2. A higher centre with slightly lower ends presents another form of regularity.
3. A lower centre with slightly higher ends is another form.

These and other orderly arrangements avoid the fault of monotony which may be farther overcome by variety in minor features and in colour. This matter of some scheme of orderliness of total heights is of much importance because it outlines the buildings, and that outline is a dominant element in the whole scene. It is inevitable that great irregularities must occur when higher or more important buildings are built beside lower ones. But this need be no source of offence when the lines of the buildings are reasonable and agreeable in themselves. It is the little needless irregularities that are irritating and unsightly. When certain so-called architectural ornaments are used, it sometimes happens that they are of a clumsy and meaningless sort such as architects and competent designers severely avoid. When they are interesting, or even merely inoffensive, they

This store front on Jasper Avenue and 106 Street in 1933 demonstrated Burgess's contention that store windows that extended too high were awkward and the upper portion often looked like "a useless and neglected appendage." (ND 3–6385a, GA)

should not be covered up with sign boards. If they are positively ugly, as they sometimes are, they should be removed.

    Many stores have windows that are so high that there seems to be some trouble in knowing what to do with the upper part. It is found to be a needless expense to fill the space with one sheet of plate glass of the whole height. A transverse bar of wood or metal is therefore carried across so as to divide the window into a large lower show window and a long low upper part, which, in many cases, looks like a useless and neglected appendage. Sometimes this is plainly painted over. Sometimes one extra and not very attractive sign is painted upon it. In reality it should and occasionally does form an opportunity for enhancing the appearance of the store. There are some simple and good ways of doing this, one of which is to divide this upper space into well-proportioned panes with substantial divisions between them. This may be varied by making these panes in the form of an interesting lattice pattern in the manner of old-fashioned transom lights.

Not much need be said here of the general design of commercial building fronts for that is, in each case, a special problem for the professional architect. It may, however, be noted that recent buildings generally avoid the large projecting head cornices that were the rule up to twenty-five years ago. Various causes have induced this practice, partly concerned with reasonable economy and partly with safety in case of fire. Wide buildings are generally stream-lined in a horizontal direction; tall narrow ones in a vertical direction, with some exceptions. The tendency towards wider windows favours horizontal stream-lining as the general preference. When narrow frontages have their main lines horizontally accentuated, there is great need to keep the windows of neighbouring buildings in the same horizontal line to avoid irritating horizontal jogs.

The fact that the ground storey serves usually a different purpose from the upper storeys suggests giving it some emphasis as a base or foot to the building. The use of dark-coloured material for the piers and shop front carries out this idea. The topmost part of the building should look an adequate and suitable head or crown to the building. This used to be assured by means of a large cornice. In modern work it may be done by a wide surface, either plain or specially ornamented by a flat decorative band or by the use of a different material.

The nature of the materials used in the buildings greatly affects the appearance of a business street, not only by their colour and texture, but also as to the impression of worth and permanence. It is to some extent unfortunate to the effects of harmony that we have so many widely differing materials at our disposal today for building. Many old towns owe much of their charm and beauty to the uniformity of their materials and methods of building. The materials now most commonly used may be graded as follows in order of their value for street architecture. Marble gives the impression of great preciousness. Certain marbles of good quality can now be got in sufficient quantity to face large buildings, and will probably be more extensively used. Granite expresses strength and endurance. Freestone buildings have a quiet beauty and usually a pleasant rich tone. Brick has a greater variety of qualities of texture and colour. This is not sufficiently realised, for it is too frequently ruined by being painted over. When painted, the colour is flat and poor and the texture becomes merely that of paint, not the valuable texture of brick. Buildings that are entirely of brick do not harmonise well with neighbouring buildings that are entirely of stone, but can be made to harmonise well when partly of stone by a good distribution of the materials. Buildings of a fairly bright red brick, which long retains its freshness, as it generally does in our climate, have a very cheerful appearance when sashes and other woodwork are painted white and the paint [is] kept fresh and clean. Artificial stones are of various qualities. Building terra cotta can have an excellent colour and is easily washed and cleaned. Terrazzo made with marble shares these qualities. Concrete is the deadest and poorest in colour of all building materials, and can only be given any tolerable colour or interest by being [covered] with stucco colouring. Stucco itself is not a building material, but merely a coat to which some pleasing effects may be given.

Of accessory materials, wood is the most important. When painted, its value lies in furnishing interesting contrasts and in harmonising otherwise discordant colours. Tiles, whether of glass, like vitrolite, or of clay, as in tessellated or mosaic work, can be smart and pretty, qualities that are of secondary value, but which are naturally highly rated for store fronts. Metal, whether in the bright form of stainless steel or chromium plate, etc., or in the form of wrought iron or bronze, often adds a welcome secondary interest.

The chaotic nature of business signs is apparent in this photo of Jasper Avenue and 106 St. in 1945. (275–1284 CEA)

Advertising Signs

Before making positive recommendations for the improvement of advertising signs in a business street, it is necessary to realise that there exist a number of influences that operate strongly and positively against such improvements. In order to combat these influences, they must be clearly stated and kept in view. Some of the most important are:

1. The excessive urge of individuals to call attention to their premises.
2. Public indifference.
3. Pressure of sign makers.
4. Indiscriminate use of standardised signs.
5. Lack of skill in the matter of design.

It is necessary to be somewhat specific on each of these points.

1. Large businesses such as department stores and businesses whose custom is not specially to be attracted by advertising signs, such as banks

Improvement of Business Street Fronts 301

Billboards intruded into urban life everywhere in the province as this photo of a billboard adjacent to a residential district in Calgary in 1941 reveals. (NA–4072–45 GA)

and trust companies, are free from the strong temptation to make a great display of signs, provided they have fine buildings such as are in themselves the best advertisement. On the other hand, small businesses with insignificant premises are strongly tempted to make a strenuous appeal for public notice by glaring signs upon their buildings. In doing this, such businesses, each endeavouring to outdo its neighbour, start a competition in loud advertising, inevitably leading to a discordant general display, in which any individual advantage is lost in the general confusion, and the neighbourhood is lowered in general estimation.

2. Public indifference amounts often to complacency and even to a kind of satisfaction and pride in seeing strenuous though disorderly efforts as evidences of energy and enterprise. The public becomes so accustomed to the chaotic appearance of streets and of shabby advertising that these are largely accepted as necessary conditions of business. Bright colours and loud noises are the natural delight of small children. General public taste has a difficulty in rising beyond these primitive instincts, or to be aroused to a positive demand for orderliness and beauty. Frequently, atrocious signs are hailed with delight on account of their

sheer badness and boldness, much as smart or bold criminals enlist a certain amount of public sympathy and admiration. Nevertheless, there are in every city a considerable number of people who are genuinely distressed by existing conditions, and would appreciate and support efforts for improvement. The better class of storekeepers are amongst those who have the greatest appreciation and desire for improvement, and these can exercise the greatest influence by their example.

3. Sign makers of various sorts naturally wish to make the greatest display to which they can persuade their clients, in order to sell more work for their own profit. This trade is a necessary and important service in which much capital is invested and great energy enlisted. Its co-operation is necessary to the improvement of the quality of advertising signs. Advertisements of large size are a great source of offensiveness. These are probably the most profitable to this trade. To call for a reduction in the plague of advertising is to diminish the profits of the trade. The only compensation would be to raise the quality and value of a lesser spread of advertising.

4. Many standard signs, generally of the nature of bill posting, are distributed over every city and town.[2] However interesting or clever any of these may be in themselves, they have the drawback that, being designed for no special situation, they appear out of place in almost any situation. In the country, their bad effect is generally recognised, and there they have been legislated against. In towns too, they produce bad effects.

5. Lack of skill in the application of advertising signs is a matter that might be remedied by the better attention of the decorator's trade to the subject. Decorators who have good skill in design are apt to exercise, and even to be required to exercise, that skill in a manner detrimental to general good effect. If the occupier of a store cares nothing for a community of effect, he is little likely to get it from the decorator he employs. One of the difficulties in the treatment of street fronts is the number of different decorative trades that are employed. Those who furnish illuminated signs have little regard for those whose business is painting, and still less for the fundamental art of architec-

ture. It is a large part of the purpose of these notes to suggest methods by which some co-operation could be effected.

Advertising signs are a necessity of business. Their primary function is to serve as a directory and guide to the public. They must appeal clearly to the eye and should do so in a pleasing manner. They have great possibilities of beauty in themselves and of adding interest and delight to the general effect of our street scenes. But who, glancing at the existing medley of signs, can deny their general effect of confusion and ugliness? Neither can it be suggested that they act efficiently as a directory to the public. What, then, is wrong, and what can be done about it?

We may consider five of the most common faults, the correction of any one of which would effect a great improvement. The correction of all of these would create a veritable revolution for the better. These corrections would not be hard to make:

1. The misplacement of signs.
2. Excessive size in relation to position.
3. Unsuitable forms.
4. Discordant colour.
5. Disregard of neighbours.

1. *The Misplacement of Signs.*

Appropriate places for signs are often disregarded. No matter how simple a building may be, it has necessarily certain features of its own, such as windows and doors with vertical and horizontal structural spaces between these. The construction of a building is a piece of craftsmanship entitled to the respect due to all honest work. If this construction is hidden or disguised by advertising boarding, the building becomes a sort of house of cards, an affair with no appearance of substance. Yet we often see even excellent masonry thus thrown into discard, and the whole effect of a good building cheapened.

A decent respect for the worth of the building itself and its good result may generally be seen in bank buildings of stone. These take care to have no defacing signs at all. The advertisement of their name and purpose most often occurs only in gold letters within the glass of their windows. They may also have a sign in gold letters, each letter fixed individually on a plain band of stone over the doorway, with the lettering perfectly fitting the plain space. The larger and better stores go very little farther than this. (Hudson's Bay Company, Johnstone Walker, Eaton's, etc.)

Let us suppose for a moment, just as an ideal, that all businesses confined their signs to letters of gold or white or any colour or illuminated letters upon the glass of their windows. This would at once clean up a vast amount of mess and save a lot of expense. There is much sound sense and reason in the proposal. It would still admit of much variety in form and in colour. It would ensure a great degree of harmony. For, each sign being securely bounded by the frame and structure of the window, the tendency to clash discordantly with neighbouring signs would be reduced to a minimum. Windows signs of this nature have the advantage that they are placed in the most readable situation. They are easy to read from the near or from the farther sidewalk and are better in that respect than over-door or over-window signs. Being well separated from one another, they do not materially interfere as over-hanging signs so generally do. As a directory and guide to the public, they are the most efficient of all signs. Owners of fine buildings will be well advised to forbid any other method in rented stores, for this permits fine buildings to produce the finest effect.

There is, however, a very human desire for excitement and liveliness that hankers after a more general display than allowed under the above proposal of restraint. How far may we go, yet not fall into total discord and confusion? To lessen restraints may give opportunity for new experiments in beautiful effects or, on the other hand, it may open the floodgates of disorder and ugliness.

Extending the field for signs beyond the window glass, it is the very general custom to place the occupier's name and occupation in a horizontal line above the doors and windows. This is the most common type of sign. Yet it is not so efficient as the sign upon the window glass because, on account of its height, it is not so easily read from the near sidewalk, although probably more easily seen from the passing car or from the opposite sidewalk.

This type of store-front sign is often misapplied to the great detriment of the general appearance of our buildings and streets. Over the doors and windows of stores there is, for constructive purposes, a plain straight head or lintel, and upon this it is possible to place a sign in such a way that it does not cover up or belie this structural feature of the building. Quite frequently, however, signs in this position are broadened so that they cover up a projecting ledge or cornice above the plain lintel. In doing this, no doubt they blazon the occupier's name more emphatically, but they utterly destroy the structural and architectural character of the building, and thereby cheapen the general effect of the establishment. There is no real farther service given by letters above a foot in height when that amount of space is provided on the building. In response to the craving for larger size, many stores are designed with much wider spaces for names. It may be reasonable enough to take full advantage of the spaces thus provided, but the provision of this excessive amount of space is not desirable. Yet there are cases where the spaces provided in the design of the building are perversely misused and the advertising signs, instead of being placed on the one level suited to them, are jogged one up, another down, another half way between in a thoroughly irritating manner (Commercial Building).

It may occasionally be necessary or desirable to place horizontal signs on the face of a building to advertise businesses in the upper storeys (Chisholm Building). There is generally here no special provision for the purpose. When it is done, it should be by making these signs of separate individual letters, each affixed separately to the wall face so as to disturb the apparent structure as little as possible. The value of this method is great and will be discussed in more detail in considering suitable forms.

While Burgess generally disliked rooftop signs, he argued that this one on the CNR station in Edmonton was appropriate to the purpose and location of the building. This demonstrated how difficult it was to develop hard and fast rules for the design of signs.
(ND 3–4048, GA)

2. Excessive Size in Relation to Position.

In regard to excessive size in signs, there is a temptation to overcall one's neighbour. If all indulge in this, the result must necessarily be a Babel. This is a case in which a legal limit might be of real service, and this is sometimes imposed. Lettering eighteen inches in height can easily be read across the widest street, and there is no good reason for exceeding this. There is also little to be gained by advertising more than can be put into one or at most two lines of lettering. There are a few cases in which larger lettering is appropriate. There is the case of a public or semi-public building across the end of a street (C.N.R. and Y.M.C.A.), and the gables of buildings which stand high above their neighbours. In this latter case, the principle of individual letters, with no backboard but affixed to the wall itself, is the most appropriate and least disturbing. The large plain surfaces of the sides of high buildings may be seen from great distances and are a tempting field for advertisement. In this situation efficiency as a guide to the public may fairly be claimed. It is too common, however, to prepare for this advertising by painting over a large area of brickwork, frequently making a border around it. It is a far preferable method to leave the brick itself as being a more valuable background than paint can possibly be, and to place individual lettering against the brick in contrasting colour and tone. Standard and picture posters in these situations are inevitably of a disturbing effect.

3. *Unsuitable Forms.*

Advertising signs tend increasingly to take the form of *projecting signs* overhanging the sidewalk. These offer certain picturesque possibilities, especially effective as night illumination, but also unfortunately produce some of the worst results. In fact they have come to be the chief cause of disorder in the appearance of our streets. In regard to efficiency for public guidance, it may be admitted that, given fair isolation, they are easily read from either near or the farther sidewalk and from a considerable distance. But when multiplied and placed near one another, they interfere greatly with one another. This multiplicity arises from their use by stores with small frontages and is farther complicated by their use to serve upper storeys. The larger the sign, especially in the direction of its height, the greater is its interference with others. If confined to a moderate size of, say, twenty inches in height, with a projection from the wall face of about forty inches, and if all were placed at a uniform level, the interference would be least and their efficiency as guides would be greater. If they could be placed at the junctions between stores rather than over the centre of store fronts, so that each store would have two signs, one at each limit of its occupancy, this would probably still more increase their efficiency. But this arrangement is not practicable on account of the need for widely spreading guy wires to steady them against wind pressure. Narrow vertical signs, say twelve inches wide between stores, would not require these tie wires, and would be very efficient. But vertical reading is not natural to us as it is to the Chinese.

Burgess contended that the illuminated vertical sign on the Corona Hotel destroyed the beauty of the building. (275–108 CEA).

Illuminated overhanging signs have almost invariably a clumsy appearance by daylight on account of the need for internal wiring and other apparatus. The attempts often made to give them fanciful forms emphasises this essential clumsiness. Simple forms are best. The clumsiness might be greatly alleviated by more cheerful treatment with gold and colour, but this is seldom successfully done. The public generally are alive to the offensiveness of the multiplicity of projecting signs. In some towns, as in Palo Alto [California], they are entirely forbidden with good effect. This is an effective remedy. A compromise might be made by permitting one such sign only on properties of not less than fifty feet of frontage. In that case stringent limitations as to size and location would not be necessary, as they would not interfere with one another, and any resulting irregularities would be picturesque rather than confusing. They might also be permitted at street corners.

In old days, when people were not so literary, lettered signs did not exist. It was then the custom, of which vestiges still linger, to distinguish tradesmen's premises by symbols, such as the mortar and pestle of the druggist, the barber's pole and dish, etc. New and appropriate signs might with advantage be designed and generally used. In that case they should be kept moderate in size to prevent the foolish and deplorable competition in bigness. They could be applied as window decoration or as surmounts over the store front name-sign, or, if as projecting signs, then no larger than could be made secure in a socket without the necessity of guy wires. They could add much to the interest of street fronts and would have considerable value as public guides.

Where a premises of several storeys in height is all in one ownership, vertical signs, either flat or projecting, may be made to increase the variety of night light effects. This may be appropriate for theatres and restaurants. When illuminated signs are thus used, they are open to the general objection to illuminated signs—that they have a clumsy effect by daylight. They should never be applied to buildings that are otherwise well-designed, for they are destructive of architectural effect. (This may be seen at the Corona Hotel, a well-designed building with a vertical illuminated sign which, although itself well designed, destroys the beauty of the building.) Such bad effects would be lessened if the signs were at the ends of the facades, not in their centres.

A very considerable amount of the general effect of advertising signs depends on their manner of lettering and framing. There are many good forms of lettering. Differences in form and colour amongst signs creates interest and variety, aids efficiency in distinguishing them and may introduce no discord in the general effect so long as they are not made too big. It is interesting, however, to notice that, a good many years ago now, the Swedish people held a great exhibition at Gothenburg, in which they made a regulation that all advertising signs must be in simple block lettering. They may have also required all to be in black and white, but block lettering alone was used. This proved to be a great object lesson to the public in the artistic value of restriction. It demonstrated how even such a multifarious affair as a trades exhibition could have a unity of effect imposed on it by the observation of a simple restriction generally applied. This was one of the Swedish experiments in co-operation.

A very great improvement in the form of signs may be made by attention to a simple principle. It has already been pointed out that there is great value to be attained by letting the main structure of a building, which is the main property asset, be clearly visible. This can be greatly aided by the practice, now becoming common, of affixing the individual letters of a sign separately to the wall itself without any obscuring background, and without any surrounding border lines or empanelment. It would be well that this method should be applied as far as practicable to all signs, whether those just over store windows or on large exposed gables. It may be claimed that many store signs are quite tastefully and prettily designed with panels and border lines around them. This may be quite true, but these borderings introduce a degree of complication and add to the general street effect of having too many things crowded together. A glance at the good effect of the simpler method is the best argument in its favour. In most cases it is quite convincing.

4. *Discordant Colour.*

Colour is the greatest delight to the eye, and it is right that we should use and enjoy it. In our business streets it is to a considerable extent supplied by the goods in the store windows. That these should be exhibited with the best effect is of first importance to business. To this end, the best stores, with few exceptions, reasonably use deep tones of colour or even black for the framing of their windows and the structural members of the buildings at the street level. This by its contrast best sets out the brighter colours of the displays in the windows. On the other hand, businesses that have no occasion to show their goods in their windows, such as restaurants or coffee shops, wish rather to attract the eye to the front of the building itself and these, therefore, generally use materials of light colouring. The deeper shades of neighbouring stores cannot disagree much with one another, but when light tones of clear colour adjoin one another, or adjoin these deeper tones, there is apt to be some discord.

This question of harmonising adjoining premises is important and, of course, cannot be done without some neighbourly co-operation or consideration. When, as frequently happens, there are several stores which form part of one building, which is designed as one whole, the only reasonable thing to do is to have all the stores of one colour in their main structural features. The signs themselves may vary in colour and style of lettering. If one of such a set of premises should be a restaurant, it may very well introduce some farther gaiety of decoration upon the common base of colour. This will be the more appropriate if it should happen to be the middle premises. In that case a degree of harmony could be made even if the middle store elected to use a light colour, say ivory, whilst those on each side used a fairly dark green. Then the centre store might make the lettering of its sign green, whilst the side stores used ivory lettering. The essence of harmony is to have *something in common* and the essence of discord is to agree with your neighbour in no way.

As regards faults in the use of particular colours, the one requiring to be specially noted is the misuse of brilliant scarlet red. This colour attracts the eye strongly. It has a high value in the general scheme of colour, but it has a special power to dominate and destroy otherwise pleasing effects when it is used in large areas. Its best use is in dispersed small areas and in relatively thin lines, especially when used against light grounds. This does not apply to modified, or shaded, or toned reds.

5. *Disregard of Neighbours.*

Disregard of neighbours is naturally the root of a thousand and one discords in all the directions above discussed: misplacement, size, form and colour. To mind your own business is excellent business advice, but minding one's business implies regard for your neighbour, which is the most important part of all business. Neighbourly consideration is obviously the fundamental condition of harmony. As said above, the essence of harmony is to have something in common with our neighbours. This applies to the appearance of our buildings.

Accessory Features

A number of features occur in our business streets, not always essential but of frequent use or occurrence. Some attention should be called to awnings and roof-top signs.

Awnings are intended to shelter delicate goods in store windows from the heat and bright light of direct sunshine. In our northern climate they are not very efficient for this purpose. In mid-winter, even at mid-day, the sun is only about thirteen degrees above the horizon. If the outer edge of an awning is ten feet from the store window and eight feet above the sidewalk, the shadow from the awning will still be more than five feet above the sidewalk at the glass of the window. Before and after mid-day the advantage is still less. The shorter the length of the awning, the less service it gives because light penetrates at the ends unless these are closed. On the south side of the street, awnings are unnecessary. On the whole, however, they are much used and must be found of appreciable service. They can add variety and gaiety to the street and may be made to add some softness of effect, just as hangings do in interiors. It seems extraordinary that so many stores have awnings that, when raised, hang at the sides of the windows in a dirty, faded condition that is quite distressing. It is advisable that awnings, when raised, should be received into a box for this purpose. A hanging valance may be left out from the box if desired. It would be well that the awnings themselves should be gay in colour and kept clean.

Signs raised upon roofs may be either of the nature of bill-post boards or of illuminated signs of special design. The bill-post type can scarcely be otherwise than offensive. For special illumination, the opportunity is great for good or ill. Few or none achieve any beauty of effect. They have the least offence when on the top of buildings which may be seen either only from a great distance, or [when they are placed] on public buildings which stand across the end of a street of considerable length. (C.N.R. Station).

NOTES

1. Marked Private and Confidential. This document was followed by a report, "Detailed Recommendations for Improvement on Jasper Avenue, Edmonton 101st to 106th Streets, August 1, 1946" (71.213, file 172, UAA) which made specific proposals for sign and building front redesign to produce a more visually interesting streetscape and eliminate clutter and inappropriate construction. There is no evidence that the report was acted upon by the city of Edmonton. The area Burgess surveyed was then part of Edmonton's central business district, with Jasper Avenue serving as the district's main street.
2. That is, billboards.

PART IV

Recollections of a Half Century

Overleaf: Cecil Burgess at 100 years of age. (Folio, October 22, 1970)

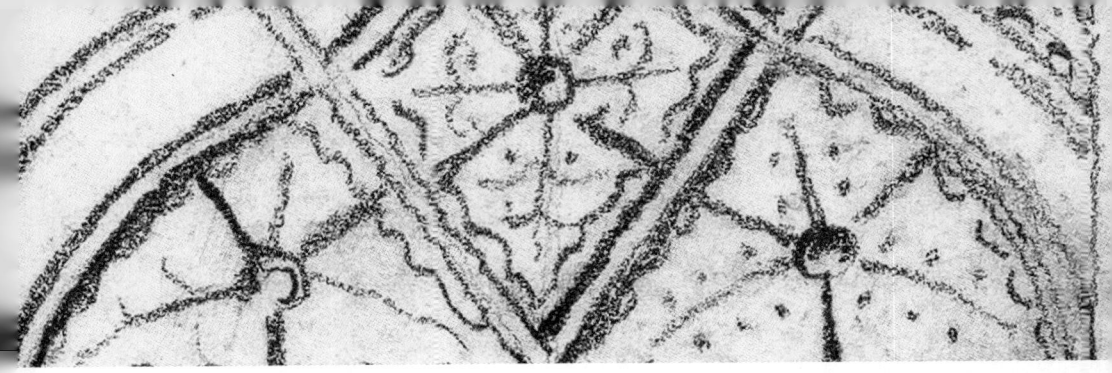

DOCUMENT 21

Recollections of a Half Century
Cecil S. Burgess

BURGESS HAD BEEN *for many years the Alberta correspondent for the Royal Architectural Institute of Canada Journal, and his memoirs were published in the RAIC Journal 34, no. 7, July 1957 issue. The typescript and published versions of the memoir are identical, and the text printed here was transcribed from the manuscript version. The published version was co-authored with W.H. Mott.*

Document 21 is the typescript of Burgess's memoirs, 71.213 file 177 UAA.

I AM WRITING this in response to a request from the editor for a reminiscent sort of article on my life and practice in Edmonton. I notice the limitation with some degree of satisfaction for it cuts out half of the enormous disarray of a past of more than eighty years.

Alberta has a provincial government, a university and an architectural association, all, today, apparently sitting pretty. But all have, in their short lives, sustained and survived staggering blows such as only the young and strong could take and still live. They tell us that the people have a voice in the government. The government has certainly a voice of its own and uses it.

On an engagement as professor of architecture, at first tentative on both sides, I arrived in Edmonton at the CNR station in the month of March 1913 and spent a night at the King Edward Hotel, there being no Macdonald or Corona then available. I next morning hired a cab and crossed the Low Level Bridge, there being no High Level Bridge then available and, by a devious trail that no longer exists, I arrived finally at an extensive wilderness in the midst of which stood two brick buildings, Athabaska Hall and Assiniboia Hall.[1] These were at that time much derided on account of their extreme plainness, but they are now probably considered too decorative by modern standards. Athabaska Hall was fully occupied by residence and class rooms, but the present large dining room, gymnasium and kitchen were under construction.[2] Assiniboia Hall was not quite completed but it was able to accommodate a number of the students and staff. There, for some months, I took up my residence. I immediately set about laying out a curriculum for the next session's calendar and also making plans for some future buildings to be immediately erected. The first of these was Pembina Hall, a residence to accommodate 150 students, a number of farm buildings for stock and a group of six residences for teaching staff, in one of which I spent many happy years. As yet there was no teaching building but meanwhile, Percy E. Nobbs was preparing, in Montreal, plans for the Arts Building. Much later the firm of Nobbs and Hyde designed the Medical Building. On these I acted as local superintending architect. On the latter building I had the picnic of collaborating with each of the professors who was to occupy the building to see that they were to get what they wanted. I doubt if they did, but if not, I want to put the blame on them, I worried them plenty. This is a usual experience of architects.

Through the years, besides those already mentioned, I designed a number of buildings for the university. Amongst these were: the south wing of the original building of the University Hospital (the provincial Public Works Department attended to the erection), the Soldiers Civil Re-establishment Hospital, the hockey rink, a janitor's cottage for the well known and respected Reg Lister, the pathological laboratory, besides a stream of alterations and extensions too numerous to relate even if I could remember them. My engagement permitted me to take on private practice so long as it did not interfere with my teaching. There were good reasons for limiting this. I designed numbers of private houses for my personal friends and I was consulting architect for the Birks Building on Jasper Avenue and for the first Provincial Administrative Building on 109 Street. Like most architects, I have planned many castles of airy fabric which have never achieved the glorious reality of glass and fibre board. The purpose of most of these was to enable the teeming mind of Dr. Tory more clearly to envisage the shape of things to come in the more or less distant future. I designed a university library, a students' union building, gymnasium and swimming pool many years before these came into being under other hands. It was the early intention of Dr. Tory that this university should be mainly a residential one. I accordingly laid out a scheme to accommodate 480 students in addition to the 450 already provided for in the three university residences. There were to be eight residences for 60 students in each. Each pair was to have its common room, each set of four its dining room. The whole arrangement was to be linked up with the great dining room which is still in use in rear of Athabaska Hall so that all matters of catering and housekeeping should be well under both central and departmental control. Between residences there were to be landscaped "quads" special to the respective residences. I had great delight in this scheme but the fates were against others sharing in my joy. My work as resident architect was in general single-handed with only occasional drafting and typing assistance. I made the drawings, wrote the specifications and typed my correspondence.

The founder and first president of the University of Alberta, Dr. Henry Marshall Tory, had, by his great natural ability, become a professor at McGill University. His favourite sport was the founding of universities. To this sport he devoted himself as some people take to mountain climbing.

When one peak has been scaled they look out for another. When one university had been well started, Dr. Tory looked around for a good place to start another. The formidable and unforeseeable difficulties are the attraction of these sports. Common sense has nothing to do with this. Something more is needed. Dr. Tory has four conquests to his credit. It has been often said that he was a man of sense and of vision. In ordinary life he had just common sense and common vision. When he undertook the planting of a university, he laid both of these aside and adopted a special sense and a special vision. This special sense was a faith in what humanity, properly appealed to, would rise to, and this special vision was the ability to focus his mental sight upon fifty years ahead. In Edmonton he looked at an area of some seventy acres covered with ragged bush, waving couch grass, with a small slough here and there, and he plainly saw there a large university. At that time the largest city in Alberta, Calgary, had a total population of 4,000. Fifty years later there was that number of students at a university that had sprung up on that wilderness, not without effort. When the university started in 1908 the population of Alberta was about 275,000, chiefly agricultural and other strenuous pioneers—too small for a university. Similarly, when the department of architecture was started in 1913, the population was too small to justify that. In 1914 there was a small enrolment. Then the war struck and it rocked the young province, the young university and the infant cradle of architecture. The Arts Building was well advanced but far from complete and that required money. The bonds of the province of Alberta, when a war was on, did not look good enough to the bankers of Canada. The dilemma was presented to the contractors, the Fuller Co. of the USA. What could they do under the circumstances? They could trust Canadians and on the security of the province of Alberta would finance the building on their usual terms of 6 percent, the principal to be paid as circumstances should permit. The work was done and Alberta justified that faith in Canada. The building was finished but, meanwhile, most of the boys and of the staff had gone to the war. Even the professor of architecture thought he owed a bit of work to King George.

After the interlude of the First World War, I returned in 1919 to Alberta wondering whether the professorship of architecture was still open for me. I seemed to be expected. The department struggled to life again. There were generally one or two students in each year of the four-year course. I had a teaching program in architecture of more than thirty hours per week. Under the stresses of the economic crisis of the thirties I was co-opted to lecture on European History. Before the session of 1935–1936 opened, I had reached the normal retiring age. Prosperity had now fairly turned the corner. The population of the province had begun its rapid increase and was now three quarters of a million. It was evident that the department of architecture could no longer be a one man job but must either cease or be fully manned and placed on a footing with those elsewhere. The governors decided that it should be closed down. I had no active part in this decision, nor do I know the various considerations that may have influenced it. I have suggested above that Dr. Tory's mental vision was usually focussed at fifty years ahead. The population of the province is now nearly a million and a quarter. The department was set up in 1913. Fifty years added to that will bring us to 1963. What of the future?[3]

The province of Alberta was created in 1905. The architects were not slow in rising to the occasion. The bill establishing the Alberta Association of Architects is dated 4th May 1906. Our association has therefore all the rights of primogeniture over the RAIC. The names of seventeen charter members appear in the bill. Nine of these are from Calgary, six from Edmonton, one each from Lethbridge and Medicine Hat. The effect of wars and economic stress upon our membership may be judged from the fact that on the roll for 1914 there are seventy-five names, sixty-four from within the province; on that of 1920 there are thirty names, twenty-five of these from within the province. By the original modest charter the association was limited to a charge of $15.00 as annual fee. Presently that youngster, the RAIC, came clamouring for $10.00 per member per annum to aid its youthful efforts. We compromised on $5.00. If that was not enough to get, it was too much to give. Our accounts were frequently in the red. By a later revision of the charter the fee now charged is $50.00 and, with over a hundred members, the association is now in a position to do things and it does them. At first, examinations for entrance to the association were conducted by a board appointed by the association. Appeals, which were not infrequent, were to the Attorney General who, too often, seemed to think that an appellant was his injured client whom he was bound to defend against a ring of robbers. This nuisance was later overcome by holding examinations under the sponsorship of the University of Alberta which commanded respect and treated the Association with the respect it deserved. The examinations are still under the aegis of the university which appoints the examiners, a number of whom are nominated by the Association.

From the cloistered bounds of the University I issued into the world's wider arena at the tender age of seventy years. I started an individual practice in which I enjoyed a little stream of minor works on which I worked lone-handed as had been my custom or my fate. I have been engaged in architecture for seventy years and have been a member of the RIBA for sixty-one. I have also been an associate of the Town Planning Institute of Canada since 1920 and have had a number of interesting adventures in town planning which do not belong to this narrative.

The above is an attempt to give, in short space, some account of the introduction of architecture into a province in which the many elements of social life had not yet settled to work smoothly together. This introduction was therefore of a somewhat pioneering adventure. In these affairs, as will be seen, I was, to some extent, personally involved.

NOTES

1. The current spelling is Athabasca.
2. Now demolished.
3. Tory's vision of fifty years hence was perhaps justified. Although the University of Alberta closed its architecture programme in 1940, the need for a programme in Alberta was seen by the establishment of one by the University of Calgary in 1971.

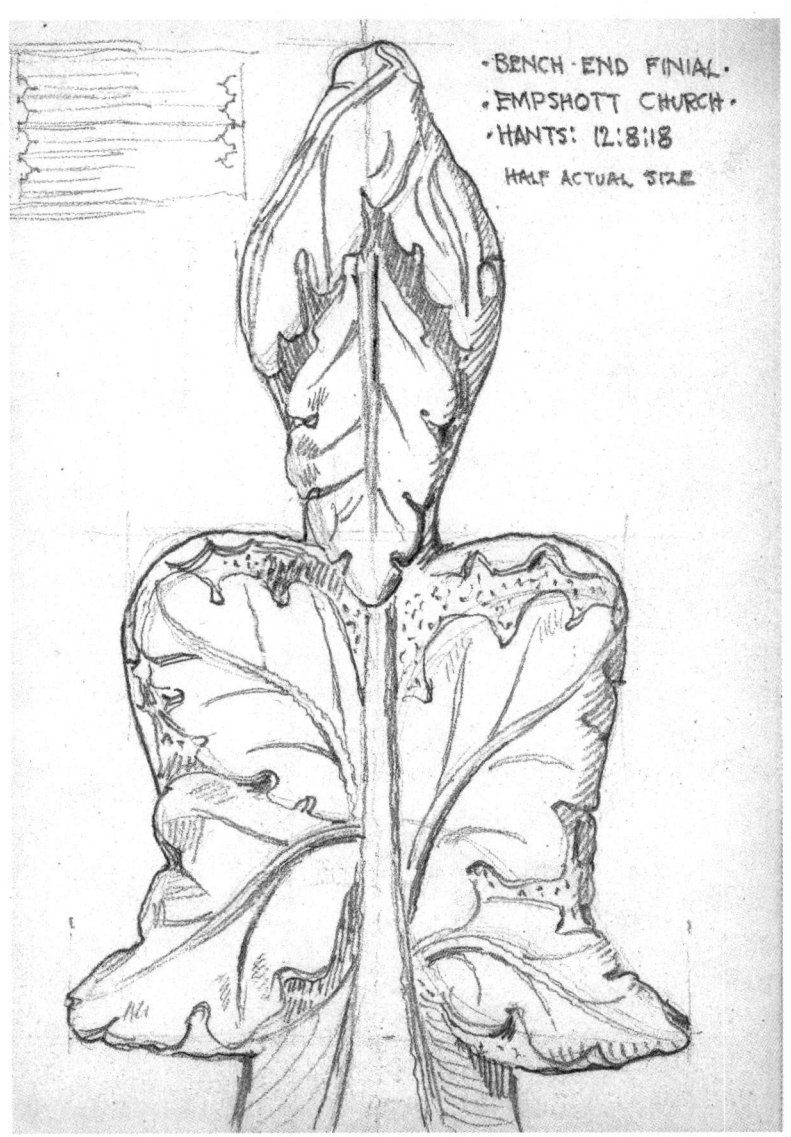

Cecil Burgess was fond of well-crafted decoration throughout his life. This fondness is shown in his 1918 sketch of an end finial on an English bench. (71.213–186, sketchbook, UAA)

Bibliography

Archival Materials

CITY OF EDMONTON ARCHIVES
City Clerk's Papers, RG 17.
City of Edmonton Papers, MS 209.
City of Edmonton Papers, RG 11.
Clipping file, "Civic Town Planning."

PROVINCIAL ARCHIVES OF ALBERTA
Cecil Scott Burgess Papers, 69.190.
Department of Municipal Affairs Papers, 71.4.
Interview with C.S. Burgess, May 1969, 69.361.

UNIVERSITY OF ALBERTA ARCHIVES
Architectural Plans 1927, 72.209.
Cecil Scott Burgess Drawings, 72.28.142.
Cecil Scott Burgess Papers, 71.213.
Ferguson Papers, 2002–45.
Henry Marshall Tory Papers, 79.112.
Interview with C.S. Burgess, October 1969, 74.19.

President Kerr Papers, 68.1.

Report of the Board of Governors of the University of Alberta for the Year Ending June 30, 1913.

Report of the Board of Governors of the University of Alberta for the Year Ending December 31, 1915.

Report of the Dept. of Extension for the Year Ending March 31, 1931.

The University of Alberta, Edmonton, Calendar, 1914–15.

The University of Alberta, Edmonton, Calendar, 1926–27.

The University of Alberta, Edmonton, Calendar, 1930–31.

Interviews

Howard and Mary Spence-Sales, Vancouver, 2002.

Books and Articles

Adams, Annmarie. *Architecture in the Family Way*. Montreal and Kingston: McGill-Queen University Press, 1996.

Adams, Annmarie and Tancred, Peta. *"Designing Women" Gender and the Architectural Profession*. Toronto: University of Toronto Press, 2000.

"Alberta Association of Architects, President's Report to Annual Meeting, September 23, 1938." RAIC *Journal* 15 (1932): 253.

"Alberta Government Administrative Building, Edmonton." RAIC *Journal* 8 (1931): 352–56.

Bayer, Walter. "Sense and Sensibility: The New Head Offices of the Underground Railway, Westminster, London." *Architectural Review* 57 (November 1929): 225–41.

Bilash, O.S.E. and Sitwell, O.F.G. "Words into Buildings: The University of Alberta, 1906–28." Society for the Study of Architecture in Canada *Bulletin* 20, no. 1 (March 1995): 4–21.

Body, Trevor. *Modern Architecture in Alberta*. Regina: Canadian Plains Research Centre, 1987.

Brady, Alexander. "A Layman's Impression of Canadian Architecture." RAIC *Journal* 9 (1932): 175.

Burgess, Cecil. "Housing." RAIC *Journal* 17 (October 1940): 182.

The Canadian Who's Who, Vol. 3, 1938–39. Toronto: Trans-Canada Press [circa 1939].

Cashman, Tony and Croll, Norman. *50 Years in Architecture*. n.p.: Schmidt Feldberg Croll Henderson, 1958.

Chan, Wah May. "The Impact of the Technical Planning Board on the Morphology of Edmonton." M.A. thesis, University of Alberta, 1969.

Cherry, Gordon E. *The Evolution of British Town Planning*. Leighton, England: Leonard Hill Books, 1974.

Clayton Research Associates and D.G. Wetherell and Associates. *Two Decades of Innovation in Housing Technology, 1946–1965*. Ottawa: CMHC, 1994.

Colquhoun, Alan. *Modern Architecture*. New York: Oxford University Press, 2002.

Corbett, E.A. *Henry Marshall Tory: A Biography*. Introduction by Douglas Owram. Edmonton: University of Alberta Press, 1992 (first published 1954).

Crinson, Mark and Lubbock, Jules. *Architecture. Art or Profession. Three Hundred Years of Architectural Education in Britain*. Manchester: Manchester University Press, 1994.

Crossman, Kelly. *Architecture in Transition. From Art to Practice 1885–1906*. Kingston and Montreal: McGill-Queen's University Press, 1987.

Davey, Peter. *Arts and Crafts Architecture*. London: The Architectural Press, 1980.

Dominey, Erna. "Wallbridge and Imrie. The Architectural Practice of Two Edmonton Women 1950–1979." Society for the Study of Architecture *Bulletin* 17, no. 1 (March 1992): 12–18.

Fedori, Marianne, Tingley, Ken and Murray, David. *The Practice of Post-War Architecture in Edmonton, Alberta. An Overview of the Modern Movement, 1936–1960*. Edmonton: n.p., 2001.

Fenske, Gail. "Lewis Mumford, Henry-Russell Hitchcock, and the Bay Region Style." In *The Education of the Architect, Historiography, Urbanism and the Growth of Architectural Knowledge. Essays Presented to Standford Anderson*, edited by Martha Pollak, 37–85. Cambridge: The MIT Press, 1997.

"Finella: A House for Mansfield D. Forbes, Raymond McGrath Architect." *Architectural Review* 66 (December 1929): 265–72.

Foran, Max. "The Mawson Report in Historical Perspective." *Alberta History* 28, no. 3 (Summer 1980): 31–39.

Gournay, Isabelle. "The First Leaders of McGill's School of Architecture: Stewart Henbest Capper, Percy Nobbs, and Ramsay Traquair." Society for the Study of Architecture in Canada *Bulletin* 21, no. 3 (September 1996): 60–66.

Gross, Alexander F. "Witness to the Passing of Victorian Architecture—The RAIC Journal, 1924–1935." Society for the Study of Architecture in Canada *Bulletin* 12, no. 1 (June 1987): 97–107.

Hitchcock, Henry-Russell. *The Pelican History of Art. Architecture: Nineteenth and Twentieth Centuries.* Markham: Penguin Books, 4th edition, 1977.

Hughes, Margaret. *Off the Record. A View of Hospital Happenings From Behind the Medical Record Desk.* n.p.: Goosehaven Publishing, 1998.

Jackson, Anthony. "The Politics of Architecture: English Architecture 1929–1951." *Journal of the Society of Architectural Historians* 24, no. 1 (March 1965): 97–107.

Johnson, Percy. "George Heath MacDonald (Class of 1911) The Story of One Graduate from McGill University's School of Architecture." Society for the Study of Architecture in Canada *Bulletin* 21, no. 3 (1996): 74–76.

Kalman, Harold. *A Concise History of Canadian Architecture.* Don Mills: Oxford University Press, 2000.

Khan, Hasan-Uddin. *International Style. Modernist Architecture from 1925 to 1965.* Cologne: Taschen Books, 1998.

Le Corbusier. "If I Had To Teach You Architecture." *RAIC Journal* 20 (1943): 17–18.

Lethaby, W.R. *Form and Civilization. Collected Papers on Art and Labour.* London: Oxford University Press, 1922.

Lyle, John M. "Architecture—A Vocation." *RAIC Journal* 10 (1933): 34–35.

Mathers, A.S. "Thirty Five Years of Practice." *RAIC Journal* (December 1955): 462–64.

McCarthy, Fiona. *William Morris. A Life for Our Times.* London: Faber and Faber, 1994.

McGill's School of Architecture: A History by Norbert Schoenauer. Montreal: McGill University, School of Architecture. At http://www.mcgill.ca/architecture/introduction/history/ (current 2005).

Nobbs, Percy. "Construction at the University of Alberta Edmonton." *Construction* (January 1921): 3–12.

———. "Planning for Sunlight." *Journal of the Town Planning Institute* 1, no. 9 (April 1922): 6–12.

———. "Architecture in Canada." *RAIC Journal* (July-September 1924): 91–94.

———. "The General Scheme for the University of Alberta." *RAIC Journal* 2 (1925): 159–64.

———. "Present Tendencies Affecting Architecture in Canada, Part I The Inheritance, Part II Modernity, Part III Adverse Influences." *RAIC Journal* 7 (July 1930): 245–48; (September 1930): 314–17; (November 1930): 388–92.

Payne, Michael. "Allan Merrick Jeffers: One of Alberta's First Architects." *Alberta Past* (Winter 1994).

"Percy Erskine Nobbs Biography." At http://cac.mcgill.ca/nobbs/bio-pen-english.htm (current 2005).

Pevsner, Nicholas. *The Sources of Modern Architecture and Design*. London: Thames and Hudson, 1968.

"Presentation of Cecil Scott Burgess." *The New Trail* 16, no. 1 (1958): 15.

Rees, Ronald. "Reconsidering Antiurban Sentiment." *Landscape* 28 (1985): 26–29.

———. *New and Naked Land. Making the Prairies Home*. Saskatoon: Western Producer Prairie Books, 1988.

"Reports on Activities of Provincial Associations. The Alberta Association of Architects." *RAIC Journal* 1 (1924): 32.

Seymour, Horace. "Town Planning Includes 'Sunlight Engineering.'" *The Canadian Engineer* 36 (April 10, 1919): 363–66

Shand, P. Morton. "Salute to Adventurers. The New Royal Horticultural Hall. Designed by Easton and Robertson." *Architectural Review* 65 (January-June 1929): 17–31.

Simmins, Geoffrey. *Ontario Association of Architects. A Centennial History 1889–1989*. Toronto: The Ontario Association of Architects, 1989.

———. *Documents in Canadian Architectural History*. Peterborough: Broadview Press, 1992.

Simpson, Michael. *Thomas Adams and the Modern Planning Movement: Britain, Canada and the United States 1900–1914*. London: Mansell, 1985.

Sir William Chambers: Architect to George III. Edited by John Harris and Michael Snodin. New Haven: Yale University Press in association with the Courtauld Institute of Art, London, 1996.

Spasoff, Nicola Justine. "Building on Social Power. Percy Erskine Nobbs, Ramsay Traquair, and the Project of Constructing a Canadian National Culture in the Early Decades of the Twentieth Century." Ph.D. diss., Queen's University, 2002.

"Status of the Profession in the Province of Alberta." *RAIC Journal* 7 (1930): 195–96.

Thompson, E.P. *William Morris: Romantic to Revolutionary.* New York: Monthly Review Press, 1961.

Traquair, Ramsay. *The Architecture of Old Quebec.* Toronto: Macmillan, 1947.

Vallance, Hugh. "Architecture in Canada." *Construction* (October 1923): 355–56.

Von Bayer, Edwina. *Rhetoric and Roses, A History of Canadian Gardening 1900–1930.* Markham: Fitzhenry and Whiteside, 1984.

W.R. Lethaby 1857–1931: Architecture, Design and Education. Edited by Sylvia Backemeyer and Theresa Gronberg. London: Lund Humphries, 1984.

Wagg, Susan. *Percy Erskine Nobbs, Architect Artist, Craftsman.* Kingston and Montreal: McGill-Queen's University Press for the McCord Museum, Montreal, 1982.

Wetherell, Donald G. and Kmet, Irene R.A. *Useful Pleasures. The Shaping of Leisure in Alberta 1896–1945.* Regina: Canadian Plains Research Centre, 1990.

———. *Homes in Alberta. Building, Trends, and Design 1870–1967.* Edmonton: University of Alberta Press, 1991.

———. *Town Life. Main Street and Evolution of Small Town Alberta 1880–1947.* Edmonton: University of Alberta Press, 1995.

Williams, Raymond. "When Was Modernism?" *New Left Review* 175 (May/June 1989): 48–52.

Winter, Robert. "The Arts and Crafts as a Social Movement." *Record of the Art Museum, Princeton University* 34, no. 2 (1975): 36–40.

Woods, Mary N. *From Craft to Profession. The Practice of Architecture in Nineteenth-Century America.* Berkley: University of California Press, 1999.

Wright, Donald A. "W.D. Lighthall and David Ross McCord: Antimodernism and English Canadian Imperialism, 1880s–1918." *Journal of Canadian Studies* 32, no. 2 (Summer 1997): 134–53.

Wright, Gwendolyn. "History for Architects." In *The History of History in American Schools of Architecture 1865–1975,* edited by Gwendolyn Wright and Janet Parks, 13–52. New York: The Temple Hoyne Buell Center for the Study of American Architecture, 1990.

Index

Aboriginal People, xli, lxxx
Adams, Holden and Pearson, 199, 200
Adams, Thomas, li, liv
Adams style, 12, 20
advertising, li–lii, lvi, 99, 107, 112–14, 113, 114, 139, 192, 204, 230–31, 295–96, 301–13
Agra, Taj Mahal, 175n1
Aklavik, Northwest Territories, xxiv
Alberta, xxviii, xl–xli, li, lxxiii, lxxxi, lxxxiii, 131–32, 186, 240–41, 261, 318, 320–321
Alberta Association of Architects, xviii, xxx, xliv–xlv, xlvii, l, lxiv, lxxx, lxxxiv–lxxxv, lxxxix n25, 321–22
Amersham, England, High and Over, 204–7, 214
Amsterdam, school, 214
Anderson, William James, 17, 29n2

apartments, liii, lxxv, 250, 274, 279–80, 290–91
architecture, as art, xxxv–xxxvii, lxvii, lxx–lxxi, 33, 90–91, 102–3, 129–30, 153–60, 172–74, 212–14; and climate, xli, lxxxiii, 28, 84–85, 112; criteria for design, xx–xxi, xxxiv, xxxvii–xl, xliii, xlix, lxv–lxxi, lxxxv–lxxxvii, 3–4, 15–26, 34–49, 56–69, 71–86, 91–103, 128, 153–54, 160–74, 181–84, 188–214, 219–26, 293–94, 296–300; drawing, xxi, xxiii, xxxv, xlv, xlix, 27, 142; and health, xxxiii, liii, lxv–lxvi, lxx, 56–59, 71–86, 94–97, 181–83, 195, 201, 204; history, xxxvi–xl, xliii–xliv, 3, 15–28, 31–32; modern, lxv–lxvi, lxviii, xciii n97, xciv n102, 86, 89–103;

Modernism, liv, lxvii–lxxii, lxxxv–lxxxvi, xciv n102, 153–54, 163–64, 177–78, 181–84, 188–91, 206, 217, 224–26, 293; practice, xxiii, xlv–xlvi, liii, lxxii, lxxxvi, xci n59, 51, 94, 144–46, 148–51; and science, xx, xxxiii, xxxv, lxv–lxvi, 56–57, 71–86, 94–97, 129–30, 147, 159–60, 181–83, 212–13, 244, 266; training, xvii, xxviii–xxx, xxxiii–xl, xlv–xlviii, lvii–lviii, lxxi–lxxv, lxxxiv, 6–7, 10, 13n3, 21, 27, 101–2, 141–42, 146–47, 150, 321

Arts and Crafts Movement, xx–xxi, xxxi, xxxiii–xli, xliii, l, lii, lxviii, lxxxiv–lxxxv, xciv n104, 3, 51, 178–79

Ashmole, Bernard, 204–5

Baines, Frank, 198
Banff National Park, lxxvii, 121n1
Baroco style, 22
Bauhaus, liv, lxvii
Beaux Arts classicism, lxxxii, lxxxviii n19
Beaux Arts training. *See* architecture, training
Berlin, Virchow Hospital, 103
Bland, John, lxxix
Blomfield, Reginald, 17, 29n2
Britain, xix–xx, xxviii, xxxiii–xxxiv, xl–xlii, liii–liv, lxix, lxxxii, 27–28, 113–14, 132, 211, 243, 269, 271, 274–75
British Columbia, lvi, 106
Brown, Murray, lxxii

Browne, George Washington, xix–xx
Brussels, Palais de Justice, 103
Buchanan, Margaret, xlvii
buildings, materials and methods, xx–xxi, xxxiii, lviii–lix, lxv–lxvii, lxix, lxxvi–lxxvii, xciii n97, 3, 10–12, 19, 25, 39–49, 68, 75–86, 95–103, 143, 151n2, 162, 164–67, 179–81, 184, 188–89, 192–211, 224–26, 262–63, 277–80
building regulation, 135, 138, 232–33, 286–92, 292n2
Burgess, Cecil Scott, xiii, lxxx–lxxxvii, 1, 87, 259, 315, 317–23; architectural work, xxiii, xxxi–xxxiii, *xxxii*, lviii–lxv, *lix, lxi, lxiii, lxiv*, 60–62; 96, 222, 318–23; early life, xvii–xxiii, at McGill, xxiii–xxiv, 3–4, 15–16; papers, xiii–xiv, xcix–c; private practice, lxiv–lxv, lxxiii–lxxvii, 267n2, 319, 323; and town planning, xlix–l, liv–lviii, lxxiii, lxxvii–lxxx, 105–6, 323; at University of Alberta, xxiv–xxv, xxix–xxxiii, xxxv–xlix, lviii–lxiv, lxxi–lxxiii, 31–32, 51, 318–23; wartime service, xliii–xliv, 320
Burgess, James, xix, lxxx
Byzantine architecture, xxxvii, 18–19, 38–41. *See also* Istanbul, St. Sophia

Calgary, Alberta, l, 105, 133, 271, 284, 302, 320, 321
Canada, xl, xlii, lxxxi–lxxxii, lxxxiv, lxxxvi, 28, 32, 194, 240, 271, 274;

as a British society, xxvi, xxxi,
xl–xlii, liii, lxxxi–lxxxiii, 52
Canaletto, 187–88
Canberra, Australia, 231; Federal
Capital, 103
Chambers, William, 17, 29n2
Chicago, Illinois, 234
Choisey, Auguste, 17, 29n2
city planning procedure. *See* town
planning
civic centres. *See* town planning
Claresholm, Alberta, xliii
Coaldale, Alberta, hospital, lxxiii
community leagues, 289–90, 292n1
Community Planning Association of
Canada, lxxvii
Connell, Amyas, 204–5
craftsmanship, xx–xxi, xxxii–xxxiv,
xxxvii–xxxviii, xli–xliii, lxxxiv, 3,
8–9, 25, 31–34, 37, 45, 47, 51–52,
54–55, 101–3, 160–62, 178–79

da Vinci, Leonardo, 187
Dant, Noel, lxxix
Darling, Frank, xxvi
Dartmouth, England, Britannia Naval
College, 104
DeStijl movement, lxvii

East and Robinson, 201, 202
Eckville, Alberta, hospital, lxxiii
École des Beaux Arts, Montreal,
Quebec, xlvi
École Polytechnique, Montreal,
Quebec, xxix

Edinburgh, Scotland, xx–xxi, 134;
Holyrood Abbey, *xviii*
Edmonton, Alberta, *xxv*, xlvi,
lxiv–lxxv, lxxviii, lxxxiv, 137, 246,
284–86, 239, 293–94, 301, 309,
318, 321
Edmonton buildings: Birks Building,
lxiii, lxiv, 319; Bowker Building
(Provincial Government
Administrative Building), *lxiii*,
lxiv–lxv, lxxxix n26, 96, 151n2,
319; Chisholm block, 306; CNR
Station, 307, 313; Commercial
Building, 306; Corona Hotel, 309,
310; Eaton's, 305; Hudson's Bay
Company, 305; Johnstone Walker,
305; legislative buildings, lxxxviii
n19, lxxxix n26; McLeod Building,
xxv, 267n2; Ottewell House,
222–23. *See also* University of
Alberta buildings
Edmonton Household Economics
Association, xlvii
Edmonton Museum of Arts, lxvi, lxx,
lxxxiii, 155, 175n2
Edmonton Rotary Club, li
Edmonton Town Planning
Commission, xvii, lxii, lxxvii–lxxx,
lxxxiv, 227–28, 246, 247n1, 269,
271, 285, 288
Edwards, William Muir, xxxi
Egyptian and Middle Eastern archi-
tecture, xl, 18, 164–65, 185; Great
Pyramid at Ghiza, 175n1; Temples
at Karnak, 175n1
Elnora, Alberta, hospital, lxxiii, *lxxiv*

Index 333

Fergusson, James, 17, 29n2
Findlay, Margaret, xlvii
Florence, Italy, San Michele, 19
Fort Macleod, Alberta, xliii
France, xxviii, 12–13, 20, 25, 52–53
furniture, xx–xxi, xli, lxiv, 53, 67, 78, 109

Garden City planning, l–li, lxxxiii, 231–32, 249–58, 269
Georgian architecture, 12, 20
Giffen, Andrew, xlv
Gothic architecture, xx, xxxvii, xciv n104, 4–6, 8, 17, 19, 22–25, 43–47, 165, 172, 178, 185, 211
Gothic Revival architecture, xxvi, 20. *See also* Ruskin, John
Grand Trunk Literary Institute, xxiii
Greek architecture, xxxvii, 4, 7–8, 18, 34–37, 43, 72, 165–66, 168–72, 184–85; Parthenon (Athens), 20, 35, 36, 49n2, 168, 175n1, 187, 211
Greenbelt, Maryland, 251–53, 256
Gropius, Walter, lxvii, 216n12

Harland Bartholomew and Associates, 234
Herbert Ellis and Clarke, 204, 205
Hill, Esther Marjorie, xlvii
Hitchcock, Henry-Russell, lxvii
Hood, Raymond, 201, 203
houses, xxxvi–xxxvii, lii–liv, 4–5, 51–69, 54, 217–18, 222–23, 243–44, 261–67, 273–84, 288; concept of home, liv, xcii n78, 51–55, 68–69, 219; design and layout, 4–5, 51–52 , 58–68, 219–26, 252, 261–67, 277–83; gardens, 65, 66, 253; government housing programmes, liv, lxxvi, xcvi n124, 245, 274, 282; home ownership, lxxvi, 274; kitchens, 63–64, 80–81, 221, 264; low cost, liii–liv, lxix, lxxiii–lxxvi, 243–45, 252, 261, 269, 274–84; 278; and social change, 52, 55–56, 217–19. *See also* Edmonton buildings, Ottewell House *and* University of Alberta buildings, Ring Houses *and* Paris, Villa la Roche
Howard, Ebenezer, l–li, lxxxiii, 249, 254–55, 258n3
Hyde, George Taylor, xxiv

Imrie, Mary, xlviii
International style, lxvii–lxviii, lxxxv–lxxxvi, xciv n104. *See also* Architecture, Modernism
Istanbul, St. Sophia, 38–39, 175n1
Italy, xxi, 19

Jasper National Park, xix, lxxvii
Jeeves, Gordon, 201, 203
Jeffers, A.M., xxx, lxxxix n26
Johnson, Philip, lxvii

Kerr, William, lxxi
Khaki College, xliv
King's College, London, xxix
Kitimat, 250

Lacombe, Alberta, *108, 110*
Le Corbusier (Charles-Edouard Jeanneret), lxvii, lxix, *190*, 214n8
Leeds, England, 244
Letchworth, England, li, 231, 253–57, 284n2
Lethaby, William, 17, 29n2, 170
Lethbridge, Alberta, lxxvii, 321
Lincoln, England, cathedral xliv, 23, 173
Liverpool, England, xxi; Roman Catholic Cathedral, 208–9, 214
London, England, xxi, 198–204, 251, 254–55. *See also* London, England, buildings
London, England, buildings: Broadcast House, 199, 214; Cathedral of Westminster, 41; Daily Express Building 204, 205, 214; Hammersmith Public Baths, 104; Head Office Underground Railway, 199, 200, 214, 216n14; Ideal House, 201–4, 203, 214; Imperial Chemical House, 198–99; National Gallery, 104; RIBA offices, 204, 214; Royal Automobile Club, 103; Royal Horticultural Hall, 201, 202, 214; St. Paul's, 48, 183, 215n6
Los Angeles, California, 234, Central Public Library, 215, 216n15
Loseley House, *54*
Ludlow, Thomas, xxiii

MacDonald, Lloyd George, xlvii
Magoon and Macdonald, xxx

Martin, Milton, 247n1
Massachusetts Institute of Technology, xxix, lxiii, lxxvii, lxxxiii
Mathers, A.S., lxxii
Mawson, Thomas, l, 105
McGill University, xxiii–xxiv, xxvi–xxvii, xxxiv–xli, xlvi, lxxii, lxxxv–lxxxvi, 7, 16, 141–42, 292n4
McKim Mead White, lxxxii, 49n3
Medicine Hat, Alberta, lix, lxxvii, 321
Middleton, Walter Thomas, xxxiii
Modernism. *See* architecture
Montmagny, France, Church, 215
Montreal, buildings: Bank of Commerce, 99, 103; Bank of Montreal Head Office, lxxxii, 99; Bonsecours Market, 12; Chateau de Ramezay, 12; Inland Revenue Office, 12; King Edward VII School, 104; Macdonald Engineering Building, xxiii; McCord Building, 12; McCord House, 13n4; Seminary of St. Sulpice, *11*, 12
Montreal, Quebec, xxii–xxiii, xxxvi, 10–13, 99, 106. *See also* Montreal, buildings
Morris, William, xx, xxxviii, lxviii, 179, 196
Mumford, Lewis, lxxxiii, 254, 281, 284n3
Myer, G. Val, 199

Nancy, France, *134*

New York City, lxvii, 37, 100, 133, 194–95, 216n11, 250, 256. *See also* New York City, buildings
New York City, buildings: Chrysler Building, 215n5; Columbia University Library, 104; Municipal Offices, 103; Pennsylvania Railroad Terminal, 37, 43, 49n3, 98, 103; Post Office, 103; Vanderbilt Hotel, 103; Woolworth Building, 103, *193*, 194
Newton, Robert, lxxx
Nobbs and Hyde, xiv, lviii, lxiv, 151n6, 318
Nobbs, Percy, xxi–xxiv, xxvi, xxx–xxxi, xxxvii, lxxxvii n7, lxxxviii n19, 3, 27, 318

Ontario Association of Architects, xlvii
Ordre des Architectes du Québec, xxiii, 4
Östberg, Ragnar, 196–97, *196*
Ottawa, Ontario, 106, 271–72; Chateau Laurier, 103

painting and sculpture, xxi, xxiii, lxxxiii, 42, 43, 45, 159, 168–70, 184–88, 198, 213, 216n14.
Palo Alto, California, 309
Paris, Gare d'Orleans, 98, 103; Opera, 104; Villa la Roche (Auteuil), *190*, 215, 215n8
Philadelphia, Walnut St. Garage Building, 214

Pointe aux Trembles, Quebec, church, 13
Prague, Roman Catholic Church, 215
Prestwich, Frank, 204
Province of Quebec Association of Architects. *See* Ordre des Architectes du Québec

Quebec, xli, 3–4, 8, 10–13
Quebec City, Quebec, 106
Queen Anne style, 20

Radburn, New Jersey, lxxiii, 249, 256–57
railways, 98, 109–11, 116n2, 307
Regina, Saskatchewan, Parliament Buildings, 103
regional planning. *See* town planning
Rembrandt Harmenszoon van Rijn, 187
Renaissance architecture, 19–20, 22, 25, 47–48, 166, 211
Richelieu, France, *134*
Rococo style, 22
Roman architecture, xxxvii, 18, 37–38, 40, 92–93, 165
Rome, buildings, Circus Maximus, 38; Coliseum, 38; Pantheon, 175n1; St. Peter's, 19; Thermae, 18–19, 38
Royal Architectural Institute of Canada, xix, xliv, lxxii, 317, 321
Royal Institute of British Architects, xxi, xxiii, xliv, 204, 323
Rule, John Ulric, xlvii–xlviii

Rule, Peter, xlvii–xlviii
Rule Wynn Rule, xlviii
Ruskin, John, xx, xxxviii, lxviii, 178
Rutherford, A.C., xxvi

Saint James Literary Society, xviii
Saskatchewan, lvi, 106
Scotland, xviii–xx, xlii, 49n4
Scott, Elizabeth, 207–8
sculpture. *See* painting and sculpture
Seymour, Horace, lvii, 127, 130, 140n2, 227
skyscrapers, lxxxii, 100, 135, 192–95, *193*
Spence-Sales, Howard, lxxix
sports, xix, 109, 121–22, 161, 290
Stein, Clarence, 250, 258n6
Stevenson, John, xlvii
Stockholm, Sweden, 196; Concert House, 197–98, 214; Stadshus, 196–97, *196*, 214;
storefronts. *See* advertising
Stratford, England, Stratford Theatre, 207–8, 214
streets layout. *See* town planning
Sturgis, Russell, 17, 29n2
Sweden, liv, lxix, lxxvi, 195–98, 269, 310

Tengbom, Ivar, 197–98
Thomas, Percy, 204
Toronto, Ontario: Canadian Bank of Commerce, 214; General Hospital, 103; Toronto Technical School, 104

Tory, Henry Marshall, xxiv, xxvi, xxix, xliv, lxxiii, lxxxviii n17, 31, 319–20
town planning, xlix–l, liv–lviii, lxv, lxix, lxxvii–lxxix, lxxxiii, lxxxiv, 105–6, 130, 211–12, 227–46, 249–58, 268–72; City Planning Procedure, lv, 228, 234–43, 271; civic centres, lv–lvi, lxxviii–lxxix, lxxxiv, 109, 136, 240; enabling legislation, lvi–lvii, lxxx, 106, 114–16, 116n3, 127–32, 227, 240–41; regional planning, lv–lvi, lxxxv, 271; relationship to architecture, xlix–l, lxv, lxix, 105, 127–28, 130, 151n7, 245; street layout and planning, lv, lxxviii, 74, 132–38, 236–38, 252–53; zoning, liv, lxxviii, 238–39, 241–42, 269, 285–92
Town Planning Institute of Canada, xlix, xcii n67, 323
towns, 106–16, 118–26, 131, 229–30, 251, 257–58
Traquair, Ramsay, xli, 3–4
Turner, Philip, xxiii

Underwood, E., l
United States, xxiv, xxix, xxxiii–xxxiv, lxxxii–lxxxiii, 192–94, 240, 251–52, 271, 274
University of Alberta, xix, xxvi, *xxvii*, xxviii–xxix, xliii–xliv, lxxi, lxxiii, lxxx, 31, 318, 320–21, 323; Department of Extension, xlii–xlv, 31–32; Faculty of Applied Science,

xxviii–xxix, lxxi–lxxii. *See also* architecture, training *and* University of Alberta, buildings

University of Alberta, buildings: Alberta College (St. Stephen's), xxx; Arts Building, *xxviii*, xxxi, *lxii*, lxiv, 151n2, 179, 318, 320; Assiniboia Hall, xxx–xxxi, 318; Athabasca Hall, xxx–xxxi, 318; campus plan, xxvi–xxvii, *xxvii*, xxxi; Medical Building (Dental Sciences), lviii–lix, 151n2, 151n6, 179, 318; Pathology Lab, 319; Pembina Hall, xxxi, *xxxii*, xxxiii, lxiv, 151n2, 318; Ring Houses, xxxi, lxxiii, lxxxix n28, *60–62*; Rink, lix, *lx*, 319; University Hospital Extension, *lxi*, lxiv, 318

University of British Columbia, xxvi, xlvii

University of Calgary, lxxiii, 323

University of Liverpool, xxix

University of Manitoba, xxix, xxxv, xlvi, xlviii

University of Michigan, xxiv

University of Saskatchewan, xlvi

University of Toronto, xxix, xxxv, xlvi–xlviii

Unwin, Raymond, 280, 284n2

urban parks, l, liv–lv, lvii, lxxviii, lxxxiv, 108–9, *108*, *110*, 116n2, 136, 239–40, 245, 281, 285

urban planning. *See* town planning

van der Rohe, Mies, lxvii

Vancouver, British Columbia, 106, 234, 236, 271

Velasquez, Diego, 188

vernacular architecture, xli–xlii, lxxxi–lxxxii, 3–4, 8–13, 9

Verona, Italy, Municipio, xxi, lxxx; Arche Scaligere, *xxii*

Wallbridge, Jean, xlvii–xlviii

Warnum, G. Grey, 204

Washington, D.C., 231, 251; Congressional Library, 104

Welwyn, England, li, 232, 253–56

Whitehorse, Yukon, lxxx

Wilson, Robert, lxxi–lxxii

Wing, Edward Lee, xlvii

Winnipeg, Manitoba, 106

women, xlvii–xlviii, 81, 141–42

World War I, xliii–xlv, lxii, lxiv

World War II, 261, 271, 273, 283–84, 292n2, 293

Wren, Christopher, 156, 170–71, 215n6

Wynn, Gordon, xlvii–xlviii

Yamaoka, Nobuichi, xlvii

York, England, cathedral, xxi, *24*

zoning. *See* town planning